Kent History Project

8

The Archaeology of Kent to AD 800

Kent History project
ISSN 1352-805X

Already published

Traffic and Politics: The Construction and Management of Rochester Bridge, AD 43-1993
eds Nigel Yates and James M. Gibson

Religion and Society in Kent, 1610-1914
Nigel Yates, Robert Hume and Paul Hastings

The Economy of Kent, 1640-1914
ed. Alan Armstrong

Faith and Fabric: A History of Rochester Cathedral, 604-1994
ed. Nigel Yates with the assistance of Paul A. Welsby

Early Modern Kent, 1540-1660
ed. Michael Zell

Kent in the Twentieth Century
ed. Nigel Yates with the assistance of Alan Armstrong, Ian Coulson and Alison Cresswell

Government and Politics in Kent, 1640-1914
ed. Frederick Lansberry

Volumes in Progress

Early Medieval Kent, 800-1220
ed. Sheila Sweetinburgh

Later Medieval Kent, 1220-1540

The Archaeology of Kent to AD 800

Edited by
John H Williams

The Boydell Press
Kent County Council

© Kent County Council 2007

First published 2007
The Boydell Press, Woodbridge,
and Kent County Council

ISBN 978 0 85115 580 7

The Boydell Press is an imprint of Boydell & Brewer Ltd
PO Box 9, Woodbridge, Suffolk IP12 3DF, UK
and of Boydell & Brewer Inc
668 Mt Hope Avenue, Rochester, NY 14620, USA
website: www.boydellandbrewer.com

A catalogue record for this book is a available from the British Library

This publication is printed on acid-free paper

Designed by Simon Coleman at White Gate Design   www.wgd.co.uk

Printed in Great Britain by Scotprint, East Lothian

The Archaeology of Kent to AD 800

Contents

Foreword

The Kent History Project is an ambitious undertaking that is presenting, through the work of dozens of academics, the first multi-volume history of the county since the work of Hasted in the late eighteenth century. This is the eighth volume in the series to be published by the County Council and it provides an authoritative survey of our current understanding of the archaeology and early history of the county.

Kent, with its beneficial geographical position facing the Continent, has a rich and exciting history. Over the centuries, numerous groups of traders, settlers, warriors and adventurers have travelled across its diverse landscapes. This book charts the impact of man on the landscape of the county and the life of its inhabitants, from some of the earliest human settlement in this country to the time when England was beginning to emerge as a nation state.

When I was Leader of Kent County Council from 1997 to 2005, Kent's present and future prosperity was a key objective. Nonetheless I increasingly realised that the special character and sense of place, which make it such an attractive County for residents and visitors, owe so much to its rich heritage and long and fascinating history. Development activity over the last twenty years, while presenting challenges to the conservation of the historic environment, has provided unprecedented opportunities for investigating Kent's archaeology, leading to fresh understandings and indeed the rewriting of several parts of the story.

Written by some of the most eminent archaeologists, this volume brings together the most recent fieldwork and research. The book includes a comprehensive review of recent work, including that occasioned by such major projects as the Channel Tunnel Rail Link. The combination of established frameworks and new perspectives makes us all realise that Kent has a heritage to be proud of, celebrate and cherish as we move forward into the twenty-first century.

I congratulate those who have brought this project to a wider audience and wish the project every success.

Sandy Bruce-Lockhart

Lord Sandy Bruce-Lockhart
Chairman of English Heritage

List of Illustrations

The authors wish to thank all those who have allowed illustrative material to be used in this volume. Full reference is hopefully made below to acknowledge duly all sources utilised.

Chapter 4
Prehistoric Kent

Chapter 5
Roman Kent

Chapter 6
Anglo-Saxon archaeology to AD 800

Notes on contributors

Martin Millett BA, DPhil, FSA, is Laurence Professor of Classical Archaeology at Cambridge University and a Fellow of Fitzwilliam College. He was previously a Professor at Durham and Southampton Universities, and worked for a period for Hampshire Museum Service. His research is focused on social and economic change in the Roman world. He has directed fieldwork and excavation projects in Britain, Spain, Portugal and Italy. His publications include The Romanization of Britain (1990), The early Roman empire in the west (1990), Roman Britain (1995; 2nd ed. 2005), and a range of fieldwork reports. He is currently the Director of the Society of Antiquaries of London.

Timothy Champion MA, DPhil, FSA, is Professor of Archaeology at the University of Southampton. He previously taught at University College, Galway, Ireland, and has been Visiting Professor at the Universities of Michigan and Zimbabwe. He is a past President of the Prehistoric Society and also a past Editor of the Society's Proceedings. He is a specialist in the later prehistory of western Europe and has been interested in the archaeology of Kent since completing his doctorate on the Iron Age of south-eastern England. Other research interests include the study of how contemporary societies understand and value the past, including such themes as heritage management, the relationship of archaeology and politics and the impact of archaeology on popular culture. Apart from work on prehistoric Britain, recent publications include Diaz-Andreu, M and Champion, T C, eds, Nationalism and archaeology in Europe (1996), and Ucko, P J and Champion, T C, eds, The wisdom of Egypt: changing visions through the ages (2003).

Martin Welch, MA, DPhil, FSA, is a Senior Lecturer in Medieval Archaeology, Institute of Archaeology, University College London. He began his career as an Assistant Keeper at the Ashmolean Museum, Oxford. He was appointed Lecturer in Medieval Archaeology in the History Department at UCL in 1978 and in 1990 was promoted to Senior Lecturer and transferred within UCL to the Institute of Archaeology. He completed an Oxford doctorate on Early Anglo-Saxon Sussex in 1979 (published in 1983 as a BAR monograph), and has produced monograph reports on excavated Anglo-Saxon cemeteries at Apple Down (West Sussex) with Alec Down and Norton-on-Tees (Cleveland) with Steven Sherlock. In 1992 he published an introductory book on Anglo-Saxon England in the English Heritage series. He is currently preparing a report on the 1976 excavation of the seventh-century Anglo-Saxon cemetery at Updown, Eastry (Kent). He has written articles and notes on a wide range of topics, chiefly relating to the period between the fourth and eighth century AD, including the study of Anglo-Saxon artefacts in Frankish cemeteries in northern France and Belgium. He was recently awarded a Leverhulme Research Grant to investigate state formation processes through archaeological evidence for the region south of the Thames between the fifth and seventh century, with particular reference to the evolution of the kingdoms of Kent, Sussex and Wessex.

Francis Wenban-Smith MA, PhD, is a Principal Research Fellow in the Department of Archaeology, University of Southampton. His current post, leading the Medway Valley Palaeolithic Project, is funded by the Aggregates Levy Sustainability Fund. After a BA in the 1980s at the London Institute of Archaeology, where involvement with the Boxgrove project stimulated an interest in the Palaeolithic, Francis took an MA in Lithic Analysis and Microwear at University College London. This was followed by a PhD at the University of Southampton, completed in 1996, focusing on the key Kentish Middle Palaeolithic site of Bakers Hole. By chance the Channel Tunnel Rail Link was then routed directly through this site, leading to the start of an active career as a Palaeolithic specialist for archaeological investigations in advance of development. Post-doctoral employment also included further years at Boxgrove. As well as many papers in academic journals, Francis has co-edited two books, Palaeolithic Archaeology of the Solent River (2001) and Lithics in Action (2004); the latter being the proceedings of the 21st anniversary conference of the Lithic Studies Society, for which Francis has recently been elected Chair.

John Williams MA, PhD, FSA, MIFA, is Head of Heritage Conservation and County Archaeologist at Kent County Council. Following a first degree in Latin he stayed on at Manchester University to undertake an MA in 'Stone Building Materials in Roman Britain'. For thirteen years he was head of the archaeology unit of Northampton Development Corporation and subsequently was awarded his doctorate for published work on the archaeology and history of Northampton. He was head of the archaeology unit of Lancaster University for five years from 1984, joining Kent County Council in 1989. A primary role has been to ensure that in the face of considerable development pressure Kent's archaeological heritage is appropriately safeguarded and investigated through the planning process. In recent years he has led a number of projects working with European colleagues to further the integration of archaeology within the planning process.

Introduction

by John H Williams

Today Kent's proximity to mainland Europe is underlined by the Channel Tunnel and the Channel Tunnel Rail Link, which speed traffic between England and the Continent: it is now quicker and easier to travel from Ashford to Brussels than to Birmingham. While improved transport links have dramatically shortened journey times to cross-Channel destinations, Kent has always had a special relationship with its continental neighbours. At times this has been a positive force, with Kent a conduit for trade and new ideas, but on other occasions the White Cliffs have symbolised defiance, with Kent being the front line in the defence of England.

Up to 400,000 years ago, when the straits of Dover were created, the chalk of the North Downs continued uninterrupted into northern France, with Britain as a peninsula rather than an island. In subsequent colder times the Channel froze over, while in warmer times Britain's island status was renewed, until, about 8,500 years ago, the final separation occurred. Throughout later periods of prehistory and carrying on into modern times there have been continuing links across the Channel and this is very much witnessed by the archaeological record.

Kent is a county of contrasts with its varying coastline, the downs and the wooded clay lands of the interior. This topography (ill. 1.1) owes much to a geology which is the most varied of any English county (ill. 1.2). Cretaceous strata were uplifted to form a dome, the Wealden anticline. This was subsequently eroded away, leaving the steep escarpments of chalk and greensand facing the Weald to the south, with more gradual dip-slopes facing northwards. Starting at the Thames in the north and journeying southwards one crosses estuarine wetlands, the undulating foothills of the coastal plain, the rolling chalk downlands culminating in a steep south-facing scarp, the greensand vale of Holmesdale with a further steep south-facing scarp, the heavy claylands of the Low Weald, the sands and clays of the High Weald and finally the coastal wetlands of Romney Marsh.

The coastal zone, the chalk downlands and the vale of Holmesdale, with their lighter soils, seem to have been attractive to settlement from earliest times. The heavier claylands of the Weald, however, have been thought to have been colonised only from the Saxon period onwards through gradual assarting and clearance of the woods and forests, although, where detailed fieldwork has been undertaken, Mesolithic and later flint scatters have been found in the Weald.

It will be interesting to see, as further field-work is undertaken in the county, whether our present perceptions of settlement history will need modifying further, for certainly archaeological work in advance of development over the last twenty years has radically increased our knowledge of Kent's past. Of particular significance have been projects such as the Channel Tunnel Rail Link and other major infrastructure works where it has been possible to uncover large areas. There a key objective has been to see how archaeological landscapes evolve spatially and chronologically, looking at relationships between sites and their contexts rather than concentrating just on the focal point of individual sites.

A clear indicator of the amount of archaeological activity in recent years is the quantity of 'grey literature' produced. This comprises the reports produced in relation to development-led archaeological evaluation work or indeed the excavations undertaken in advance of the construction works themselves. While some projects will be more formally published the key record for many investigations is the grey literature, copies of which are housed in the Historic Environment Record maintained by the Heritage Conservation Group of Kent County Council. The Record and the grey literature are available for public access. Between four and five hundred pieces of grey literature are currently being added to the Record each year. One of the important features of the present publication is the extensive use made by the contributors of this material, thereby demonstrating the significant

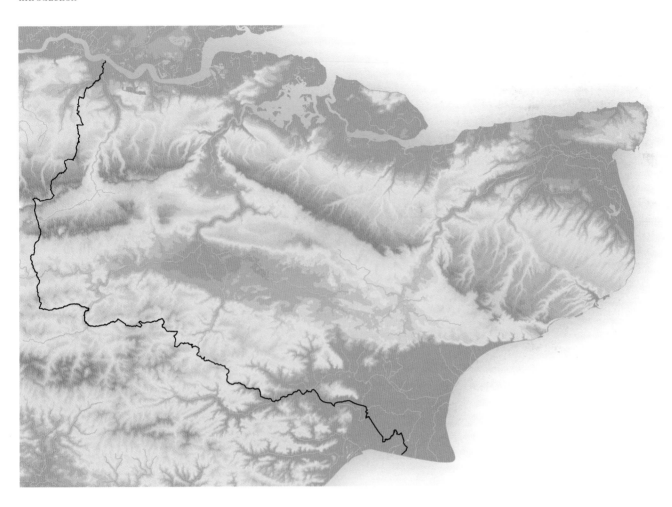

1.1 Kent: relief and drainage

contribution that development-led archaeology can make to furthering understanding of the past.

As noted at the beginning of this introduction a recurring theme throughout Kent's prehistory and history has been the relationship between Kent and mainland Europe and this is brought out in the various chapters. The need to look at Kent in a non-insular broader European context has been underlined during the various cross-Channel European projects in which the Heritage Conservation has been engaged in recent years, notably in relation to archaeology and spatial planning. The more general message, however, is that Kent has a key role in helping understanding both of England's past and of its continental neighbours.

This volume has been a long time in gestation and it is important to acknowledge the contribution of all those who have made its production possible. In the first place I would wish to remember Alec Detsicas, who was the original editor of this volume. Ill health, however, overtook him and indeed Alec subsequently died in 1999. His contribution to Kent's archaeology as editor of *Archaeologia Cantiana* and more generally was considerable. Secondly the various authors have had to cope with an ongoing flow of new archaeological material and editorial intervention, but they have been extremely successful in incorporating the most recent archaeological work, and we have all been most grateful for the assistance of the organisations and individuals who have freely given access to their work, much of it before final publication. Stuart Cakebread, Paul Cuming, Lyn Palmer and Andrew Richardson in particular have helped with copy-editing and sorting out the illustrations and relevant permissions. Casper Johnson has provided four

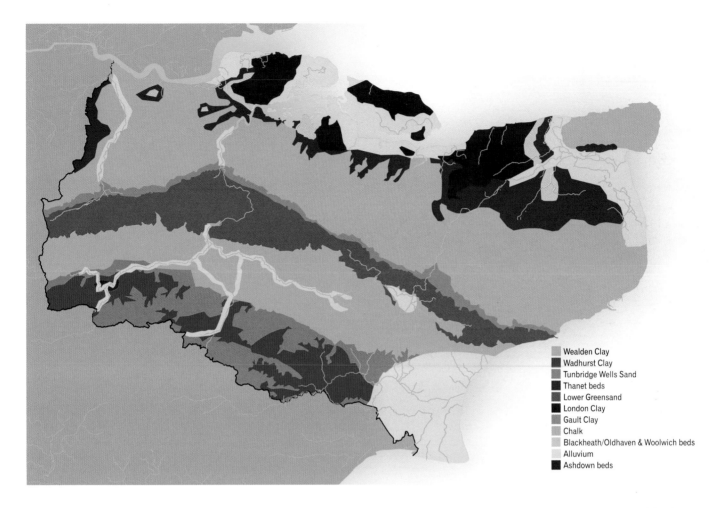

Wealden Clay
Wadhurst Clay
Tunbridge Wells Sand
Thanet beds
Lower Greensand
London Clay
Gault Clay
Chalk
Blackheath/Oldhaven & Woolwich beds
Alluvium
Ashdown beds

1.2 Kent: solid geology

reconstruction paintings especially for the volume. Ian Coulson, the general editor, has been helpful in a variety of ways. I have much enjoyed working with Linda Loe, Simon Coleman and the other staff at White Gate Design in translating ideas and images into graphic reality. To subscribers there is an apology for the delay in this volume seeing the light of day – I hope that the wait has been worthwhile. Finally in an archaeological volume such as this there is a thank you to those who across the millennia created the material which has been dug up, to those who have excavated and interpreted this material and indeed special thanks to my colleagues in the Heritage Conservation Group in Kent County Council who in recent years have contributed so much to the effective management of Kent's archaeological heritage.

The growth of archaeology in Kent

by Timothy Champion

The first recorded excavation of an archaeological site in Kent was some time before 1542, when the aptly named William Digges opened a barrow near Barham, between Canterbury and Dover, for King Henry VIII (Kendrick 1950, 105). He discovered a large urn containing a cremation, as well as what he thought were shields and helmets; he had probably found a Bronze Age primary cremation and Anglo-Saxon secondary burials (Grinsell 1992, 363). It is not clear whether he was seeking treasure or evidence of the past, but it was the time when an intellectual interest in the past was born. In 1533 King Henry had appointed John Leland as King's Antiquary and he travelled through Britain, mainly recording topography and family histories, but also describing some archaeological sites.

Somewhat later, William Camden set out to investigate Roman remains in Britain, though he found himself increasingly drawn into the problems of the pre-Roman period. In Kent, William Lambarde (1536-1601) drew up a more detailed account of the topography of the county in his *Perambulation* (1576). The new spirit of enquiry into the past is evident in their works, but their knowledge of the history of Britain before the Saxon period and of possible sources of evidence for it was severely limited. They knew and described the surviving Roman forts, but little else. Reculver, Richborough and Lympne were all well known monuments, as was the Roman pharos, or lighthouse, on the Western Heights at Dover, now demolished and built over; curiously, the eastern lighthouse, still surviving within Dover Castle, does not seem to have been recognised as Roman until the eighteenth century (Wheeler 1929). Although there was some debate as to how these sites should be reconciled with place names recorded in late Roman documentation, there was no doubt that they were indeed Roman. The Roman historians provided a framework within which the sites of that period could be interpreted, but for the centuries before and after there was as yet no basis for understanding.

The late seventeenth and eighteenth centuries witnessed a wave of enthusiasm for antiquarian

scholarship (Sweet 2004). The antiquaries, though often the subject of ridicule, devoted their energies to collecting and recording the evidence of the past, most often on a very localised basis. At first their main sources of evidence were written documents and the standing buildings of the medieval period, and their principal interests were in the history of landed estates and of civil and ecclesiastical authority. During the course of the eighteenth century, however, the significance of other archaeological remains, both sites and objects, began to be appreciated, and their field of enquiry widened and stretched further back in time.

In Kent, the early antiquarian histories, such as Harris's history of the county (1719) or Lewis's history of Thanet (1723), make few references to any archaeological remains earlier than the medieval period, except of course for the Roman forts. William Somner had already shown that the defences of Canterbury were Roman in origin (1640) and he also published a posthumous account of the Roman forts of the county (1693). His work was followed up by John Battely, who recorded inscriptions from Richborough and wrote a detailed account of Richborough and Reculver (1711). The antiquarian, William Stukeley (Piggott 1985; Haycock 2002), best known for his work at Avebury and Stonehenge, also made regular tours round Britain in the 1720s; in Kent he visited Canterbury and the Roman forts, but also recorded prehistoric earthworks on the chalk downs, now destroyed, as well as the remains of the Medway megaliths (Stukeley 1724; 1776) (ill. 2.1). Awareness of archaeological remains grew throughout the century: when William Boys wrote his history of Sandwich (1792) he described sites in the immediate neighbourhood, including not only Richborough, but also the foundations of the Roman temple at Worth to the south of the town.

The Roman period may have been the most important in the eyes of the eighteenth-century antiquaries, and certainly the one where it was easiest to make sense of the visible antiquities in the county, but important progress was also made in laying the foundations for understanding the early

Kits Coty house 15. Oct. 1722. The N.E. Prospect.

The View

The lower Coty house

The Groundplot

Stukeley delin:

F. Kirkall sculp.

2.1 William Stukeley's illustration (1722) of Kit's Coty House (above) and attempted reconstruction of Lower Kit's Coty House (below): compare ill. 4.7 and ill. 4.8.

Anglo-Saxon period. Many areas of Kent, especially the downs between Canterbury and Dover, still retained large clusters of burial mounds, and, as in many other parts of the country, these attracted the attention of the antiquaries. Unlike most other regions, however, where the barrows were mostly prehistoric, in Kent a significant quantity were of Anglo-Saxon origin. Excavations were undertaken from the beginning of the eighteenth century, but it was only towards the end of the century that the true nature of what was being recovered was appreciated. In 1730, Dr Cromwell Mortimer, secretary of the Royal Society, was exploring some barrows at Chartham Down, and attributed the burials to Roman soldiers who had been killed in Caesar's invasions; such was the quality of the objects included in the graves, that it was unthinkable that they could be anything but Roman.

Among those who came to see the excavations was the young Bryan Faussett (1720-1776), of Heppington, near Canterbury. Some years later, he began his own campaign of investigation, and between 1759 and 1773 explored nearly 800 graves in East Kent, including cemeteries such as Gilton, Barfriston and Kingston Down. He carefully preserved the grave goods discovered and kept meticulous records of his excavations, quite extraordinarily good by the standards of the time (Hawkes 1990) (ill.2.2). Unfortunately, although his work was known to other antiquaries, it was not published at the time, but, when it was eventually published (Faussett 1856) as *Inventorium Sepulchrale*, it became, and has remained ever since, an indispensable source of primary information (Rhodes 1990). Despite, however, the quality of Faussett's excavation and recording, he still attributed the remains he had discovered to the

Roman period, not to Caesar's soldiers but to 'Romans Britonized' or 'Britons Romanized'.

Among those who knew of Faussett's work was James Douglas (1753-1819) (ill. 2.3). A man of many talents and an enquiring mind, he served as an engineer in the army and later was ordained (Jessup 1975). While stationed at Chatham, he became interested in archaeological sites being destroyed in the course of the construction of defences, and from 1779 to 1793 he carried out a series of excavations of Anglo-Saxon burials, mainly at Chatham Lines and in Greenwich Park. His military training had taught him the importance of surveying and accurate planning and, like Faussett, his excavation and recording were well ahead of his time. Douglas, however, realised the true chronology and origin of these burials: arguing from the nature and distribution of the cemeteries in the areas of initial Saxon occupation, and from the occasional association in them of Roman coins of a date as late as the sixth century, he astutely rejected the accepted interpretation of them as Roman and rightly placed them in the pagan Saxon period. The publication of his results as *Nenia Britannica* (Douglas 1793) was a major landmark in British archaeology, but his views on Anglo-Saxon burials were not widely accepted for another fifty years.

By the end of the eighteenth century, therefore, considerable progress had been made in investigating and recording the prehistoric, Roman and Saxon archaeology of Kent, though it was only for the Roman period that there was sufficient understanding for the sites and objects to be properly appreciated. The state of archaeological knowledge at that time, a century on from Lambarde, is well reflected in Edward Hasted's massive *History and Topographical Survey of the County of Kent* (1797-1801). Hasted (1732-1812) came

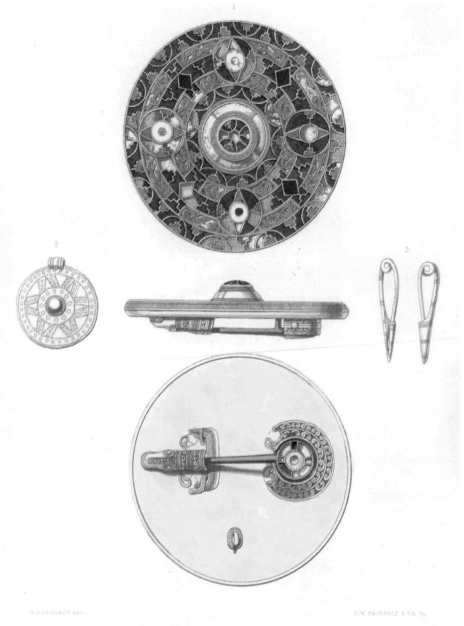

from a Kent land-owning family (Black 2001) and his work reflects the traditional interest in manorial and ecclesiastical organisation, but he also commented on social and economic history and on historic buildings and antiquities. He tried to visit each of the 400 parishes in the county to inspect them for himself. His information is presented on a parish basis, and at the end of each parish section he gives details of the antiquities known there; thus

2.2 The Kingston brooch, as illustrated in Roach Smith's publication of Faussett's *Inventorium Sepulchrale* (compare the photograph in ill. 6.30).

2.3 James Douglas, who correctly inferred the post-Roman date of the Anglo-Saxon burials of the sixth and seventh centuries AD.

never been experienced before. Kent in particular, as well as providing space for its own expanding towns and military and naval establishments, was well placed to produce building materials such as sand, gravel, cement and bricks to meet the insatiable demands of London. Some antiquarians continued to excavate new sites, but much was destroyed by development. Sometimes attempts were made to record what was being destroyed, but more often objects were collected later from workmen; much presumably went completely unrecorded. The rapid increase in the availability of artefacts, whether properly provenanced or not, encouraged the habit of forming personal collections of local antiquities.

In the early part of the century it was again the Roman and the early Anglo-Saxon periods that attracted the most interest. Lord Albert Conyngham dug a 'considerable number' of barrows in the large cemetery on Breach Downs in 1841 (Conyngham and Akerman 1844), and Douglas's idea that these burials were of Saxon date was beginning to gain credence; detailed analysis of the associations of the pottery and metal-work had shown that they belonged to the fifth and sixth centuries AD, not the Roman period (Rhodes 1990, 49), and, with the publication of Akerman's *Archaeological Index* (1847), the argument was finally resolved. Roman sites were increasingly disturbed and, because of the comparative ease of identifying coins and pottery of that period and the importance attached to them, they were more often preserved and collected. In East Kent, William Rolfe, the grandson of William Boys, the historian of Sandwich, formed a large collection of antiquities (Matson 1962); he himself excavated at Richborough *c.* 1846, but much came from other sites. His collection was sold to the wealthy Liverpool goldsmith and collector, Joseph Mayer (Gibson and Wright 1988), and then on again to the archaeologist Sir John Evans. In Maidstone, a local doctor, Thomas Charles, was an active excavator and collector; he dug the Roman villa at The Mount, Maidstone (Charles 1843; Kelly 1992; Houliston 1999). At his death, he bequeathed his house and his collections to the town of Maidstone, where it formed the basis for Maidstone Museum.

in his account of St John's parish in Thanet, he describes the old port of Margate and the recent explosion of new development as it emerged as a fashionable sea-bathing resort. He then records the discovery of what we would now recognise as a late Bronze Age axe hoard, as well as Roman coins and burials, and subsequently, in his treatment of St Peter's, gives details of the prehistoric burials found in the excavation of the Hackendown Banks barrows in 1743 (Hasted 1797-1801, Vol. X, 329-32 and 368-9). Hasted, however, did not attempt to do more than record these finds, and had very little idea about how they should be interpreted, apart from the obvious Roman remains.

The pace of exploration quickened in the nineteenth century. All over England, urban and industrial expansion and the construction of canals and railways, as well as the beginnings of mechanised ploughing, turned over the soil in a way that had

2.4 Members of the British Archaeological Association excavating barrows at Breach Down during the Canterbury Congress of 1844.

Though many of the excavations were partial or poorly recorded, others were more informative. The Roman villa at Hartlip had been discovered in the eighteenth century (Hasted 1797-1801, Vol. VI, 16-17), and further excavations took place in 1845 and 1848 (Smith 1852b). One of the most remarkable projects of this period was the total excavation of a bath house at Boughton Monchelsea, near Maidstone, in 1841 (Smythe 1842). The excavator, Charles Smythe, a local solicitor and Town Clerk of Maidstone, also dug an important walled cemetery at Lockham, but his verbose account of it had to wait forty years for a brave editor to prepare it for publication (Scott Robertson 1883).

The central decades of the 1800s saw some of the most important intellectual and organisational changes in the study of the past in England. The biblical chronology of a six-thousand-year-old world was finally abandoned as a combination of Darwin's biology and prehistoric archaeology showed that the world and the human species were both enormously older than that. The Three Age System began to provide a structure for thinking about this much longer past, with its successive Stone, Bronze and

Iron Ages extended still further when Sir John Lubbock divided the Stone Age into Old and New phases, or Palaeolithic and Neolithic (Lubbock 1865). Just as important were changes in the way the past was studied, as the amateur enthusiasm for antiquarianism gave way to the professional discipline of archaeology (Levine 1986): national and local organisations were formed, permanent institutions for research and preservation were established, specialist journals were published, conferences were held and eventually professional career opportunities emerged.

Perhaps the most important event for the future development of archaeology in Kent, albeit indirectly, was the foundation of the Archaeological Association in December 1843 (Wetherall 1994). A group of archaeologists, including Albert Way, Thomas Wright and Charles Roach Smith, had grown increasingly frustrated at the inertia of the Society of Antiquaries of London and their failure to prevent the destruction of the archaeological heritage, and formed a new organisation, intended to be more active. Its inaugural meeting was held in 1844, and the location selected was Canterbury, a clear indication of the city's archaeological importance. The meeting was an academic and social success, attended by more than 200 people. To coincide with the event, Lord Albert Conyngham arranged for a further eight barrows on Breach Downs to be opened (ill. 2.4), and the still unpublished Faussett collection in the family home at Heppington was also made accessible to the visitors. Shortly after the Canterbury meeting, the Association, for a variety of financial, social and personal reasons, split into two successor organisations, the Archaeological Institute and the British Archaeological Association. Charles Roach Smith, who was respected as one of the leading archaeologists of the period, allied himself with the latter.

Charles Roach Smith (1806-1890) was in business in London as a wholesale chemist, but devoted much of his time to archaeology. He formed a large collection of Roman antiquities, mostly recovered during redevelopment work in London, which he sold to the British Museum in 1865, where it became the nucleus of their Romano-British collection. He took a particular interest in the archaeology of Kent and, when he eventually retired from business, moved to Strood, near Rochester. He attempted to persuade the British Museum to acquire the Faussett collection when it was offered to them in 1853, and was furious at their refusal. It was eventually acquired by Joseph Mayer and displayed in the museum he founded in Liverpool (Macgregor 1998). Mayer also financed the publication of the collection, edited with a short introduction by Roach Smith (Faussett 1856). Through his own research and his support for that of others he made a major contribution to our knowledge; his work on the Roman period, especially pottery and buildings, was fundamental to all later research. He also appreciated the archaeological importance of the North Kent marshes, both for the history of Thames embankment and additionally on account of the buried or submerged evidence of earlier periods (Smith 1880).

Alongside these national organisations, many counties founded archaeological societies (Piggott 1974). Kent was not among the first wave, but the Kent Archaeological Society eventually came into being in 1857 (Jessup 1956), largely due to the energetic and diplomatic efforts of the Revd Lambert Larkin, Rector of Ryarsh, who defeated attempts to link Kent and Sussex in a single society. The Society provided the institutional basis for the promotion of archaeology in the county. It brought together a wide range of people with interests in the past, and disseminated knowledge through its meetings and its publications, especially *Archaeologia Cantiana*. It also laid the foundation for future research through forming its own collection of local antiquities and a library and archive, and sponsored new excavations on a series of Roman and Saxon sites. Despite inevitable problems of financing such an ambitious programme of investigation and publication, the Society played a major role in developing the practice of archaeology in the county in the later decades of the century, a role that, with some occasional fluctuations in its fortunes, it has continued to play to the present day.

Another major innovation was the establishment of local museums. The collection and preservation of antiquities had hitherto been a matter for interested individuals, many of whom built up large and valuable collections. From the early nineteenth century, however, it became accepted that this was a public function, and local museums were founded by borough authorities or county archaeological societies. Several towns in Kent set up their own museums: the first was in Dover, founded in 1836, followed by others in Maidstone, Canterbury, Rochester, Dartford and elsewhere. The Maidstone Museum, opened in 1858, was created from the bequest of Dr Thomas Charles's house and collection; the building also housed the growing collection of the Kent Archaeological Society. These museums acted as important institutions for the promotion of research, and also for presenting Kent's past to a wider audience.

The archaeological work carried out in the later

part of the nineteenth century largely reflected earlier interests, with a continuing concentration on the Roman and Saxon periods. Some sites were investigated or recorded in the course of their destruction, but research on unthreatened sites became more common. The Kent Archaeological Society sponsored further excavations of Saxon cemeteries, as at Sarre (Brent 1863; 1866; 1868), and T. Godfrey Faussett (later T. G. Godfrey-Faussett), great-grandson of Bryan Faussett, carried out well-recorded work at Bifrons (1876; 1880). Despite this activity, other sites were destroyed with minimal recording; perhaps the richest of all Saxon cemeteries, that in the King's Field at Faversham, was lost to railway construction and other work, though the artefacts collected were acquired by the British Museum.

Charles Roach Smith played an important role in promoting Roman research. He published a further review of knowledge about the three major forts at Reculver, Richborough and Lympne (1850) and subsequently excavated at Lympne (1852a). Knowledge of villas and other buildings slowly increased, with excavations such as those at Boxted (Payne 1883) and Maidstone (Smith 1876), but it was not until near the end of the century that an entire villa plan was exposed, at Darenth (Payne 1897).

Knowledge of the prehistory of Kent developed more slowly. Important Bronze Age barrow excavations took place at Ringwould, near Deal (Woodruff 1874), and the late Iron Age burials recovered from a sand pit at Aylesford by Arthur

Evans (1890) played a major role in the development of knowledge of that period. The most significant progress, however, was the recognition of the archaeology of the Palaeolithic period and the particular importance of the deposits in the Ebbsfleet valley in West Kent. Much of the credit for this is due to Flaxman Spurrell. The work of the French archaeologist, Jacques Boucher de Perthes, in the valley of the Somme near Abbeville had revealed tools made by humans securely stratified with the bones of extinct animal species, and the implications of these discoveries were widely publicised by Lubbock's *Pre-historic Times* (1865). It seemed likely that the geologically similar gravels of the Thames and its tributaries would contain similar finds. Stone tools had been noted for some time in the region of Reculver and Herne Bay, but it was the careful fieldwork of Spurrell, recording the findspots of the tools and correlating them

2.5 Benjamin Harrison outside Oldbury rock shelter.

with the gravel terraces of the Thames, that marked the first systematic understanding of the Pleistocene sequence in west Kent (1883). He also published what is probably the first attempt at refitting struck flakes to reconstruct an original flint nodule (1880a). Another important figure in the development of west Kent archaeology was Benjamin Harrison of Ightham (Harrison 1928), who spent a lifetime exploring his local landscape and building up extensive collections of artefacts, which he housed in a museum over his draper's shop in the village (ill. 2.5). He is now best remembered for claiming that flints from the chalk plateau, which he called 'eoliths', were very early and crudely made human tools. These are now recognised as purely natural stones but Harrison did make many important contributions to our knowledge of the early prehistoric archaeology of his region.

One of the most active archaeologists of the later nineteenth century was George Payne (1848-1920), who was born and raised in Sittingbourne. He showed an early interest in archaeology, and was introduced to Roach Smith, who was an important influence on his later work. Payne energetically recorded the antiquities discovered in the quarries, brickfields and building sites of north Kent and also carried out further fieldwork. By the 1880s he had amassed a large collection of antiquities, which he offered to Sittingbourne in an attempt to found a local museum. This was frustrated and his collection passed to the British Museum. In 1888 Payne moved to Rochester and continued his career of exploration and recording in the field. Here his ambitions for a museum were more successful, and he was the prime mover in the foundation of Rochester Museum as a focus for the collection and display of local antiquities. From 1889 to 1904 he was Chief Curator of the Kent Archaeological Society's collections in Maidstone, but his main enthusiasm was for fieldwork.

Two of Payne's ideas for the development of the organisation of archaeology were strikingly ahead of their time. He collated a list of all the archaeological sites and findspots in Kent with an associated map, the methodology used by most subsequent regional records before computers. The published version (Payne 1888) included an annotated map, a gazetteer with bibliographical references, and a very brief introduction. The map and the list were updated by subsequent Curators, and Payne's initiative deserves to be recognised as the first County Sites and Monuments Record in Britain. Another of his ideas was less successful, though no less far-sighted. In 1892 he suggested that a post should be created with county-wide responsibilities for archaeology, to be funded by the local borough authorities. The boroughs predictably refused to contribute, but the idea was a remarkable forerunner of the County Archaeologist structure that became established almost a century later.

The archaeology of Kent owes much to outstanding figures such as Charles Roach Smith, George Payne and Flaxman Spurrell. Many, however, of the greatest names in archaeology in the nineteenth and early twentieth centuries, who had connections with Kent through living or working there for a longer or shorter time, had somewhat variable impacts on the archaeology of the county. Charles Darwin and John Lubbock were neighbours near Bromley but they made no direct contribution to the study of Kent's past, however great their indirect influence. General Pitt Rivers, though before he changed his name from Lane Fox, served as an instructor at the army School of Musketry at Hythe, and returned to East Kent to excavate near Broadstairs on the Isle of Thanet in 1868 (Pitt Rivers 1868) and at Caesar's Camp, Folkestone, in 1878 (Pitt Rivers 1883); although minor projects compared to his later researches in Cranborne Chase, they played an important part in the evolution of his field methods (Bowden 1991, 57-94). The young Flinders Petrie, later to be celebrated as the founder of modern Egyptology, grew up in Kent near Woolwich and learnt his surveying techniques on Kentish earthworks (Petrie 1880); in 1877 he gave a lecture to the Royal

Archaeological Institute, where he met the then Col. Lane Fox, and also Flaxman Spurrell, who was to become a close friend and collaborator (Drower 1995, 22-26). Another whose reputation now rests on a later career in the Near East was John Garstang, who conducted a short excavation at Richborough in 1899 (Garstang 1900).

By the start of the twentieth century, therefore, the state of archaeology in Kent was probably as good as for any county in England. The summaries written for the *Victoria County History of Kent* show the enormous progress made in the century since Hasted. The prehistoric section (Clinch 1908) is rather disappointing, but reveals an increased understanding of the Palaeolithic and the Bronze Age, especially the metal-work. The Saxon section (Smith 1908) provided a narrative of the accumulating evidence for that period, demonstrating in particular the wealth and importance of the sixth- and seventh-century cemeteries. The Roman section (Haverfield *et al.* 1932) was delayed until a later volume, and was of a completely different scale of detail and interpretation; although the general improvement in knowledge of Roman Britain in the intervening years was partly responsible for this difference, it was also a reflection of the amount of research devoted to Roman Kent in the previous two centuries compared to other periods. In the decades leading up to World War II, however, much less progress

2.6 Excavations at Coldrum in the 1920s.

was made, despite some important excavations and spectacular discoveries. Urban and industrial development continued, especially along the north coast and in the suburban fringes of London, but too often without the same level or quality of observation and recording.

The lack of visible field monuments of the prehistoric period held back research on this period compared to other regions of Britain. Small-scale work was undertaken at Coldrum (Bennett 1913; Filkins 1928), in the western group of Medway megaliths (ill.2.6), and at Julliberrie's Grave in the Stour valley (Jessup

1937; 1939), but there were no further excavations of Bronze Age barrows or significant settlement sites. Elsewhere, hillforts provided a major focus for field research on the Iron Age; Kent has few such monuments, but excavations were carried out at Bigberry (Jessup and Cook 1936) and Oldbury (Ward Perkins 1944). Nor were there any important excavations of Anglo-Saxon cemeteries. Perhaps the greatest progress was made in the Roman period. A long series of excavations was begun at Richborough (Bushe Fox 1926; 1928; 1932; 1949), and a large cemetery at Ospringe (Whiting *et al.* 1931) and a massive villa at Folkestone (Winbolt 1925) were explored. The pace of development slowed in Canterbury, resulting in fewer opportunities for excavation, but little was done to synthesise or publish the results of the previous century's work. In Dover, however, Wheeler's careful collation of earlier observations (Amos and Wheeler 1929; Wheeler 1929) set knowledge of the town's Roman phase on new foundations and paved the way for further research.

The Second World War brought most archaeological work to a stop, and the following decades saw only slow progress. Excavations, however, began in 1944 and 1945 respectively in the bomb-damaged areas of Canterbury (see box adjacent) and Dover (Threipland and Steer 1951; Threipland 1957; Rahtz 1958). Archaeological work, especially excavation, had hitherto been almost exclusively the preserve of the amateur, possibilities for professional employment being extremely limited – to staff from museums or the Office (later Ministry) of Works – but these people had many other commitments and restricted time for fieldwork. The excavations at Bigberry by Norman Cook of Maidstone Museum and at Richborough by J P Bushe-Fox of the Office of Works had been some of the first by professional archaeologists, but research in advance of the construction of military sites during the war, as at Manston airfield, and the redevelopment of bombed towns provided new opportunities for professionals. Funds for such

Exploring Canterbury's past

The site of the present-day city centre of Canterbury has been occupied continuously since the first century BC. The structures of each successive phase have been overlain, and in part destroyed, by those of later generations; medieval and later cellars have been especially destructive. The earliest layers of the Iron Age, Roman and Anglo-Saxon periods survive in places, but often at considerable depths.

Redevelopment has provided the opportunity for increasing our knowledge of Canterbury's past; where it has been carried out with archaeological research and recording, that knowledge has been realised, but where there was no record, the evidence has been lost forever. Where there has been little recent redevelopment, there have been few opportunities for exploration. Thus in the north-eastern quarter of the city, now occupied by the Cathedral precinct, there have been few chances to glimpse the Roman streets and buildings that are known to lie underneath. Conversely, the area to the south, around and to the south of St George's Street, was worst affected by bombing in World War II, and its destruction and subsequent rebuilding have made it archaeologically the best known sector of the Roman and medieval city.

The seventeenth-century antiquary, William Somner (1640), was able to use historical evidence and standing remains to deduce that the city defences were of Roman origin. Some of the defences and gates were recorded by later scholars such as Stukeley (1724) and Gostling (1774), but little attention was paid to remains below ground. At the end of the eighteenth century Canterbury suffered its first demolitions to improve traffic flow: most of the gates were demolished, as was the east end of St Margaret's church, and in 1806 Guildhall Street was created to improve access to the north. No record was made of the antiquities destroyed or revealed, but archaeological awareness improved rapidly. The suburban expansion of the city and the construction of the railways encroached upon the outlying Roman cemeteries, such as Martyr's Field, but many objects

were recorded and recovered (Brent 1860; 1861). One of the most remarkable contributions to Canterbury archaeology was made by the City Engineer, James Pilbrow, in 1868. The construction of a drainage system meant the digging of ditches up to 5 metres deep along many of the city's streets, cutting through prehistoric, Roman and medieval layers. Pilbrow's careful observations and accurate recording (1871) allowed the first attempt to map the streets and buildings of the Roman town.

The destruction of the eastern half of the city in the bombing of 1942 provided another opportunity for research, and excavation had begun by 1944. The Canterbury Excavation Committee carried out annual projects until 1957, mainly in the cellars of bombed out buildings. During the 1960s, redevelopment continued, but archaeological rescue work was very small-scale, much being done by the local postmaster, Dr Frank Jenkins. In 1975 a new professional organisation, the Canterbury Archaeological Trust, was established to carry out archaeological operations, and it has monitored the redevelopment of city sites since then. Many of these sites have been very extensive, requiring investigation on a much larger scale than previously, such as the series of excavations on the Whitefriars site.

2.7 The 'Big Dig': large-scale excavation (2000-2003) of medieval and Roman Canterbury before the redevelopment of the Whitefriars shopping centre.

work, however, were scarce and much still depended on the efforts of enthusiastic amateurs such as Ronald Jessup and Frank Jenkins. Roman villas continued to stimulate interest and activity: the Lullingstone villa, with its mosaics and evidence for Christianity, attracted much public attention (Meates 1955; 1979; 1987). Iron Age hillforts were also a focus, with excavations at High Rocks, near Tunbridge Wells (Money 1968), Caesar's Camp, Keston (Piercy Fox 1969), Squerryes, Westerham (Piercy Fox 1970), Quarry Wood Camp, Loose (Kelly 1971) and Castle Hill, Tonbridge (Money 1975; 1978), followed by further work at Bigberry (Thompson 1983) and at Oldbury (Thompson 1986).

The words used by a number of speakers at a conference held in 1979 to review the archaeology of Kent (Leach 1982) are indicative of a sense of frustration at the lack of progress: 'The archaeology of the Neolithic period in Kent has been neglected' (Clarke 1982, 25); 'If the prehistory of Kent has been neglected in favour of the later periods, the Bronze Age has perhaps suffered worst' (Champion 1982, 31); 'Iron Age studies in Kent and the immediately adjacent territories have remained in something of a doldrum' (Cunliffe 1982, 40). Such gloomy assessments may have been somewhat over-pessimistic, especially in view of some of the work being done at the time by local amateur groups, but they were not totally unrealistic.

Transformation of the organisation of archaeological activity in Kent and our knowledge of the county's past had in fact already begun. As elsewhere in England, the rate of the destruction of the archaeological heritage had increased rapidly and had attracted public and political attention (Jones 1984). One response was the increasing professionalisation of archaeological practice: organisations with a core of full-time professional staff, such as the Canterbury Archaeological Trust, the Trust for Thanet Archaeology and the Kent Archaeological Rescue Unit (Philp 2002), were set up or emerged from previously amateur groups. Key work included

Archaeology and the Channel Tunnel

Most archaeological investigation is focused on a single site or development plot, but projects such as railways, major road schemes or pipelines provide an opportunity for a very different sort of insight into the past. They are linear transects across the countryside, often through areas where little is known about the archaeology, and thus offer us unique evidence for the history of human exploitation of the landscape. In Kent, the topography of the county has determined the major routes of the communication network. Roads and railways run predominantly east to west along the north coastal plain or at the foot of the scarp slope of the downs and through the valleys of the Darenth, Medway and the Stour, with major crossings of the Medway near Rochester or Maidstone: even the modern addition of motorways and a railway to the Channel have followed the same basic routes. So, although archaeological discoveries along these routes tell us much about the nature and density of human occupation in Kent, the results are relevant only to these specific zones: other areas, such as the high chalk downlands or the clays of the Weald, may well have very different histories which need to be investigated separately.

The building of such major infrastructure projects has always caused disturbance and destruction to the archaeological remains along the route, but the nature of the response by archaeologists has varied greatly. Most of Kent's railways were constructed in the period from the 1840s to the 1860s (Jessup 1958, 162-171), when it was not possible to mount a systematic programme of excavation; much was recovered during the operations, especially around Faversham and Canterbury, but records are poor and much more must have been lost without trace. Improvement of the road system for motor traffic took place piecemeal throughout the twentieth century, again with little organised archaeological response. In the second half of the century, however, the construction of the motorways represented a new stage in road building, much of it along new alignments. The archaeological response was better,

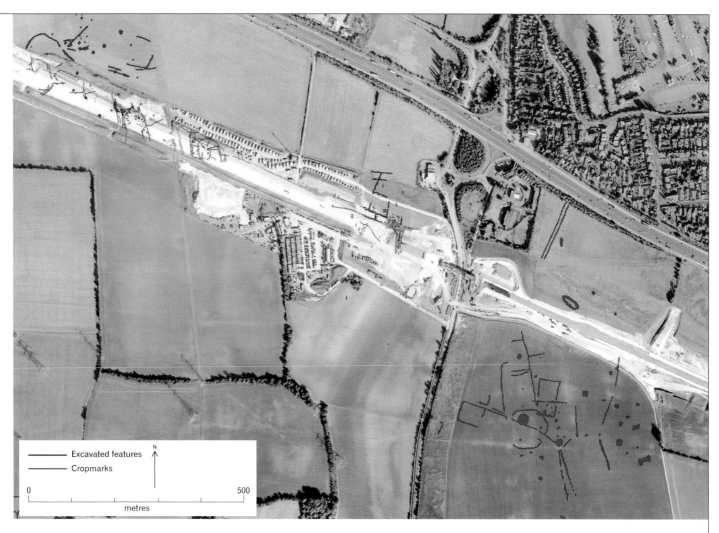

Excavated features
Cropmarks

N

0   500
metres

but still variable; rescue work in advance of the construction of the M20 included the total excavation of an Iron Age settlement site on Farningham Hill (Philp 1984, 7-71).

The biggest development project in Kent has been the construction of the Channel Tunnel Terminal and subsequently the Channel Tunnel Rail Link. The construction of the terminal involved the development of a large area at the foot of the downs, producing important archaeological and environmental evidence, including Bronze Age burials and Iron Age occupation sites, as well as a large sample of an organised early Bronze Age landscape, with a trackway and the fence lines of an enclosure (Bennett 1988).

The later construction of the Rail Link was one of the biggest engineering undertakings in the county

since the original railways, and the associated archaeological investigation probably the biggest such project in Britain. It involved preliminary documentary research and detailed survey of the entire route to minimise the impact on the archaeology, and the preparation of a research design to identify the problems that could be answered; then further investigation of the sites with the highest potential, and finally the excavation of more than forty of the most important sites. These included neolithic structures at White Horse Stone, Bronze Age burial monuments, later Bronze Age and Iron Age settlement sites, especially at White Horse Stone and Beechbrook Wood, the Roman villa at Thurnham, and the vast Roman cemetery at Pepper Hill near Springhead, and important Saxon burials at Saltwood, all of which are discussed later in this volume.

2.8 Vertical view of the Channel Tunnel Rail Link excavations south of Gravesend with the excavated features highlighted in purple and unexcavated cropmark evidence in red.

major programmes of work elucidating Canterbury's urban development (Blockley *et al.* 1995), the discovery of the Roman fleet bases at Dover (Philp 1981; 1989) and the excavation of the Bronze Age boat at Dover (Clark 2004).

Another response was the increasing acceptance by local government during the 1970s and 1980s of its responsibility for archaeology. This was largely co-ordinated at county level and Kent, following the example of other counties, appointed a County Archaeological Officer in 1989; a century after George Payne's original suggestion, a team was built up in the County Council's Strategic Planning Service to maintain a Sites and Monuments Record, to advise planning authorities on the impact of development proposals, and to give other advice on archaeological and heritage matters. The publication of Planning Policy Guidance Note 16 on archaeology and planning in November 1990 brought about a fundamental change in the relationship between archaeology and development and provided a much firmer basis for the conservation and investigation of archaeological sites. PPG 16 requires either the preservation *in situ* of potentially significant archaeological remains or their investigation as part of the development process. Additionally the growing professionalism of archaeology was reinforced.

By the early 1990s the impact of these changes was generally becoming evident, and particularly in a county such as Kent, with its wealth of archaeology being subjected to increasing development pressure. The volume of archaeological activity had grown dramatically; almost all of it was in advance of development and carried out by a variety of professional organisations to specifications and standards set by the county archaeological team. The large scale of development in the countryside, both for infrastructure works, such as the Channel Tunnel Rail Link and various major road schemes (see box pages 20-1), and also housing and industrial development, was a contributory factor in the

development of the technique of 'strip, map and sample', where the landscape dynamics of archaeology, both spatially and chronologically, assume considerably greater importance. Extensive areas have been investigated, providing significant new insights into how archaeological sites relate both to their immediate context and also their wider hinterland (*Current Archaeology* 168 (2000)).

This increase of archaeological knowledge, reflected in the Sites and Monuments Record and its associated archive of reports, was thus largely determined by modern development activity. New information related mainly to those areas affected by economic growth or regeneration projects, such as the north coast, the Medway towns, Thanet and around Ashford, with less new information about other areas such as the Weald, where there was much less redevelopment.

This recent explosion of knowledge can best be seen by comparing the vision of Kent's past presented in this volume with earlier attempts to summarise the county's past, such as Jessup's pioneering book (1930) or the rather gloomy conclusions of the contributors to the 1979 conference (Leach 1982). It is important to recognise the efforts of early antiquarians such as Bryan Faussett and James Douglas and their nineteenth-century successors Charles Roach Smith and George Payne, but our knowledge of the archaeology of Kent has been totally transformed since the 1980s.

The Palaeolithic archaeology of Kent

by Francis Wenban-Smith

Introduction

The Palaeolithic is the earliest period of human history, yet several factors make its study unique. The Palaeolithic has an immensely long duration, much longer than any subsequent period. In Britain, it covers the time from initial colonisation by early hominins, possibly as long ago as 800,000 years, to the end of the last ice age *c.* 10,000 years ago. Although very recent compared with the 4,600 million years since the molten earth began to solidify, and the 65 million years since the global extinction of dinosaurs, this is still extraordinarily far back in time (ill. 3.1). If one imagines the history of Britain as a football match, the Palaeolithic represents all ninety minutes of normal time. Later prehistory, including the entirety of the Neolithic, the Bronze Age and the Iron Age, occurred during five minutes of extra time and the period that has elapsed since the start of the Christian calendar is not much more than a particularly long blast of the final whistle.

The British Palaeolithic coincides with the second half of the Pleistocene geological period, often known as 'The Ice Age'.[1] During the Pleistocene the climate underwent numerous and repeated dramatic changes, oscillating between glacials, episodes of severe cold, and interglacials, episodes of warmth. Thus, rather than a single Ice Age, there were repeated ice ages throughout the Pleistocene, separated by interglacials. At the cold peak of glacial periods, ice sheets hundreds of metres thick would have covered most of Britain, reaching on occasion as far south as London and rendering the country uninhabitable. At the warm peak of interglacials the climate would have been warmer than the present day; mollusc species that now inhabit the Nile were abundant in British rivers, and tropical fauna, such as hippopotamus and forest elephant, were common in the landscape. For the majority of the time, however, the climate would have been somewhere between these extremes.

This history of dramatic climatic changes had a major impact upon the landscape of Britain. During periods of cold climate, glaciers carved out major valleys, cutting through pre-existing sediments and pushing earth and rocks before them. So much of the global water supply was locked in ice sheets that global sea levels fell, leading to rivers cutting new channels at lower levels, and leaving behind sediments from previous channels high above the banks of the new channels. The lack of vegetation meant that the landscape was more vulnerable to mass movement of deposits. A range of events, from seasonal snow melts or rainstorms to more dramatic floods or freezes associated with the pivotal points of climatic change, would have caused major bodies of sediment to slide downhill, denuding high ground and filling hollows in low ground.

The present landscape of Britain is the result of almost two million years of these processes, although relatively little change has taken place since the end of the last ice age. The evidence of occupation from the post-glacial occupation of Britain, embracing initial Mesolithic hunter-gatherers, later prehistoric Neolithic and Bronze Age societies (cf. Chapter 4) and all subsequent periods, is reflected in artefact finds and structural features that have been left, or created, on the surface of this post-glacial landscape. A few post-glacial sedimentary formation processes, such as the formation of alluvial floodplains, peat bogs or colluvial deposition, have led to the deeper burial of post-glacial evidence, but, for the most part, strip away the topsoil and one can find evidence of Mesolithic occupation, Bronze Age houses or Roman villas. Evidence for the Palaeolithic, in contrast, is buried within the older, underlying sediments. Although this evidence is sometimes close to the surface, where further deposition has not occurred, or where subsequent erosion has led to the ancient sediments being exposed, it is often buried more deeply, under five, ten, or even twenty metres of ancient river gravel, cliff collapse or mass slope-movement deposits.

The process of burial has often also led to major disturbance of the evidence that has been preserved. Artefacts can be transported significant

[1] For the dating framework for the Pleistocene and Palaeolithic in Britain see ills 3.9 and 3.16. Dates for the Palaeolithic are often referred to as years BP – *Before Present*. Dating is also sometimes defined in terms of marine isotope stages (MIS) (pages 35-7).

Timeline

3.1 Timeline; note that the timescale is logarithmic, increasing by a factor of 10 with each downward step.

Million years ago			
Present	HOLOCENE	Norman Conquest (AD 1066) Roman Invasion of Britain (AD 43)	HISTORIC TIME
		Bronze Age (4,000 to 3,000 BP) - Pyramids Neolithic (6,000 to 4,000 BP) - Stonehenge	LATER PRE-HISTORY
0.01	PLEISTOCENE (ICE AGES)	End of last Ice Age (10,000 BP) Extinction of Neanderthals (35,000 BP)	PALAEOLITHIC
0.1		Evolution of anatomically modern humans in Africa (125,000 BP) First hominins in Britain (750,000 BP)	
1		Spread of early Homo into Europe and Asia (1,500,000 BP)	
	TERTIARY	First stone tools in Africa (2,400,000 BP)	PRE-HUMANITY
10		Proliferation of early bipedal hominins in Africa (5,000,000 to 3,000,000 BP)	
		Separation of Africa and America (40,000,000 BP) First primates and expansion of mammals (60,000,000 BP)	
100	MESO-ZOIC	Extinction of dinosaurs by asteroids (65,000,000 BP) Age of the dinosaurs - (225,000,000 to 65,000,000 BP)	
	PALAEO-ZOIC	First animals	
1,000	PRE-CAMBRIAN		
		First plants and algae (3,000,000,000 BP) Earth solidifies from molten state (4,600,000,000 BP)	
5,000			

28

distances, losing the geographical context and spatial patterning that might be used to reconstruct behaviour. Evidence from different episodes of activity can also be mixed together, making it more difficult to use the sparse evidence that we do find to interpret Palaeolithic behaviour and lifestyle. Furthermore, artefacts that have been buried once can be reworked and reburied by later depositional events. This causes uncertainty over whether evidence that is found together is of the same broad age, or comprises material from tens of thousands of years apart, misleadingly combined into a single deposit.

The evidence itself is very limited in character. There are no written or oral records of the Palaeolithic period and we are limited to the remains that survive in the deposits of the period, as well as, for its final part, enigmatic paintings on the walls of caves and rock-shelters. The majority of the evidence comprises stone tools, and waste from their manufacture. These are relatively indestructible, although they often show wear and tear from their history of, sometimes violent, burial and post-depositional disturbance. Other evidence is only rarely preserved. Organic materials such as artefacts made of wood or plant fibres, or faunal dietary remains, are much more vulnerable to decay, and require particular conditions of burial and ground chemistry to survive.

Given all these difficulties, one might consider study of the Palaeolithic a futile task; those in the discipline would probably prefer 'challenging'. The great age and rarity of Palaeolithic evidence in themselves provide a fascination to many. The Palaeolithic is also another world, a world populated by exotic beasts, hunted by extinct forms of hominin in a landscape and climate alien to our experience. Nonetheless, evidence of this world pervades and underlies many of the drabber parts of our present industrial and urban landscape, exposed on occasion in road cuttings, building foundations or even our gardens. Certain aspects of the Palaeolithic may always be beyond our reach, but the interest and the challenge of

studying the Palaeolithic lie in making the best of the very limited evidence that we do have, combining 'hard' Quaternary science with the 'soft' theorising of the humanities to provide tiny glimpses into this other world.

Before looking at the Palaeolithic of Kent, some background information will be useful. The following two sections provide, firstly, a brief summary of how the British Palaeolithic fits into the wider global and European picture, and secondly, consideration of the particular significance of Kent for British Palaeolithic research. Clearly the former has to be a very thumbnail outline, but a number of references are provided for those who wish to pursue the wider picture further. There then follows an outline of the dating and climatic framework of the Pleistocene period, with discussion of the range of depositional processes that have affected Palaeolithic material and the consequent implications for interpretation of the evidence. The Palaeolithic in Britain is then reviewed, with major cultural trends and the accompanying hominin evolutionary development being outlined. One of the difficulties, or challenges, of the discipline is that we are dealing with a period that encompasses, over 500,000 years, the arrival of one hominin species, their evolution into Neanderthals, extinction of the Neanderthals and arrival of the first modern humans. Finally, against all this background, it will be possible to present a survey of the Palaeolithic in Kent.

The global and European context
The Palaeolithic begins in the east African Rift Valley over two million years ago, with the manufacture of simple stone chopping tools by Australopithecines, a group of bipedal apes with a brain capacity not very different from the modern chimpanzee. Since then, these apes have taken over the world, evolving into a range of progressively more recognisably human forms while colonising ever-increasing swathes of the earth's surface. They have developed more sophisticated technologies, first in stone and then

in other materials, and most recently they, or rather we, have harnessed the atomic forces of the universe.

The initial hominin expansion out of Africa took place between 1.5 and 1 million years ago, and involved eastward migration across southern Europe into Asia (Dennell 2003). The hominins at this stage, named as *Homo erectus* or *Homo ergaster*, and much more recognisably human than their Australopithecine ancestors, were capable of inhabiting a range of tropical and subtropical regions, but could not yet cope with the seasonality of the higher European latitudes. The long winter and more restricted growing season meant that a hominin could not rely upon the wide range of plant and animal foodstuffs available year-round in more tropical regions. Survival in more northerly latitudes such as Britain would depend upon the ability to exploit a more restricted variety of seasonally available resources, such as rhinoceros or deer in winter and nuts or berries in autumn. Physiological factors must also have restricted expansion of the hominin range; the tropical-adapted *Homo* would have been, and still is, vulnerable to the cold in higher latitudes. Expansion into these latitudes would have depended upon solving these problems by some means. This could have been any, or most likely a combination of, physiological evolution (new mental capabilities, body shape, body fat, increased body hair), social/behavioural evolution (food sharing, group-building/maintenance), or technological evolution (clothing, hunting equipment).

Initial expansion into Britain and Europe seems to have consisted of very occasional forays during periods of warm climate between 800,000 and 500,000 BP. A few very early sites of this age are known in France and Spain, as well as one recently discovered in Britain at Pakefield on the Norfolk coast (Parfitt *et al.* 2005). The evidence consists of very simple cores and flakes recovered from deposits that indisputably date to an interglacial substantially older than MIS 13, although how much older is uncertain. These were presumably made by a form of *Homo*

erectus/ergaster, known to be present in Central/Eastern Europe from at least 1,000,000 BP. The only other evidence in north-west Europe that may come from this period is from the site of Saint-Malo-de-Phily, in Brittany, north-west France, where a heavily abraded simple chopper-core has been recovered from fluvial gravels that have been tentatively dated to *c.* 600,000 BP (Jumel and Monnier 1990). These pioneer populations failed to establish themselves, however, and soon died out.

Following these isolated occurrences of very early hominin presence, there then was a major range expansion northward into Britain and northern Europe between 600,000 and 500,000 years ago, and from this point the region is almost continually settled, although with some population movement at its northern fringe, and probably in highland zones, caused by expanding and retracting ice sheets. There are a number of sites, dating from *c.* 500,000 BP, associated with the early western European *Homo heidelbergensis*, named after a jawbone found in a quarry at Mauer, near Heidelberg, in Germany. Several other sites from this period also contain evidence of stone tool manufacture (Roebroeks and van Kolfschoten 1994; 1995), among them Boxgrove in West Sussex where an extensive area of undisturbed lithic evidence is associated with abundant faunal remains and palaeo-environmental indicators, as well as fossil remains of two individuals (Pitts and Roberts 1997; Roberts and Parfitt 1999). These comprise two lower front incisors from one individual, and a shinbone from another. Hominin remains from this period are so rare that the Heidelberg and Boxgrove finds comprise the full skeletal record of this early north-west European ancestor. A slightly less limited quantity of material, including Neanderthal remains from continental Europe (Stringer and Gamble 1993) and a notable pre-Neanderthal skull from Swanscombe in north-west Kent (cf. box pages 50-1), represents the remainder of the Palaeolithic until the arrival of modern humans in its final stages.

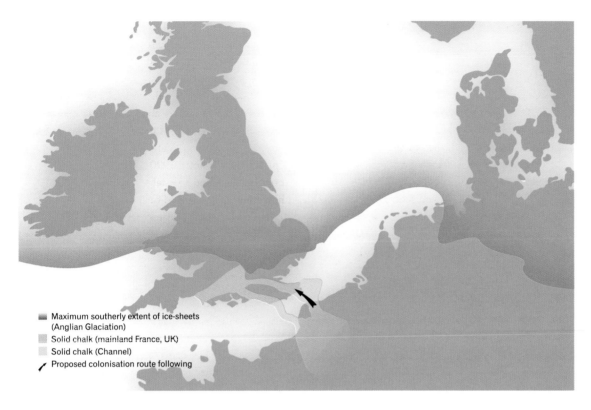

Maximum southerly extent of ice-sheets
(Anglian Glaciation)
Solid chalk (mainland France, UK)
Solid chalk (Channel)
Proposed colonisation route following

3.2 Map showing the southern extent of the Anglian ice sheet, and the migratory route across the straits of Dover.

After 500,000 BP, Palaeolithic occupation became more frequent in Britain, although certainly not continuous. Periodic deteriorations in climate would have made Britain uninhabitable, and existing populations must either have died out, or moved southward to the continent. Britain would then have become inhabitable again as the climate ameliorated. Sea levels would, however, have risen with the warming climate, and, once the straits of Dover had been created through breaching the Dover–Calais Chalk ridge, probably in the Middle Pleistocene *c.* 400,000 years ago (Gibbard 1995), access to Britain would have been effectively obstructed during warm periods. The potential of hominins and other fauna to recolonise would have been governed by a sensitively balanced combination of the distribution of the refuge population, its rate of range expansion as climate changed and the rate of sea level rise. Once a population had returned to Britain it would then be isolated from the Continent by high sea level until the following

climatic deterioration. This history of contact with the northern European mainland, of abandonment and recolonisation of Britain, or of extinction of its population, is still poorly understood.

The significance of Kent

Kent is a particularly significant county for the study of the Palaeolithic in Britain. It is the closest part of the country to the European mainland and this may well have made it the first part of Britain to have been visited and settled by *Homo*. Early in the Palaeolithic the Dover–Calais strait had not yet been formed, and there would have been a highway of chalk downland, rich in flint raw material for tool manufacture and grazed by abundant herbivores, leading along the north-eastern side of the Wealden anticline and continuing into what is now northern France (ill. 3.2). Whether or not evidence for such pioneering colonisation survives in Kent has long been the subject of debate and is considered below. Due to its proximity to continental

3.3 Investigation of Pleistocene exposures at Barnfield Pit in 1906. The figures are thought to be Reginald Smith of the British Museum and Henry Dewey of the Geological Survey.

hominin refuges, Kent would also have continued to be one of the first regions to be recolonised following the periodic abandonment of Britain which accompanied climatic fluctuations.

Kent was also relatively unaffected by glaciation, the ice sheets that repeatedly grew during glacial episodes never reaching further south than London and south Essex (ill. 3.2). Indeed the main reason that the Thames Estuary is in its current position is that the Thames was diverted southward by ice sheet growth from its original route across East Anglia. Advancing ice would have erased any archaeological traces under or immediately in front of it. Thus, having been beyond the reach of the destructive effects of ice sheets, Kent, along with other southern counties, preserves a rich record of geological deposits with Palaeolithic archaeological evidence. The valleys of rivers such as the Thames, the Medway and the Great and Little Stour, and numerous minor

tributaries, such as the Darent and the Beult, contain, preserved as terraces on the valley-sides, ancient fluvial deposits with archaeological evidence from the whole of the Palaeolithic.

More recently, the situation of Kent adjacent to continental Europe, and the role of the navigable Thames Estuary as a key means of access to Britain, have placed parts of the county at the heart of urban development and the increasing industrialisation of the British landscape. This has had both advantages and disadvantages for advancing understanding of the Palaeolithic. The combination of population growth and infrastructural and industrial development since the nineteenth century has led both to considerable disturbance of deposits containing Palaeolithic archaeological evidence, and at the same time a relatively high level of investigation and recording (ills 3.3, 3.4). The growth of Palaeolithic archaeology as a discipline in the late nineteenth century was characterised by the enthusiasm of a number of amateur researchers. While only the richest could afford to indulge an interest in the classical archaeology of Greece and Italy, the evidence of the Palaeolithic was all around and offered a more socially inclusive and widely accessible intellectual pursuit.

Many of the best of these amateurs were active in Kent, systematically investigating quarries, rail cuttings and house foundations for Palaeolithic evidence. Although all cannot possibly be mentioned here, the activities of Spurrell in particular were exemplary in the amount of material found (cf. Chapter 2), the recording of the locations and stratigraphic contexts of his finds, and their study and interpretation. The work of Spurrell (e.g. 1880a; 1880b; 1883), and subsequently of others such as Harrison, Stopes, Cross and Marston, has led to the discovery and recognition in Kent of a number of highly significant Palaeolithic sites, the investigation of which has underpinned the development of understanding of the British Palaeolithic as a

whole, and not just its manifestation in Kent. Kent has by a long way the highest number of Palaeolithic artefacts and find-spots recorded of any county in Britain: over 40,000 artefacts, almost 14,000 of them handaxes, from 475 sites are present in museum collections across the country (cf. ill. 3.17).

Pleistocene climatic and dating frameworks
The Pleistocene
Study of the Palaeolithic is inseparably entwined with study of the Pleistocene. Scientific investigation of Pleistocene, or 'drift', sediments began early in the nineteenth century. These sediments were distinguished as soft rocks of sands, clays and gravels, generally between five and twenty metres maximum thickness, overlying the much deeper 'solid' geology of the earth's crust. They were not present everywhere, but outcropped in certain places, such as along the flanks of modern river valleys. It became clear that they represented evidence of a relatively recent part of earth's geological history, but a period

3.4 Early quarrying at Barnfield Pit.

3.5 Handaxes from
(a) the Somme, northern
France (H 169mm),
(b) Hoxne, Suffolk (H 190mm)
and (c) Preston Hall Aylesford
(H 161mm).

(a)　　　　(b)　　　　(c)

well before any historically recorded era, and one where the landscape and climate were wholly unfamiliar. The sediments were often recognisable as, for instance, river gravels, lake-bed clays or shingle sea-beaches, but they were found in inexplicable situations in the modern landscape: river gravel and lake-bed sediments on hilltops, or shingle beaches well inland from the present-day coastline and fifty metres above the current sea level. Remains of Roman buildings and Neolithic monuments were dug into their top part, and they contained evidence of extinct animals such as mammoths, straight-tusked elephant and woolly rhinoceros. Other remains, such as pollen, seeds and molluscs, often showed that the sediments were formed under quite different climatic conditions from the present day, frequently much colder and almost arctic, although sometimes warmer. The sediments were attributed to 'The Ice Age', on the basis of the cold-climate evidence they contained, their presumed formation by catastrophic flooding caused by the melting of snow and ice, and other evidence demonstrating the movement of erratic rocks by glaciers in the British landscape. We now know, however, that these deposits represent a series of ice ages, with intervening periods of warm climate – a geological period we call the 'Pleistocene'.

After this basic geological framework was in place, it was recognised that certain curiously pointed and symmetrical flint objects – handaxes (ill. 3.5) – that were found in Pleistocene sediments, must have been made by humans, and thus that humans must have been present in this early era, despite the absence of historical sources and in contradiction with religious texts.

Investigation of the Pleistocene is fundamental to Palaeolithic research because it tells us everything about the context of a site, allowing investigation of key questions such as:
• How old is the site?
• How was the site formed?
• How disturbed are the artefacts?
• What was the prevailing climate?
• What was the contemporary landscape?
• What plants and animals were available as resources?

Dating techniques

Absolute, or chronometric dating techniques depend upon understanding the change of some property of a material through time. Relative dating techniques depend upon fitting sites without any absolute dating evidence into a framework based on geological relationships and zoological correlation or biostratigraphy. For instance, the evolutionary development and extinction dates of certain species of vole are particularly well understood, leading to the so-called 'vole clock' for the British Pleistocene. As long as there are a few sites in these frameworks that have absolute dating and so can act as fixed points, other sites can be dated by comparison, provided relevant evidence is present.

Several chronometric techniques applicable to the Pleistocene have been developed (Smart and Frances 1991), the most frequently used being carbon 14, optically stimulated luminescence (OSL), uranium series and amino acid racemisation dating (ill. 3.6). Carbon 14 and uranium series dating depend upon measuring the radioactive decay through time of certain unstable isotopes. OSL dating depends upon the continuing natural rearrangement through time of electrons within buried sand grains under the influence of background cosmic radiation. By heating a sand grain, and finding out how much energy is given off by the return of electrons to their original sites, one can establish how long the sand grain has been buried. Amino acid dating depends upon identifying the ratios of left-handed and right-handed optical isomers in shell proteins. A living shell has a natural imbalance, whereas after death the balance begins to revert to an even split. Measuring the degree of imbalance can therefore give an indication of time elapsed since death. Each technique has its limitations of range and accuracy, and none works reliably for the early part of the Palaeolithic. Often the main limitation is that suitable material for applying any of them is not present at a site. In such a situation dating has

to depend upon correlation with other sites of known date. This is usually done by geological correlation based on the location of the site in relation to other sites, or zoological correlation.

The climatic and environmental framework

Alongside dating techniques, other key elements of Pleistocene research since the nineteenth century have concerned the development of a fuller understanding of climatic changes through the period, and the association of changing climate with fluctuating sea level, terrestrial sedimentation and the evolution of the landscape. By collating information from a few locations across the globe where a continuous sedimentary record is preserved, such as the Chinese loess plains, the Antarctic ice cap and the Pacific seabed, a complete and dated framework of climatic changes through the Pleistocene has been developed (Shackleton and Opdyke 1973; 1976; Berger et al. 1984). The beginning of the Pleistocene, approximately 1.8 million years BP, is marked by deterioration in the climate. Over sixty numbered cold and warm stages have now been recognised relating to the time following this initial cooling, based on fluctuating proportions of the oxygen isotopes O18 and O16 in deep-sea foraminifera (ill. 3.7). By convention odd numbers represent warm stages and even numbers cold ones, and stages are counted back from the present. We are therefore currently in marine isotope stage (MIS) 1, which represents the 10,000-year warm period since the end of the last ice age. If it were not for the impact of global

Main chronometric Pleistocene dating techniques

Technique	Material	Age range	Accuracy
Carbon 14	Organic remains (plant, bone)	Up to 40,000 BP	2-3%
OSL	Sand	Up to 400,000 BP	5-10%
Uranium series	Bone	Up to 400,000 BP	5-10%
Amino acid racemisation	Mollusc shells	20,000 to 400,000 BP	5%

3.6 Main chronometric Pleistocene dating techniques.

Global marine oxygen isotope stage framework

3.7 Global marine oxygen isotope stage (MIS) framework, showing Pleistocene stages, timescale and sea-level change.

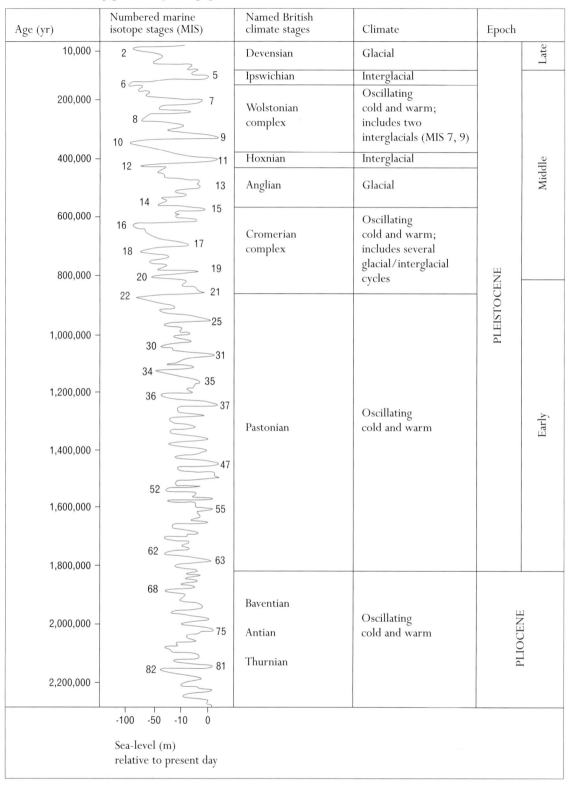

Age (yr)	Numbered marine isotope stages (MIS)	Named British climate stages	Climate	Epoch	
10,000	2	Devensian	Glacial	PLEISTOCENE	Late
	5, 6	Ipswichian	Interglacial		
200,000	7, 8	Wolstonian complex	Oscillating cold and warm; includes two interglacials (MIS 7, 9)		Middle
	9, 10				
400,000	11, 12	Hoxnian	Interglacial		
	13	Anglian	Glacial		
	14, 15				
600,000	16, 17	Cromerian complex	Oscillating cold and warm; includes several glacial/interglacial cycles		
	18, 19				
800,000	20, 21				
	22, 25				
1,000,000	30, 31	Pastonian	Oscillating cold and warm		Early
	34, 35				
1,200,000	36, 37				
1,400,000	47				
	52, 55				
1,600,000					
	62, 63				
1,800,000	68	Baventian		PLIOCENE	
2,000,000	75	Antian	Oscillating cold and warm		
	81, 82	Thurnian			
2,200,000					

-100 -50 -10   0

Sea-level (m)
relative to present day

warming caused by modern use of fossil fuels and other chemicals, then we might well be heading for the next ice age, since the Pleistocene record shows that peaks of climatic warmth, such as we are experiencing, have often only lasted 5,000-10,000 years.

The earliest Palaeolithic evidence in Britain occurs early in the Middle Pleistocene, at *c.* 700,000 – 800,000 BP (MIS 17-19) (cf. ills 3.7 and 3.16). Since then there have been at least seven major cold stages, alternating with interglacials. Only a small proportion of the Pleistocene time-span, however, is taken up by peak glacial or interglacial conditions. The majority of the Pleistocene consisted of conditions in between glacial cold and present-day warmth, with numerous minor cold and warm oscillations lasting hundreds or thousands of years. It should also be remembered that even the shortest climatic oscillations of the MIS framework would have been too long to be noticed at the scale of a human lifespan. It is possible that a few major events might have been marked by catastrophic events noticeable by individuals, such as major floods associated with rapid climatic warming at the start of MIS 5e. It is also possible that the prevalence of flooding myths in religious texts and folk stories is a distant oral record of flooding and climate change at the start of the present interglacial 10,000 years ago. Nonetheless the major climatic variability recognisable by hominins through the Palaeolithic would have been seasonal.

As the Pleistocene climate varied, there were corresponding changes in landscape, fauna and flora. Study of preserved remains such as tree pollen, molluscs and insects allows reconstruction of the Pleistocene climate and environment. During the more prolonged and intense cold stages of the Middle and Late Pleistocene, increased quantities of water across the globe became bound up as snow and glacial ice in mountainous and polar regions. The amount of water frozen was sufficient to lead to substantial drops in global sea level, to as much as 100m below that of the present day. The tree line would have migrated southward, and the plant and animal populations dramatically changed, with species evolving to adapt to the cold, dying out or migrating. Mean annual temperatures in Britain would have been between –5 and –10°C, with the winter temperature as low as –25°C and the summer temperature not exceeding 10°C. The landscape would have been a treeless plain, dissected by hills and fast-flowing rivers with gravel beds and banks, probably with quite rich grassland and small shrubs in the summer, when not covered by snow and ice.

Conversely, during interglacial periods substantial quantities of global snow and ice would have melted, leading on occasion to sea levels higher than the present day. The climate in Kent would have been up to 3° C warmer than now, similar to Spain or France. The landscape would have been heavily wooded, although intensive grazing by large herbivores may have maintained open patches of grassland on the chalk downland and along river floodplains. The rivers would have been relatively quiet-flowing, although still substantial, with fine-grained sand and silt sediments filling the beds, and spreading over the banks during seasonal flooding to form rich alluvial floodplains.

Pleistocene sediments and site preservation
It is only through the sediments that survive from the Pleistocene, and the archaeological and environmental evidence they contain, that we have any knowledge of the Palaeolithic. Sediments have been deposited through a range of processes relating to the fluctuations in sea level and climate through the Pleistocene, and have been formed under both glacial and interglacial conditions, as well as during transitions between these climatic extremes. They only accumulate, however, in certain locations in the landscape, and then are vulnerable to subsequent reworking or destruction. Consequently our knowledge is initially restricted by the limited circumstances where sediment formation has incorporated archaeological material and where sediments

Climate

Terrace sequence

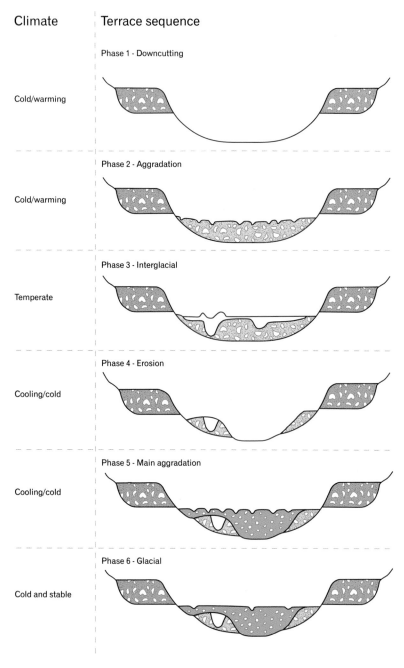

Phase 1 - Downcutting

Cold/warming

Phase 2 - Aggradation

Cold/warming

Phase 3 - Interglacial

Temperate

Phase 4 - Erosion

Cooling/cold

Phase 5 - Main aggradation

Cooling/cold

Phase 6 - Glacial

Cold and stable

3.8 Pleistocene river terrace formation.

evidence, confuses the spatial distribution of evidence from various areas of activity and combines material from different phases of occupation and possibly periods. Other processes bury material gently, preserving faunal remains and individual areas of activity. The swiftness of burial will affect whether single episodes of activity are represented, or an accumulated behavioural palimpsest. Although many types of Pleistocene sediment have produced Palaeolithic evidence in Britain (Wymer 1995), in Kent there are only four main types:

- River terrace deposits
- Mass movement colluvial/solifluction deposits
- Aeolian/loessic deposits
- Residual deposits.

River terrace deposits

During cold periods, the reduction in vegetation and the action of seasonal freezing and thawing led to decreased sedimentary stability, and increased river flows and sediment-carrying capacity. Abetted by geological uplift and the drop in sea level due to more of the global water supply being tied up in snow and ice, river channels eroded downward, leaving terraces of older deposits high above the banks of the new channel (ill. 3.8). Over the course of the Pleistocene, the recurrence of cold–warm cycles led to repeated downcutting of the Thames and its tributaries, leaving a series of successively older terrace deposits on the valley sides up to 150m above the level of the present-day channel. Crucially for dating, these terraces are thought to correspond with major stages of the Pleistocene marine isotope stage framework (Bridgland 1994), with each terrace containing fine-grained sediments from an interglacial stage, sandwiched by coarser-grained sand and gravel sediments from the onset and end of glacial stages. The coarser sands and gravels represent phases of faster water flow with mobilisation and transport of pebbles on the river bed, regular migration of the narrow channels containing water and frequent rearrangement of sand and gravel bars

survive to the present day. Interpretation of the evidence we do have is then dependent upon understanding of how it has become buried. Different burial processes have different implications for any archaeological evidence. Some processes lead to substantial mixing and transport of material, and this destroys fragile between the water channels. The finer-grained sediments represent slower-moving bodies of water, when small particles of silt and fine sand accumulate on the river bed and alluvial floodplain without being washed away.

The process of river terrace formation is significant for the Palaeolithic, since Pleistocene river terrace deposits are one of the commonest sources of Palaeolithic artefacts. Rivers provided, or were the key to, many of the most significant resources for early hominins. The water would have attracted game animals to drink, besides also being needed by the hominins themselves. The beds of rivers would often have contained abundant pebbles, usable both as a source of raw material for stone tools and as percussors for their manufacture. Where a river channel cut into Chalk bedrock, or secondary deposits rich in derived flint nodules, a ready supply of larger, fresher flint for knapping would have been exposed at the riverbank and on its bed.

When hominin activity was taking place at a time of faster water flow and sand/gravel deposition, any archaeological evidence left at a river would most likely have been quickly incorporated in the sands and gravels by seasonal spates. It was then liable to have been further transported and rearranged, as water channels, sand banks and gravel bars migrated across the floodplain. Thus evidence from fluvial sand/gravel deposits has generally been disturbed, and does not represent *in situ* evidence of activity on a palaeo-landsurface. This does not, however, mean that it is of no use for archaeological interpretation. Fluvial deposits that contain archaeological material from a reasonably wide catchment area provide a more representative sample of the range of artefacts produced over the period of occupation than evidence from a single undisturbed site, which might represent just one event. Each downcutting phase would lead to some reworking of older artefacts into the new channel-bed, but the majority would be left in the correct part of the terrace sequence, preserved for the future. Older derived specimens are likely to be a rare component of assemblages from a terrace body, and also be distinctive through their greater degree of abrasion. Thus the stone tool evidence in sequences of river terraces in different basins can give a useful insight into the overall trajectory of regional cultural change and hominin presence through the long Palaeolithic period.

Although most fluvial deposits are coarser sands and gravels, beds of finer-grained silts and fine sands also occur within terraces. These occasionally bury, or include, temporarily exposed landsurfaces on which hominins were active. The quieter deposition of these sediments means that any archaeological evidence is left undisturbed. Such sites are extremely rare, with fewer than twenty known in England, but several of them are in Kent, notably Swanscombe, Crayford (now in Greater London) and Baker's Hole (cf. boxes pages 50-1, 56-8). Such sites provide more detailed information about behaviour at a particular place, complementing the more disturbed evidence from fluvial gravels. The two types of evidence combine to provide a fuller picture of the Palaeolithic than would be possible from either on its own.

Mass movement colluvial/ solifluction deposits

Mass slope-movement deposits have formed by a range of processes, for example rapid, high-energy landslip events that incorporate rocks and pebbles of all sizes alongside finer-grained sands and silts, or gradual, low-energy events where fine-grained sediments creep slowly down a slope. Consequently the Palaeolithic remains they contain have varied depositional histories and interpretative potential. In general, colluvial and solifluction deposits occur at the base of slopes, on the surface of valley sides, in dry valleys and in hollows in the landscape, anywhere, in fact, where sediment destabilised by severe climatic conditions and/or de-vegetation has slipped downslope and accumulated. Despite their sometimes coarse nature, many colluvial/solifluction deposits have slipped only a short distance, leading to the relatively gentle burial of archaeological material. Others have moved a longer distance, and may also include derived material from significantly older deposits, for instance when a landslip cascades down a dry valley tributary across a series of terrace deposits of different ages.

Aeolian / loessic deposits

Kent is unique within Britain for the quantity of loessic sediments preserved on the chalk downland and high ground within the Weald. These sediments are very fine sands and silts, gathered by wind and then deposited at particular parts of the landscape where wind-speed dies. From the Palaeolithic archaeological point of view loessic deposits are potentially significant because they form progressively, burying any archaeological evidence very gently and preserving it undisturbed. Although they are not so well developed as the thick loessic sediments of north-east France, substantial areas of sediment mapped across Kent as Head Brickearth are of loessic origin, and often of substantial age. The loess in northern France has produced frequent rich and spectacular Palaeolithic archaeological sites; the equivalent resource in Kent has been less subject to archaeological investigation due to its lack of recognition, although a background noise of stray finds gives a hint that more careful investigation could reveal important sites.

Residual deposits

Residual deposits can be found capping high ground where there has been little Pleistocene deposition, but the surface has been subject to exposure throughout the Pleistocene, leading to the development of sediments. These probably represent remnants of soils built up throughout the Tertiary and Pleistocene and periodically subject to sub-aerial weathering and degradation accompanying climatic oscillations. Any artefacts within residual deposits may have been reworked within the sediment by repeated freezing and thawing, but not been subject to down-slope

movement or fluvial transport. Accordingly any archaeological evidence found in residual deposits such as Clay-with-flints, which often caps chalk on high ground in Kent, has probably been deposited close to where it was found. There is rarely, however, any precisely stratified material, and Neolithic, Mesolithic and Palaeolithic finds can all be contained within the same horizon. Thus the archaeological material from residual deposits comes from a palimpsest representing 500,000 years of intermittent occupation.

The chronological and stratigraphic framework

Pleistocene deposits in different regions of Britain have been dated and related to the overall MIS framework, based on stratigraphic relationships, chronometric dating, zoological correlation, and mapping of river terrace gravel sequences. Certain key deposits have been identified as coming from particular isotope stages, and the site-names of these deposits have been adopted for the different glacial and interglacials of the MIS framework (ill. 3.9). This is a difficult subject, however, and the Quaternary scientific community is continually revising its attribution of particular sediments to particular isotope stages (e.g. Mitchell *et al.* 1973; Bowen 1999).

The key link between Kent and the wider framework is provided by deposits of the Anglian glaciation at Hornchurch, in south-west Essex, being cut into by those of the highest terrace of the Lower Thames, the 100-foot, or Swanscombe, terrace. This terrace, which contains a number of important Palaeolithic sites, then continues eastward into northern Kent. Several lines of evidence link the Anglian deposits to ice advances associated with MIS 12, and the Swanscombe deposits to the subsequent interglacial MIS 11. Starting from this key relationship, the succession of lower terraces in the Thames valley in northern Kent has been tied into the sequence of younger isotope stages (Bridgland 1994). Terrace sequences in Thames tributaries such as the Darent and the Medway can also be fitted into this

British Pleistocene chronological and stratigraphic framework

3.9 British Pleistocene chronological and stratigraphic framework.

Epoch	Age (BP)	Marine isotope stage (MIS)	Stratigraphic stage (Britain)	Climate
Holocene	Present — 10,000	1	Flandrian	Warm — full interglacial
Late Pleistocene	— 25,000 — 50,000 — 70,000 — 110,000	2 / 3 / 4 / 5a–d	Devensian	Mainly cold; coldest in MI Stage 2 when Britain depopulated and maximum advance of Devensian ice sheets; occasional short-lived periods of relative warmth ('interstadials'), and more prolonged warmth in MIS 3 – when modern humans colonised north-west Europe
	— 125,000	5e	Ipswichian	Warm — full interglacial
Middle Pleistocene	— 190,000 — 240,000 — 300,000 — 340,000 — 380,000	6 / 7 / 8 / 9 / 10	Wolstonian complex	Alternating periods of cold and warmth; recently recognised that this period may include more than one glacial–interglacial cycle, and that there may be distinct changes in faunal evolution and assemblage associations through the period that may distinguish its different stages.
	— 425,000	11	Hoxnian	Warm — full interglacial
	— 480,000	12	Anglian	Cold — maximum extent southward of glacial ice in Britain; may incorporate interstadials that have been confused with Cromerian complex interglacials
	— 620,000 — 780,000	13–16 / 17–19	Cromerian complex and Beestonian glaciation	Cycles of cold and warmth; still poorly understood due to obliteration of sediments by subsequent events
Early Pleistocene	— 1,800,000	20–64		Cycles of cool and warm, but generally not sufficiently cold for glaciation in Britain

Further information Jones & Keen 1993

framework by relating the channel profiles of different terraces to the points of confluence, and through independent dating of specific terraces in the tributary systems, by, for example, OSL or zoological correlation. The major problem on most sites, however, is to tie down dating firstly within a regional framework, and secondly within the national and international MIS framework.

The Palaeolithic in Britain
The nature of the evidence

Our understanding of the Palaeolithic is hampered by the fact that the earliest written texts post-date the end of the Palaeolithic by thousands of years. Unlike in later periods, there is no evidence in Britain, and very little elsewhere, for structures such as huts, houses or monuments, leading to the

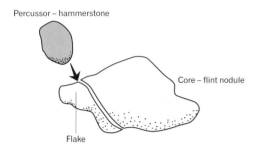

3.10 Hard hammer knapping – striking a flake from a flint nodule.

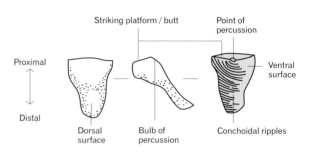

3.11 Hard hammer flake characteristics.

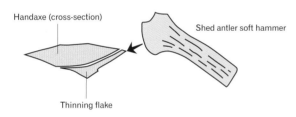

3.12 Soft hammer knapping – striking a flake from one face of a handaxe.

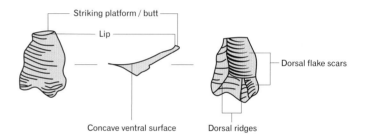

3.13 Soft hammer flake characteristics.

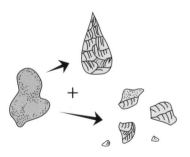

3.14 Handaxe and waste debitage.

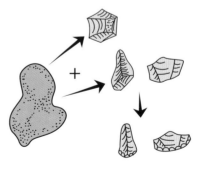

3.15 Core, waste debitage, scraper and backed knife.

Stone tool manufacture

Pieces of raw material need to be struck with a percussor for flakes to be removed from a core. A rounded piece of stone weighing 250g to 1kg is generally used. Percussors made of stone are grouped together as hard hammers. Percussors can also be made of softer organic material such as wood, bone or the proximal ends of shed antlers (soft hammers). Hard hammers and soft hammers are used in different ways and for different purposes (ills 3.10, 3.12), and flakes produced by each type of hammer have distinct identifying characteristics (ills 3.11, 3.13).

There are two fundamentally different approaches to the manufacture of lithic artefacts. Firstly, one can take a piece of raw material and remove flakes to leave a finished core-tool, such as a handaxe — the flakes removed, or debitage, are essentially waste products (ill. 3.14). Alternatively, one can focus on producing flakes of a desired size or shape. These can then be used with no modification or can be further worked (retouched) into a flake-tool, such as a scraper or backed knife (ill. 3.15) — in this instance the core and unused flakes left behind from the original piece of raw material are the waste products, as well as tiny flint spalls from retouching.

Further information
Wymer 1968; Waddington 2004

basic presumption that lifestyles were essentially mobile, with regular movement around a wide regional landscape. Finds from caves and rock-shelters do, however, indicate that these locations were often visited, particularly in the Middle and Upper Palaeolithic. The main evidence for the Palaeolithic consists of artefacts and other remains discarded or lost in the course of this way of life, and subsequently buried under or within geological sediments. It is only under rare circumstances, however, that this material has accumulated at a point in the landscape with the right conditions for it to be preserved, for instance on the edge of a river floodplain just before a major flooding episode, or at the foot of a slope just before a minor landslip. One should, therefore, always remember that for any phase of the Palaeolithic, only tiny parts of the landscape have survived, and even these may not always happen to contain archaeological evidence.

Stone tools and waste flakes from their manufacture constitute the main type of evidence. Certain types of stone are dense and fine-grained, so that, when struck or 'knapped', they break to leave a sharp edge, useful for numerous tasks, such as shaping wood and cutting plant material or animal flesh. Throughout the Palaeolithic, hominins learned to find suitable raw materials, and to control the knapping process to produce a range of tools (box, adjacent). In Britain the main material used was flint, which occurs as nodules within Chalk, and is particularly suitable for stone-tool manufacture, being very sharp and easy to knap compared with many other types of stone used across the Palaeolithic world. Chalk and flint are common across much of Kent, which would have made the region a suitable landscape for occupation, with flint nodules easily available through exposure by natural erosive processes such as river action, landslips or coastal processes.

Although stone artefacts can be damaged by some burial processes, as, for example, when they are caught up in a river channel or crushed under an ice sheet, they are essentially indestructible and resistant to biological decay, which is why they

The Palaeolithic in Britain

Archaeological period	Human species	Lithic artefacts and other material culture	MI Stage	Date (BP)	Geological period
Upper Palaeolithic	Anatomically modern *Homo sapiens sapiens*	Dominance of blade technology and standardised tools made on blade blanks Development of personal adornment, cave art, bone/ antler points and needles	2–3	10,000– 35,000	Late Pleistocene
Middle Palaeolithic	Early pre- Neanderthals initially, evolving into full *Homo neanderthalensis* after MIS 5e	Continuation of handaxes, but growth of more standardised flake and blade production techniques (Levalloisian and Mousterian) Development of a wider range of more standardised flake-tools, and towards the end, the development of *bout coupé* handaxes Use of wooden spears and basic hafts for lithic tools	3–5e 5e–8	35,000– 125,000 125,000– 250,000	Middle Pleistocene (later part of)
Lower Palaeolithic	Archaic *Homo* — *Homo* cf *heidelbergensis* initially, evolving towards *Homo neanderthalensis*	Handaxe dominated, unstandardised flake core production techniques and simple unstandardised flake-tools Occasional industries without handaxes, based on large flake blanks made by unstandardised core-reduction techniques Use of wooden spears	8–13	250,000– 500,000	
	?? *Homo erectus/ ergaster*	Very simple core and flake industries — one site on Norfolk coast at Pakefield	14–17	500,000– 800,000	Middle Pleistocene (early part of)

Further information
Wymer 1968, 1982; Stringer and Gamble 1993

constitute the bulk of Palaeolithic evidence. This can of course pose problems, since one always has to consider, when interpreting stone artefacts, whether they have been moved from where they were discarded, and whether they represent mixed material from different periods of the Palaeolithic. Under certain circumstances, organic remains such as bone or wood are also preserved. These are normally not a direct result of human use and abandonment, but represent the natural environmental background of contemporary animal and plant species, preserved by chance in the same deposits as the stone tools. Bone fossils do, however, occasionally show cut-marks and evidence of breakage, indicating exploitation for food. Bone, antler or wooden artefacts have also very occasionally been found. These include, even from the very early Palaeolithic, wooden spears, hafted flint tools, and antler percussors for knapping. In the Upper Palaeolithic, paintings and decoration on cave and rock-shelter walls provide an extra dimension for interpretation. Upper

Palaeolithic sites also sometimes have more sophisticated organic remains, such as bone needles, points and pieces of bone carved with delicate engravings of animals. These rare discoveries serve as a constant reminder that at most sites we are missing major elements of the evidence, and that we should not overlook this when interpreting human society and behaviour from the ubiquitous stone tools and waste flakes that predominate through the Palaeolithic.

Periods of the Palaeolithic

The Palaeolithic has been divided into three broad, chronologically successive stages, Lower, Middle and Upper, based primarily on changing types of stone tool (ill. 3.16). This framework was developed in the nineteenth century, before any knowledge of the types of human ancestor associated with the evidence of each period, and without much understanding of the timescale. The tripartite division has, however, stood the test of time, proving both to reflect a broad chronological succession across wide areas of Europe, and to correspond with the evolution of different human ancestral species.

Human ancestors

The Lower and Middle Palaeolithic saw the gradual evolution of an Archaic hominin lineage from the first colonisers of Britain (*Homo heidelbergensis*) into Neanderthals (*Homo neanderthalensis*) up to the middle of the last, Devensian glaciation (*c.* 35,000 BP). Around this time Neanderthals were suddenly replaced in Britain and north-west Europe by anatomically modern humans (*Homo sapiens sapiens*), who are associated with the later Upper Palaeolithic. The Upper Palaeolithic is also characterised by major cultural developments, such as bone and antler tools and the representation of animals in paintings on cave walls or as small antler or bone carvings. The suddenness of this change, the physiological differences between Neanderthals and modern humans and DNA studies (Cann 1988) all suggest that modern humans did not

evolve from Neanderthals, but developed elsewhere, probably in Africa *c.* 150,000 BP, before colonising other parts of the world and replacing any pre-existing Archaic populations.

In Europe, there must have been occasions when the two hominin lineages came into contact. The nature of these interactions and the possible role of modern humans in the extinction of the Neanderthals remain open to speculation. Interbreeding of any sort is unlikely. The DNA evidence suggests a clear African origin for all present-day Europeans. Attempts to interpret certain fossil specimens as evidence of inter-breeding are highly dubious, being based on over-interpretation of the natural range of variation, or on immature specimens whose subsequent physiological development cannot be predicted. Neanderthal genocide is another unlikely scenario. There is no evidence of Neanderthal–modern human conflict, either from skeletal pathology or archaeological remains. Populations would have been so low that the types of tribal conflict characterised as genocide in the present day would have been inconceivable. It is most likely that the influx of modern humans upset the ecological balance of Neanderthal adaptation in some way, making co-existence impossible, and leading to their extinction with minimal direct interaction.

The Lower and Middle Palaeolithic in Kent

The range and distribution of sites

Kent is the richest county in England for Lower and Middle Palaeolithic archaeological evidence, with almost 450 recorded find-spots and 30,000 artefacts. In addition to these, Henry Stopes' massive collection stored at the National Museum of Wales in Cardiff includes further Kent material. Recent study has established that the Stopes Collection contains over 10,000 Palaeolithic artefacts, with approximately half of these being handaxes from the Swanscombe area (Wenban-Smith 2004a). Stopes also collected material from 27 sites not otherwise known to have produced

Lower and Middle Palaeolithic finds in Kent

Sediment class	Find-spots	Handaxes	Cores	Debitage	Total
Fluvial/alluvial	105	11,043	593	21,748	33,384
Colluvial/solifluction/aeolian/ derived	302	2,295	136	4,017	6,448
Residual	68	257	5	284	546
Total	**475**	**13,595**	**734**	**26,049**	**40,378**

Palaeolithic finds. Overall, then, more than 40,000 artefacts are known from Kent, with over 13,000 handaxes (ill. 3.17).

The distribution of known sites is inevitably initially constrained by the location of Pleistocene sediments, and then secondarily influenced by the amount of their disturbance and investigation. Three main groups of Pleistocene sediments have produced Lower or Middle Palaeolithic evidence in Kent (ills 3.17 and 3.19):

• Fluvial/alluvial
• Colluvial/solifluction/aeolian (and derived surface finds)
• Residual.

Fluvial/alluvial sediments

Pleistocene fluvial sands and gravels survive as terraces on the valley flanks above the current courses of larger rivers such as the Lower Thames, the Medway and the Stour. Concentrations of deposits occur in the north of the county, near Dartford, on the Hoo peninsula and on the Blean north of Canterbury. There are also small terrace systems associated with Thames tributaries, such as the Cray and the Darent, and inside the Weald, with headwater tributaries of the Darent and the Medway, such as the Eden and Beult. Spreads of alluvial floodplain deposits also outcrop at the confluence of the Cray and the Darent with the Thames at Dartford, and at certain drainage pinch points along the course of the Medway, such as east of Tonbridge.

Although only around 20% of Kent sites are located in fluvial deposits, they have produced almost 80% of the Palaeolithic finds. The Thames deposits in north-west Kent are of particular significance, and finds from a few sites in the Swanscombe area have made a disproportionately high contribution, in numbers as well as quality of information, to current knowledge of the Lower Palaeolithic in both Britain and Kent (cf. box, pages 50-1). Terraces of the Stour in the area of Canterbury have also produced abundant finds, whereas those on the Hoo peninsula and within the Weald, at the heads of the Medway, Darent and Stour, have produced almost nothing in comparison. Whether this is a genuine reflection of artefactual content and the distribution of Palaeolithic activity, or a result of patterns of modern quarrying and investigation is uncertain.

Colluvial/solifluction/aeolian sediments

These deposits comprise a variety of sediment types, from coarse-grained solifluction gravels to fine-grained silty sands mapped as Head Brickearth. The large areas mapped as Head Brickearth include both aeolian and colluvial deposits. In north-eastern Kent there are substantial bodies of sediment, mapped as brickearth capping the chalk, that probably include a significant proportion of undisturbed aeolian material. Some areas capping the higher ground of the Hythe and Folkestone Beds in the northern Weald may also have in situ aeolian elements, but they may have been sufficiently affected by exposure during the Pleistocene that they should be regarded as residual. The majority (almost 65%) of Kent Palaeolithic sites are find-spots related to colluvial/solifluction/aeolian deposits, although most have produced only small numbers of finds, and collectively less than 20% of the total.

Residual deposits

Residual Clay-with-flints is one of the commonest Pleistocene sediments in Kent, capping wide areas of the North Downs chalk bedrock. Head Brickearth deposits capping higher outcrops of the Hythe and Folkestone Beds within the northern Weald can probably also be regarded as residual, although they may include an aeolian element. Clay-with-flints has produced reasonable quantities of handaxes, mostly from ploughed field surfaces. Although 15% of find-spots are from Clay-with-flints, the deposit accounts for only 2% of artefacts. This reflects the large number of finds of single handaxes, and the difficulty of attributing accompanying debitage to the Palaeolithic, due to its uncertain age.

The Lower Palaeolithic

The handaxe is the definitive artefact of the Lower Palaeolithic (ill. 3.5). Although there were periods within the Lower Palaeolithic when handaxe manufacture was not practised, for instance the Clactonian horizons at Swanscombe (cf. box, pages 50-1), and although there was often a small element of crude core and flake-tool production alongside handaxe manufacture, there is a significant period of time, between MIS 13 and 8, when lithic technology was dominated by the manufacture of large quantities of handaxes. Lower Palaeolithic sites are abundant on the high terraces of the Lower Thames in the Dartford region and the middle terraces of the Stour around Canterbury. Isolated finds, and occasionally richer sites, also occur in numerous other fluvial, colluvial/solifluction/aeolian and residual deposits across the county. The evidence from the fluvial terraces makes the greatest contribution to our overall picture of the Lower and Middle Palaeolithic in Kent, since, despite issues of derivation and disturbance, these deposits are the most reliably dated (ill. 3.19).

The earliest evidence

The earliest evidence for the occupation of Britain comes from the site of Pakefield on the Norfolk coast, dating to a pre-MIS 13 interglacial (Parfitt *et al.* 2005). Following this, there are several sites in southern England dating to MIS 13, *c.* 500,000 BP, such as Boxgrove in West Sussex (Roberts and Parfitt 1999), High Lodge in Suffolk (Ashton *et al.* 1992) and Westbury-sub-Mendip in Somerset (Andrews *et al.* 1999). Unfortunately, there are no

Major Middle Pleistocene fluvial deposits and key Kent Lower/Middle Palaeolithic sites

MIS (?)	Mid. Thames	Lower Thames		Medway		Stour	
	Fluvial deposits	Fluvial deposits	Key sites	Fluvial deposits	Key sites	Fluvial deposits	Key sites
14/13/12	Black Park	Dartford Heath?	-	(T4) High Halstow? Clinch Street/ Farm Dagenham Farm	-	T3 – Fordwich	Fordwich
12/11/10	Boyn Hill	Orsett Heath	Barnfield Pit	(T3) Shakespeare Farm	Shakespeare Farm	T2 — 100 ft	Sturry
10/9/8	Lynch Hill	Corbets Tey	-	(T2) Newhall	-	T2 — Sturry	Sturry
				Stoke		T1 — Chislet	-
8/7/6	Taplow	Mucking	Crayford Ebbsfleet Valley	Middle Stoke/ Grain Binney	Cuxton		

3.18 Major Middle Pleistocene fluvial deposits and key Kent Lower/Middle Palaeolithic sites.

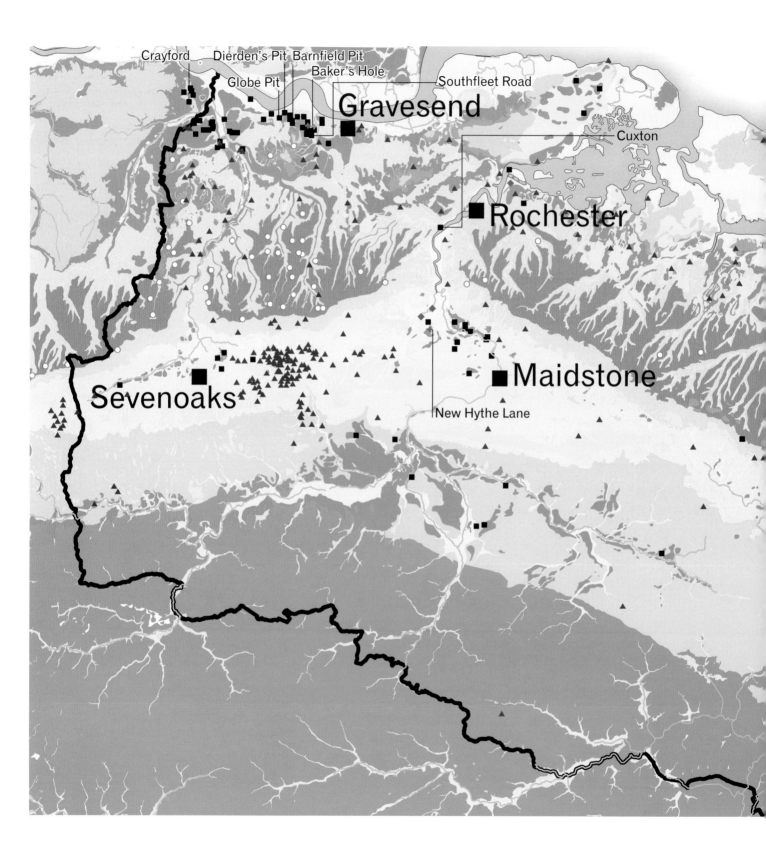

Crayford
Dierden's Pit
Barnfield Pit
Globe Pit
Baker's Hole
Southfleet Road
Gravesend
Cuxton
Rochester
Maidstone
New Hythe Lane
Sevenoaks

3.19 Pleistocene sediments and Palaeolithic finds across Kent, showing: named sites in text, Levallois sites, *bout coupé* sites, major rivers, major towns.

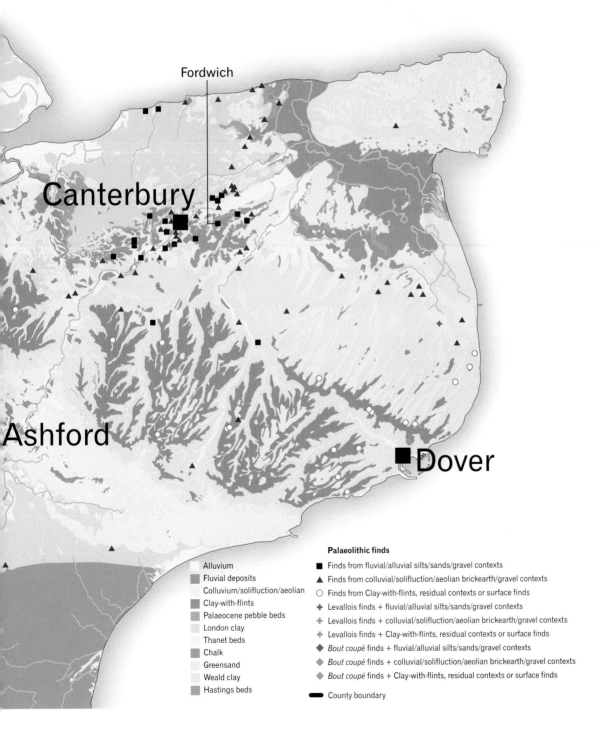

Fordwich

Canterbury

Ashford

Dover

Palaeolithic finds

■ Finds from fluvial/alluvial silts/sands/gravel contexts

▲ Finds from colluvial/solifluction/aeolian brickearth/gravel contexts

○ Finds from Clay-with-flints, residual contexts or surface finds

✚ Levallois finds + fluvial/alluvial silts/sands/gravel contexts

✚ Levallois finds + colluvial/solifluction/aeolian brickearth/gravel contexts

✚ Levallois finds + Clay-with-flints, residual contexts or surface finds

◆ *Bout coupé* finds + fluvial/alluvial silts/sands/gravel contexts

◆ *Bout coupé* finds + colluvial/solifluction/aeolian brickearth/gravel contexts

◆ *Bout coupé* finds + Clay-with-flints, residual contexts or surface finds

▬ County boundary

Alluvium

Fluvial deposits

Colluvium/solifluction/aeolian

Clay-with-flints

Palaeocene pebble beds

London clay

Thanet beds

Chalk

Greensand

Weald clay

Hastings beds

3.20 Clactonian core.

Barnfield Pit, Swanscombe

Summary

Barnfield Pit was one of the first Lower Palaeolithic sites in Britain to be excavated, with, in the early 20th century, systematic screening for artefacts and careful attention to the stratigraphic context of material (ill. 3.3). Several major subsequent investigations have taken place, demonstrating a deep sequence of mostly fluvial deposits, which contain lithic artefacts in association with a range of biological evidence including molluscan, avian, fish and mammalian remains — amongst which latter the Swanscombe skull.

3.21 Handaxe from the Lower Middle Gravel at Swanscombe (H 149mm).

Stratigraphy and archaeology

The archaeologically significant deposits consist of a series of fluvial sand and gravel deposits (Lower and Middle Gravels) divided by a horizon of laminated sands and silts (Lower Loam), representing alluvial floodplain deposition interspersed with periods of short-lived landsurface exposure. These deposits have produced abundant and well-documented archaeological and biological material, with the Lower Loam containing undisturbed Clactonian flint flakes and cores lying where they were discarded. These are overlain by a less-understood series of deposits (Upper Loam, Sand and Gravel) that may also have produced some archaeological material, although its provenance is less securely recorded.

3.22 Stratigraphic and archaeological summary of the Barnfield Pit sequence, Swanscombe.

Stratigraphic and archaeological summary of the Barnfield Pit sequence, Swanscombe

Phase	MIS	Stratigraphic unit	Height OD	Palaeolithic archaeology
III	10–8? 11	Upper Gravel Upper Loam	c. 33–34m c. 32–33m	No reliably provenanced material; reports of white-patinated ovate handaxes are based on preconceptions that these were more advanced, and so would come from a younger horizon than the pointed forms that predominate in the Middle Gravel
II	11	Upper Middle Gravel Lower Middle Gravel	c. 28.5–32m c. 26.5–28.5m	Mostly pointed handaxes with thick partly trimmed butts, often large and well-made but also small and crude cores, debitage and *ad hoc* flake-tools – 'Acheulian' (Swanscombe Skull level)
I	11	Lower Loam Lower Gravel	c. 25–26.5m c. 22–26.5m	Cores, debitage, *ad hoc* flake tools, and very occasional crude proto-handaxes – 'Clactonian'

The Swanscombe skull

Three refitting parts of a skull were found at the base of the Upper Middle Gravel at Barnfield Pit (ill. 3.4) on separate occasions between 1935 and 1955. The skull shows some Neanderthal-type features, suggesting physical evolution from *Homo* cf *heidelbergensis* towards Neanderthals had already begun at the time of deposition of the Swanscombe sequence. To what extent this was accompanied by behavioural change remains unknown, and a major research question in Palaeolithic archaeology.

Climate and environment

The Lower/Middle Gravels and Lower Loam contain abundant biological evidence. This reflects a warm climate, and indicates surrounding woodland, probably with open grassy spaces caused by heavy herbivore grazing, and nearby presence of substantial water bodies reflected in the bird remains. Large mammal species present include macaque, wolf, beaver, straight-tusked elephant, cave-lion, two types of rhinoceros, horse, wild boar and four types of deer (red, roe, fallow and giant). Small mammals include rabbit, pine marten, mouse and four types of vole (water, field, northern and pine). Bird remains found include osprey, giant cormorant and duck.

Date

Most of the deposits — Lower and Middle Gravels, Lower Loam and Upper Loam — date to the Hoxnian interglacial around 400,000 years ago (MIS 11). They represent the earliest remnants in Kent of the new course of the Lower Thames, after it had been diverted south by the Anglian ice sheet. The uppermost part of the sequence (Upper Gravel) is probably a later solifluction deposit, and may be considerably younger.

Further information

Smith and Dewey 1913; 1914; Swanscombe Committee 1938; Wymer 1968; Stringer 1985; Ovey 1964; Bridgland 1994; Conway *et al.* 1996; Wenban-Smith and Bridgland 2001

3.23 Swanscombe skull (back view).

3.24 Swanscombe skull (right side view).

3.25 Fossil faunal remains from Swanscombe deposits: fallow deer (*Dama dama*) (above); straight-tusked elephant *Palaeoloxodon antiquus* molar (below).

3.26 Lower Palaeolithic handaxes
– ranges of types:
(a) crude pointed (Fordwich)
(H 150mm),
(b) *bout coupé* (Ashford) (H 96mm)
and
(c) *ficron* (Cuxton) (H 307mm)

(a)

(b)

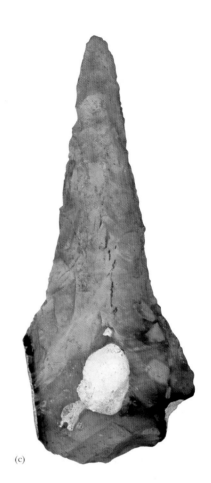

(c)

reliably dated sites of this period in Kent, although Kent is one of the most likely routes by which Britain was originally colonised from the Continent, since the English Channel had not yet been formed and there would have been a land bridge of Chalk downland between Calais and Dover.

The strongest contender for having produced the first evidence of human activity in Kent is the site of Fordwich, where reasonably abundant Palaeolithic handaxes have been found 125 feet above the present Stour, in a terrace of Pleistocene river gravels mapped as Terrace 3. The crude form of some of these handaxes (ill. 3.26a) and the height of the terrace have long been thought to reflect a great age. There has, however, been no independent dating due to the absence of datable material. The refinement of the handaxes from Boxgrove (Roberts *et al*. 1997) emphasises that one should be wary of jumping to conclusions about age on the basis of perception of handaxe quality and shape, which may also have been

constrained by the quality of the raw material or the needs of the task at hand. Nonetheless, the most recent assessment of the date of the Fordwich terrace (Bridgland *et al*. 1998) places it in the period MIS 14–12, which would make it contemporary with other early sites such as High Lodge and Boxgrove, despite the contrasts in handaxe shape. Much of the earliest Kent evidence, however, may be represented by stray handaxes within the residual Clay-with-flints deposits, which cap the North Downs along the likely route of initial migration, but the difficulty of dating individual artefacts from this palimpsest means that the earliest evidence is likely never to be reliably isolated from the mass of later artefacts.

Post-Anglian occupation
There are no deposits in Kent formed during the severe cold of the Anglian glaciation. Considering, however, that there was a substantial ice sheet visible across the Thames Estuary in

Essex, it is hard to imagine human occupation at this time, and the pre-Anglian inhabitants must either have migrated southward to the Continent, or died out. The ground would have been frozen solid across the county, and probably deeply buried by snow and ice. Following the end of the glaciation, the Thames laid down a substantial series of deposits in north-west Kent from Dartford to Gravesend. They can be correlated with the Boyn Hill terrace of the Middle Thames, and are dated to the Hoxnian interglacial, MIS 11, lasting from *c.* 425,000 to 350,000 BP. Despite their antiquity and limited extent, they contain some of the best evidence for the Palaeolithic in Britain, with good survival of faunal remains, numerous artefacts and the preservation of undisturbed deposits at certain horizons. Barnfield Pit at Swanscombe (box, pages 50-1) in particular has produced significant evidence and been the subject of much research, although many other nearby sites have also been productive (Wymer 1968).

A major recent discovery has been the site at Southfleet Road, Ebbsfleet, where archaeological investigations in advance of the Channel Tunnel Rail Link have identified undisturbed evidence of the butchery of an elephant, associated with a non-handaxe Clactonian flint industry. Although, at the time of writing, analysis of the excavated material has hardly begun, it is already clear that the site is broadly the same age as the Clactonian horizons of the Lower Loam at Barnfield Pit. Interpretation of the Clactonian is a contentious issue (box, page 54). Clactonian sites are recognised by the absence of handaxe manufacturing evidence, as well as the presence of numerous cores and large utilised flakes, often with notches. It has been periodically argued since the 1970s that they do not represent a genuine cultural phenomenon (i.e. a human group that never made handaxes), but just reflect limited knapping activity in one part of the landscape of a group that sometimes did and sometimes did not. As more sites of this specific date without handaxes are found in different parts of the

landscape, the case for a distinctive Clactonian culture becomes stronger. At Southfleet Road, the quantity of finds without any indication of handaxe manufacture and the frequent examples of large cores and notched flakes provide further support for the long-standing view that Clactonian assemblages represent the evidence of a human group present in south-east England in the first part of MIS 11, *c.* 400,000 years ago. The key question now is whether the appearance later in the same interglacial of sites with abundant handaxes (such as in the Lower Middle Gravel at Swanscombe) represents internal cultural development of the indigenous British population, or an influx of handaxe-makers from the Continent. The former is most likely, since sea levels would have been high in the middle of MIS 11, restricting access from outside Britain, and there are also occasional signs of proto-handaxe manufacture at Clactonian sites.

Despite the abundance of immediately post-Anglian Thames gravels in north-west Kent, and the proliferation within them of Palaeolithic remains, there is a relative lack of material from the following climatic cycle of MIS 10/9/8. No Thames horizons of this period have been recognised in Kent, although the varied typological range and fresh condition of the substantial handaxe collections from the Globe Pit (Greenhithe) and Dierden's Yard (Ingress Vale) give a hint that they might not come from deposits of the same age as those at Barnfield Pit, but from younger channels in their surface. Deposits on the north side of the river at Purfleet in Essex that date to this period contain similar archaeological material to that from the Swanscombe terrace, apart from the Levalloisian material present in their upper parts (White in Schreve *et al.* 2002).

The post-Swanscombe climatic cycle is represented in north-east Kent, in the Stour and Medway valleys. Gravels at Sturry, north-east of Canterbury, mapped as Terrace 2, have produced abundant artefacts including a range of handaxe types similar to those from Swanscombe (Dewey

The Southfleet Road Clactonian elephant butchery site

Clockwise from top left:

3.27 Excavation of the elephant in progress.

3.28 Clactonian flake *in situ* in the ground.

3.29 Vole teeth from tufaceous deposits just beside the elephant skeleton.

3.30 Mollusc remains from the same tufaceous deposits.

Summary

Archaeological excavations in advance of the Channel Tunnel Rail Link revealed an undisturbed Lower Palaeolithic site *c.* 400,000 years old at Southfleet Road, in the Ebbsfleet Valley. The skeleton of a single extinct Straight-tusked Elephant (*Palaeoloxodon antiquus*) was preserved in the muddy sediment near what was then the edge of a small lake, surrounded by Clactonian flint tools, lying undisturbed where originally discarded. The evidence was then buried under clays associated with the continuing build-up of lake margin sediments. Finally, these deposits were buried by a series of river gravels, reflecting a significant change in the local landscape, possibly related to wider climatic change. In contrast to the underlying deposits, the river gravels contain abundant Acheulian handaxes.

Climate and environment

Sieving of the sediments at the site has produced a wide range of evidence that reveals the climate and local environment. Beaver, sticklebacks, frogs, newts and aquatic molluscs confirm the presence of standing water. Wood fragments preserved in the sediment, pollen grains from ferns and a number of trees, and teeth from a woodmouse indicate an interglacial climate, similar to or warmer than the present day, with the lake surrounded by woodland, probably with some open areas due to heavy herbivore grazing.

Dating

The deposits contain several species that allow the site to be dated. Of particular importance is the co-occurrence of narrow-nosed rhinoceros (*Stephanorhinus hemitoechus*) and pine vole (*Microtus subterraneus*). This pine vole has been extinct in England for the last 400,000 years and the narrow-nosed rhinoceros, although now extinct, is only known in Britain from deposits younger than 450,000 years BP. Taken together, these species indicate that the lake margin sediments containing the elephant are of similar age to the Phase I deposits at Barnfield Pit, Swanscombe, and date to the early part of MIS 11, the Hoxnian interglacial.

Further information

Wenban-Smith *et al.* 2006

and Smith 1925). Site records suggest that there may be two terraces, one contemporary with the MIS 11 Swanscombe terrace, and the other, with its base at *c.* 22m OD, perhaps corresponding with MIS 10/9/8. Both the identification of two Sturry terraces and the overall correlation of the Stour terrace staircase with the Lower Thames sequence are, however, uncertain, and further observations are required to clarify the situation.

The Medway contains a series of terraces lining the valley from where it breaks north through the North Downs scarp at Halling, through Rochester and Frindsbury, to the Hoo peninsula. The sequence is best preserved on the Hoo peninsula, where at least nine different terraces have been identified (cf. ill. 3.18). Two handaxes (one pointed and one ovate) have been found in the Shakespeare Farm terrace (Bridgland and Harding 1984), probably equivalent in age to deposits at Swanscombe, and there are also stray finds from younger terraces. Further up the Medway, Frindsbury (Cook and Killick 1924) and Cuxton (Tester 1965; Cruse 1987; Wenban-Smith 2004b) have produced significant material. Frindsbury, which is probably an undisturbed flint-working site, lies on Chalk bedrock above the third terrace, sealed by a clayey brickearth, which is probably of mixed colluvial/aeolian origin. Since, however, the site was not in fluvial deposits, it cannot be associated with the third terrace, and so is of uncertain age. Two handaxes were found, in addition to numerous piles of flint flakes in fresh condition, many of which can be refitted together, demonstrating a significant non-handaxe flake-core industry, apparently contemporary with the handaxes. A quartzite pebble with surface battering reflecting its use as a knapping percussor was also found. This is of interest since quartzite would not have been available locally, and is scarce in the region. Its presence must reflect both recognition of its suitability for knapping, and its deliberate transport to the knapping site, both of which required thinking and planning ahead, abilities often doubted for Archaic hominins, but for which the evidence is becoming increasingly strong (Wenban-Smith 2004c).

The site at Cuxton, in contrast, is reliably associated with fluvial deposits of the Medway,

and has produced a large number of handaxes (ill. 3.26c), as well as debitage from their manufacture. The dating of the site is problematic, but extrapolation of the Hoo peninsula sequence upstream to Cuxton suggests a correlation with the Stoke terrace, which most likely belongs to MIS 8. Some have suggested that the site is much younger, dating to the middle of the last Ice Age *c.* 60,000 BP, MIS 3 (Cruse 1987), but this would be surprising in view of the prevalence of handaxes, and the absence of typical Middle Palaeolithic evidence, which predominates in all reliably dated sites younger than MIS 7. Cuxton, however, is unlikely to be older than MIS 8, *c.* 250,000 BP, which makes it of particular interest for demonstrating the repeated occurrence in Britain of the basic Lower Palaeolithic technological package, comprising handaxes, occasional cores and ad hoc flake-tools, over a period of 250,000 years and through at least two major glacial–interglacial cycles.[1]

One of the intriguing aspects of the Lower Palaeolithic is the wide variety of handaxe shapes and sizes within the constant core-tool theme. Attempts have been made to find some consistent patterning through time in handaxe shapes, or to relate them to raw material availability. To date, however, these have foundered, with too many sites always contradicting the hoped-for patterns. This may be because patterning is being sought at an inappropriate spatial scale, for instance across the country rather than within smaller regions, or because the chronological resolution of sites is too loose to build them reliably into the MIS framework. Nonetheless, one fact that does seem to be clear is that, when large assemblages of handaxes from specific horizons with a restricted time-range are studied, there is usually a clear predominance of a particular shape that cross-cuts factors such as raw material source and shape. This seems to indicate that shape is a deliberate construct of the knapper, rather than an accidental and inevitable outcome determined by the initial shape of the raw material.

[1] Recent results from OSL dating indicate a date at *c.* 230,000 BP, early MIS7 (Wenban-Smith *et al.* forthcoming).

The Middle Palaeolithic

After, or towards the end of MIS 8, *c.* 250,000 BP, there are several changes in material culture. There is a proliferation of Levallois technology, with an emphasis on the production of flakes from carefully prepared cores. Two of the best British Levalloisian sites occur in Kent, notably the classic sites of Baker's Hole (box, adjacent) and Crayford, now in Greater London (box, page 58). Levalloisian material is also known in the Medway terrace deposits in the area of New Hythe, but it is uncertain whether it originates from Terrace 2 or 3. Early Levallois techniques, as evidenced in material from chalk solifluction deposits at Baker's Hole, involved the preparation of large tortoise-cores, by flaking one face into a dome, and striking from this face a single large flake, which was often then transformed into a flake-tool like a hand-axe. Later in MIS 7, as evidenced from Burchell's sites at Baker's Hole, and also probably Crayford, although it is not possible to be sure how the dates of the material from Baker's Hole and Crayford compare, Levallois techniques developed to involve the removal of a series of large blades from one face of the core.

It is possible that Levalloisian technology originated in north-west continental Europe, where it was present much earlier than MIS 8 at sites such as Cagny-La-Garenne, and was brought to Britain during MIS 8, when the Channel was sufficiently low to allow population movement. Interestingly, the later MIS 7 blade variant seems to have been present in south-east England earlier than on the Continent, where it occurred abundantly in MIS 6 (Révillion and Tuffreau 1994). There is no evidence for human presence in Britain during the interglacial of MIS 5e, between *c.* 125,000 and 115,000 BP, when the climate was warmer than the present day, and conditions would probably have been very amenable to occupation. This must reflect the decline of the British population during the prolonged and extreme cold of the preceding MIS 6, and the lack of enough time for population movement back to Britain during the rapid

Baker's Hole

Summary

Baker's Hole comprises an area of quarrying in the Ebbsfleet Valley between Swanscombe and Northfleet with several separate Middle Palaeolithic sites. The first material to be discovered was large numbers of classic Levalloisian tortoise cores and flakes from a Chalk solifluction deposit. Later investigations by Burchell led to the recovery of large quantities of blades and cores, with very few classic tortoise cores and Levallois flakes, from fluvial channel deposits that probably stratigraphically overlay the chalk solifluction deposits. Investigations by Carreck in the 1950s identified deposits in yet another part of the site that contained no artefacts, but abundant biological evidence including molluscs and large mammals — especially mammoth, horse and red deer.

Dating

The Ebbsfleet Valley is cut down through the Swanscombe 100 foot terrace and so all sediments within it are younger than MIS 11. The sequence within the Ebbsfleet Valley comprises a complex mixture of colluvial and solifluction deposits that have slid down into the valley from the higher ground around it, and fluvial deposits representing short-lived bouts of activity by the palaeo-Ebbsfleet that have incised a small-scale terrace sequence into the valley flanks. It is most likely that the classic Levalloisian tortoise core and flake material from the Chalk solifluction deposits dates to late in MIS 8. The other sites investigated by Burchell and Carreck both probably date to within MIS 7, although their relationship to each other and precise position within this multi-part MI Stage remain uncertain.

Investigations for the Channel Tunnel Rail Link

Between 1997 and 2003 a significant amount of archaeological investigation was carried out in advance of construction of the Channel Tunnel Rail Link. Little artefactual material was found, but Pleistocene sediments rich in biological evidence

were investigated at several locations. Analysis is still in progress, but it is clear that the sequence within the Ebbsfleet Valley is remarkably complex and varied, and includes sediments from at least as early as MIS 7, through MIS 5 and 4 to the Holocene.

Further information

Spurrell 1883; Smith 1911; Burchell 1933; 1954; 1957; Wenban-Smith 1995; 2001

Clockwise from top left:

3.31 Levallois tortoise core and flake.

3.32 Coombe Rock at Baker's Hole as seen by Reginald Smith in 1911.

3.33 Coombe Rock exposed during the Channel Tunnel Rail Link fieldwork.

3.34 Channel Tunnel Rail Link excavations in progress.

Crayford brickearths

Summary

The brickearth quarries at Crayford, in historic north-west Kent, but now in the London metropolitan area, were well-known in the mid 19th century as a source of fossil molluscan and faunal remains. In 1880, at Stoneham Pit, Spurrell discovered a layer of mint condition flint artefacts towards the base of the brickearth. He succeeded in fitting these back together to reconstruct the original flint nodule, confirming the undisturbed nature of the site and allowing better understanding of the methods and objectives of the flint knapping strategy. Some of the flint flakes were resting above the jaw of a woolly rhinoceros and mammoth bones were also found at the level of the flint artefact horizon. Other archaeological material was found from the same stratigraphic horizon in other nearby brickearth pits.

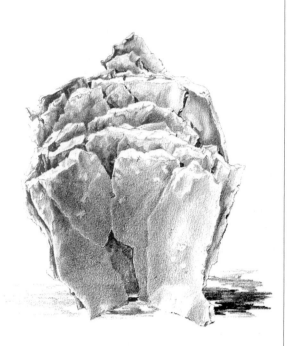

3.35 Refitting blade sequence and core. (Spurrell 1880a, P1 II, fig 1.)

Stratigraphy

Spurrell's main artefact horizon came from a dipping clayey lamination within a body of clay-laminated sands at the base of the main brickearth, where it abutted a steep cliff of Chalk bedrock. The sands overlay the surface of a body of fluvial gravel with a thickness of at least 4m and lying between *c*. 4m and 8m OD. Spurrell identified bands of artefacts both above and below his main horizon. Chandler also found mint condition artefacts on the surface of the gravel, right at the base of the brickearth. This suggests that a landsurface was exposed for a period of time on the surface of the gravel, and that human activity took place at this time, and then continued during the build-up of the basal brickearth deposits.

Archaeology

Spurrell's Stoneham Pit assemblage contained several hundred flakes and at least twenty cores, as well as micro-debitage. The material is dominated by the production of large blades from one face of a core, similar to some of the material from Baker's Hole, but lacking the classic tortoise core and Levallois flake element. Damage to the rhinoceros jaw found by Spurrell, and extraction of one of its teeth, which was found nearby, suggest human attempts to access the marrow for food.

Dating

The upper part of the brickearth that buries the site contains a fluvial horizon at *c*. 13–15m OD, known as the Corbicula or Cyrena bed, with molluscan and small vertebrate evidence suggesting a temperate period within MIS 7. The gravel underlying the base of the brickearth is attributed to the basal Taplow/Mucking gravel formation, associated with downcutting and gravel aggradation at the end of MIS 8 and the start of MIS 7. This suggests a date for the main archaeological evidence early in MIS 7.

Further information

Spurrell 1880a; 1880b; 1884; Hinton and Kennard 1905; Kennard 1944; Cook 1986; Bridgland 1994;

warming and sea level rise at the end of MIS 6. It seems possible, therefore, that the later Levalloisian blade-dominated knapping approach developed in England during MIS 7 and then returned across the Channel when populations retreated southward as conditions deteriorated during MIS 6. It then persisted alongside classic tortoise-core techniques, these latter usually on a smaller scale than before, and involving the recurrent production of several Levallois flakes from single cores, as, for example, at the northern French site of Hermies (Vallin and Masson 2004).

Following the high sea level and climatic optimum of MIS 5e, the return to colder conditions in the Devensian glaciation and associated dropping sea level in the Channel re-opened access from the Continent, where occupation was prolific through the period, accompanying the climax of Neanderthal dispersal and activity. There are few Kent sites that can be attributed to this late phase of the Middle Palaeolithic. Levallois material from New Hythe Lane, Aylesford, which is small and in fresh condition, is similar to the last glacial material from north-east France, and may represent early Devensian occupation in Britain. Its context, however, is uncertain, and it may be a small-scale application of the classic MIS 8–7 Levalloisian. Evidence from other sites in England and Wales indicates that a distinctive form of handaxe, known as *bout coupé* (ill. 3.26b), may reflect a specific period of late Neanderthal occupation of Britain, in the second half of the Devensian, during MIS 4 and 3 (White and Jacobi 2000). Excavations in slope deposits near the Oldbury rock-shelter have produced at least one *bout coupé* handaxe in association with debitage reflecting a Mousterian discoidal core technique, which is thought to be characteristic of MIS 4 and 3 on the Continent (Cook and Jacobi 1998). Two *bout coupé* handaxes (from Johnson's Pit and Clubb's Ballast Pit, both in the Maidstone area) are probably associated with mid–late Devensian gravels, and several others have been found across the county (ill. 3.19). These stray finds probably represent

the evidence of the last of the Neanderthals, at least in England.

Lifestyle and appearance

Study of the Lower and Middle Palaeolithic is inevitably dominated by stone tools, since they are the main evidence we have. Having constructed a framework based on changes in lithic material through time, there are still numerous questions over what these Archaic people were like and what they were actually doing. In fact one of the fundamental questions concerns whether we can think of them as 'people' at all, or whether we need to try and imagine some kind of bipedal chimpanzee, technically skilful, but lacking a level of consciousness that we would regard as typically human. Despite their lack of achievements often regarded as defining 'humanity', such as animal carvings and dramatic pictures on cave walls, we should not jump to the conclusion that they lacked a human degree of consciousness. Firstly, consider the implications, or rather the non-implications, of the lack of material evidence for technological and artistic development. Anatomically modern humans have been around for over 100,000 years, yet it is only in the last 30,000 years that cave-painting has proliferated, and only in certain parts of the world, establishing that its absence does not necessarily imply a lack of human capability. Furthermore during the last 10,000 years developments such as writing, pottery, use of metals, television, computers and space travel are not so much signs of an evolving species, but of development of technical and information-storage systems, which in turn facilitate increasingly swift and complex technological change. No one would argue that the diverse peoples of the world today are not all part of the human species, yet there are considerable contrasts, in an archaeological sense, in visible material culture between nomads of the Saharan desert, inhabitants of the Amazon rainforest and the denizens of twenty-first-century Kent.

It is also necessary to consider the positive

implications of the evidence that we do have. Chimpanzees and other animals have developed a range of tool-using behaviours that exploit the innate potential of naturally found objects, sometimes with a small amount of trimming or modification, for instance trimming twigs from a branch to leave a denuded stick. The ability to make even the simplest stone tools requires, however, the much greater ability to foresee the transformation of an innately useless lump of blunt and asymmetrical material into an entirely different sharp-edged object. Even with a clear intention in mind, the ability to achieve the desired end-product depends upon an understanding of how one specific type of stone will fracture when hit, and the ability to transmit this knowledge from one generation to the next. These abilities were developed two million years ago in Africa.

Manufacture of the sophisticated tranchet-sharpened handaxes by some of the earliest inhabitants of Britain at Boxgrove 500,000 years ago depended on visualising how the removal of single flakes would contribute to the shaping of the final artefact. Each time the flint nodule is struck, a short-term tactical objective is sought within the context of the overall strategic goal. Although knapping depends upon being able broadly to predict how a flint nodule will fracture, there is always some uncertainty. Tiny variations in the force or location of percussion, together with the almost incalculable complexity of how a single flaking blow will impact on the nodule as a whole, affected by factors such as supporting hand pressure and overall three-dimensional shape and balance of the nodule, lead to a certain amount of unpredictable variation. As knapping progresses, short-term objectives are being continually developed and modified to reflect the specific, and sometimes unwelcome, outcomes of attempted individual flake removal. In fact, making a handaxe is very similar to playing chess, with the same mixture of deliberate planning, often several moves ahead, and almost unconscious strategic action, based on years of

experience. It seems inescapable that the Archaic hominins of the Lower and Middle Palaeolithic were capable of thought processes broadly similar to modern humans, and that their lack of technological development was fundamentally ignorance and lack of necessity rather than stupidity.

This has implications for how we understand their behaviour. While some still see the Archaic world as one of a fifteen-minute attention-span, with tools made, used and abandoned as required, it is questionable whether such strategies could have worked in the seasonal climates of north-west European latitudes with their patchily distributed raw material resources. Moreover, there are sites which show clear patterning as locations of handaxe manufacture/export or handaxe discard incompatible with a strategy of tool use and discard to meet immediate expediencies (Wenban-Smith 2004c). We can, therefore, reasonably imagine an Archaic world involving foraging parties going on excursions, targeting specific resources, tooling up at certain well-known raw material sources en route or in advance, and habitually returning, laden with food, to specific base locations or temporary camps for overnight stays. Some scarce or labour-intensive equipment, such as knapping pebbles or wooden spears, was probably either cached at specific locations around the landscape or carried and cared for as personal equipment.

Socially, these Archaic humans would have functioned within a group, and life would have been dominated by the three S's, namely sex, status and subsistence. Much like today, maintaining and negotiating social status and sexual relationships within the group would probably have been at the heart of daily existence, embedded within day-to-day subsistence activities. Items of personal equipment such as handaxes and spears, rather than watches and cars as today, could well have been significant weapons in this social battleground, and the incredible attention paid to the size and symmetry of certain handaxes or Levallois cores probably reflects their function in the social arena rather than any practical concerns in relation to butchering efficiency. Cut-marks on animal bones from certain sites, and in particular Boxgrove, confirm the long-standing assumption that meat-eating was central to diet, an argument supported by our omnivorous dentition and the necessity for a high protein diet to support our brain development (Aiello and Wheeler 1995; Stanford and Bunn 2001). There is no sign of the use of fire until late in Neanderthal development, so, through most of the Lower and Middle Palaeolithic, meat would have been eaten raw, emphasising the continual need to acquire it fresh.

A number of studies over the last decades have suggested for the Lower Palaeolithic group sizes reaching 20–40 individuals with a home territory of c. 30 x 30 km, with group sizes increasing to 60–80 and territorial range to c. 50 x 50 km in the Middle Palaeolithic (Gamble and Steele 1999). In respect of group organisation and gender roles, little agreement has been reached, and discussion has often been reduced to recognition that there are dangers in uncritically extrapolating present arrangements and prejudices back into the prehistoric past, with the further problem that present arrangements are highly varied in societies around the world.

Concentration on prehistoric life as a world of male lithic production and hunting parties has been justifiably criticised, often on the basis not that the role of females has been unfairly misrepresented, but rather not considered at all. Certain inescapable facts must, however, have influenced division of activity on a gender basis. Newborn young would have been dependent upon parental support for their survival, and, although one can envisage exceptions, this must usually, and especially initially, have involved close attention by the mother, the only parent equipped for breastfeeding. While still probably reasonably mobile and able to provision themselves with gathered resources, nursing and heavily pregnant mothers would have been constrained in wider-ranging and more physically arduous activities,

such as locating and hunting the larger herbivores that were the preferred meat sources.

While there is no reason a priori why other females could not have participated fully in these activities, the incapacity of heavily pregnant females and new mothers would probably have led to increased male involvement, and this is certainly the case in chimpanzee societies, where males habitually range over wider distances and are more involved with hunting (McGrew et al. 1996). The greater muscle bulk and explosive performance capabilities of muscle fibres in the male physique would also have enhanced the likelihood of success in both hunting and the subsequent scramble for meat from a carcass. This would probably have had consequent societal benefits of high group status and sexual access, not to mention personal nutrition. Thus, if hunting is a key part of Lower Palaeolithic adaptation, and many sites and nutritional studies suggest that was the case (e.g. Stanford and Bunn 2001), then there are grounds for arguing for a gender-based structuring of group activity, and for development of alpha-male leadership in Lower Palaeolithic society. Paradoxically for some unduly androcentric perspectives, a division of labour between more mobile male hunting parties and more residential female-dominated groups might mean that the majority of lithic production at residential base sites, if such sites can be identified, would reflect female rather than male activity.

Finally, what was the size of these early humans and what did they look like? The fragments of skeletal material that we have are sufficient to confirm a fully bipedal hominin with a brain size approaching our own, or even exceeding it in the Neanderthal era. The tibia from Boxgrove indicates the extreme robustness of at least one very early Briton, perhaps similar to an international rugby player, and the fairly large number of continental Neanderthal remains gives a clear image of the general robustness, heavy brow ridges, long head and forward-jutting face of the final Archaics. Skeletal material from the intervening period, however, is restricted to very few specimens, none of which allows facial or post-cranial reconstruction. Look around the diversity in any gathering of more than a few people in the present day, and it is clear that the small quantity of material we have is insufficient for any generalisations concerning whole Archaic populations. It is possible that post-cranial proportions would have varied with climatic change, with cooler conditions encouraging squatter body shapes, as is the case with Neanderthals. The large size of many handaxes, hammerstones and waste knapping debitage provides an indicator, based on experience from modern experimental knapping, that Archaic hominins would have been more robust and stronger than the majority of the present-day population.

There are no archaeological indications of any form of clothing and, bearing in mind the cold climate, usually colder than the present day, one has to consider how survival was possible without fire or protective clothing in the latitudes of north-west Europe. A number of animals that colonised more northerly latitudes from a tropical origin developed increased fat and body hair to aid survival. These included the woolly rhinoceros and woolly mammoth, the remains of which have been found in the arctic permafrost. It seems highly likely, therefore, that Archaic humans would have been adapted in a similar way, and possessed increased subcutaneous fat and a thick furry pelt over the whole body.

The Upper Palaeolithic in Kent

The Upper Palaeolithic commences with the arrival of modern humans and their associated range of lithic and bone/antler artefacts, characterised as Aurignacian, after the site of Aurignac in France (Mellars 2004). The first influx into Europe seems to have occurred from the south-east in MIS 3, *c.* 40,000 BP. There are a number of British sites with Upper Palaeolithic evidence dating between *c.* 30,000 and 26,000 bc (uncalibrated radiocarbon years), particularly

Kent's Cavern in Devon and Paviland Cave on the Gower peninsular in Wales (Jacobi 1999). Early Upper Palaeolithic sites in Britain are concentrated in the south-west, and it seems possible that the route of Upper Palaeolithic colonisation of Britain was by the Atlantic seaboard. There is no Upper Palaeolithic evidence in Britain during the coldest part of the last glaciation, the Last Glacial Maximum, or LGM, between *c.* 26,000 and 13,000 BP (Otte 1990), and this major break in human presence marks the end of the period covered in this chapter. Britain was resettled *c.* 13,000 BP, corresponding with a brief phase of climatic amelioration before the final end of the last glaciation. Evidence of this Late Upper Palaeolithic period and its manifestation in Kent is considered next, in chapter 3.

There are very few sites in Kent with any evidence of the earlier phase of British Upper Palaeolithic settlement, and none with reliably provenanced and published material. To the south of Kent in the southern Weald, a collection of flint artefacts found early in the 1900s at Beedings, near Pulborough (West Sussex) cannot be directly dated, but they are similar to material from the pre-LGM earlier Upper Palaeolithic on the Continent (Jacobi 1986). Over two thousand flint artefacts in fresh condition were found in sand-filled fissures of the Hythe Beds within the Lower Greensand. There are several refitting pieces within the surviving collection of almost 200 artefacts, which is dominated by tools. The collection probably represents a palimpsest of archaeological remains, probably from repeated visits over maybe several hundred years. The site location would have afforded a north-east view across the central Wealden plain, and Jacobi has suggested that the site may represent a field camp or monitoring point used by hunters operating within the mammoth steppe of the Weald. The situation of the site highlights a type of context that may produce similar material elsewhere, and contemporary sites might be present in Kent in fissures in the Hythe Beds in the northern part of the Weald.

So far as Kent is concerned, a blade-point similar to material from Beedings is known from Conningbrook Manor Pit, at Kennington, near Ashford (pers. comm R Jacobi), suggesting occupation before the LGM. The site of Park Farm, also near Ashford, is known to have produced a tanged point during excavations by the Canterbury Archaeological Trust in 1994. The point could date to either before or after the LGM, and this might be resolved by comparison with material from other British assemblages. A leaf point found at Bapchild, near Sittingbourne, and now in the Burchell collection in the British Museum is the only other Kent evidence from the pre-LGM part of the Upper Palaeolithic (pers. comm R Jacobi). There is, however, no information on its provenance. Other Upper Palaeolithic material from Bapchild, comprising backed blades and end-scrapers (Dines 1929), may date from the post-LGM Upper Palaeolithic (cf. Chapter 4). There is, however, some confusion over the provenance of this material too, since it is reported by Dines to have been found in association with bones of goat, pig and deer, as well as fire-cracked flints and disc-scrapers, all of which sound very Neolithic.

Conclusions

Although representation of the pre-LGM Upper Palaeolithic is sadly lacking, the quantity and variety of Lower and Middle Palaeolithic evidence in Kent is exceptional. Southern Britain was at the northern margin of the habitable world, and was probably unoccupied for substantial periods of the Palaeolithic, due to cold climate or inaccessibility across the Channel. Continental Europe would have provided a refuge area from which Britain was regularly repopulated when climate and overland connection allowed. Once populations had reached Britain, they may well have become isolated from the Continent. Thus the archaeological record most likely contains a combination of material similar to that on the nearby continental mainland and unique

developments of the isolated British populations. The situation of Kent, adjacent to the Continent and to the south of any ice sheet, makes the Kent evidence a key resource in improving our understanding of when Palaeolithic settlement, extinction and recolonisation occurred, and of what cultural changes were associated with this settlement history.

While the current level of understanding has been bought at the price of destruction of much evidence, there still remain abundant potentially significant deposits. The extent of previous research means that we are now comparatively well-informed about the distribution of these deposits, although of course one should always be prepared for interesting finds in unexpected places. Kent is now on the threshold of a further major phase of increased development. This is both a threat and an opportunity. Our current knowledge is based on a combination of the results of amateur collecting which continues to the present day, chance finds (which should always be reported to a local museum since the records of such finds can combine over the years to highlight unsuspected areas of archaeological interest), research excavations carried out by local amateur groups or institutions such as the British Museum, and excavations in advance of development. The implementation of Planning Policy Guidance Note 16 in 1990 has made archaeological investigation in advance of development a central part of the spatial planning process. This has led to a more systematic approach to evaluation of potentially significant sites before any development commences, followed by appropriate investigation before or during development, and analysis and publication following development. It cannot be over-emphasised how significant a step this has been for archaeological investigation of all periods, and the quantity of work carried out since 1990 highlights how much has been, and could still be, lost without such controls.

This review has highlighted the great contribution made to our understanding of the

Palaeolithic in Britain by excavations and discoveries in Kent, particularly for the Lower and Middle Palaeolithic. There remain, however, a number of key areas where evidence is lacking, and which should be priorities for further research:

- lack of good evidence from the earliest stages of the Lower Palaeolithic, before the Anglian glaciation
- improved dating and correlation of Lower Thames, Medway and Stour terrace formations
- discovery of more/better Middle Palaeolithic sites
- more precise dating of the development of different facies of Levalloisian technology through MIS 8 and 7, and the relationship of these to different sub-stages of MIS 7
- discovery of any Upper Palaeolithic sites
- more detailed mapping and better understanding of brickearth and Head deposits, with differentiation of aeolian, fluvial and colluvial deposits
- improved understanding of changing access/connection to mainland Europe, and integration of the Kent Palaeolithic record with that of north-east France and Belgium.

In light of the attention now paid to archaeological investigation in advance of development, there is great cause for optimism that a future review of the Kent Palaeolithic may include a number of new sites that will have made a major contribution in some of these areas.

Acknowledgements

I am grateful to all in the Kent County Council Heritage Conservation team who have helped with different aspects of preparation of this paper, in particular John Williams for inviting me to contribute and suggestions throughout, Lis Dyson for information on a number of recently discovered sites, Paul Cuming for information from the Kent Historic Environment Record and Stuart Cakebread for preparation of draft site distribution figures. Useful information on finds from particular sites has been provided by Jodie Humphrey, John McNabb and Keith Parfitt. Finally I would particularly like to thank Helen Glass (Senior Archaeologist for Rail Link Engineering) for permission to use copious material from the CTRL investigations in the Ebbsfleet Valley, Roger Jacobi for his very helpful comments on an early draft, and for information and discussions on the evidence of the Upper Palaeolithic in Kent, and Siân Jones and Yvonne Marshall for discussions on possible gender organisation and roles in early hominin society.

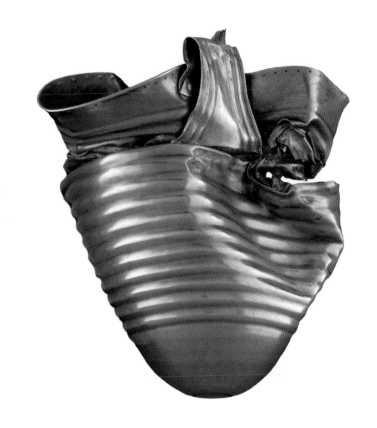

Prehistoric Kent

by Timothy Champion

Introduction

This chapter covers a period of 14,000 years, from the first reoccupation of Britain after the Ice Age to the Roman Conquest beginning in AD 43. It was a period that saw Britain become an island separate from the European mainland and Kent take on something like its present-day shape and size.

One of the commonest ways of organising our knowledge of the pre-Roman past has been to divide the prehistoric period into phases according to the Three Age System. The three phases, the Stone Age, the Bronze Age and the Iron Age, which can in turn be divided into early, middle and late sub-phases, have proved to be successful for grouping the material remains of prehistory and arranging them in a chronological sequence. This system, however, has not been adopted as the scheme for the presentation of Kent's prehistory in this chapter, though terms such as Bronze Age metalwork and Iron Age pottery are retained. The Three Age System emphasises technological progression, but these stages do not necessarily match other, possibly more significant, changes such as those in subsistence economy, settlement patterns and social organisation. The first section of this chapter, 'After the Ice Age', covers the final stages of the Upper Palaeolithic and the Mesolithic; there was considerable continuity in the hunter-gatherer economy, as well as in lithic technology. The second section, 'The first farmers', deals with the earlier Neolithic, which saw the beginnings of agriculture and the construction of major monuments. The third section, 'A world of monuments', discusses the later Neolithic and the early Bronze Age periods, which saw a proliferation of new types of monuments, individual burials and symbolic artefacts. The fourth section, 'Ordering the landscape', covers the middle and late Bronze Age and the earlier part of the Iron Age; wholesale changes in the archaeological record demonstrate the adoption of a fully sedentary agricultural economy. The fifth section, 'The approach of Rome', describes the major social changes that characterise the later Iron Age, culminating in the rise of dynastic rulers.

For the first 10,000 years of this period, evidence is sparse and limited almost entirely to stone tools. Chronology depends on radiocarbon dating, but there is no agreed method of calibrating these dates to calendar dates, and dates are still generally quoted in radiocarbon years Before Present (BP), as in the previous chapter. From about 4000 BC, however, with the adoption of farming and a more sedentary way of life, archaeological evidence becomes more plentiful and more varied. There is also an agreed calibration method for radiocarbon dates, and from that point onwards the dates quoted below are in calendar years BC.

After the Ice Age

When the last Ice Age was at its height, the so-called Late Glacial Maximum of *c.* 18,000 BP, much of northern Britain was covered in ice, sea level was as much as 100 metres lower than today, and north-western Europe was unoccupied. The human population had migrated southwards, and their nearest refuge was in south-western France. As the climate began to improve, the glaciers retreated and sea levels rose (box, pages 70-1). The improvement in the climate was, however, by no means uniform. A sudden rise in temperature about 13,000 BP was followed by a period of two thousand years of warmer climate, the Windermere Interstadial, during which temperatures dropped steadily from their initial peak until a sudden decline about 11,000 BP ushered in the return of Ice Age conditions. This colder period, the Loch Lomond Stadial, persisted until the final retreat of the glaciers about 10,000 BP and the start of the current interglacial phase, the Flandrian.

At the start of this period, Kent did not exist in any meaningful sense. Britain was joined to the Continent by a broad strip of land exposed by the low sea levels, and the area of the modern county comprised the higher zones overlooking the lowlands now under the English Channel and the North Sea. As sea level rose, these lowlands were submerged, Britain was isolated and Kent began

4.1 Map showing hypothetical reconstruction of the Mesolithic coastline of the Thames estuary after Britain had become an island, *c.* 6000 BC.

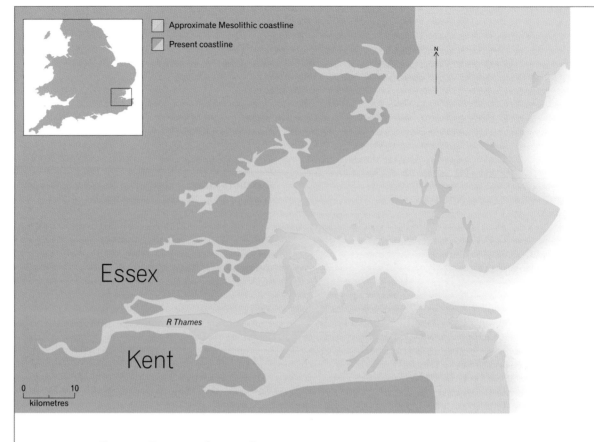

Approximate Mesolithic coastline

Present coastline

N

Essex

R Thames

Kent

0   10
kilometres

4.2 Graph showing radiocarbon dates for post-glacial rise in sea level at locations in south-eastern England (horizontal axis in millennia BP, vertical axis in metres below OD).

Post-glacial sea level

Rising temperatures after the Last Glacial Maximum melted the glaciers over northern and central Britain, leading to a rapid rise in sea level. Detailed studies of these processes in the Thames estuary (Devoy 1978; 1980), the East Kent fens (Long 1992), and for Romney Marsh (Long and Innes 1993) all show the same picture: a period of very rapid relative rise in sea level, followed by a period of slowing in the rate of rise, and then a levelling off, though with some differences in chronology (Fulford *et al.* 1997, 32-34).

Southern England became a more hospitable place and human populations returned. Gradually, however, the low-lying lands were flooded and Britain became an island. Much of the evidence for the human recolonisation of Britain is concealed under the waters of the North Sea and English Channel, though occasional finds during fishing and more recently by maritime archaeologists have begun to document this phase (Coles 1998; Flemming 2004).

Coastlines continued to evolve. Sheppey and Thanet became islands and the major river valleys such as the Thames, Medway, Stour and Rother were flooded, creating wide estuaries. As the rate of flow in these rivers slowed down, their sediments were deposited, filling the valleys with alluvium. In the south, shingle spits protected the sediment deposits, initiating the creation of Romney Marsh (Eddison and Green 1988; Eddison 1995; Eddison *et al.* 1998; Long *et al.* 2002) and later the Dungeness promontory (Long and Hughes 1995).

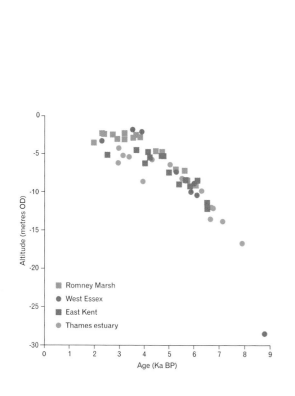

In east Kent, a shingle spit also developed northwards from Deal; the Lydden Valley was covered with alluvium, and the Wantsum channel gradually silted up, though it remained navigable until the Saxon period (Hawkes 1968). In the estuaries of the Thames and Medway, coastal marshes were formed. Fluctuations in sea level produced changing environments and at times the marshes offered land for grazing or industries such as pottery and salt production.

At the same time, Kent suffered continuing coastal erosion. The impact has been particularly severe on the chalk cliffs of east Kent and Thanet and on the softer rocks of the north coast west of the Wantsum (So 1965; 1966; 1971).

to emerge as the south-eastern promontory of England. This period also saw similarly dramatic changes in the climate, environment and population of the area. At the start, tundra conditions prevailed, uninhabited by humans. Later plant and animal life returned, and woodland succeeded grassland. The human population also returned, but numbers were small until about 8000 BP.

Recolonisation

As the climate improved, humans recolonised northern and north-western Europe from their southern refuges (Housley *et al.* 1997). Current evidence suggests they reached Britain about 12,600 BP. The earliest archaeological traces of human occupation during the Windermere phase are best known from caves in the Peak District and Somerset, though there is increasing evidence for open-air sites. The stone tools found at these sites are a late variant of the Magdalenian tradition of the continental late Upper Palaeolithic, but no large assemblage has been found in Kent. Two shouldered and truncated points, apparently found at Oare near Faversham (Jacobi 1982, 12 and Fig. 4), are an important addition to the evidence of this phase, but nothing else is known about their provenance or associations (ill. 4.3). A slightly later tradition of stone tools, dating to *c.* 12,000 to 11,000 BP and related to the Federmesser

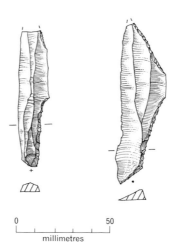

4.3 Shouldered and truncated points from Oare, near Faversham, rare evidence for the human reoccupation of Britain.

industries of the north European final Upper Palaeolithic, is characterised by small curve-backed points and end-scrapers. Tools of this tradition are found more widely in Britain, but again no large assemblage is known from Kent. The problematic collection of stone tools from Bapchild, near Sittingbourne (Dines 1929), which has already been mentioned at the end of the previous chapter, included characteristic convex-backed points and other tools of this phase.

During the colder period of the Loch Lomond Stadial, an open tundra environment developed and reindeer returned, but Britain was probably once again abandoned by the human population for a millennium. It is only shortly before 10,000 BP that there is clear evidence of human activity, marking the final recolonisation of the British Isles. The last phase of the final Upper Palaeolithic is marked by stone tool assemblages containing long blades, sometimes bruised as though used for heavy chopping, either for butchery or for tool preparation, as well as tanged points; though organic items are mostly absent in Britain, finds of wooden implements with similar tools in Germany show that points were used for arrows and that the bow had become an important hunting weapon. Finds of long-blade industries are commonest in south-eastern England, often on river terraces and near to flint sources. In Kent, such assemblages are known from Riverdale, near Canterbury (Barton 1988), and from the lower of two 'floors' excavated at Springhead (Burchell 1938; Jacobi 1982, 13 and Figs 5-6).

The evidence from Kent for this critical period in the history of the human occupation of Britain is very limited. The few finds of stone tools are clear signs of human activity, but there is no evidence of other types of material culture or of how food was procured. From contemporary finds elsewhere in northern Europe, objects of bone, antler and wood are known, but none has survived in Kent, if they ever existed. Hunting and gathering strategies must have changed greatly as the climate and environment changed, but

there is little actual evidence. South-eastern England must have played a central role in the return of human populations to Britain, but in the earliest millennia after the Ice Age, when sea levels were still comparatively low, a very broad land bridge existed, perhaps stretching as far, in terms of present-day geography, as from Hampshire to Lincolnshire. Much of the evidence for the human recolonisation of Britain may now be lost under the North Sea and English Channel.

Hunter-gatherer communities

Though the end of the last Ice Age is conventionally set at *c.* 10,000 BP, it was not until some centuries later that new stone tool technologies characteristic of the early Mesolithic were developed (Barton 1991). These include some tool types similar to those in earlier industries, but also new forms: simple microliths, probably used as blades and tips in arrows, saw-edged blades and axes. These new tools, which show some similarities to the microlithic and blade industries of Scandinavia, seem to have been designed for working wood, perhaps an indication of the changing environment as climate improved. These early Mesolithic tools are best known from sites further west, and although there are a number of microliths in Kent that might belong to this period, there is only one site with an assemblage. A small collection of stone tools from Ditton, near Maidstone (Clark 1932, 70-71), including three obliquely backed pieces and an adze-sharpening flake, is probably best assigned to this period.

A second, slightly later, phase of Mesolithic activity, starting about 9000 BP, is marked by assemblages including the characteristic hollow-based microliths known as Horsham points. These tools are limited to south-eastern England, mainly to the Wealden area; several finds extend the distribution into Kent, such as that from Harrietsham (Jacobi 1982, 15 and Fig. 7). This variation in the form of stone tools may represent the stylistic production of one social group, whose hunting territory extended across the Weald.

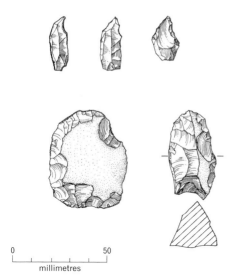

0
50
millimetres

4.4 Mesolithic flints from below the Chestnuts megalithic tomb, Addington.

It is not until the latest phase of the Mesolithic, from about 8000 BP, that finds become more plentiful. These later Mesolithic industries are marked by geometric microliths; the lithic industries of Britain show fewer similarities to those of the Continent than before, suggesting that with rising sea levels and the increasing isolation of Britain, cultural development was taking its own course. Finds from field-walking and excavation are comparatively common and widespread, though rarer on the high chalk Downs. This quantitative increase in evidence perhaps indicates a real increase in population levels in Kent; how much this was a response to the loss of lower-lying land to the rising sea is unknown. Among the find-spots are some more extensive sites with larger collections of stone tools (Jacobi 1982, 16-17). These may represent preferred sites in the landscape to which the mobile hunting groups regularly returned. The largest concentration of Mesolithic finds is at Addington (ill. 4.4), and it may be no coincidence that a Neolithic tomb was later built at this site.

It is disappointing that the evidence for the Mesolithic, like the earlier post-glacial periods, is almost entirely restricted to stone tools. There is no evidence for their food procurement strategies, except for some hazelnut shells. Nothing is known of any objects of bone or antler,

let alone other organic materials. The one exception is a wooden paddle, now lost, found at Swanscombe (Jacobi 1982, 14). It was apparently associated with Mesolithic implements, and is the earliest known implement of this kind in Britain. It is an intriguing reminder of the importance of water transport, especially as the sea level rose and Kent became a maritime peninsula.

The first farmers

The beginnings of agriculture, or in even more dramatic terms, the arrival of the first farmers, is often seen as a major turning point in prehistory: as progress from hunting and gathering to food production, from mobility to sedentism, and from a world in which material possessions were an encumbrance to one in which productive crafts could flourish. The first farmers were thought to have initiated the process of woodland clearance, the most important factor in the shaping of today's landscape. Recent research, however, suggests that this interpretation needs considerable modification (Thomas 1999). The human impact on the natural environment during the Mesolithic period was much greater than previously imagined, and Neolithic clearances extended an already existing practice. Studies of the early Neolithic economy show that, although arable and pastoral farming were important, the hunting and gathering of wild resources still played a major role in food supply (Entwistle and Grant 1989; Moffett et al. 1989); the presence of cattle and pig in significant quantities at sites of ceremonial importance may not give a true picture of everyday food supply. The continued lack of evidence for substantial permanent settlement sites has encouraged the idea of continued mobility of occupation (Whittle 1997). There certainly were new ideas and practices: domesticated animals and cultivated cereal crops, a new concern for monument building and ancestors, and perhaps an interest in parts of the landscape little frequented by people in the Mesolithic. In other things, however, old ways may have persisted: continued reliance on wild resources; small social groups and a comparatively egalitarian society; a mobile pattern of settlement, though perhaps increasingly tied to certain places, especially where crops were being grown, thus altering the nature of traditional rights to use the landscape. Less emphasis is now placed on the evolutionary trends of the period, whether economic, technological or social, and more on understanding the meaning of monuments and artefacts, and the nature of existence in a changing world.

By this period, Kent had taken on approximately its present shape, though sea levels continued to rise and the coastline continued to retreat. Human activity was beginning to have a major impact on the environment; the woodlands were felled, but clearances were seldom permanent. The population was growing, but the density was still very low and settlement was mobile rather than permanent. The first domesticated animals, sheep, goat and pigs, were reared and domesticated cereals such as wheat and barley played an increasingly important part in human diet. In contrast to the slight evidence for human settlements, major monuments of earth and stone were constructed.

Farming the landscape

Though the onset of the Neolithic is often associated with clearance of the woodland, the actual evidence for human impact on the natural vegetation is very sparse. There is only one environmental sequence that spans the period from the Mesolithic to the early Neolithic, that from the Devil's Kneadingtrough, Brook, near Ashford (Kerney *et al.* 1964). Other deposits at Sugar Loaf Hill, Folkestone, and Wateringbury show agricultural activity in prehistory, but the sequences are not continuous or well dated (Kerney *et al* 1980); the environmental sequence from Holywell Coombe, Folkestone, is particularly good for the earlier periods, but lacks evidence for later prehistory (Preece and Bridgland 1998; 1999). There are important sequences from elsewhere, such as Godwin's

profiles from Wingham and Frogholt (Godwin 1962), but they do not start until the second millennium, by which time some clearance has already taken place. At Brook, deposits on the scarp slope of the Downs reflect conditions higher up on the chalk; they show that clearance had begun before about 3000 BC, but it was followed by regeneration of the woodland. A major episode of renewed clearance followed later; dating evidence is poor, but it was probably not until the early first millennium BC. Unfortunately there are as yet in Kent no detailed studies of the colluvial deposits on the chalk of the North Downs comparable to the research of Martin Bell (1983) on the South Downs.

Some indication of the extent of early agriculture can be gained from the setting of two of the major Neolithic monuments discussed below. Both Coldrum in the western Medway group and Julliberrie's Grave in the Stour valley lie on top of well-developed lynchets, which must have been formed by hillwash from ploughing that took place before their construction. Neither monument is precisely dated, but by comparison with others in southern England they should date to quite early in the Neolithic, around the middle of the fourth millennium.

There is almost no evidence for the actual details of food procurement in the Neolithic of Kent. The animal bones from a small pit at Wingham (Greenfield 1960) included domesticated ox, sheep or goat, and pig, and among the fills of another pit at Ramsgate were marine shells (Dunning 1966), but it is not at all clear whether such pit fillings constitute a representative sample of domestic debris.

Apart from flint implements, which are often found in dense scatters, the most plentiful evidence of Neolithic activity is a series of pits, which are often taken as indicators of human settlement (Dunning 1966). This may in fact be so, but the pits and their filling are not simple domestic features (Barber 1997). They are mainly small, shallow and round-bottomed, not well suited to storage, unlike the much larger pits of the Iron Age, interpreted as grain stores; a few, such as that at Nethercourt Farm, Ramsgate, were much larger, and may have originally had a more utilitarian function, though in this case the filling included two inhumations. In some cases the filling shows clear signs of deliberate selection and careful placement of artefacts. At Mill Road, Deal (Dunning 1966, 1), the pit was of an unusual conical shape, and more than a metre deep. On the base were five pots, packed around with flints, the central one of which contained a large stone 'grain crusher'; half-way up the filling was a layer of flint flakes, including some that had been polished, presumably from a polished flint axe. At Wingham (Greenfield 1960) the pit filling included pottery, animal bone, a comb made from red deer antler, a bone point and part of a saddle quern and rubber, as well as charcoal. The pots were fragmentary when deposited, but included a high proportion of rim sections. The flints were fresh and unpatinated, and all from a single nodule; they could be refitted to show that no tool had been extracted.

Earlier finds in east Kent, summarised by Dunning (1966), show a concentration on the brickearths around Deal, though this may be a product of the work of local archaeologists. A cluster of features at Grovehurst, near Sittingbourne (Payne 1880), has sometimes been interpreted as the remains of hut circles or an even more substantial structure, but they were probably just pits. The recent increase in archaeological work has brought surprisingly few further pits to light. At Preston near Sandwich, a feature containing pottery and flint, and interpreted as a hearth, was revealed in a water-main trench (Ogilvie 1977, 97), and another pit with early Neolithic pottery was found in similar operations at Bogshole Lane, Herne Bay (Canterbury Archaeological Trust 1996). A small pit with Neolithic pottery a long distance from the modern shoreline at Minnis Bay (MacPherson-Grant 1969) shows how far coastal erosion has affected Thanet. An important collection of early Neolithic pottery has also been recovered from pits in roadworks near Monkton in Thanet.

These pits are typical of a phenomenon well known in the British Neolithic (Thomas 1999, 64-74). The digging and filling of pits was not primarily a part of domestic occupation, but a means of bestowing significance on a place, whether a place of occupation or feasting or periodic assembly, by creating a physical symbol of the human events that had taken place there. Domestic debris, including burnt material, is common but the careful selection of items means that it is not necessarily an easy guide to the domestic or agricultural economy.

A small number of sites in Britain have produced evidence for much more substantial timber buildings. Two structures revealed by the Channel Tunnel Rail Link at White Horse Stone are important additions to this list (Booth, Champion *et al.* forthcoming), though even now only about forty such sites are known in Britain (ill. 4.5). These structures are often interpreted as houses and have a generic similarity to the massive timber long houses of the early Neolithic period on the Continent, but the nature of their occupation is not clear (Darvill 1996). They are very uncommon, so may not represent the typical domestic residence; they are also very substantial in comparison to other traces of domestic activity, and do not fit well with the perception of Neolithic life as still partly mobile. They may not have been lived in but may have had some alternative function for the community.

The larger structure at White Horse Stone has a particular resemblance to continental prototypes in the plan of its post-holes and post-trenches. It dates to around the middle of the fourth millennium, but it cannot be accidental that much later pits containing Peterborough ware and grooved ware were found within the outline of the earlier house. Both buildings are also very close to a group of presumably contemporary megalithic long barrows discussed below, and that location cannot be random. It is quite probable that the structures had a role that was more communal and ceremonial than purely residential and domestic, though such stark divisions may not have made sense in the Neolithic.

4.5 White Horse Stone
Neolithic long-house.

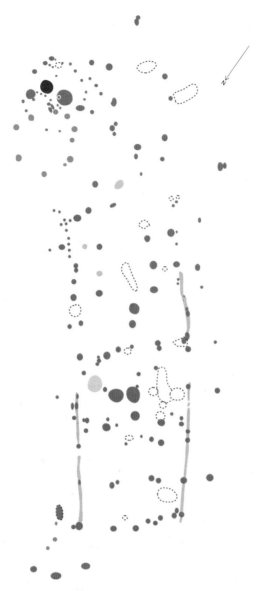

Wall foundation gullies
Post-holes
● without finds
● with grooved ware
● with early Neolithic plain bowl?
● with Peterborough ware
◖ circular structure
⬭ root disturbance/sarsen removal marks

0   5

metres

Celebrating the ancestors

The most important monuments of the Neolithic
in Kent are two groups of barrows. Though badly
damaged, they are still some of the most visible
remains of prehistory in the county, and have been
striking elements in their local landscapes since
their first construction. The two groups, which
are very different in the structural techniques
employed, are centred on the Medway valley
north of Maidstone, and on the Stour valley (ill.
4.6). Monuments outside these groups are rare.
A probable mortuary enclosure at Tollgate in west
Kent was identified in operations in advance of
construction of the Channel Tunnel Rail Link, but
it was not excavated (Booth, Champion *et al.*
forthcoming). Other possible long barrows or
mortuary enclosures have been identified in air
photographs, mainly in Thanet and East Kent, but
none has been confirmed.

The Medway megaliths are now in a very
ruinous state of preservation, but were once some
of the largest and most impressive of early
Neolithic funerary monuments anywhere in the
country (Ashbee 1993a; 1999; 2000). The group
is divided into two separate clusters, one to the
west and one to the east of the Medway. The

western group comprises three certain monuments, Addington and the Chestnuts close to each other and Coldrum a short distance to the north; two others may have existed close to Coldrum, but they are now reduced to a long spread mound of chalk and a line of sarsen stones respectively. Coldrum is the least damaged of all the Kent megaliths, but has still suffered badly (Ashbee 1998). It originally comprised a chamber built of large sarsen slabs at the east end of a long mound, with the entrance to the chamber flanked by a curving stone facade. It was built on top of a massive lynchet which was already well developed. The monument was severely damaged in the Middle Ages, when the chamber was slighted and the facade pulled down. Details of the eastern end are thus unclear; the chamber may

originally have been bigger. To the west of the chamber is a sarsen curb, also partly destroyed. This may represent not the outline of the original mound, but an earlier mortuary chamber pre-dating the mound. Coldrum would thus be a multi-period site, with a mound and kerb now largely lost. At the Chestnuts (Alexander 1961) ploughing has also removed most of the long mound. Again, there is a chamber built of large sarsen slabs with a facade, at the east end of a long mound of sand. The Addington barrow is divided into two by a road, but was originally a similar long mound with a kerb of sarsen stones and flanking ditches. There was a chamber of sarsen slabs at the east end.

The other cluster lies at the foot of the scarp slope of the North Downs east of the Medway. It

4.6 Map showing the two groups of Neolithic tombs in Kent: the Medway megaliths and the Stour Valley earthen long barrows.

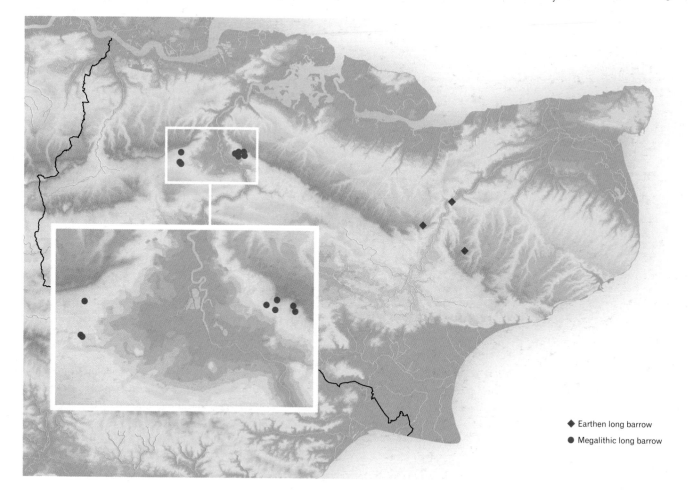

◆ Earthen long barrow

● Megalithic long barrow

comprises four certain monuments and two possible ones. Kit's Coty House (Ashbee 1993b) is perhaps the best-known monument in Kent (ill. 4.7). The three stones covered by a capstone are all that survive of the original chamber and probably represent its rear portion; the stones give some idea of the scale of the structure. The front portion of the chamber and a possible facade have been destroyed; there are sarsen stones nearby which could have come from the monument, and one recorded by William Stukeley in the 1720s, known as the General's Tomb, was particularly massive. The mound and flanking ditches have now been ploughed flat, but can be seen in aerial photographs. The neighbouring monument of Lower Kit's Coty House survives as a jumble of large sarsen stones, sometimes known as the Countless Stones (ill. 4.8). It represents the remains of a large rectangular chamber, now collapsed or pulled down, at the east end of a mound which would have been at least 20m wide. The third monument is known as the Coffin

Stone, an appropriate name for a huge slab of sarsen, which is all that remains of the original chamber. It was at the east end of a mound which can still be traced for a considerable length. The Warren Farm site (Ashbee 2003) is now largely destroyed, but earlier records suggest that the end of a sarsen-built chamber had survived; it was orientated east-west, and was presumably at the end of a long mound, though no trace of it remains. Two other sarsen stones nearby, one now removed, known as the Upper and Lower White Horse Stones, may also have been the remnants of two further monuments of the same type.

These Medway megalithic long barrows conform to the same general plan and were originally massive. They were all aligned east-west, with a stone chamber at the east end of the mound and probably a stone facade flanking the entrance to the chamber. Addington was about 70m long, Kit's Coty House is known to be about 80m long, and the Coffin Stone's mound may have been 90m. At Lower Kit's Coty the mound was even wider, and if it was in the same proportions, may have been even longer. The chambers were also large, using the sarsen slabs locally available: the largest of all may have been at Lower Kit's Coty, where the chamber was probably over 5m long, 2.5m wide and nearly 3m high.

Only Coldrum and the Chestnuts have been excavated in recent times, though there are records of finds from in or around several of the other monuments. Pottery is said to have been found at Addington and Kit's Coty House and both pottery and bones at Warren Farm. Bones, including skulls, were recovered close to the Coffin Stone. Excavation of the Chestnuts produced both burnt and unburnt bone together with flint and pottery. There were both early and late Neolithic sherds, suggesting a lengthy period of usage. A series of investigations at Coldrum has revealed pottery, flint and human remains including skulls; excavation in 1910 produced the remains of twenty-two individuals of both sexes and a wide age range. The chalky nature of the bones suggests they may have been buried

4.7 Air photograph of Kits Coty House: the remains of the chamber (see Stukeley's drawing, ill. 2.1) are in the square fenced enclosure, and the long, light-coloured soil mark stretching to the left marks the site of the original mound.

4.8 Lower Kits Coty House: the ruinous remains of what may have been one of the largest of the Medway megaliths (compare Stukeley's speculative reconstruction in ill. 2.1).

elsewhere before being brought to Coldrum.

The other group of long barrows in Kent is focused on the Stour valley and is made up of three monuments. The site referred to as Julliberrie's Grave has been known to antiquarian scholarship since the sixteenth century, but it is only more recent fieldwork that has led to the other two discoveries. The sites at Boughton Aluph and Elmstead (Parfitt 1998b) remain unexcavated and are known only as earthworks.

Julliberrie's Grave comprises a mound 2m high and 15m wide with flanking ditches; the mound survives to a length of 45m, but the northern end has been severely damaged by chalk quarrying and it may originally have been substantially longer. Excavation revealed that the mound was made up of a central spine of loam, capped with chalk rubble. Finds included flint flakes and animal bones, as well as a flint axe of Scandinavian type.

No burials were found, but it is possible that the most important part of the monument had been lost at the truncated northern end. On the other hand, it is now recognised that long barrows were not just funerary monuments, and that many may never have contained a burial. It is also possible that the site had a long history of ritual activity. A pit, without finds, was discovered under the mound, and another pit was dug into the mound at a later date. Although sarsen was available in the vicinity, there is no evidence that it was used in any of these monuments.

These two groups, on the Medway and the Stour, are differentiated by the presence or absence of sarsen and would fall into separate classes according to the standard classification of long barrows: megalithic and non-megalithic respectively. The best comparisons for the Medway group are in north Wiltshire and

Berkshire, where sarsen was similarly used in monuments such as the West Kennet long barrow (Piggott 1962) and Wayland's Smithy (Whittle 1991). The earthen, or non-megalithic, long barrows frequently had equally long and complex histories (Kinnes 1992); the Medway sites form one regional group in a widely distributed pattern. In reality, though, there are two architectural variants on the same theme: the massive sarsen chambers are stone versions of those in wood, and vice versa. Sarsen would most likely be used only where it was available, as in the Avebury region and the Medway valley, but even where it was available it was not always employed. In form, long barrows recalled the long houses of the early Neolithic cultures on the Continent, in their length and mass and the presence of flanking ditches. If they were seen as houses for the ancestors, they were not tombs in the ordinary sense: they were not the primary resting place of the recently dead. Long barrows were monuments with long histories and many ritual functions. One of these was to be the resting place of the bones of the ancestors, but perhaps only temporarily and after burial elsewhere. The bones deposited in long barrows are often carefully selected, not whole skeletons, but critical parts. Over the long use of the monument the bones may have been brought out for use in ceremonies and returned for safe keeping many times, before perhaps being swept aside and replaced by others. Information about the contents of the Kent monuments is sadly very poor, but the evidence from Coldrum suggests that the funerary deposits may have been capped by domestic debris containing pottery, as at West Kennet, before the tomb was closed. Even then the sites may have continued in use. They would have been prominent features in the landscape and the space in front of the facades would have been an appropriate setting for further rituals. The close clustering of the monuments in Kent is an unusual feature of their distribution. It would argue against their interpretation as territorial markers for dispersed social groups, but would

certainly suggest that particular locations had special meaning within the landscape.

The Medway and Stour long barrows, though familiar monuments in the local landscape, are some of the least known and most seldom cited in wider debates on the British Neolithic. Yet they should be some of the most important. Despite their present ruinous and unimpressive condition, they were some of the largest and most impressive monuments of the British Neolithic, especially in the size of their sarsen chambers. Whatever explanation is adopted for the origins of agriculture in Britain, the beginning of the Neolithic involved some undisputed innovations from the Continent: the domesticated cereals and sheep were not indigenous. Kent, as the British side of the shortest crossing, must have played a significant role. There is no evidence for the date of the Medway and Stour barrows, but as the nearest to the Continent, and as those perhaps most similar to the long houses, they deserve more attention than they have received.

There is little other evidence of Neolithic activity in the area of these monuments to suggest why their locations were chosen or how they affected human use of the landscape around them. The Chestnuts tomb was situated on the large Mesolithic site at Addington, though the excavator noted a layer of sterile sand between the Mesolithic artefacts and the monument; there was also a comparatively large collection of early Neolithic pottery from the old ground surface below the monument, suggesting some type of activity before construction (Alexander 1961). Its siting may represent the continued use of a place whose age-old importance was still remembered. The barrows remained important landmarks in the later landscape, and two of them, the Chestnuts and Julliberrie's Grave, were reused in the Roman period. At the Chestnuts a small structure of the fourth century AD was interpreted as a shepherd's hut. At Julliberrie's Grave four first-century AD burials had been placed in the ditch of the barrow, but other deposits also seem to be of a ritual nature:

domestic debris, including first- and second-century pottery, and bone and oyster shells, had been placed there, and there were also collections of later Roman coins. The barrows, especially those in the group east of the Medway, certainly had a local significance well into the Middle Ages, shown not only by their names and the legends attached to them, but also by what appears to have been a concerted attempt to destroy them in the twelfth or thirteenth century (Ashbee 1993a).

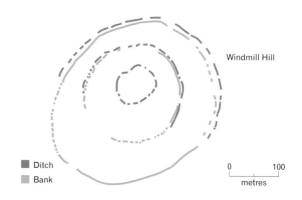

4.9 Causewayed enclosures in Kent compared to the complete plan of Windmill Hill, Wiltshire: Kingsborough Farm is partially excavated; Ramsgate is known from partial excavations and air photographs.

Communal monuments

For a long time it was a matter of considerable surprise that Kent did not have certain evidence of any of the other major categories of Neolithic monuments of the middle and late fourth millennium well known in southern England, especially no causewayed enclosure and no cursus (e.g. Barber 1997). That gap has now been filled with the recognition of three certain and two probable causewayed enclosures and a probable cursus (Dyson *et al.* 2000; Oswald *et al.* 2001). Such discoveries emphasise how little is yet known of Kent's prehistory and suggest that further surprises may await us.

The causewayed enclosure at Chalk Hill, near Ramsgate, was first identified from air photographs and subsequently confirmed by partial excavation in advance of road works (Shand 2001) (ill. 4.9). The enclosure was about 150m in diameter, surrounded by three rows of interrupted ditches. There was a very clear patterning to the carefully placed deposits in the

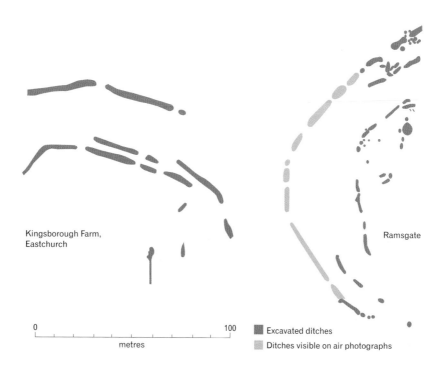

ditches. The inner one contained cremated bone, the middle one flint implements such as scrapers and arrowheads, especially at the terminals of the ditch sections, and the outer ring bones, shells and pottery, possibly the remains of feasting (ill. 4.10). There were also two human skulls. The other two confirmed sites, at Eastchurch on the central ridge of the Isle of Sheppey, were unsuspected until encountered in an excavation undertaken in advance of house construction.

4.10 Placed deposits of animal bones, including cattle skulls, in the ditch of the Ramsgate causewayed enclosure.

It may be pure coincidence that the three excavated examples of this type of ceremonial monument all lie on what would have been off-shore islands in the Neolithic; they are certainly in areas responsive to aerial photography and which are experiencing heavy development pressure. Both conform well to one of preferred locations for such monuments (Oswald *et al.* 2001, 91-102). Nearly eighty examples are now known in England, and almost a third of them are located on valley sides, on the slopes just below the crest of a hill, and orientated towards lower land. The Chalk Hill site is on the south slope of the Isle of Thanet, and would have commanded a view across the eastern mouth of the Wantsum along the east coast of Kent, past present-day Sandwich. The Eastchurch sites occupy similar locations on a ridge on the Isle of Sheppey, with views across the Swale and the Thames.

In addition to these three verified examples, there are two other probable examples of causewayed enclosures identified from air photographs. One at Tilmanstone would also have been on a hillslope looking down towards a valley; the other at Burham in the Medway valley north of Maidstone would fit well with another of the other common locations for these monuments; more than a third of all such monuments are sited on low rises in the floors of river valleys (Oswald *et al.* 2001, 91-102, 152-153). That at Burham would also be only about 3km from the group of megalithic long barrows east of the Medway.

The Kent sites thus conform well to the general pattern of knowledge emerging about these sites (Oswald *et al.* 2001). In size, form and location they are reasonably typical, and their ditches show the same care in the selection and placing of deposits. Domestic debris, possibly from feasting, is common, and so too are fragments of human skeletons, especially skulls. The sites played a major role in the communal rituals of the fourth millennium, and their locations were places of great significance in the landscape.

Overlying the enclosure ditches at Chalk Hill were two further ditches, also containing flint and pot, but then cutting right across the enclosure were

The first to be recognised also had three circuits of ditches which contained placed deposits of flint and pot; it was on the south-facing slope of the ridge, looking across the Swale towards mainland Kent. As development continued, a second causewayed enclosure was discovered a short distance to the north; it lies on the north-facing slope, with views across the Thames estuary.

two parallel ditches about 35m apart. They also date to the Neolithic and may well represent a small part of a cursus. The full length of such a monument is unknown, even from air photographs. To the east it would disappear into a valley leading down to Pegwell Bay and to the west it would be orientated approximately towards the complex of barrows at Lord of the Manor, which might have a Neolithic origin. Two other causewayed enclosures are similarly overlain by cursus monuments, Etton, Cambridgeshire, and Fornham All Saints, Suffolk (Oswald *et al.* 2001, 134-135 and Fig. 8.2). Though apparently representing an abandonment of the earlier monument, it might equally suggest the continued remembrance of its existence and the renewed importance of the site as a place of ceremonial significance.

Material objects

Until the recent excavations of the causewayed enclosures there were few good assemblages of artefacts to encourage detailed study of the material culture of the Neolithic. The small pits generally produced few objects, and the barrows had been badly destroyed; most of the excavations were old, and only the Chestnuts had been examined with modern methods. Flint implements are comparatively plentiful, but there have been few attempts at systematic collection and study. Recent work has now begun to remedy that situation, and detailed examination of the excavated objects will add immensely to our knowledge of the period.

Apart from flint and pottery, other objects such as the antler comb and the bone point from the pit at Wingham are very rare. The pottery all falls within a fairly small range of undecorated bowl forms generally typical of the early Neolithic (Dunning 1966; Clarke 1982, Fig. 9). There are so far no detailed studies of early Neolithic flint assemblages.

Flint axes are widely distributed (Clarke 1982, Fig. 8), and occasionally deposited in ways that seem to have a special significance. Caches of deliberately buried axes are known from Pembury and probably Saltwood (Pitts 1996, 356 and 367). A flint axe was buried in the mound of Julliberrie's

4.11 Neolithic stone axes from Kent (all in Maidstone Museum): from left to right, Group IX (Northern Ireland), from Sittingbourne (L. 96 mm); Group VI (Great Langdale, Cumbria), from Rolvenden (L. 135 mm); Group I (Mounts Bay, Cornwall), from Murston (L. 116 mm); Group VII (Craig Llwyd, Gwynedd) roughout, from New Hythe (L. 163 mm).

Grave, and another was deposited in the ditch of a small circular monument at Weatherlees Hill, Thanet (Hearne *et al*. 1995, 250). Pitts (1996, 322 and Fig. 3) has shown that in Kent, Sussex and Norfolk over 80% of Neolithic axes are of flint, part of a more general pattern of exploiting locally available resources. Both Sussex and Norfolk have well-documented Neolithic flint mines, but none has yet been discovered in Kent (Barber *et al*. 1999). Axes made from more exotic rock sources are comparatively rare (Woodcock *et al*. 1988). Several of these sources have not yet been identified, but many of the axes may have come from the south-west of England. Though the numbers are small, the network of contacts is shown by axes deriving from Cornwall, Wales, the Lake District and even Northern Ireland (ill.4.11).

A world of monuments

In much of Britain from about 3000 BC new types of monument began to be built. Settlement sites are still very rare, and for the next 1,500 years the archaeological record continues to be dominated by ceremonial sites. Henges, which constituted a rather varied class of monuments, were circular, often with a ditch and an external bank. The largest of these were in Wessex, such as Avebury or Durrington Walls, or the abnormal Stonehenge, but in various forms they were widespread. They were communal monuments for the practice of important ceremonies. New types of burial monument also came into use. These were round barrows containing individual burials. Though commonest in the early Bronze Age, they began in the late Neolithic.

It would be easy to contrast the long barrows of the early Neolithic with the round barrows of later periods. The long barrows are known to have held multiple burials; they were the final resting place for parts of human bodies after funerary rituals, possibly elsewhere, and were the focus for repeated ceremonial acts. The round barrows, on the other hand, could be seen as individual funerary monuments for the single event of the primary interment of the body. Such a contrast,

however, would be far too simple. Recent research on round barrows has shown how long and complex were their life histories (Woodward 2000). Many show extended sequences of acts, over many centuries, the construction of the barrow often being quite a late episode. Many of the ceremonial acts were not concerned with burial of the dead, and some barrows may never have had a single burial. Rather, they were places for the enactment of important rites and ceremonies, some of which included burial of the dead. The dead, however, were treated as individuals, suggesting a different approach to the idea of ancestors and their use in the legitimation of the rights of the living.

The chronology of the period from approximately 3000 BC to 1500 BC, which in traditional archaeological terminology includes the late Neolithic and the early Bronze Age, has now been fixed with some degree of certainty by radiocarbon dating. Dates for the main pottery types and the early assemblages of copper and bronze objects have been determined in sufficient quantity for precise periods of usage to be suggested (Needham 1996). There is a growing number of radiocarbon dates available for sites in Kent, and, where diagnostic pottery or metalwork is found, other sites can be dated by inference. Unfortunately, much less study has been undertaken on lithic assemblages in Kent, and where sites are characterised only by their flint artefacts, it is often not possible to date them more precisely than 'late Neolithic or early Bronze Age' or even 'prehistoric'.

In this period Kent began to assume its present form as sea levels stabilised. Clearance and regeneration of the woodland continued. Flint tools suggest a dense level of activity in some areas, especially the chalk downs of east Kent, though evidence for actual settlements is still slight. Round barrows became a common feature of the landscape. Kent maintained long-distance contacts by sea, across the Channel and around the coasts of Britain. Some people had access to exotic materials such as gold, amber, jet and copper.

Elusive settlements

Evidence for settlement of this period is again very fragmentary (Brück 1999b). Since human populations were probably still not fully sedentary, their settlement sites were not as substantial as later, and they have suffered badly from the effects of human and natural processes. Agriculture has been a major agent of destruction; some sites have been destroyed by ploughing, while others have been concealed by the hillwash it caused. Natural processes of coastal change have also been dramatic. Coastal erosion has been severe, especially along the north coast, while in other areas alluviation has concealed prehistoric sites; buried beneath the surface in the Lydden Valley in east Kent are older land surfaces which have produced evidence of beaker and Bronze Age occupation (Halliwell and Parfitt 1985).

Most of the evidence for later Neolithic settlement is again in the form of shallow pits with characteristic pottery. The Ebbsfleet and Mortlake styles of Peterborough ware are the commonest in Kent. The Ebbsfleet style was originally discovered at the eponymous site in west Kent (Burchell and Piggott 1939; Sieveking 1960). Peterborough sherds are known from Castle Hill, Folkestone (Rady 1990, 42), and from Chalk Hill, Ramsgate (Hearne et al. 1995). Other sites producing similar pottery include Cheriton (Smith and Philp 1975) and Baston Manor, Hayes (Philp 1973, 5-19), where a wide range of late Neolithic decorated pottery was discovered; a pit found during construction of a pipeline at Monkton (Perkins 1985) contained a layer of clam shells, above which were flint flakes, animal bone and late Neolithic pottery. Ditches containing Peterborough ware with beaker sherds and a barbed and tanged arrowhead, found at Oaklands Nursery, Cottington, Thanet (Perkins 1998c), and another curving ditch or gulley with late Neolithic pottery at Chislet (Canterbury Archaeological Trust 1996) suggest the possible existence of more substantial sites and structures. At Chilston Sandpit, Lenham, an occupation area including shallow pits, post-holes, gullies and ditches was

located (Holmes and Bennett 2003); it had been badly truncated, but a small collection of flint and pottery assigned it to the late Neolithic or early Bronze Age.

The other main tradition of late Neolithic pottery, grooved ware, is found more commonly on settlement sites, as well as on the major ceremonial henges of Wessex, but it is rare in Kent. Small pits containing grooved ware are known at Mill Hill, Deal (Parfitt 1990), and from sites on the old ground surface of the Lydden valley below the later alluviation (Halliwell and Parfitt 1985).

A notable rarity is a large sub-rectangular enclosure dating to the beaker period. The site, at Minster in Thanet, comprised a ditched enclosure about 80 by 40 m, and its ditches contained beaker pottery and a flint assemblage, including a barbed and tanged arrowhead. The site was identified but not further excavated, so nothing is known about its interior (Boast and Gibson 2000). Beaker settlement of a different form is known at Greenhill, Otford (Pyke 1980; 1981). Pits, possibly from tree clearance, contained beaker pottery and flints, as well as some Peterborough pottery, probably derived from a focus of occupation nearby.

The commonest form of evidence for human activity at this period is provided by the widespread distribution of worked flint. This is most abundant on the chalk downlands between Canterbury and Dover, but is a frequent find elsewhere. The flints cannot often be dated more precisely than late Neolithic or early Bronze Age, and the relationship between surface finds and any subsurface features is unknown. Little research has yet been done on the distribution or significance of these assemblages, or even on their typology and technology. Analysis of one such surface assemblage from Lyminge (Wilson 1999) showed two main phases of production. There was a Mesolithic component, including Thames picks and burins, but the majority of the items were of late Neolithic or early Bronze Age date, including scrapers and arrowheads. The presence of cores and freshly struck flakes suggests that flint knapping was taking place on site.

Another frequent, but enigmatic, element of the Bronze Age landscape in many other parts of Britain is the occurrence of quantities of burnt stone, often accumulated in mounds (Hodder and Barfield 1991). Various suggestions have been made for their use, including cooking and saunas, but their function, or functions, are still unclear. A few finds of piles or dumps of burnt flint have now been made in Kent: at Chartham Hatch (Allen 1999) a pit containing a large mass of fire-cracked flint has been radiocarbon-dated to the middle of the third millennium BC, while at Crabble Paper Mill, Dover (Parfitt and Corke 2003a), pits containing large quantities of calcined flint, located in an area of ashy soil with much charcoal and some struck flint flakes, produced very similar dates. A shallow pit containing calcined flint found at Honeywood Parkway, Whitfield, near Dover (Parfitt 2004a), has been dated to the late third millennium. It is very likely that such sites were much more frequent than the few so far recorded and dated would indicate.

One of the most important pieces of early landscape history was revealed in the construction of the Channel Tunnel terminal. At Holywell Coombe, to the west of Folkestone at the foot of the scarp of the chalk Downs, deep layers of colluvial deposits were interleaved with old ground surfaces (Bennett 1988). Buried within this stratigraphy was a layer belonging to the beaker period. It showed evidence of early agriculture in the form of ard marks, overlain by an organised landscape. A trackway had been worn hollow by constant use, and bones of cattle and pig, as well as marine shells such as mussels, winkles and limpets, were trodden into the surface. Dense masses of post-holes marked out the fence lines of small enclosures and possibly of buildings. Evidence for settlement organisation of this sort at this period is very rare anywhere in England. At the former North Barracks, Deal (Parfitt and Corke 2001), a series of ditches containing pottery and flint-working debris has been interpreted as a multi-phase field system of the early Bronze Age, but otherwise there are very few glimpses of how the landscape was organised.

The true extent of human activity in this period is unknown. The known barrows are most densely clustered on the chalk of Thanet and east Kent, but they may originally have been much more widespread. Little systematic collection of flint material has been undertaken. Gardiner's (1990b) survey of the archaeological evidence from the Weald omitted Kent since evidence had not been systematically collected in the way that it had in Sussex and Surrey. There is, however, no reason to think that conditions were fundamentally different there, and human interest in the Weald may have been more intense than can currently be documented. Indeed, it is in the early Bronze Age that the scatter of archaeological material seems to reach its peak, before a decline in the middle and late Bronze Age.

Henges

Field monuments of this period survive only in very small numbers; thanks to aerial photography, many more sites have now been identified, but there are still no certain henges, though the evidence for their existence is growing steadily. It is only very recently, however, that the first causewayed enclosures and a possible cursus of the early Neolithic have been discovered, and it may well be only a matter of time before the first true henges are confirmed. On the other hand, henges are not yet well known north of the Thames either. Air photographs in Kent suggest the possible presence of such monuments, but we should also be aware of the likelihood of regional diversity in the development of Neolithic societies. The lack of henges may be real, or it may be a quirk of prehistoric research.

Perhaps the most persuasive evidence for a henge is at Ringlemere, near Sandwich. The site was originally located when a gold cup was found with a metal detector (see below). The site showed evidence of a small mound, later identified as one of a group. The obvious assumption was that this constituted the remains of a badly plough-damaged early Bronze Age barrow with one or more burials, but, on further investigation, it was found to be a much more complex monument (Parfitt and Needham 2004). The core of the mound and the old ground surface contained large quantities of grooved ware pottery and occasional beaker sherds; shallow pits dug into the subsoil also contained grooved ware. One pit gave a radiocarbon date in the centuries before 2600 BC. The ditch was also very large, with a diameter of 42m, and with at least one entrance; the pattern of silting also suggested the possibility of an external bank. All these features suggest that what was originally a henge monument may have been remodelled with a mound at some later stage, and that the gold cup and other objects were deposited there, perhaps as much as a millennium after its first construction.

The recognition of one probable henge raises the question of whether there were more. The diameter of the ditch of the Ringlemere monument is much greater than the average for known Bronze Age barrows, and aerial photography has shown a number of other sites which are of the same scale. The possibility of the reuse of a henge as a later barrow also raises questions about the early phases of some of the more complex barrows already excavated, but no site has produced the quantities of grooved ware seen at Ringlemere. A round barrow at Eythorne was also built over an area with a high concentration of grooved ware, but it was not fully explored and the nature of the earliest structural phases is unknown (Parfitt 2004b).

The celebration of the dead

By far the commonest monuments of this period, or of any period of prehistoric Kent, are the round barrows. The number of these known has increased dramatically in recent years, due largely to the impact of aerial photography. A survey in 1960 (Ashbee and Dunning 1960) listed 30 barrows from 21 locations in east Kent, mostly still upstanding in some form. Grinsell (1992) catalogued 170 barrows, though he was aware that

this included only a small selection of the ploughed-out sites then beginning to be recognised, especially in Thanet. Today, there are probably over 800 barrows known, though that is certainly an underestimate of the total that once existed. Only certain soils are responsive to air photography, particularly the chalk downlands of Thanet and the area between Canterbury and Dover; others, such as the Greensand and the soils of the Weald, are unresponsive and the sites there may be under-represented. Furthermore, previously unknown ploughed-out ring ditches are still regularly found in the excavation of other sites (ill. 4.12).

The known distribution of barrows is, of course, affected by these biases in recognition. The vast majority of those so far recorded are on the chalk of Thanet and east Kent. Though many of them are located on ridges, there is no particular concentration on the crest of the North Downs escarpment; only in Thanet do they seem to cluster in cemeteries along the ridges of the island. A comparatively small number are known

4.12 Air photograph of ploughed-out Bronze Age barrow cemetery at Birchington.

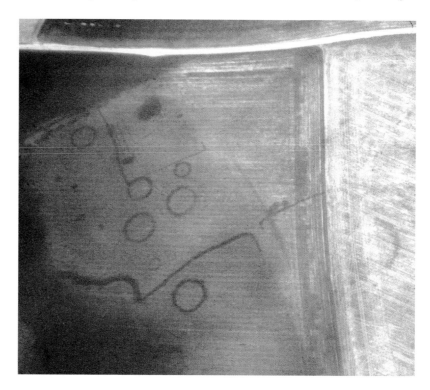

from the dip slope of the North Downs in west Kent. Even fewer are known from south of the Downs, though important clusters of barrows have been revealed in operations for the Channel Tunnel terminal at the foot of Castle Hill, Folkestone (Canterbury Archaeological Trust 1992, 365), and for the Channel Tunnel Rail Link at Saltwood (Booth, Champion *et al.* forthcoming). This presents a sharp contrast with the pattern observed on the South Downs (Field 1998), where scarp-top barrows are common, and there are some large clusters of barrows on the Greensand of West Sussex. Only further fieldwork will tell whether these differences are real, or the result of differences in archaeological visibility.

The vast majority of barrows have been badly damaged by the plough and survive now only as ring ditches cut into the subsoil. This means the loss of most of the evidence for burials or other activities in the mound above ground level. In most cases evidence of burials has survived only because they were placed in graves cut into the chalk or other bedrock or into the filling of the ditches. Many ring ditches show no evidence for any burial, but it is impossible to tell if there had originally been a burial on the old ground surface or higher in the mound, or if the barrow had been built and used for non-funerary purposes. Ploughing has also often damaged the surface of the underlying chalk, removing any fragile traces of timber structures that might have been part of the history of the monument.

The severe degradation of many of Kent's barrows is in stark contrast to their survival in other chalkland areas of southern England such as Sussex and especially Wessex, where monuments survived due to the comparatively limited extent of arable farming, and the long-term use of the downlands as sheep pasture. When the eighteenth-century antiquaries started excavating in Kent, the barrows they opened were almost exclusively Anglo-Saxon; there are few hints that they found much that was prehistoric. Some barrows had clearly survived in some recognisable form, though not necessarily intact, to serve as the focus

for Anglo-Saxon cemeteries. Though medieval and later ploughing had certainly had a serious effect on them, in some cases the barrows had been ploughed out much earlier: the ring ditches at Dumpton Gap, Broadstairs (Hurd 1909, 431), Hartsdown, Margate, Site 2 (Perkins 1996), Hillside, Gravesend (Philp and Chenery 1997), the Whitfield-Eastry by-pass (Parfitt, Allen and Rady 1997) and Barrow 1 on the Bridge by-pass (MacPherson-Grant 1980), are cut through by Iron Age ditches, and at Castle Hill, Folkestone (Canterbury Archaeological Trust 1992, 365), all three barrows were overlain by a settlement of early Iron Age date. In all these examples it seems likely that the mounds had been greatly reduced or even completely removed by ploughing in prehistory. The great variability in the survival of the barrows needs further examination as part of the landscape history of Kent, but clearly Kent had a very different long-term environmental history from other areas of southern England.

The near-total absence in Kent of barrows surviving as earthworks has meant that barrow studies have not progressed as fast as in some other areas. The increasing pace of development in recent years has led to a greater number of excavations, but other lines of research have been neglected. Elsewhere, recent barrow studies have focused on questions of location, grouping, setting in the landscape and intervisibility (Woodward 2000; Garwood 2003). Little of this has yet been done in Kent. Field's (1998) study of the location of barrows in south-eastern England used a very restricted set of data for Kent. He suggested that, contrary to the usual perception of barrows being located on high chalkland, many barrows in south-eastern England were located in lower positions in valleys, along ridges near water. This would be true for the group of three barrows at Castle Hill, Folkestone (Canterbury Archaeological Trust 1992, 365), and even more so for the three barrows spaced out along a ridge at Saltwood (Booth, Champion *et al.* forthcoming). Many of the barrows on the chalk Downs are grouped in cemeteries. At Monkton (box, pages 90-1), road improvements cut a long swathe through such a cemetery and showed that the construction of the barrows was only one element in the long-term ceremonial use of this landscape. There is still an enormous amount to be learnt from research of this kind. Indeed, given the very damaged state of many of the barrows and the limited evidence they can offer, this may be a much more productive approach.

Only when barrows have been excavated is it possible to tell anything of the structural sequence and internal features. Despite the very degraded state of many of them, it is occasionally possible to see that some had very long and complex histories, with multiple structural phases. Ditches were recut, enlarged or multiplied; sometimes stratigraphic succession demonstrates the sequence, but elsewhere, where multiple ditches do not intersect, it is not clear whether we are dealing with one complex phase or a succession of adaptations. In many barrows there are multiple burials in graves cut into either the subsoil itself or very often the soft filling of the ditch; any burials placed higher in the mound may have been damaged or destroyed by later ploughing. Individual graves might be reused, and further burials can also be found in the area immediately surrounding a barrow. Some of the best evidence for the use and reuse of barrows and the spaces around them comes from the barrow cemetery at Monkton.

Evidence for other internal structures is very rare. Chalk rubble and turf were common mound materials, but flint was also used. At St Margaret's, near Dover, the core of the barrow was a flint cairn, and at Ringwould the central burials in one barrow were covered by a thick layer of flints (Woodruff 1874); at Wouldham a layer of flints covered the central pit containing the cremation (Cruse and Harrison 1983). Garwood (2003) has noted the frequent destruction of flint-cored barrows in Sussex in the search for building materials, and it is possible that a similar process was at work in Kent. At West Langdon near Dover, excavation showed

some large stones laid in a sort of pavement (Woodruff 1874). Evidence for timber structures is rare: post-holes, probably from wooden structures associated with the burials, are known at Wouldham (Cruse and Harrison 1983).

Though the damaged state of most of the barrows makes it difficult to be certain, it is possible that some of them never contained burials. Excavation of one of the barrows that still survived at Ringwould (Woodruff 1874) produced no evidence for a burial; the careful description and drawing of the other barrow there and the burials it contained suggest the absence may be genuine. Nor need all the deposits made in a barrow site have been associated with burials (see below).

The presence in the barrows of burials dated by pottery or radiocarbon shows that the main period of use for that purpose was during the currency of beaker and collared urn pottery, perhaps 2100 to 1500 BC; burials accompanied by middle Bronze Age pottery show continued use of some of the barrows down to about 1100 BC. These burials, however, do not necessarily define the beginning and end of the building and use of such monuments. The location of barrows at sites where concentrations of grooved ware show their earlier significance in the late Neolithic has already been mentioned, but the construction of the barrows may not begin until the early Bronze Age. Perkins (2004), however, has drawn attention to a group of barrows in Thanet which, it is suggested, may have origins in the late Neolithic. The barrows, with diameters of 20 to 40m, are much larger than the average Bronze Age barrow in Kent. They show signs of an initial phase which later underwent major structural modification, at a time when the original ditch was substantially silted up through natural causes; such alterations might include the redigging of the ditch, the digging of a new concentric ditch or the slighting of an original causewayed entrance. All this had taken place before the use of the monument for burials, sometimes datable to the beaker period. In most cases, later use has made it

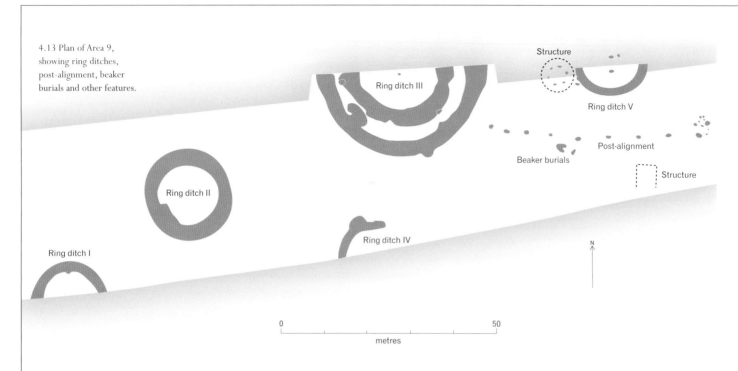

4.13 Plan of Area 9, showing ring ditches, post-alignment, beaker burials and other features.

Ring ditch III

Structure

Ring ditch V

Post-alignment

Beaker burials

Structure

Ring ditch II

Ring ditch IV

Ring ditch I

N

0   50

metres

4.15 Ring ditch III during excavation.

Monkton barrow cemetery

Road widening in the Isle of Thanet cut through a large barrow cemetery at Monkton. Ten barrows were excavated, and although they had been badly truncated by ploughing, they give a very good example of the range of structures and practices seen in such monuments (Canterbury Archaeological Trust *et al.* 1996; Clark forthcoming).

Several of the barrows were simple ring ditches, some with evidence for recutting of the ditch or refurbishment of the mound. In one case, a barrow was replaced by a new one, which cut through the filled-up ditch and the mound of the earlier structure. Evidence for burials in the mounds was sparse, but the area around them contained inhumations and cremations.

Others were more complex. Barrow III started as a ring ditch, followed by a timber post-circle, probably associated with a line of posts along which two crouched inhumations had been placed; then a double ring ditch had been dug; and the mound at some stage refurbished. Fragments of beaker pottery suggest the original presence of burials. The first of

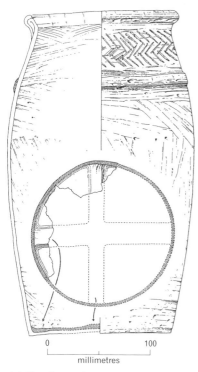

4.14 Trevisker urn from
Cornwall, found in ring ditch X,
outside the area in plan.

the inhumations placed along the row of posts contained a group of 217 thin disc-shaped beads of Whitby jet. This grave was cut by another: no skeleton had survived, but it contained a beaker and a copper alloy bracelet.

Barrow X was a single ring ditch, with a pit containing a middle Bronze Age cremation burial near the inner edge of the ditch. In the filling of the ditch had been placed a Trevisker urn, imported from Cornwall (Gibson *et al.* 1997). Also in the ditch fill were a copper alloy bead and a jet bead, possibly derived from destroyed burials. Nearby was a group of inhumation burials; three were accompanied by beakers and one also contained a copper alloy bracelet.

The fragmentary remains of pottery, including beaker, collared urn and small perforated cups, suggest that there had been a series of burials, but the barrows were only part of a ceremonial landscape which also included post circles, post rows and isolated burials. The whole complex was also in use for at least 800 years, possibly more.

difficult to determine the form and function of the original monument, or to fix its true chronology. It is possible that the first phase of the structural sequence may have been in the late Neolithic, and it is also possible that the monuments originally had a non-funerary function. In one case, the site of Lord of the Manor 2D near Ramsgate (Perkins and Macpherson-Grant 1981), an apparently quite early monument was reused for the burial of a crouched inhumation, but was not otherwise subject to major modification. It consisted of a ditch with a diameter of 23m and a causewayed entrance to the south-west, enclosing an internal bank and other enigmatic features including post-holes and a hearth. Whatever its function, it does not appear to have been funerary; its absolute dating is also unknown. Whether it is typical of the monuments that were later modified and used for burial in the early Bronze Age will only be known with more excavated examples and more high-precision radiocarbon dates.

It may also be possible to see some sequential development in the construction of barrows, and Perkins (2004) has drawn attention to a second group of possibly very early barrows, also in Thanet. Small, oval monuments, with ditches built in conjoined segments, enclose more than one burial pit; in some cases there is evidence for a flint cairn, the disturbance and removal of skeletal material and flat graves nearby. At Manston, near Ramsgate, a ploughed out barrow was excavated in 1987 (Perkins and Gibson 1990); the central burial was a crouched inhumation with a beaker, a flint knife and a perforated jet button, radiocarbon-dated to just before 2000 BC, but this may not have been the primary burial. At South Dumpton Down (Perkins 2004, 77-79), a small, oval barrow contained a double burial pit with a complex series of seven crouched inhumations; the second-earliest was accompanied by sherds of food vessel, while a beaker was associated with one of the burials higher up. These oval barrows certainly belong early in the sequence, but the absolute chronology of the structures, rather than the burials, remains to be firmly fixed. The barrow on the Whitfield-Eastry by-pass (Parfitt, Allen and Rady 1997) had a similar oval plan, and an early, possibly even late Neolithic, date has also been suggested for its original construction.

In some cases it is known that barrows continued in use for a long time. The Whitfield-Eastry barrow had several structural phases, but the radiocarbon dates for the burials demonstrate that there was a millennium between the earliest inhumations and a cremation deposited in the late Bronze Age. In the case of the barrow at Manston, mentioned above, the beaker burial was followed by a secondary crouched inhumation, but the area inside the ditch also contained some post-holes of unknown date, and seven small pits. In five of these, sherds of late Bronze Age pottery had been placed on the bottom, with a flint nodule on top. This must have been a deliberate set of deposits, which were placed well over a millennium after the central burial. Despite what was said above about barrows having been destroyed possibly already by the Iron Age, others certainly survived as prominent features of the landscape. In some cases they were selected as the focus for Anglo-Saxon cemeteries, more than two thousand years later (below, page 227).

Not all burials of this period are found in surviving barrows or associated with ploughed-out ring ditches. Some are found in graves cut into the subsoil without any trace of a barrow, as in the cemetery at Monkton described above. In these cases it is sometimes not clear whether there was originally a mound without a ditch, or whether the grave had been flat, perhaps with some other sort of marker. A more unusual burial rite is represented by a group of three crouched inhumations found at Aylesford in the 1880s, buried in cists made of slabs of tufa and sandstone (Ashbee 1997). There is no direct dating evidence, and no parallel for the cists, but the form of the burial suggests a date in the Bronze Age.

After the work of the nineteenth-century antiquaries such as Woodruff (1874; 1877), there was very little excavation of barrows for the next hundred years. The information from modern excavations has grown steadily, but the true complexity of these monuments still remains to be explored. It was certainly not a case of the simple introduction of a new burial rite and a new type of monument for single burial. Barrows reused places of significance in the late Neolithic; some of the earliest monuments may have been for multiple burials; barrow burials and flat graves existed side by side; barrows show episodes of building and deposition unconnected with burial. The barrows of Kent have certainly suffered more damage than those in other parts of Britain, but many of them have shown evidence of long and complex histories. We have only just begun to explore the detailed story of Kent's distinctive tradition in the early Bronze Age.

A world of exotic goods

Many of the burials are not accompanied by grave goods, so cannot be easily dated except by radiocarbon; as yet, however, only a small number of barrows or burials have been dated in this way. Where grave goods are included, the commonest item is pottery, but there are a number of other types of object included in the barrows, frequently of exotic origin and presumably of considerable value.

The earliest graves with grave goods are those with beaker pottery. Clarke (1970) listed over thirty beakers for the county; many of these are complete and may well be from burials, but documentation is poor. More recently a number of beaker burials have been excavated (ill. 4.16). These mainly conform to the normal mode of burial, crouched inhumation with head to the north. A distinct regional pattern in Kent seems to be a tradition of beaker flat graves without any trace of a mound, as at Monkton. There is a variety of other grave goods associated with the beakers. The burial at Manston with a flint knife and a perforated jet button has been mentioned above. Another Thanet burial, at Chalk Hill, Ramsgate, produced a beaker and a jet pendant

(Shand 2001). At Monkton grave goods included copper alloy bracelets and jet beads. A stone wristguard is known from a beaker burial at St Peter's (Grinsell 1992, Broadstairs and St Peter's 6), and an assemblage from Sittingbourne (Payne 1883a), comprising a wristguard, a copper alloy knife and a bone pendant, would be a classic beaker group, but it lacks a beaker. The beakers themselves are mostly of types common in eastern England, rather than those found in Wessex. The rapid growth of excavation from the 1980s has led to a considerable increase in beaker finds and a detailed appraisal of them is needed; typological study combined with the few radiocarbon dates so far available suggest that most of the beakers are early types, with a surprising scarcity of later forms.

Biconical urns are found occasionally. At Wouldham (Cruse and Harrison 1983) a biconical urn was inverted over a primary cremation in a central grave pit. They are also known from older excavations: at Capel-le-Ferne another was similarly inverted, but high up in the barrow mound, over a secondary cremation (Ashbee and Dunning 1960). At Ringwould a biconical urn was also inverted over a secondary cremation with a bead of faience and a small perforated 'incense cup' (Woodruff 1874). Similar slotted or perforated cups, well known from contexts in Wessex, have also been found at Tilmanstone and Luddington Wood, and also at Lord of the Manor Site 4, where there was the tip of a copper alloy awl inside (Perkins and Macpherson-Grant 1981); sherds of such vessels are also known from Castle Hill, Folkestone, and Monkton. They have a very distinctive form, and may well have been for the burning of aromatic or psychedelic substances.

Collared urns are also frequently present in these graves. Longworth (1984, 216-217) lists ten certain or probable grave finds, mostly from older excavations such as those at Westbere (Brent C 1866) and Ringwould (Woodruff 1874; 1877). More recently, a collared urn was discovered inverted over the cremation of an adult male, in the pit of what may have been a flat grave at

4.16 Double beaker burial excavated at Northumberland Bottom, near Gravesend: both burials were flexed inhumations, accompanied by a beaker vessel; the lower, with head to the north was probably female, the upper, with head to the south was probably male.

Otford (Pyke and Ward 1975). The top part of another inverted urn, the base removed by ploughing, was recorded in Site 3 of the Lord of the Manor group, Ramsgate (Perkins and Macpherson-Grant 1981). Collared urns were interred in a rather standardised manner, inverted over a cremation, rarely with any other grave goods; a flint flake was found at Westbere, and one of the burials in the Whitfield-Eastry by-pass barrow (Parfitt, Allen and Rady 1997) contained bone 'tweezers', a type otherwise limited almost entirely to Wessex graves (Proudfoot 1963).

Not all the objects placed in the barrows necessarily accompanied a burial. At Monkton, a Trevisker urn from Cornwall had been placed in the ditch of one of the barrows (Gibson *et al.* 1997). Perhaps the most spectacular object from the whole of prehistoric Kent is the small gold cup from Ringlemere, near Sandwich (Varndell and Needham 2002), found with a metal detector in 2001, and dating to around 1800-1600 BC (ill. 4.17). It is one of a very small group of metal

4.17 The Ringlemere gold cup.

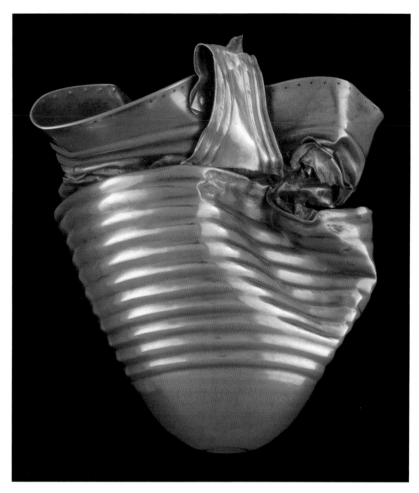

Apart from the Sittingbourne dagger grave, the bracelets from Monkton and the fragment of an awl from Lord of the Manor, there is one other important find. Two flat graves were recorded at Aylesford in the 1890s; one may originally have had a bronze object, but the other contained a flat axe and two triangular daggers (James 1899; Ashbee 1997). There are other dagger blades from the county (Gerloff 1975), but the circumstances of their deposition are unknown. They may have been from graves, or they may have been from other deposits; the discovery of an early Bronze Age copper alloy knife from the Medway (Kelly 1987) suggests that the deposition of metalwork in rivers and other wet places had already begun by then. There is only one known hoard of bronze of this date, from Buckland, Dover, containing three flanged axes and a tanged spearhead (Megaw and Hardy 1938).

cups from early Bronze Age Europe, though other examples are known made from shale and amber; its closest parallel is with a gold cup from a cist at Rillaton, in Cornwall. The Ringlemere example, however, does not seem to have been deposited with a burial. As described above, the original structure at the find-spot was possibly a henge, modified at some later date with the addition of a central mound. Though the site had certainly been damaged and the cup misshapen by ploughing, in subsequent excavation there was no trace of a burial and no other objects of possibly similar date, except for two pieces of amber (Parfitt and Needham 2004). It seems as though the cup and the amber had been placed in a barrow without a burial.

Metal is comparatively rare in these graves.

This was a world in which many exotic or unusual materials were in use, and many of them found their way into graves or barrows, even if only in broken or fragmentary form. Thus as well as pottery, barrows include items of gold, amber, copper alloy, jet, faience, stone and bone. The early Bronze Age from about 2050 to 1700 BC (Period 3 in Needham's (1996) chronological system) is characterised by graves containing a wide variety of personal ornaments in many different materials. The biggest concentration of such graves is in Wessex, termed the Wessex

Culture by Piggott (1938), but it is now clear that such burials are not exclusive to that region. There are several other well-known clusters of such graves, especially in Yorkshire, the Peak District and parts of Scotland (Clarke *et al.* 1985). The concentration of the items of gold, amber, jet, faience and early copper alloy objects in east Kent is unique in south-eastern England (Champion 2004). The parallels with the Wessex graves are also matched in the more mundane items such as the perforated incense cups from several sites and the bone 'tweezers' from the Whitfield-Eastry barrow. All this evidence suggests the existence of another centre of power and wealth in the region in the early Bronze Age, and that at least some people in Kent were well aware of the latest fashions in personal ornament and funerary ritual and able to acquire the necessary materials.

Occasionally more unusual and less obviously valuable items are found in the graves, though they presumably all had some special significance. At North Foreland, Thanet (Perkins 1999), the burial of a child inserted into the ditch of a barrow was covered with a large fragment of whale bone. A grave at St Margaret's with a crouched inhumation also included marine shells and a nodule of ironstone (Woodruff 1874). Ironstone was also found in a grave under a barrow at Cherry Garden Hill, Folkestone (Stebbing and Cave 1943). Woodward (2000) has emphasised the importance of the exotic nature and unusual material represented by the very diverse grave goods deposited in the barrows, and has also stressed the range of colours they would originally have presented to the eye.

Kent and the outside world

It is clear that Kent was not isolated at this time. Quite the opposite: the archaeological record shows a wide range of contacts, and, as one would expect from its nodal position, these extend westwards along the south coast and northwards into eastern England, as well as across the Channel. It seems very reasonable to suppose that many of these contacts were made by sea. Those across the Channel inevitably had to be, and travel within Kent itself also required it: Thanet was still an island, and the river estuaries such as the Stour were much wider then. Communication along the coast, across the estuaries or inland up the rivers would have been easiest, especially with loads to carry. One striking piece of evidence is the sewn-plank boat, discovered at Dover in 1992, of a type well documented in the British Bronze Age (Clark 2004b) (box, pages 96-7). Harbours may not have been needed, with boats beached on suitable shores (Parfitt 2004c).

The external links can be plotted to some extent by the nature of the materials and the parallels for the ideas and practices witnessed in Kent. The Trevisker urn from Monkton, which must have originated in Cornwall, and a piece of Dorset shale found in the Dover boat demonstrate the links along the south coast. Connections to the east of England are shown by the presence of jet, from Whitby. South-eastern England has no native source of copper or tin, so all the metalwork found there must be made from imported materials. The copper may have come from western England, Wales or Ireland, or possibly from sources on the Continent. Nor are there sources of gold or amber in south-eastern England. The gold for the Ringlemere cup, wherever it was manufactured, must have come from a remote location, while the amber came originally from the Baltic.

Kent's external links were not limited to valuable raw materials or exotic items. Similarities in local practice demonstrate networks of social links through which passed information and knowledge. Though our understanding of the geographical and chronological variability of beakers is not yet well developed, it is clear that the Kentish beakers are akin to those found further north in eastern England rather than those of Wessex. On the other hand, the similarities in the rich graves of Kent to those of Wessex and other parts of Britain show Kent as one node in a much more far-flung pattern of shared ideas and

4.18 Reconstruction of the Dover Bronze Age boat.

4.19 The Bronze Age boat during excavation.

The Dover Bronze Age boat

In September 1992 contractors working on the A20 main road through Dover revealed timbers at a depth of about 6 m below ground level, quickly identified as the mid-section of a prehistoric boat. In all, a section about 9 m long from a boat that was originally almost 12 m in length was recorded and retrieved. After conservation, the boat is now on display in Dover Museum (Clark 2004b).

The boat, dating to about 1600 BC, is an example of a type of vessel now well known from the British Bronze Age (Wright 1990; van der Noort *et al*. 1999). It was made from massive planks shaped from three-hundred-year old oaks. The side planks were sewn on to the bottom planks with yew withies, and the ends were formed of large planks of oak, to produce a shape like a modern punt. The planks were carefully trimmed, the seams were caulked with moss and thin strips of oak, and the stitching sealed with beeswax and animal fat.

Eventually, when the boat had been used and repaired, but was by no means worn out, it was taken to its final resting place, dragged upstream through shallows into a backwater of the River Dour. It was partly dismantled, a piece of Dorset shale was placed inside it, and domestic debris including flint flakes, pottery and animal bones deposited on either side of it. In time the boat settled into the accumulating silts of the Dour, preserving it for the next three and a half thousand years.

The boat is the largest and most complex object known from prehistoric Kent and gives a very clear idea of the level of woodworking skill that existed in the Bronze Age. Sea transport must have been very important for the inhabitants of prehistoric Kent, but apart from the Mesolithic paddle from Swanscombe (cf page 73), the Dover boat and occasional finds of prehistoric logboats (McGrail 1978), such as those at Erith, Maidstone and Murston, little trace of this activity has yet been found.

practices. At an even wider scale, Kent plays a pivotal geographical role in many of the processes that characterised western Europe in the late Neolithic and early Bronze Age. Though the detailed development of the bronze industry is distinctively British, it shares many traits with the Continent, which must be the result of constant interaction. Other cultural practices similarly show long-term contact across the Channel: the raising of burial mounds, especially with timber structures, is best paralleled in the Netherlands, while the use of beakers and their associated artefacts links England into a network of shared ideas found all over western and central Europe. Though we may not know the precise social mechanism or geographical routes through which these ideas were transmitted, we can be sure that Kent played a key role in their dissemination.

Ordering the landscape

The centuries in the middle of the second millennium BC witnessed a profound change in many features of human society in southern England, and indeed in its very nature; these changes were also seen in much of the British Isles and the neighbouring area of north-western Europe. The changes did not happen all at once, nor would they have seemed particularly sudden to people alive at that time. Nevertheless, with the advantage of hindsight offered by archaeology, it can be seen that within a comparatively short period of a few centuries, human society underwent what was probably the most important transformation since the repopulation of Britain after the last Ice Age.

Monuments of the kind that had dominated the archaeological record of the fourth and third millennia were no longer built or rebuilt, and there is little evidence that they were used or respected at all. The tradition of constructing round barrows and depositing in them a series of individual burials came to an end. Instead, the remains of domestic settlement sites and land divisions dominate the archaeological evidence. The scale of woodland clearance was greatly

4.20 Prehistoric pottery from Kent: from the top, middle Bronze Age Deverel-Rimbury ware, late Bronze Age plainware, late Bronze Age decorated ware (all from Kemsley), and early Iron Age pottery (from Dumpton Gap).

expanded, and the land was divided and enclosed. Though arable crops had been grown and domesticated animals had been reared for over two thousand years, it was only now that agriculture became the dominant means of livelihood, and intensification transformed the face of the landscape and the very nature of existence. Settlement evidence becomes increasingly common, suggesting a new emphasis on permanent sedentism and an abandonment of mobility. The new architecture and organisation of sites provided a new setting for the routines of everyday life. Agriculture offered the possibility of a new range of crafts to exploit its by-products, such as the spinning and weaving of woollen textiles.

Although the surviving evidence for this new phase of the past seems rather domestic and utilitarian in contrast to the prevailing ritual nature of the previous millennia, it would be wrong to think that this was a secular age and that the evidence of a farming economy, clearly ancestral to that of the recent past, is easy to understand in modern terms. Detailed study of the material from many of the settlement sites of this period suggests that it was not the casual discard of rubbish, but the careful choice of selected artefacts for deposition in what were seen as important locations. In this way the practice of structured deposition, first seen in the early Neolithic causewayed enclosures, was continued in very different circumstances. The best-known form of this practice of deliberate deposition was the burying of hoards of bronze, and it is particularly difficult to explain the discarding of such wealth in terms of a modern sense of values.

The chronology of the period from 1500 to 300 BC, including the middle and late Bronze Ages and the early Iron Age, is based on metalwork and pottery. The sequence of middle and late Bronze Age metalwork has been established by typological studies and radiocarbon dating (Needham et al. 1998), and the chronology of Iron Age brooches is also well known

Pottery of the middle and late Bronze Age and the early Iron Age

The pottery sequence in Kent follows that generally established for southern and south-eastern England (Barrett 1980; Needham 1996): Deverel-Rimbury pottery in the middle Bronze Age (1500-1150 BC), followed by plain and then decorated phases of post-Deverel-Rimbury pottery, and finally early Iron Age pottery.

Deverel-Rimbury pottery is characterised by thick-walled vessels in heavily flint-gritted fabrics, mainly large bucket urns with a few finer jars. It is well documented in funerary contexts from the county (MacPherson-Grant 1980; Champion 1982), but there are as yet few published domestic assemblages such as that at Coldharbour Road, Gravesend (Mudd 1994).

The post-Deverel-Rimbury plain ware phase (c.1150-800 BC) is marked by finer fabrics and thinner-walled vessels, still mostly flint-gritted, in a wider range of forms, including ovoid jars, hemispherical bowls and sharply angled bowls. This phase is characterised by assemblages such as the later material from Coldharbour Road (Mudd 1994), Hoo St Werburgh (Moore 2002) and some of the pottery from the ring-ditch enclosure at Mill Hill, Deal (Stebbing 1934; Champion 1980, 233-237 and fig. 6), as well as some of the sites located in the A2 improvement scheme near Bridge and Barham, south-east of Canterbury (MacPherson-Grant 1980, especially Sites 1, 5 and 8, Pit 20).

In the post-Deverel-Rimbury decorated phase (c. 800-500 BC) the pottery is characterised by the increased use of ornamentation, especially finger-nail and finger-tip impressions on the rim and shoulder of vessels. The best example in Kent is the assemblage from Monkton Court Farm, Thanet (Perkins et al. 1994).

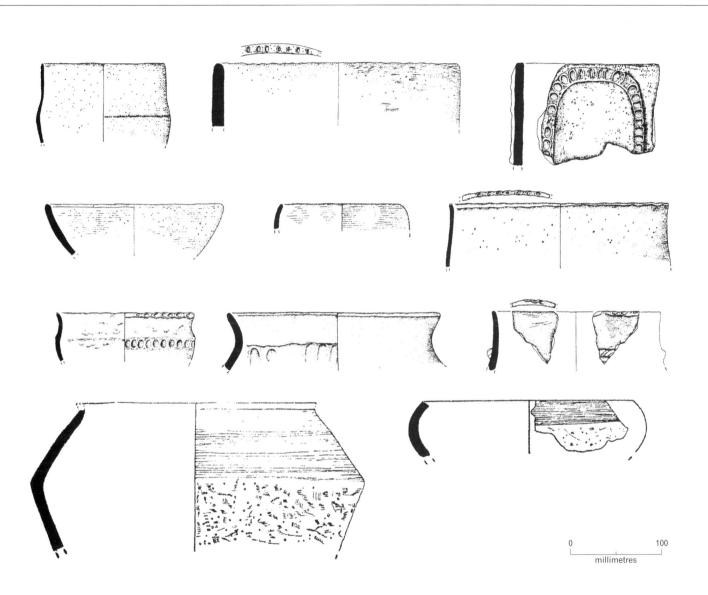

Pottery of the early Iron Age (*c.* 500-300 BC) is best known in east Kent, where a distinctive tradition has been recognised, characterised by pots with deliberately roughened ('rusticated') surfaces and others with geometric patterns of decoration, sometimes executed in polychrome painting. This 'East Kent rusticated tradition' (Macpherson-Grant 1989; 1991) is closely paralleled by assemblages in northern France and Belgium, e.g. Leman-Delerive (1984), van Doorselaer *et al.* (1987), Hurtrelle *et al.* (1990), especially the early La Tène pottery excavated during Channel Tunnel operations on the other side of the Channel (Blancquaert and Bostyn 1998).

(Haselgrove 1997), but bronze finds are rare on settlement sites or in burials of this period. The chronology of settlement sites of this period in Kent is therefore based largely on pottery, though there are few well-established associations of pottery and metalwork, few stratified sequences and a limited number of radiocarbon dates to anchor a somewhat speculative typological sequence of ceramics (box, pages 98-9).

In this period the landscape of Kent took on its modern appearance. The coastal marshes were formed as the river estuaries silted up. The woodlands were cleared everywhere except in the Weald. The land was divided into fields and permanent settlements were built. The pattern of settlement distribution and land use that was to dominate Kent for many centuries was adopted: the majority of the population lived along the northern dip slope of the Downs and the Greensand vale, while the high downland was used for wood pasture. Population density increased and so did the complexity of the agricultural economy.

Dividing the landscape

The evidence for human modification of the environment becomes much more plentiful after the middle of the second millennium. Many excavations produce dug features such as pits and ditches, but unless the investigation is on a sufficiently large scale, it is often difficult to interpret this evidence. Nevertheless, many of these features do seem to belong to extensive systems of land division or to smaller enclosures around settlement areas, suggesting a much more intensive mode of farming and a more permanent and sedentary mode of settlement.

There is still a comparative dearth of environmental evidence for the history of human exploitation of the landscape of Kent (Scaife 1987), but what there is suggests a coherent picture of intensified activity from about the middle of the second millennium BC. At Wingham the woodland seems to have been substantially cleared by the beginning of the second

millennium, but there was arable activity in the late Bronze Age and early Iron Age; at Frogholt considerably increased clearance is shown from about the beginning of the late Bronze Age (Godwin 1962). Weatherlees Hill, now on the south coast of Thanet but probably then an island in the Wantsum, shows a slightly different picture of the later prehistoric environment before the alluviation of the Wantsum Channel. In the middle and late Bronze Age there was still much oak and hazel woodland, though with some clearance and possible cereal agriculture. More extensive clearance and cereal cultivation is dated to the late Iron Age and early Roman period (Hearne *et al.* 1995).

The fate of earlier prehistoric monuments of Kent, especially the round barrows, has already been discussed in the previous section. Many of them were destroyed in later periods of prehistory, and this not only supports the picture of intensified arable farming but also tells us something about attitudes to earlier monuments.

In parts of Kent, the intensification of human exploitation is shown by the proliferation of organised systems of land division, typically surviving as lengths of ditch, sometimes in the form of rectilinear fields, elsewhere more irregular enclosures. There is no evidence to suggest that these fields were all part of a larger system, nor is there yet in Kent anything to match the very complex landscape of field systems and enclosures dating to the late Bronze Age that has been explored at Hornchurch on the other side of the Thames from Gravesend (Guttman and Last 2000). There is, nevertheless, more than enough evidence to show that parts of Kent, including especially the north coast and the Gault and Greensand zone to the south of the scarp of the North Downs, were exploited in this way in the later Bronze Age.

It is clear that these field systems were not all established at once, and that during the life span of this episode of landscape history, which lasted perhaps seven or eight hundred years, there were significant changes in the focus and nature of these managed landscapes within the county. At Shrubsoles Hill in Sheppey (Coles *et al.* 2003), for instance, there were successive phases of land division within the later Bronze Age. These changes can only be glimpsed at the moment, and the chronology is obscured by the problems of ceramic dating discussed above.

Some of the Kent sites certainly began in the middle Bronze Age. At Coldharbour Road, Gravesend (Mudd 1994), the primary fills of a large ditch system were associated with Deverel-Rimbury pottery; the system had a long life, as shown by the presence of later pottery and later radiocarbon dates from higher levels in the ditch fills. Along the north coastal strip there are indications of other sites with similar Deverel-Rimbury ceramic associations: several sites in the Hoo peninsula, Kemsley Fields near Sittingbourne (Willson 2001), Shrubsoles Hill in the Isle of Sheppey (Coles *et al.* 2003) and, further east, Churchwood Drive, Chestfield (Allen 2002). Other sites in the same region have a less clearly defined chronology, but are certainly of middle or late Bronze Age date. The same chronology applies to sites in the Greensand belt, as sites near Ashford such as Westhawk Farm (Booth and Lawrence 2000) and Brisley Farm (Stevenson and Johnson 2004) show (ill. 4.21).

Field systems of this date are known in the Greensand zone between the Medway and the English Channel, and along the north coast from London as far east as the Herne Bay region. Despite much recent investigation, no definite example has been found in Thanet, and very few

possible examples of late Bronze Age or early Iron Age date on the chalklands east of Canterbury; parallel ditches observed at Wick Wood, Barham (Willson 1984), may be from such a field system, as also may some of the ditches explored in the widening of the A2 near Bridge (MacPherson-Grant 1980). Instead, a different pattern of

Westhawk Farm

0   50
metres

Brisley Farm

0   50
metres

4.21 Bronze Age field systems from Westhawk Farm and Brisley Farm, near Ashford: the sites are less than 1km apart and the near coincidence of orientation suggests the possibility of large-scale landscape organisation.

settlement is found in these regions, described below.

Field systems of this sort have now been recognised in several regions of southern England. Pryor (1998) has argued that they were designed for intensive sheep rearing, and the occasional evidence in Kent for droveways and wells would support the idea of animal husbandry. One of the most important aspects of the intensification of agriculture at this time was the increasing exploitation of animals for purposes other than food, and wool would have been an important product. This certainly fits well with the first regular appearance of artefacts connected with the spinning and weaving of woollen textiles at the end of the early Bronze Age: cylindrical loomweights of typical middle Bronze Age shape are known from Hayes (Philp 1973, Fig. 19, 151-2) and a growing number of other sites. The excavation of a series of timber-lined wells at Swalecliffe (Masefield *et al.* 2003; Masefield *et al.* 2004) produced important evidence for the environment and the economy. The wells were in successive use for 500 years from 1200 to 700 BC, showing a long-term stability in the patterns of land use in the late Bronze Age. They would have supplied water for animals being grazed on the coastal pasture, including the rearing of cattle, sheep and pigs; wheat and barley were cultivated in the vicinity.

Yates (1999; 2001) has shown that such fields existed throughout the Middle and Lower Thames valley and has suggested a pattern of localised clusters of such systems associated with large enclosures and concentrations of metalwork deposited in hoards and rivers. The distribution of metal finds in Kent is discussed in more detail below, but the precise relationship of fields, enclosures and metal remains to be explored in detail. There are serious problems with establishing a precise chronology, and there is as yet little evidence for the integration of settlement enclosures and fields. As will be discussed below, the main area of middle Bronze Age hoard deposition is one so far devoid of

fields. The quantity of evidence is growing steadily, and future work will shed much light on this critical period in the history of Kent.

It is a striking feature of the emerging pattern of prehistoric occupation in Kent that the areas where these field systems are found show very little sign of subsequent occupation during the Iron Age (Champion 2007). The Bronze Age finds from the ditches date the process of abandonment and silting up, so they may already have been disused within the Bronze Age, and the next observable phase of usage is often a further system of fields or enclosures with fills dated to the late Iron Age or early Roman periods. Not only is there no evidence of field systems or other patterns of land division, but there is little evidence of any sort of occupation. The same pattern has been noted north of the Thames: in the Southend peninsula, where traces of middle and late Bronze Age occupation very similar to those in Kent are abundant, sites of the early Iron Age and even more so of the middle Iron Age are very uncommon (Wymer and Brown 1995, 157). In the Greater London area, too, early Iron Age sites are rare in comparison to the plentiful sites of the middle and late Bronze Age (Wait and Cotton 2000, 105). On the other hand, the areas of east Kent where no Bronze Age fields are found are the areas where the densest pattern of occupation in the Iron Age is also located.

A further implication of this evidence is that there are, in the current state of knowledge, no systems of field divisions that can be securely dated to any phase of the Iron Age before the last. Aerial photography has shown many so-called 'Celtic' field systems, especially on the chalklands of east Kent, but none of these has been dated, and they could as well be of Roman origin as any earlier. Despite the excavation of a growing number of Iron Age sites, there have been few detailed studies of the agricultural economy, but there is little reason to think that it was significantly different from that seen elsewhere in southern England, with a mixed arable and pastoral regime adapted to the specific environment (Hambleton 1999). How that was actually practised is not at all clear.

Unless these results are a random product of the present state of research, or of current misunderstandings of the chronology, they suggest that there were very marked regional and temporal differences in long-term land-use history within the county and within the whole of the lower Thames estuary region (Champion 2007). We still know little about the history of the chalk Downs, but the investment of labour in the construction of fields in the late Bronze Age suggests a period of intensification very different from what followed in the Iron Age, when human impact on the landscape was apparently much less.

We still know very little about the details of how this landscape was being exploited or about the food supply in this period. At the middle Bronze Age site at Westwood Cross, Broadstairs (Allison 2005), there was plentiful evidence for the consumption of a range of shellfish, especially mussels, though fish and shellfish are remarkable for their almost total absence thereafter until the end of the Iron Age. Cereal remains from this site and from Princes Road, Dartford (Hutchings 2003), show that spelt wheat was already present in the second millennium. Spelt is generally thought to have replaced another wheat variety, emmer, by the Iron Age, but its presence this early is unusual. The transition from emmer to spelt, however, was not as complete as elsewhere, especially in Wessex; plant remains from a late Bronze Age site at the Guston roundabout near Dover (Allison 2005) and from an early Iron Age site at Whitfield show that emmer was cultivated throughout the first millennium BC.

Settling down

Sites of human occupation become very much more common from the middle Bronze Age onwards, reflecting a greater commitment to permanent residence arising from increased reliance on intensive agriculture and investment in major enterprises such as the construction of

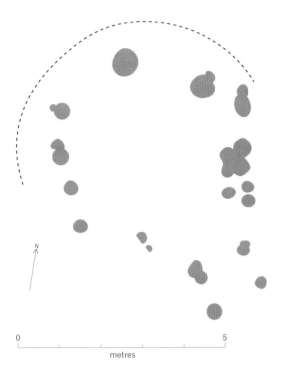

4.22 Middle Bronze Age roundhouse from East Valley Farm, near Dover

fields. Longer-term commitment to one location would in turn have encouraged developments in domestic architecture and other craft activities, all of which would have left more physical remains. Nevertheless, details of the internal arrangement of sites are still limited. Plough damage has been severe, and many of the sites have only been very partially excavated.

Middle Bronze Age settlement in southern England is often characterised by the presence of enclosures, round houses and other features such as fences and ponds (e.g. Brück 1999a). This picture, however, is based on evidence from further west, mainly from Wessex but also Sussex (Hamilton 2003, 70-71). Despite much recent excavation in Kent, very little evidence for this pattern is known, and what there is comes from a limited area in the east of the county. The only middle Bronze Age round house so far known is from East Valley Farm north of Dover (Parfitt and Corke 2003b) (ill. 4.22); it was nearly 6m in diameter, and built with an inner ring of posts and an outer wall of stakes, with a porch to the southeast. The easternmost part of Kent has also

4.23 Middle Bronze Age enclosure at South Dumpton Down, Thanet.

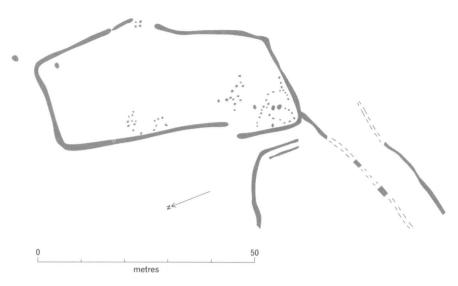

0 _____ 50
metres

produced evidence for settlement enclosures of this date. Two examples have been excavated in Thanet: at South Dumpton Down a roughly rectangular enclosure of *c.* 50m by 20m was totally excavated, with occupation in the interior demonstrated by pits and post-holes (Perkins 1995, 468-470) (ill. 4.23), while at Westwood Cross, Broadstairs (Gollop 2005), the enclosure was larger, measuring *c.* 50m by 40m, though no internal features survived. At Eastry part of an enclosure, including the entrance, was excavated; Deverel-Rimbury pottery was found in the ditch, and the presence of a collared urn may even suggest a slightly earlier date (Willson 1993). A length of enclosure ditch at Broadstairs (Perkins 1998b) may be part of a similar site. The concentration of enclosures in north-eastern Kent coincides with a striking cluster of middle Bronze Age hoards there (Perkins 1988). In an analysis of middle Bronze Age settlement patterns in southern England, Ellison (1981) predicted the existence of a major site of this period in Thanet; the concentration of metalwork deposits has grown since then, but no single site has been located, and Needham and Ambers (1994) have cast doubt on the reliability of such a prediction. Nevertheless, Thanet and East Kent do show a pattern of enclosure and deposition in the middle Bronze Age that is quite distinct from most of the rest of Kent.

Other evidence of middle Bronze Age settlement is more enigmatic. In some cases, as at Hayes Common (Philp 1973), there are pits and short sections of ditch, but no sign of domestic architecture; often, however, the only trace of occupation comprises isolated pits, as at Iwade

(Willson 2002) or Kent International Business Park, Thanet (Perkins 1998a). A pit from Ramsgate (Hawkes 1942) contained two imported bronze pins. Whether these pits are the remains of storage or refuse disposal activity, or are more akin to the pits of the early Neolithic as symbolic indicators of settlement, is uncertain. It is clear, however, that the classic model of middle Bronze Age settlement, derived from Wessex and Sussex, does not fit most of what is known in Kent.

Evidence for occupation or non-agricultural activities associated with the field systems is sparse. Pits and other small features are known at sites such as Shrubsoles Hill (Coles *et al.* 2003), Kemsley Fields (Willson 2001) and Churchwood Drive, Chestfield (Allen 2002), but possible traces of domestic architecture are rare. At Willow Farm, Broomfield (Helm 2003b), part of a post-built round house was found, and at Shelford Quarry, near Canterbury (Boden 2004), there were traces of a roundhouse, four-post structures and other possible rectangular buildings. The same lack of domestic architecture in the later Bronze Age, and in particular the disappearance of the classic middle Bronze Age roundhouse, have been noted in Sussex (Hamilton 2003, 73-75), but the implications are far from clear.

The ceramic chronology for the first millennium BC still needs to be improved, but it seems that

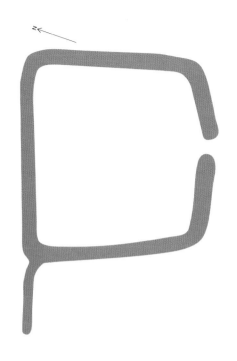

4.24 Comparison of late Bronze Age enclosures at Lofts Farm, Essex (left), and Highstead, Kent (right): Lofts Farm has been totally excavated, while Highstead is known from air photographs and minimal excavation.

towards the end of the late Bronze Age a much wider variety of settlement types was in use, including enclosed and unenclosed sites. One of the most striking is the circular enclosure typified by Essex examples such as Springfield Lyons or the two sites at Mucking, and often called 'ringforts'; they show great care in the division of internal space and the location of structures, and are dated to the early part of the first millennium BC, from about the ninth century (Needham 1992). The site at Mill Hill, Deal, is a good example, though little is known about its interior (Stebbing 1934; Champion 1980, 233-237). These 'ringforts' may be a very specific case of a wider class of late Bronze Age enclosures. Others are rectangular, such as Lofts Farm in Essex (Brown 1988), and a possibly similar site is known in Kent at Highstead (Champion 1980, 237; Bennett, Macpherson-Grant and Couldrey 2007) (ill. 4.24). Others again are sub-circular, such as two more enclosures at Highstead, or one at Hartsdown, Margate (Perkins 1996); another example was found in the Ramsgate Harbour Approach Road excavation, next to the Neolithic causewayed enclosure (Dyson *et al.* 2000) (ill. 4.25). Much bigger enclosures also existed,

such as the sub-rectangular example at Eddington Farm, Herne Bay (Shand 2002). Excavations at Kingsborough Farm, Sheppey (Wessex Archaeology 2002), have shown a series of sub-circular late Bronze Age enclosures of varying size, used for both occupation and funerary purposes.

Unenclosed sites are also known, though their nature makes them more difficult to recognise and they may be under-represented in the record. Sites of this sort were excavated on the Thanet Way between Whitstable and Herne Bay (Allen *et al.* 1997); South Street consisted of pits, post-holes and a hearth, while Radfall Corner had remains of a trackway and a possible structure. The large occupation area at Monkton Court Farm (Perkins *et al.* 1994) also belongs to the end of this phase. In both enclosed and unenclosed settlements, evidence of buildings is again very scarce.

The proliferation of enclosed settlement towards the end of the Bronze Age marks a significant change in the organisation of human occupation of the landscape. Such enclosures were used to demarcate space for various activities, including domestic, agricultural and funerary ones, but some of the more elaborate sites, such

4.25 Comparison of late Bronze Age oval enclosures with interrupted ditches at Highstead (top, showing simplified interpretation of one phase) and Ramsgate (bottom).

0   50

metres

large and very complex occupation area at Dumpton has also produced sections of other curvilinear enclosures, and possibly also of unenclosed settlement. These sites are characterised by pits and post-holes, though no complete structures have been revealed. Large areas of hilltop at North Foreland (Diack *et al.* 2000; Diack 2003) and possibly Fort Hill, Margate (Perkins 1997, 227), seem to have been enclosed by ditches, though the ditches are slight and not of the scale typical of hillforts elsewhere. At North Foreland, an extensive area of Iron Age settlement has been excavated, mostly belonging to the earlier part of the period, but with some later features; there was a fairly clear zoning of different structures, with clusters of post-holes separated from pits and a group of four-post structures enclosed by a small rectangular ditch.

At other locations in Thanet and elsewhere in the east of the county, reports of Iron Age occupation are mostly limited to exposures of pits or small sections of other features, possibly ditches. There are no reliable enclosure plans, and the probability is that many of the settlement sites of this period were unenclosed. This is confirmed by those sites where larger-scale excavation has occurred. At White Horse Stone (Booth, Champion *et al.* 2007) (ill. 4.26), pits and post-holes were spread over a large area, with some measure of clustering to indicate the ordered use of space within the site. There were distinct clusters of pits and of four-post structures, and elsewhere there were groups of post-holes which suggested the presence of roundhouses, though no certain plans could be identified. Two sites in north Kent have produced evidence of a different kind. At Highstead (Bennett, Macpherson-Grant and Couldrey 2007), following the late Bronze Age enclosures, the unenclosed Iron Age occupation was marked by a row of roundhouses, and some post-built features including four-post structures and an unusual rectangular building (ill. 4.27). The roundhouses were indicated by circular or near-circular drainage gulleys surrounding them; little or nothing of the structure of the

as the circular ringfort at Mill Hill must have made a considerable statement about the status of the occupants.

The same diversity of site type continues into the Iron Age, though, despite much work, the nature of settlements in this period still remains elusive. In Thanet rectangular enclosures of the Iron Age have been reported from South Dumpton Down (Perkins 1995, 468-470), Hartsdown (Perkins 1996) and elsewhere. The

Metalworking area

Lynchet

Chalk quarry pits

Cremation

Bridleway (possible Roman road)

Late Bronze Age/early Iron Age

Roman

Medieval - post-medieval

Burials

0   50

metres

house itself remained. Similar evidence of a cluster of roundhouses has also been found at a site a short distance to the west of Highstead, at Underdown Lane, Eddington (Jarman 2005). These are the only examples so far known in Kent of the unenclosed roundhouse cluster and the roundhouse drainage gulley, types of settlement and structure characteristic of the early to middle Iron Age in many other parts of southern and eastern England.

In the western part of the county, west of the Medway, almost nothing is known of early Iron Age settlement, although investigations for the Channel Tunnel Rail Link at Tollgate and Northumberland Bottom produced the first definite evidence of occupation of this date (Booth, Champion *et al.* forthcoming). It is

possible that this area was comparatively lightly occupied then, but it is also possible that it was more densely populated, yet in a way that is not easily visible archaeologically.

4.27 Early Iron Age roundhouses at Highstead.

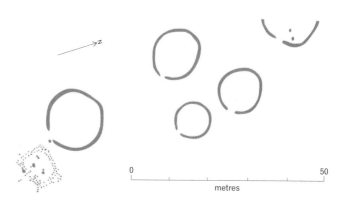

0   50

metres

New technologies

The new commitment to increased permanence of settlement and intensified agriculture both permitted and encouraged the development of new technologies. Older crafts continued to be practised. Some settlement sites produce simple stone tools and it seems likely that they were contemporary products, not residual. Other crafts have left little or no trace. Woodworking must have been important, but few wooden products survive; the Dover boat (box, pages 96-7) is a rare example. Bone was also exploited for tools such as Iron Age weaving combs (Hurd 1909, Fig. 2; Parfitt 2000), though Kent has so far produced fewer such objects than other areas of southern England. Pottery had been made since the Neolithic, but from the later Bronze Age onwards pots were more plentiful and were produced with a wider range of forms and decoration and for a wider range of functions, especially the preparation and serving of food, suggesting a new social importance for eating and drinking.

Metal objects had been present in Kent since the beaker period, but there is no indication that any of these early items were actually made there. It is not until the late Bronze Age that there is evidence of manufacture rather than use. As discussed below, much of the bronze metalwork has been found in contexts that suggest some form of ritual deposition, but many of the hoards were assembled for reasons to do with bronze production. They typically contain many items that have been broken up into small pieces as though for recycling, as well as ingots of new copper metal; the hoard from the Isle of Harty (Evans 1881, 442) also contains moulds made of bronze for casting socketed axes. A middle Bronze Age palstave from near Maidstone (Barber 2003, 120 and Figs 35-6), made of lead and useless as a tool, would have served as a pattern for making a mould. Actual clay mould fragments are also known from ditch fills at two late Bronze Age sites: for a ring at Mill Hill, Deal (Champion 1980, 237 and Fig. 6) and for the multiple casting of pins and possibly other objects at Highstead (Bennett, Macpherson-Grant and

Couldrey 2007). Production, circulation and deposition of bronze largely ceased around 750 BC, though it did not disappear from use completely; it was used for brooches and other small items, though they are very rare until the late Iron Age.

Iron began to be used early in the first millennium BC, but it too is far from common before the very late Iron Age. That may be due partly to the fact that prehistoric iron is much harder to recognise than bronze, but, even allowing for that, finds are rare. Furthermore, iron was not used in the same way as bronze, and in particular was not, at least in the early Iron Age, deposited in hoards. Iron may have replaced some of the functions of bronze, but it does not appear to have had the same significance.

Although the Wealden iron deposits were exploited before the Roman period, there is nothing to suggest that this began much before the late Iron Age. Other sources may well have been used, though they were of lower quality and more localised. Pits on the chalk Downs above Wye appear to have been dug to extract marcasite, a form of iron ore, and these contained Iron Age pottery. Perhaps more important is the evidence for ironworking found at a late Bronze Age site at South Street, south of Herne Bay (Allen *et al.* 1997), which is among the earliest in the country. One of the most surprising finds from the early Iron Age site excavated at White Horse Stone was a deposit of iron objects accompanying a cremation burial (Booth, Champion *et al.* forthcoming) (ill. 4.28). It included an iron knife, a curved blade, four awls and a whetstone. The rarity of such a find, and the quality of the craft skills displayed, suggest that the very limited number of early finds may have been the result of a lack of deposition rather than of a restricted quantity or a low technical level of production. These finds together hint at a longer and more competent history of iron production in Kent, even before the use of the Wealden ore sources.

Two other important industries were developed during the middle and late Bronze Age, allied to agriculture. One was the production of salt,

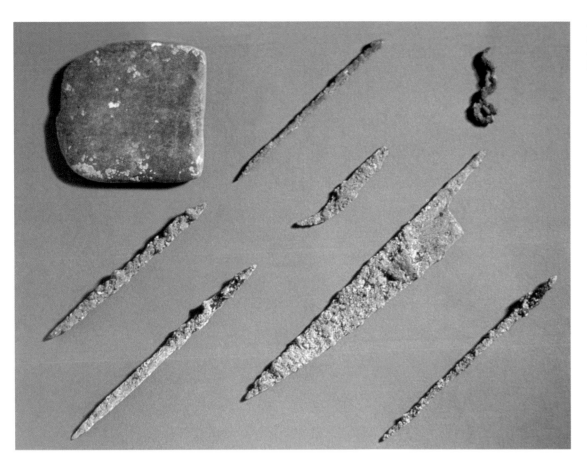

4.28 Iron tools and whetstone deposited with an early Iron Age cremation burial at White Horse Stone.

especially along the Thames coast, for preserving meat (box, page 110). The other was textile production. The intensive rearing of sheep from the middle of the second millennium stimulated the production of wool. Though actual textiles rarely survive, the equipment for spinning and weaving is commonly found on settlement sites: ceramic spindle whorls and loomweights, at first cylindrical, then conical and finally triangular in the early Iron Age. As textiles replaced skins and furs for clothing, new styles of dress, combined with patterns and dyes, offered many new opportunities for adornment and the display of personal identity.

Changing rites

Over much of Britain the formal burial rites of the early Bronze Age began to disappear around the middle of the second millennium. In southern and south-eastern England, however, they were continued in one final phase lasting *c.* 1500 to 1100 BC, characterised by cremations, often in pots of the Deverel-Rimbury tradition. These were sometimes secondary deposits in earlier barrows, though in other cases new barrows were built, or the cremations were placed in flat cemeteries. In contrast to earlier times, barrows of this period were typically small, and the burials they contained were seldom accompanied by anything other than the pot in which they were placed. Despite the continuity of barrow building, the rites associated with the disposal of the dead were clearly taking on a different meaning.

Though the evidence is not as good as in many other areas of southern England, Kent clearly shared this tradition. The best recorded example of Deverel-Rimbury burials is Barrow 2, one of a badly damaged pair excavated on the A2 at Bridge

4.29 Map showing areas of prehistoric salt production and distribution.

■ Zone where salt dried and transported in vase-shaped containers
■ Zone where salt made in troughs

Salt production

Many regions of Europe saw a growth in salt production in the later Bronze Age. On the Atlantic and North Sea coasts of Britain and Europe the method used was evaporation from sea-water. The evidence for this industry (Morris 1994) is largely made up of distinctive types of pottery called *briquetage*. The salt was extracted by heating the sea-water in pans over a fire, and some *briquetage* is the remains of this process. It often shows evidence of exposure to fire; many of the pieces have a distinctive dark red or even purple colour and a white surface deposit. There are two main forms, the pans or troughs used to hold the water, and the pedestals that supported them. Other *briquetage* comprises the remains of crude pottery containers used to transport the salt.

The earliest evidence for the salt industry in Kent is from the late Bronze Age. Open rectangular troughs are known from Minnis Bay (Worsfold 1943, fig. 8, no. 10), and pedestals from sites such

as Hoo St Werburgh (Moore 2002, fig. 4), while similar troughs are known from Iron Age contexts at Highstead (Bennett *et al.* 2007). The Kent industry was similar to those known in Essex (Fawn *et al.* 1990) and Lincolnshire (Lane and Morris 2001). Later *briquetage* from Iron Age sites such as White Horse Stone (Booth, Champion *et al.* forthcoming) was in the form of pottery containers, from unknown production sites in north Kent.

The human nutritional need for salt is mostly met by normal food intake. Specialised production of salt is usually related to other needs; salt was important for the tanning of leather, but its major use was for the preservation of foodstuffs. There is little evidence for an interest in fish until the very end of the Iron Age, and salt was probably used for preserving meat. Drying or smoking may have been practised, but salting was another alternative, especially suitable for pork. Such meat may have been used for storage for later consumption, but it may also have been for trade.

(Site 9) (MacPherson-Grant 1980). It was 14m in diameter and contained ten burials in the interior and a further six outside to the north. Some were contained within pots inverted over the cremated remains, but in other cases the ashes were simply deposited in a pit. The accompanying pottery comprised heavily flint-gritted bucket urns typical of the Deverel-Rimbury tradition, and would normally be dated *c.* 1500-1150 BC. It is quite possible, however, that the barrows, like those of the earlier period, were in use for a considerable period of time. Radiocarbon dates from Barrow 2 suggest that the practice of unurned cremation extended the use of the barrow beyond the date of the pottery. Barrow 2 also shows that the rites practised there were not limited to human remains. The ditch contained evidence for other types of deposition, including a small tub-shaped pot in a concentration of flints at the top of the primary silts and a deposit of burnt flint and ash in the upper fill. Other Deverel-Rimbury cremations are known throughout the county, especially in the east, from Kingsdown Cliffs, Ringwould, and Sholden Bank, Deal (Stebbing 1936; 1937), Tankerton (Worsfold 1927, 230), Hartsdown Site 13, Margate (Perkins 1996), as well as in the Monkton barrow cemetery. A more elaborate burial was found at Godmersham, where a crouched inhumation had been partly cut away by a small cist of chalk blocks containing an inverted urn, apparently superimposed on an earlier one (Bradshaw 1966).

One anomalous burial is reported from near Ramsgate; a group of bronze armlets and a ribbed bracelet was apparently found with an inhumation (Rowlands 1971, 184). If it is a genuine grave group, both the rite and the contents make it stand out; the bronzes have clear continental parallels, especially with northern France. Even more enigmatic is the report of a flat grave near Walmer (Parfitt 1994) which contained two pins, possibly also of this date. These burials surely indicate cross-Channel connections, if not actual people from the Continent.

By *c.* 1000 BC, however, this formal burial tradition disappears, and for much of Kent there is no regularly recognisable burial practice for about a thousand years. This does not mean that the dead were treated with disrespect, and it is helpful to distinguish once again, as with the long barrows of the early Neolithic, between rites associated with the treatment of the dead and those associated with the final consigning of the remains to the ground. There is some evidence for the latter, from which it is possible to make some inferences about the former, but the treatment accorded to the majority of the population is unknown, beyond the fact that it has left no regular trace in the archaeological record.

Unurned cremations are known from several late Bronze Age sites, including Shrubsoles Hill (Coles *et al.* 2003) and Kingsborough Farm (Wessex Archaeology 2002), both in Sheppey, and Shelford Quarry, Broad Oak, just north of Canterbury (Boden 2004). Elsewhere, human remains are known from settlement sites: at Minnis Bay, parts of a human jaw and a femur were incorporated in pit fills (Worsfold 1943, 39). Whether the initial rites accorded to the dead were excarnation or cremation, human remains were used in a variety of ways: as Brück (1995) has argued, their deposition is akin to the deposition of other significant categories of goods such as metal, and has less to do with the disposal of the dead and more to do with the symbolising of rights to important resources.

None of the occupation sites of the early Iron Age has yet been fully analysed, but sites in Kent seem to show the same sort of evidence as those elsewhere in the south, where fragments of human bone occur relatively frequently and whole skeletons are occasionally found in pits. Such pit burials are known from Dumpton Gap, where one body had a dog under the head as a pillow, at South Dumpton Down and at White Horse Stone. That site also produced a cremation burial of the early Iron Age, accompanied by a large group of iron objects and a collection of charred grain.

A tradition of formal inhumation existed in east Kent and Thanet, which can be well

4.30 Part of the late Bronze Age hoard of bronze objects found at Crundale.

4.31 Middle Bronze Age gold torcs from the River Medway at Aylesford (all in Maidstone Museum): top, bar torc of round section with grooves to simulate twisting; middle, complete twisted torc with square section; bottom, two parts of twisted torc, broken in antiquity

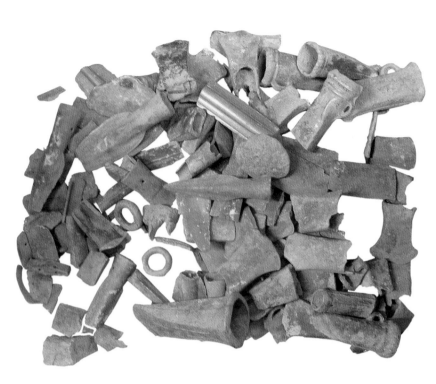

documented in the late Iron Age and will be discussed more fully below; radiocarbon dates (Parfitt 1998) suggest it may have started in the middle of the first millennium BC. Elsewhere in Kent, however, there is no other evidence for a formal rite of human burial.

Consuming wealth

Perhaps the most conspicuous legacy of the middle and late Bronze Age is the large collection of metalwork, mostly bronze but also some gold, much of it deposited in hoards, and only rarely found on settlement sites. It was a period with good access to these exotic metals, and they played an important role in social and economic activity. Bronze was the medium for weapons, tools, ornaments and vessels (Barber 2003), while gold, of which there was a particular concentration in Kent in the late Bronze Age, was used for ornaments of high symbolic value (Eogan 1994). Previous discussion of the bronzes has concentrated mostly on the hoards, dividing them into classes such as personal hoards, merchants' hoards, craftsmen's hoards or scrap hoards for recycling. While it is important to consider why a hoard collection was brought together, this does not explain why it was deposited in the ground. Older explanations such as concealment at a time of trouble have now given way to alternative theories which stress the predominantly ritual deposition of all metalwork, including finds from sites and rivers as well as hoards, and single finds as well as multiple assemblages. Though many of the finds from Kent have limited information about the circumstances of burial or recovery, the evidence that does exist tends to support this interpretation. There has been a recent explosion of new finds in Kent, mostly by metal

detectorists; older maps (such as Champion 1982, Figs 13-14) are out of date, but though these new finds have greatly increased the quantity of data, and altered the detailed distribution, they have not greatly affected the larger patterns.

There are marked concentrations of metal finds (Perkins *et al.* 1994, Fig. 24). In the middle Bronze Age most of the bronze metalwork occurs along the north coastal zone, with a major clustering in Thanet, and with minor groups in the Medway Valley and around Canterbury, Ashford and Dover. Gold bar torcs (Eogan 1994, 53-57 and Fig. 32) mirror this to some extent; finds from the River Medway, Chatham and Gillingham, and from near Canterbury and Dover, fit the pattern, but there are no gold objects from the north-east of the county. In the late Bronze Age, the distribution of bronze is more concentrated along the north coast, a pattern reinforced by recent finds (ill. 4.30). The clustering of hoards around the mouth of the Medway and especially on either side of the Wantsum channel has been confirmed. Gold finds again partly reflect this pattern (ill. 4.31); hoards of bracelets from Aylesford and Walderslade

(Eogan 1994, 84-91 and Fig. 38) reinforce the importance of the middle Medway Valley, but other finds from Bexley and Little Chart are from areas that otherwise are not well known for late Bronze Age objects. Again, it is curious that there are no gold objects in the area of the main concentration of bronze hoards; perhaps two different systems of storing and displaying wealth were in operation in Kent.

Recent research on bronze finds has tended to focus on deposition, whether of single finds or hoards (Barber 2003, 43-78). Many bronze items have been found in wet places, especially the Medway, where deposition began in the early Bronze Age (Kelly 1987). Engineering and dredging work associated with the naval base at Chatham has yielded many bronze finds, especially swords, from the river bed, while the middle stretch of the river around Aylesford is characterised by gold. At Thurnham, a middle Bronze Age rapier was deposited in a water-hole (Booth, Champion *et al*. forthcoming). A similar watery connection may have been significant in the placing of a bronze sword of *c*. 1000 BC at Shatterling, where it was found laid on a bed of pebbles through which water was welling up (Perkins 1995, 472). At a Bronze Age riverside site at Princes Road, Dartford (Hutchings 2003), deposits in wet contexts included domestic refuse such as Deverel-Rimbury pottery and also bronze pins of the final Bronze Age, suggesting a period of use spanning several centuries. These practices recall those elsewhere in England: not far westward at Nine Elms, Vauxhall (Cotton and Wood 1996, 14-16), where two spearheads were found adjacent to a substantial wooden jetty, and elsewhere at Shinewater Park, Eastbourne (Greatorex 2003), or most spectacularly at Flag Fen (Pryor 2001). The concentration of gold finds at Aylesford fits the same pattern; some were certainly from the river, including a group of four bracelets reportedly found there in a wooden box (Pretty 1863).

Finds from dry-land sites have received less attention, but recent work in Kent has produced

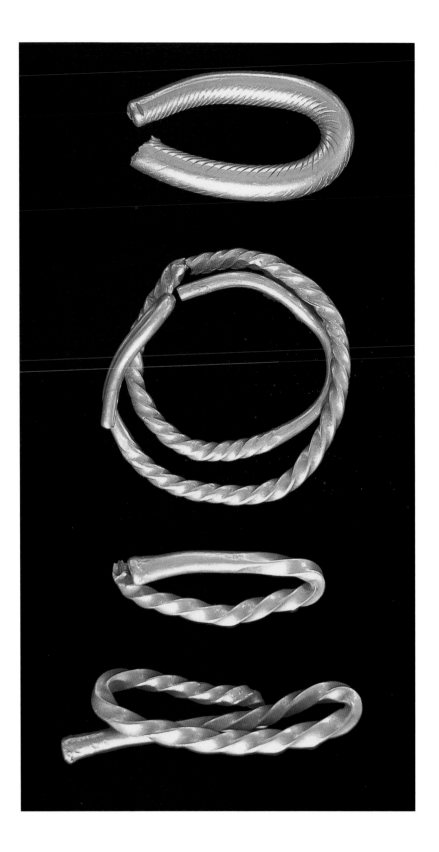

some evidence for the context of metalwork deposits. Some were certainly found in settlement sites. In the middle Bronze Age, the St Mildred's Bay hoard was deposited in the filling of a shallow ditch in a site on the foreshore (Perkins 1988), and the palstave hoard from South Dumpton Down had been buried in a pit dug into the fill of the large Deverel-Rimbury enclosure ditch; a group of four palstaves arranged in a fan shape was covered by a block of flint, on which in turn were laid another palstave and a bracelet (Barber 2003, 60). At Shrubsoles in the Isle of Sheppey a middle Bronze Age spearhead was placed in the ditch fill of a field system (Coles *et al.* 2003). A group of three pins of continental affinity was placed in a pot in the filling of a pit at Ramsgate (Hawkes 1942) and the Birchington hoard of palstaves (Powell-Cotton and Crawford 1924) was also in a pot in a pit, but it is more difficult to know whether these older finds were isolated or part of a larger occupation area.

A similar pattern is found in the late Bronze Age. A small hoard was found in a pit dug into the filling of a ditch at Bogshole Lane (Helm 2003a), and the large hoard from Minnis Bay was probably also deposited in a pit in a settlement (Worsfold 1943). Deposits of bronze items and metalworking evidence in enclosure ditches at Mill Hill, Deal (Stebbing 1934), and Highstead (Bennett, Macpherson-Grant and Couldrey, 2007) also follow this pattern. The two groups of gold bracelets from Bexley were also found in pits, possibly within a settlement site (Clinch 1908, 338). One unusual phenomenon within the concentration of late Bronze Age bronze deposits in north-eastern Kent is the presence of multiple hoards at Monkton Court Farm (Perkins and Hawkes 1984; Perkins 1991b; Perkins *et al.* 1994, 289-297) and Ebbsfleet (Perkins 1992, 303-304; Hearne *et al.* 1995, 274-278). Though the precise details of the context of deposition and the relationship to the other occupation features are less than clear, it seems likely that the act of placing metal objects in, or near to, an area of occupation may have been a regular occurrence.

The context of many bronze and gold finds is still unknown, but the evidence suggests that, as well as in rivers, metal objects were often deliberately deposited in or near settlements. In many cases, such as Shrubsoles Hill, South Dumpton Down or Bogshole Lane, it is clear that these rites were enacted at a very late date in the history of the site, when ditches were already largely silted up. They represent the final act, marking the transition from occupation to abandonment.

Deposition of bronze and gold ceased around 700 BC. For more than 500 years, until the reintroduction of gold in the form of coins in the late Iron Age, there is no trace of this metal in the archaeological record. Although bronze continued to be available and was used for small items like brooches, such objects are extremely rare, again until the late Iron Age.

External links

Kent continued to be closely linked to other parts of southern England, especially to Essex, and to the Continent opposite. All Kent's bronze and gold had to be imported, and the most graphic evidence for this trade is the scatter of bronze objects found on the seabed at Langdon Bay, Dover (Muckelroy 1980). This must represent the cargo of a ship that foundered as it tried to enter the estuary of the Dour around 1100 BC. The items were all of types largely unknown in England, but deriving from central France. The bronze was being shipped in bulk as a commodity, and would have been recast in England into forms acceptable here. Evidence such as this is not common, and neither are actual imports. The middle Bronze Age pins and armlets from Ramsgate and the late Bronze Age pins from Dartford noted above are rare examples. Nevertheless, the general similarity in the forms and technology of bronze objects shows the degree of contact across the Channel. Chemical analysis of bronze can also indicate such contacts; though there was much recycling and mixing of metal from different origins, some batches stand out. Thus the metal used to make many of the objects of the Wilburton phase, *c.* 1150-1020 BC, which was derived from an Alpine source, was kept relatively pure (Northover 1982), and an entry through Kent or the Thames estuary seems very probable. In the Iron Age, however, the bulk of southern England's supply of copper seems to have come from western Britain or Ireland. Ireland was probably also the source for the gold. Many of the objects, especially the late Bronze Age bracelets, are of distinctively British type, but there are two which, because of their precise form, are likely to be imports from Ireland: a 'dress-fastener' from Aylesford and a bracelet from Walderslade (Eogan 1994).

External links were not limited to the acquisition of exotic and valuable materials, however, and more mundane items show a variety of relationships. Kent was an important source for quernstones from the Bronze Age onwards: querns of Greensand and a ferruginous sandstone from the Folkestone beds were found at North Shoebury in Essex and they may have been exported more widely through eastern England (Wymer and Brown 1995, 72). Other items of material culture indicate, not so much the trading of actual objects as the sharing of a common cultural tradition of technology or style, especially with the region north of the Thames. One characteristic item of some late Bronze Age domestic assemblages are small perforated clay plaques (Champion 1980, 237; Perkins *et al.* 1994, 311-312); their function is unknown, but they have been found on sites in north Kent and Essex. Whatever they were for, they demonstrate a distinctive and short-lived technological innovation and a regional estuary-based network of cultural interaction in the late Bronze Age.

Larger-scale patterns of interaction are evident in the cross-Channel distribution of some artefact types. This is particularly marked in the early Iron Age, when east Kent ceramics are characterised by assemblages with rusticated surfaces, and fine wares with patterns of painted and incised decoration. The forms, fabrics and decoration have parallels in northern France, particularly with the pottery excavated at sites found during Channel Tunnel operations (Blancquaert and Bostyn 1998). In the same period the distinctive triangular clay loomweight known throughout southern and eastern England (Champion 1975) is matched by examples in north-western Europe (Wilhelmi 1977; 1987) and bone combs (Tuohy 1992) are also found on the Continent, demonstrating a network of interaction and shared cultural tradition across the southern North Sea and English Channel.

The approach of Rome: two centuries of change

Earlier navigators from the Mediterranean had described the offshore islands of Britain, but when Julius Caesar and his troops landed on the coast of Kent in late August 55 BC, it entered the recorded history of Europe. Although Caesar's two visits in 55 and 54 BC did not result in permanent conquest, which had to wait nearly a century until AD 43, his first landing has assumed iconic significance as a turning point in British history. That he landed near Deal may indeed be taken as symbolising the importance of Kent as a major axis of contact with the Continent throughout prehistory. The years before the arrival of Claudius's army in AD 43 were marked by many political and social changes, but Caesar's intervention did not initiate them: they had been under way for at least a century.

Establishing a chronology for the period from 300 BC to the Roman invasion in AD 43, including the later part of the middle Iron Age and the late Iron Age, is easier than for earlier periods: associations of pottery and metalwork in settlement and burial contexts are more frequent, the comparative continental chronology is more precise (summarised by Haselgrove 1997, 56), and datable continental imports are more common. The late Iron Age is marked by the use of brooches of late La Tène type and innovations in pottery, including new forms and the progressive introduction of wheel-thrown manufacturing techniques (box, adjacent). This had already begun by the end of the second century BC, though there are still very few good assemblages from domestic rather than funerary contexts to document it in detail. These innovations are best seen in east Kent, and changes in ceramic technology and burial rite had less impact in the west before the Conquest.

A firmer chronological foundation is given by the increasing number of imports from the better-dated milieu of the early Roman Empire. The presence of imported pottery, especially Gallo-Belgic fine tablewares, and new styles of brooch from about 15 BC, gives a more solid basis for the last half-century before the Roman Conquest. It is still possible that the dates given to the imports may be conservatively late, but even uncertainty over a decade or two makes the chronology of the late Iron Age much more precise than for any earlier phase.

In these final centuries before the Roman Conquest, Kent experienced a quickening of the pace of political and economic change. The landscape was again divided into fields and enclosures, and exploitation of the Weald for its iron began. New types of settlement appeared, and the predecessors of Canterbury and Rochester were founded. Dynastic rulers came to power. Kent continued to exploit its unique position as the nearest part of England to the Continent; trade flourished and new sites emerged around the coast to import ceramic and bronze tableware, as well as wine. Ultimately, it was the landing place for the invading Roman armies of Caesar and Claudius.

A landscape with hillforts

The limited environmental evidence suggests that the process of clearance that began in the Bronze Age continued into the Roman period, but there is little detailed information about the nature of the agricultural economy. The evidence from Farningham Hill in west Kent is therefore particularly important (Philp 1984, 71). It showed

Pottery of the middle and late Iron Age

Pottery is again the key evidence for establishing the chronology of sites. In the western part of the county there are large middle Iron Age collections characterised by bowls with S-profiles and foot-ring bases, best described at Farningham Hill (Couldrey, in Philp 1984, 38-70), but also found at other sites such as Oldbury hillfort (Ward Perkins 1944; Thompson 1986), Crayford (Ward Perkins 1938) and Greenhithe (Detsicas 1966). Similar middle Iron Age assemblages from further east, however, are very rare. One such was found at Bigberry hillfort, just west of Canterbury (Thompson 1983); this included foot-ring bowls and jars, and examples of curvilinear decoration. Decorative techniques in Kent included impressed lines, stamped circles and rows of comb-stamped dots.

From about 100 BC new forms and new technologies were introduced, part of a regional tradition of pottery production found over much of south-eastern England (Thompson 1982). Some of the pottery was wheel-turned rather than hand-made. Some of the new forms found in cemeteries such as Swarling (Bushe Fox 1925) include cups and tall pedestal urns, but a wider range of forms is found elsewhere. Large domestic assemblages are still rare, but the pottery from Canterbury (Blockley *et al.* 1995) may be representative. These new forms are rare in the west of the county, and older traditions may have survived, but they certainly were in use, as, for example, at Thong Lane, Gravesend (French and Green 1983).

From 15 BC new styles of pottery reached southern Britain. These included Arretine ware from Italy, the earliest Samian from southern Gaul, and the products of the Gallo-Belgic factories in northern France. The forms included cups, bowls, platters, beakers and flagons, which were table wares for the serving and consuming of food and drink. The imports are commonest in major centres such as Canterbury, but the forms, especially the platters, were quickly copied in local fabrics and are found throughout the region.

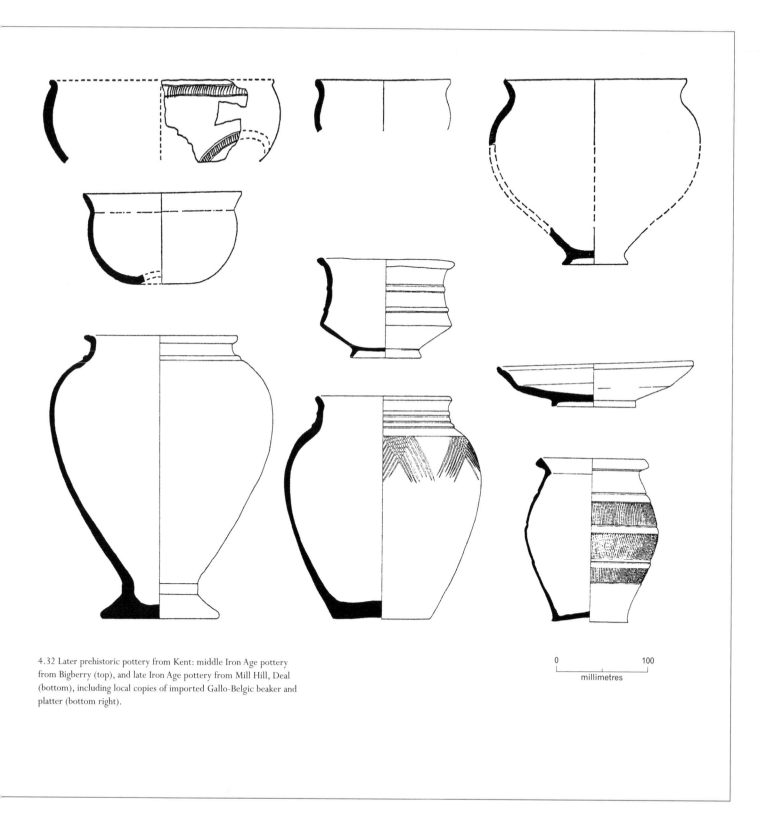

4.32 Later prehistoric pottery from Kent: middle Iron Age pottery from Bigberry (top), and late Iron Age pottery from Mill Hill, Deal (bottom), including local copies of imported Gallo-Belgic beaker and platter (bottom right).

0   100
millimetres

the presence of cattle, sheep and pig, but supplemented by the hunting of red deer, roe deer and wild boar, suggesting the presence of woodland somewhere nearby. Wheat and barley were grown. Not far away at Wilmington (Scaife 1987, 169), the wheat crops included both spelt and emmer, as well as some barley and oats. The cultivation of emmer alongside spelt continues the practice seen above in earlier parts of the first millennium BC. They seem to have been grown as a mixed crop, though in other parts of England wheat production had switched to single crops of spelt and to autumn sowing, with spring sowing of barley, thus spreading the labour of ploughing and sowing and potentially increasing productivity. The Greek geographer, Strabo (4.5.2), lists agricultural products such as corn, cattle and hides among Britain's exports, but there is too little evidence to judge whether Kent played a part in this trade.

Human settlement did, however, expand spatially, and there is much more evidence for human interest in the Weald in the late Iron Age. The mainly pastoral and wooded nature of land use and the comparative lack of modern development pressure make the identification of archaeological sites much more difficult than further north, but material of late Iron Age date has been recorded at Ulcombe (Aldridge 2005) and Biddenden. One objective was certainly the iron ores of the region, and the extraction industry is of pre-Conquest origin, but there may have been other motives, though the nature of the agricultural economy is unknown.

One sign of interest in the resources of the Weald may be the construction of hillforts. In some parts of England, notably Wessex and Sussex, hillforts were constructed from early in the first millennium, and some were densely occupied centres of regional organisation. This model has often been taken to typify the British Iron Age, but it is a highly regional one, and Kent, like much of the rest of eastern England, did not follow it. The difference is well illustrated by the contrasting histories of hillfort building in Sussex to the south of the Weald and in Kent and Surrey to the north

(Hamilton and Manley 2000). The hillforts of Kent belong to the middle and late Iron Age and show little evidence of dense occupation; they were not built on the high scarp or other prominent places of the North Downs, but in most cases on the fringes of the occupied area.

The hillforts lie mainly west of the Medway. The largest, enclosing almost 50 hectares, is Oldbury, near Ightham (Ward Perkins 1944; Thompson 1986); it is located on a prominent outlier of the Greensand ridge, looking southward to the Weald (ill. 4.33). Occupation may have begun by the third century BC, but continued until the Roman Conquest; the defences may be as early. Internal occupation is sparse, but the fort contains a natural spring and pond. There is a concentration of coin finds in the area and there are reliable reports that at least some came from within the defences. They are, however, gold coins, not smaller denominations, and the site may have been, among other things, a special place for ritual activity.

The two small forts at Castle Hill, Tonbridge (Money 1975; 1978), are an unusual pairing. There is little evidence for dense occupation and, on the basis of pottery and radiocarbon dates, both forts seem to belong to the middle Iron Age. Squerryes Camp, Westerham (Philp 1970; Piercy Fox 1970), is also situated on an outlier of the Greensand; it had a massive bank with a sandstone revetment and a complex gateway with several phases of construction. Again, there is little trace of internal occupation, but the pottery suggests a date in the middle or late Iron Age. The hillfort at High Rocks, Tunbridge Wells (Money 1960; 1968), lies further into the Weald; though occupation continued into the Roman period, it started in the middle Iron Age.

These forts show long and complex structural histories in the later Iron Age, but so far little sign of dense occupation. This evidence from Kent is matched by that from Surrey, where the hillforts show similar siting and use (Hamilton and Manley 2000). From the Medway westwards, they lie on the Greensand or further south, on the fringe of areas that were not heavily occupied until the later

Iron Age, and looking south towards the area of the Weald. This was an area that was beginning to be more heavily exploited in the late Iron Age and the forts were in some way connected with this southward expansion, perhaps visible places where rights to the landscape were maintained.

In east Kent the only proven hillfort is Bigberry, near Canterbury. Suggested hillforts underlying the later defences of Dover Castle (Colvin 1959) and Caesar's Camp, Folkestone (Pitt Rivers 1883), are unverified. Bigberry (Jessup 1932; Jessup and Cook 1936; Thompson 1983) occupies a prominent position overlooking the Stour, and may have been the fortified place attacked by Caesar in 55 BC. Its origin, however, is earlier than that; its ramparts are not well dated, but pottery from the interior could extend from the second century BC to the first AD. The presence of pottery, including an imported Roman amphora, and a possible structure suggest some sort of occupation, in addition to its possible defensive role. Recent interpretation has concentrated on Bigberry as a

precursor to Canterbury as a regional capital and as an early oppidum (see below), an idea supported by the discovery of a collection of ironwork, including slave-chains and a firedog. The lack of intensive occupation and the absence of coinage, however, make this unlikely. The ironwork has sometimes been taken as the evidence of elite occupation (e.g. Thompson 1983, 252), but it is more likely a ritual hoard (Manning 1972, 230). Other finds (Thompson 1983, 259), including a piece of horse harness deposited in a silted-up waterhole, an iron ard in a house gully and an iron anvil set upright in the ground, support the idea of Bigberry as a place of ritual activity, not of aristocratic residence.

Settlement sites dating to the final phases of the Iron Age are more plentiful throughout the county than for the preceding period; this may be due to the problems of recognition and of pottery chronology discussed above, or it may be due to a real change in the nature and density of human occupation. In the west, sites with middle Iron Age

4.33 Defences of the hillfort at Oldbury.

4.34 Plan of the middle and late Iron Age enclosure at Beechbrook Wood, near Ashford.

0   50

metres

pottery are known, but of varying form. A large collection of pottery was excavated at Crayford (Ward Perkins 1938), but apart from the presence of pits little is known about the nature of the occupation. Excavations at Stone Castle Quarry, Greenhithe (Detsicas 1966), showed a series of enclosures dating to the later Iron Age; one phase included a curvilinear enclosure that would have surrounded a house. A large site with similar enclosures, some recut several times, is known from the Isle of Grain (Philp 2002b, 139-141). Such sites with multiple curvilinear enclosures are well known elsewhere in lowland England, but are rare in Kent. A different type of site was discovered at Farningham Hill (Philp 1984), where a sub-rectangular enclosure was completely excavated, revealing the interior evidence for structures and pits; the ditches must have been mostly filled up by the end of the second century BC, but some activity seems to have continued until about the time of the Roman Conquest. In east Kent the ceramics of the early Iron Age rusticated tradition are rarely, if ever, found with those of the wheel-turned, grog-tempered phase of the late Iron Age in a context which suggests unbroken continuity. This implies a chronological hiatus, but it is difficult to identify sites of this period. One important exception is the settlement at Beechbrook Wood, near Ashford (Booth, Champion *et al.* forthcoming), which was surrounded by multiple ditches (ill. 4.34). It is a distinctive type of site known elsewhere in Britain, but so far unique in Kent.

Evolution of settlement

Sites of the late Iron Age are much better documented than earlier phases. The densest areas are again the northern coastal strip and the Greensand zone, many of the sites overlying late Bronze Age activity; Thanet is still occupied, though perhaps not as densely as before. Many of the sites have been found in small-scale evaluations and have only been partially excavated. Nevertheless, it is a consistent theme that these sites are characterised by ditches. It is sometimes difficult to tell whether these are ditches for formal fields or paddocks or whether they demarcate enclosed settlement sites, or perhaps both. It is clear, however, that the landscape was once again being divided and reorganised. Enclosure complexes are known at Hillside, Gravesend (Philp and Chenery 1997), Charing Sand Pit (Keller 1990), Glebelands, Harrietsham (Jarman 2002) and Highstead (Bennett, Macpherson-Grant and Couldrey 2007). Much larger areas of settlement have been explored at Brisley Farm, Ashford (Williams 2003, 226 and Fig. 6), showing successive large-scale patterns of organised enclosures and houses. Many of these sites continued in use well into the Roman period, and the pattern of early Roman settlement was established before the Conquest.

Individual settlement enclosures have been excavated at Thurnham (Booth, Champion *et al.* forthcoming), where an Iron Age site preceded the Roman villa (see page 154-5); this consisted of roundhouse gulleys and four-post structures in a rectangular enclosure. At the Kent International

Business Park (Perkins 1998a) and on the Whitfield-Eastry by-pass (Parfitt, Allen and Rady 1997) two more rectangular enclosures were excavated, though with less structural evidence. Such enclosures are well known from aerial photographs in east Kent, and the secure dating of these examples to the late Iron Age may indicate the chronology of the others.

Among the sites of the late Iron Age, some are of a different nature by virtue of their form, the material found there or their later histories. These sites, like others in south-eastern England, have been seen as important central places, exercising some of the economic and political functions of Roman towns. As symbols of pre-Conquest urbanisation, they have been termed *oppida*, the Latin word for towns used by Caesar to refer to some of the major Iron Age sites he encountered. Some did indeed develop into Roman provincial capitals, but that status should not be simply extended back to the Iron Age without a critical examination of the site evidence. Five such sites have been identified in Kent: Canterbury, Rochester, Quarry Wood Camp at Loose, Bigberry and Oldbury. The last two sites, discussed above, have none of the characteristics of an *oppidum*, such as comparatively dense occupation or signs of economic significance, and are more properly considered with the rest of the hillforts.

Quarry Wood Camp (Kelly 1971) is a massively enclosed site at the heart of a set of earthworks that cut off a long stretch of the valley of the Loose stream, including springs and areas of marsh (ill. 4.35). Excavation has produced material of the first century BC, including an imported amphora, but there is nothing to suggest continuity into the first century AD. With its earthworks and valley bottom location, the site is comparable to some of the major late Iron Age sites of Hertfordshire such as Verlamion, the predecessor of St Albans (Haselgrove and Millett 1997). Other contemporary sites are now known in its immediate neighbourhood, and it may have played a key role in the region. There is a

concentration of coin finds in the general area, but their connection to the site itself is unclear.

The late Iron Age predecessor of Canterbury has been difficult to find since occupation has been continuous on the same site, destroying or concealing the earliest layers. Pre-Roman layers have been found in several locations, such as the Marlowe Theatre Car Park (Blockley *et al*. 1995), Rose Lane (Frere 1954) and the Whitehall area (Frere *et al*. 1987, 45-54) to the west of the Stour. The starting date of this occupation is unclear. The Whitehall area was not occupied before the early first century AD, but the Marlowe site may be much earlier. An enclosure surrounded by three ditches was found, with internal features including a round house that had three structural phases before the site was levelled about AD 50. Much of the artifactual evidence for this phase, including pottery, brooches and coins, was found redeposited in later features, but the brooches in particular suggest a date in the middle of the first century BC (Blockley *et al*. 1995, 955-982).

The nature and status of Canterbury in the late Iron Age is uncertain. It seems more like a cluster of dispersed and variable settlement complexes than the formally planned layout of Silchester, and has not produced the sorts of important ritual monuments found at Colchester or St Albans. Its economic importance cannot be denied. It has a long list of coins (Haselgrove 1987, 139-145), and coin mould fragments suggest some were minted there (Blockley *et al*. 1995, 1102). There is a series of imported pottery including amphorae (Arthur 1986) and Gallo-Belgic tablewares, as well as many brooches and at least one rich burial (see below). Its peak seems to have been in the first century BC, though this may be a quirk of available excavation sites. The triple-ditched enclosure at the Marlowe Theatre Car Park site is an unusually impressive feature, and may have been a high-status residence; an enamelled piece of horse harness, one of the very few items of decorated Iron Age metalwork from Kent, was found very close to this site in the nineteenth century (Pilbrow 1871, 159) (ill. 4.36). It has also

4.35 Plan of earthworks at
Quarry Wood Camp, Loose.

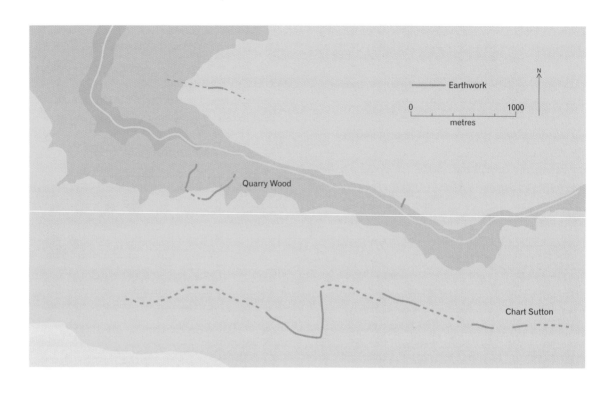

4.36 Strap-union from horse
harness found in Canterbury:
it is made of bronze with red
enamel inlay, though now
badly corroded (H 100mm).

been suggested that a concentration of Iron Age
occupation under an area that later became a
Roman temple enclosure may indicate a religious
function in the pre-Roman period (Bennett *et al.*
2003).

Canterbury, like other such sites in south-
eastern England, may also have been the focus for
important changes in everyday life. Though the
Marlowe site has produced a round house of
traditional Iron Age form, such buildings may
already have begun to seem old-fashioned.
Rectangular buildings were being introduced in
the late Iron Age (Rodwell 1978), and the remains
of such structures have been found at Whitehall
and in Palace Street (Frere *et al.* 1987, 47 and
81). Another form of structure is represented by
the sunken-floored building at Whitehall Road;
this form recurs in Roman contexts in Kent. Also
found at Whitehall were examples of fired clay
objects generally called 'Belgic bricks'. These have
been found at several late Iron Age sites, and seem
to have had a structural function, though their
precise use is unknown. Daub was also found with

plaster attached, suggesting a new style of finishing a building. At least in Canterbury, if nowhere else in Kent, the very fabric of the everyday surroundings was changing, with new styles of architecture and building technology.

Pre-Roman Rochester underlies the Roman and medieval city and is even more enigmatic. Pre-Conquest layers have only been located on one site in the High Street, but these produced coin moulds similar to those at Canterbury (Harrison 1991). There is no evidence to suggest an origin as early as Canterbury, but so little has yet been found that certainty is impossible.

By the end of the Iron Age, a further series of important sites had developed on the coast, distinguished especially by imported pottery and associated cemeteries (Rigby 1995) and by concentrations of coin finds (Holman 2005). A site must have existed at Folkestone from the first century BC, indicated by imported pottery including amphorae, and possibly exploiting the Greensand for quern production (Keller 1989). Cemeteries with pre-Conquest imports at Dover, Faversham and near Sittingbourne suggest the presence of others, as yet unlocated. Parfitt (2004c) has drawn attention to a series of coastal sites in east Kent, such as Worth and Richborough, with important concentrations of Iron Age coins, and suggested that they may have been ports. Other clusters of settlement developed along the Stour north-east of Canterbury; cremation burials have long been known from Sturry and Westbere, and early Roman sites such as Hersden may have late Iron Age origins (Williams 2003, 227). Settlements along the north Kent coast are less well known, but sites such as the complex of enclosures at Castle Street, Sittingbourne (Clark 2004a), may represent the counterparts of the cemeteries. These sites are characterised by the presence of imported amphorae and Gallo-Belgic finewares, and represent an important reorientation of the settlement pattern towards the coast and cross-Channel trade.

Burials

Throughout the first millennium BC much of England shows no formal means of disposing of the dead that is archaeologically recoverable. There are some regional exceptions, but for most of the south-east it is not until the first century BC that a new cremation burial rite occurs. This Aylesford burial tradition, named after the site in Kent where it was first recognised in the late nineteenth century (box, pages 124-5), is centred on Essex and Hertfordshire, but extends to north and east Kent, and is now increasingly recognised in south central England (e.g. Fitzpatrick 1997). Its adoption was an important part of the changes that affected south-eastern England in the late Iron Age.

East Kent and Thanet, however, show signs of a very localised tradition of inhumation burial that started rather earlier in the Iron Age and persisted alongside cremation. The best explored site is at Mill Hill, Deal, where inhumation and cremation burials have been recovered in quarrying and building operations for more than a century, and a larger-scale excavation has revealed a further cluster of three small cemeteries (Parfitt 1995). Burials in this area were mostly inhumations and radiocarbon dates show that they had begun by at least the third century BC (Parfitt 1998c). Burials are also known from other sites, especially in Thanet. The rite practised was extended inhumation, frequently without grave goods. There is usually no sign of a mound or marker of any sort. If this tradition is seen as an extension or adoption of burial practices on the Continent, then it might date from even earlier than the third century, since inhumation was giving way to cremation by then.

Among the burials at Deal, and dating to about 200 BC, was the spectacular grave of an important male (ill. 4.37). He had been buried with a sword and shield and had a bronze crown on his head. Such warrior burials are found occasionally in England, but recall practices much more common across the Channel, even though the shield and the crown are specifically of British types.

Two more warrior burials have been found at Brisley Farm, near Ashford (Johnson 2003) (ill. 4.40). In an area of dense late Iron Age occupation, the burials of two adult males, both with sword, spear and shield, were found in small square enclosures, probably originally with barrows. These were attached to a larger rectangular enclosure, with pottery and animal bone in the ditches showing evidence of feasting. Pottery in the graves suggests a date not long before the Conquest. Though the burials may be related to the earlier tradition of inhumations and warrior graves in Britain, they have close affinities to sites on the Continent, and may be yet another sign of contacts across the Channel in the later part of the Iron Age.

The new tradition of cremation was also adopted from the Continent (Collis 1977). Though there were regional variations in the precise details of the rites, in Kent the cremated remains were usually placed in a pot, accompanied by a limited range of unburnt grave

4.37 Grave 112 from Mill Hill, Deal: warrior burial containing (1) sword, (2) shield, (3) crown, (4) bronze brooch decorated with coral, (5) bronze suspension ring decorated with coral, and (6) bronze strap-end decorated with coral, possibly with the ring part of a strap to suspend the sword.

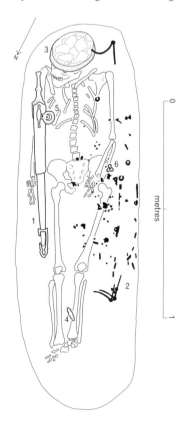

Aylesford

In November 1886, Arthur Evans, later the excavator of Knossos in Crete, visited Aylesford, investigating reports of discoveries made there (Evans 1890). He was able to recover the richest burial of all, which had only recently been dug up. The British Museum subsequently acquired the contents of this grave, and material from several others. The surviving documentation is poor, causing considerable confusion around the contents of the major grave groups (Birchall 1964; Birchall 1965, 243-244; Stead 1971, 260; Thompson 1982, 588-602; Rigby 1995, 179-180).

Three graves are of particular significance, now known as Graves X, Y and Z (Birchall 1965). Grave X contained a large wooden vessel with iron bands and iron ring-handles, around 40 inches (*c.* 1 m) in diameter, even larger than the decorated Marlborough bucket (Jope 2000, 96-99 and pl. 146). This vessel is said to have contained a number of pottery vessels; these may have been cremation urns, but it is more likely that the ashes were placed separately in the wooden bucket with the pots as an accompaniment.

Grave Y, recovered by Evans, had been lined with chalk and contained a bucket in which the cremated remains had been deposited with three brooches (Stead 1976, 402), as well as a series of pots. The stave-built wooden bucket (Stead 1971) was covered in bands of sheet bronze, decorated with a frieze of horses. The grave also contained two imported bronze items, a jug and a long-handled pan or patera, both probably made in Italy (Boube 1991; Feugère and de Marinis 1991).

Grave Z contained a bronze-mounted wooden tankard with bronze handles, together with several pots.

Evans's publication of the Aylesford graves was one of the first serious studies of Iron Age art in Britain and the first significant publication of a late Iron Age cemetery. Further excavations were carried out on a small cemetery at Swarling, south of Canterbury, in 1921 (Bushe Fox 1925) and these two sites were taken to typify the late Iron Age cremation rite, sometimes referred to as 'Aylesford-Swarling' burials.

4.38 Grave Y at Aylesford, as
originally illustrated by Arthur
Evans, reconstructed from
accounts by quarry workmen.

4.39 Objects from grave Y:
bronze-bound bucket in its
modern reconstruction, and
imported Italian jug and pan.

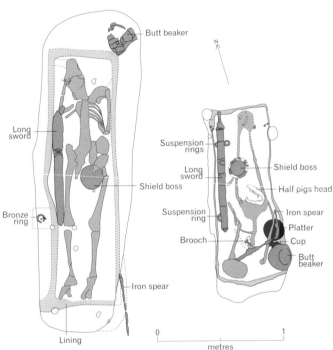

4.40 Late Iron Age warrior burials from Brisley Farm, near Ashford

goods, including other pottery vessels and brooches. Richer graves are not common, but those that are known are discussed below. The earliest brooches in the graves (Stead 1976) would now be dated to a point early in the first century BC, and it is quite possible that the cremation tradition was established by then. The local tradition of inhumation continued alongside, and the two rites are sometimes found in the same cemetery, as at Mill Hill (Parfitt 1995), or the poorly recorded cemetery at Highstead near Sittingbourne (Vale 1987, 368), or a small group of burials inserted into the ditch of the Neolithic long barrow at Julliberrie's Grave (Jessup 1937; 1939).

There is limited evidence for the relationship of burials to contemporary settlement sites. In contrast to the earlier Iron Age, where human remains are often found in settlement sites, the organisation of formal cemeteries, such as those at Aylesford or Swarling away from areas of

occupation, seems like a significant separation of domestic and ritual activity. The change, however, is less clear-cut. Some cremation burials are still found in settlement contexts: at the Marlowe site in Canterbury, a cremation was placed in the ditch of one phase of the round house (Blockley *et al.* 1995, 629), and cremations have been found in the silted-up ditches of other sites. Unburnt fragments of human corpses also occur in late Iron Age contexts. At Chalk Hill, Thanet, human vertebrae were found in a late ditch fill, though the accidental disturbance of an earlier deposit cannot be ruled out (Hearne *et al.* 1995, 265 and 301). At Thong Lane, Gravesend (French and Green 1983) a fragment of human skull was found in one feature.

Among the cremations a small number stand out by virtue of their grave goods, but none are as richly furnished as the so-called Welwyn graves found to the north of the Thames, which typically contain imported pottery including amphorae

(Stead 1967). This has led to suggestions that Kent was isolated after the Caesarean wars and denied access to Roman trade. Such a view cannot be sustained. Foreign trade was not the only source of power and grave goods are not a simple reflection of such power. Gold, perhaps the most important economic and political item, was never deposited in the graves, and there is plenty of evidence for imported pottery, including amphorae, in Kent, though the latter never occur in burials (Pollard 1991). That must have been a matter of cultural preference; the nature of burial rites and the selection of appropriate grave goods differed in Kent from practices north of the Thames.

Few graves with cremations in ceramic urns contain more than minimal grave goods; a burial at Chilham (Parfitt 1998a) contained a bronze mirror, and one from a small cemetery at Harrietsham included a bronze bowl (Jarman 2002). More commonly, the graves that stand out are distinguished by details of the rites rather than by quantities of grave goods. The body was cremated in a costume with ornaments or with a covering such as a skin, and a portion of the ashes and the burnt goods were collected; they were not placed in a pot, but piled up or put into a bag, perhaps fastened by a pair of brooches. One such burial was found at Palace Street in Canterbury when sewer trenches were dug in 1868 (Pilbrow 1871, 161). It contained iron bars, perhaps from firedogs, and the cremated remains were piled under an inverted bronze bowl imported from Italy, probably in the first half of the first century BC; it is the only example of such a bowl known in England.

In other burials the ashes, probably in a bag, were placed in a bucket. At Aylesford (see box), Grave Y was such á burial; it also contained two bronze items imported from Italy, a jug and a pan (Evans 1890). These are normally thought to be for the serving of wine, but their original use was for washing at communal meals. Another bucket burial was excavated at Swarling, but without any imports (Bushe Fox 1925, Grave 13). Two more

bucket burials have been found at Alkham, near Dover (Philp 1991), one of which included a toilet set (James and Rigby 1997, Fig. 80). An isolated cremation found at Westhawk Farm, Ashford, was another burial containing a bucket, but the burial rite is different, the ashes being placed in a wooden box; the imported bronze vessels and a *terra nigra* dish suggest a date near the time of the Roman invasion (*Britannia* 32 (2001), 380-2).

The majority of these burials seem to belong to the middle decades of the first century BC, though the brooches in one of the Alkham burials may be somewhat later. In the half-century before the Conquest there is a distinct change in the symbolism of burials; richer burials are marked by the inclusion of imported pottery associated with new styles of eating and drinking, and these are mainly located in cemeteries around the coast (Rigby 1995). The warrior inhumations at Brisley Farm and the bucket burial at Westhawk Farm, both near Ashford and mentioned above, all date approximately to the time of the Conquest; so too does a handle escutcheon of an imported bronze bucket found at Hales Place, Canterbury (Hawkes 1975), almost certainly from a burial. It looks as though the political crisis of invasion and conquest elicited a symbolic response that drew on older ideas of warrior burial and bucket burial.

The distribution of cremation burials suggests a major divide between the east and the west of the county. To the east, sites are frequent. Very few have been found west of the Medway, and those are mostly late; a similar situation is found in Surrey. The divergent histories of the two halves of the county have been noted before, but it is particularly noticeable in their different rates of adopting this new practice.

Ritual and religion

Another significant development in the late Iron Age was the separation of ritual activity from the domestic sphere and the foundation of specialised ritual sites such as temples. Important collections of metalwork were still deposited in rivers and lakes (Fitzpatrick 1984), though there is little sign of such activity in Kent, but there is less emphasis on structured deposition in settlement sites. Temples were another innovation and an example of the late Iron Age continental practices being imitated.

In west Kent, Springhead developed in the Roman period into a small town with a major ritual function, growing up around the headwaters of the Ebbsfleet. Its origins are obscure, but it certainly began before the Conquest (Williams 2003, 222-225). A large ditch separated domestic settlement from the area overlooking the spring, and terraces were cut on the hill slope above the water (box, pages 160-1).

At Worth, near Sandwich, a Romano-Celtic temple, with masonry structures dating to the Roman period, was excavated in the 1920s (Klein 1928). There is a large collection of pottery from the excavation, much of it of early Iron Age date. More recent observations have confirmed the presence of a wide area of occupation of later Iron Age date around the temple; the temple itself was surrounded by an enclosure with a massive ditch 4.5m wide and 1.6m deep, first dug in the late Iron Age (*Britannia* 21 (1990), 364). Finds from the area include imported amphorae and fine tablewares, and a considerable quantity of coins. The site clearly has a long and complex history, with an important phase of occupation late in the Iron Age. There is no conclusive proof of an Iron Age temple, but the discovery of miniature bronze votive shields, well paralleled on other temple sites and in a large Iron Age hoard from near Salisbury (Stead 1998), suggests a ritual function for the site.

The introduction of coinage

One more innovation of great significance in the late Iron Age was the introduction of coinage. Here too, south-eastern England was integrally linked with much of western Europe, which began to copy the Mediterranean use of coins as a means of storing and transferring wealth and specific coin types, especially those of Philip of Macedon, as the prototypes for indigenous designs. These coins began to be produced in continental Europe in the third century BC. Kent was the earliest part of Britain to share in this trend, though in the later history of its coinage it was eclipsed by south central England and the areas north of the Thames (Holman 2000) (ill. 4.41).

Small quantities of some of the early continental series are known from Kent, as also are a few coins from Greek and Carthaginian cities in the Mediterranean. There is no real reason to doubt that these were brought to Kent in late prehistory, and they clearly demonstrate the links the region had to the Continent. The more plentiful production of local coins began in the late second century BC, though it is sometimes difficult to tell whether coins were manufactured in Britain or in northern France. The earliest coins fall into two different groups. One comprises high-value gold coins called staters, though some smaller fractional denominations are known. The earliest series, Gallo-Belgic A and B, are concentrated in west and east Kent respectively, though later ones are more widespread. Gallo-Belgic E is particularly common; it was produced to finance the war against Caesar in the 50s BC, and demonstrates the far-flung political ramifications of those events. Further series of uninscribed gold coins were produced in Kent down to about 25 BC. These early gold coins are found mostly as stray finds or in hoards, almost never as finds from settlement sites.

The other group of early coins was made of potin, a high-tin copper alloy, copied from a prototype coin of Marseilles (Haselgrove 1988). The earliest of these are found in similar contexts to the gold coins, especially in hoards in north Kent. The final series, from about 50 BC, is much more frequent on settlement sites. The usage, perhaps even the value, of these coins seems to have changed during the first century. Potin coins were not produced after about 25 BC, though they continued to circulate for some time.

Age. The bronzes were of lower value and used in a very different way from the precious metal issues. Like the later potin coins, they are most frequently found in settlement sites, and not in hoards. Most Iron Age coinage was not used like modern coins, for everyday commercial transactions. The gold and silver issues were of very high value, and were used for storing or measuring wealth and transferring it in a limited range of interactions, such as dowries, ritual offerings, conspicuous demonstrations of personal generosity, rewards to clients or mercenaries, or political gifts. The lower-value coins, the later potins and the bronzes, were very different, and were used for everyday transactions, though to nowhere near the extent of today's money economy. They are found in some quantities on a large site such as Canterbury, but are also found on smaller settlements, suggesting that the use of coinage had penetrated quite deeply into the local economy.

From about 25 BC various series of coins were produced with inscriptions. Some are recognisable as personal names, probably of rulers, though the meaning of others is less secure. The first of these coins in Kent were inscribed with the name of Dubnovellaunus. A different series with the same name was produced in Essex and there has been a considerable debate, as yet unresolved, as to whether they are one and the same person. Some comparatively rare inscribed series may be local to Kent, but they were soon replaced by coins of Eppillus, a ruler whose name is also known from Sussex, and then those of Cunobelin and Adminius, successive rulers of the region north of the Thames. If the inscribed coinages give us a true reflection of the extent of a ruler's political authority, then Kent was under the sway of various outsiders from Sussex or Essex for most of the last seventy years before the Roman Conquest.

The latest of the uninscribed and the inscribed series of coins included gold, silver and bronze denominations, a complicated trimetallic coinage that was not common elsewhere in the late Iron

From Caesar to Claudius: trade, politics and culture

The final two centuries of the Iron Age saw major changes in the nature of society in south-eastern England, including imports from the classical world, the emergence of new types of settlement, the adoption of coinage, the appearance of a new mode of formal burial, and new styles and techniques for the production of pottery. Less obvious are new fashions for dressing and adorning the body, witnessed by the proliferation of brooches (Haselgrove 1997) and a new concern for bodily hygiene, seen in the use of toilet instruments and possibly vessels for washing (Hill 1997). The evidence from Canterbury suggests new styles of domestic architecture. The use of inscribed coins and the presence of a sherd with a two-letter graffito at Canterbury (Blockley *et al.*

1995, Fig. 269, no. 11) also suggest at least a limited level of literacy (ill. 4.42).

Previous explanations for these changes have invoked immigrants from the Continent (the 'Belgae'), but these theories have given way to an emphasis on trade as an external driver for cultural and political change, seeing the cross-Channel links as essentially commercial. This sort of analysis has also stressed the concentration of imports in central places of political power or in the graves of the rich and powerful; imported Roman goods would be both an indicator of power and its source. Recent critiques of this view question whether graves are such a simple indicator of status, whether such a concept of commercial trade is anachronistic, whether trade can be separated from wider political relations, and whether the local population should be assigned such a passive role (Woolf 1993; Willis 1994).

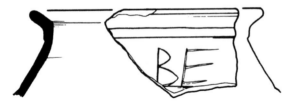

4.42 Graffito on late Iron Age pottery sherd from the Marlowe Theatre car park site, Canterbury.

There is no doubt that goods were brought into Britain from the Roman world, and the broad pattern of that trade is well known (ill. 4.43). The earliest items were wine amphorae, at first in southern central England and then from the early first century BC mainly through the south-east (Peacock 1971; Peacock 1982; Fitzpatrick 1985; Pollard 1991). Towards the end of the first century other pottery followed, mainly fine tablewares. Bronze jugs and pans from Italy also arrived, but in much smaller quantities, and probably as special gifts rather than trade goods. As we have seen, the bronze items were limited to richly furnished graves, but the amphorae are found, not in burials, but on settlement sites, and not necessarily major ones. Grave contents were

carefully selected and are not a good indicator of trade.

If goods were arriving, can we see what was traded in return? It is almost impossible to find material items of British origin on the Continent. They could have been organic: Strabo (4.5.2) lists corn, cattle, hides, hunting dogs and slaves among the exports from Britain. The slave trade is well documented by a find of collars and chains among the Bigberry ironwork (Thompson 1983, 274). But the question itself is wrong. The concept of balanced trade is a modern one. Trade does not need to balance, and indeed probably will not, if it is only the material symbolisation of a larger set of political relationships. Often left out of such discussions of cross-Channel interaction is the most important item of all, gold, and the most important type of relationship, the political. Traded items need to be put into a much wider picture of social and political interaction across the Channel, in which the local population of prehistoric Kent is given a far more active role in deciding the future of its own society.

Unfortunately, we know little about the political relationship of Britain and Gaul in the late Iron Age. In his account of the conquest of Gaul, Caesar gives us a few clues. He tells us (*D.G.B.* IV, 20, 1) that Britons were regularly fighting against him in France, and the wide circulation of the Gallo-Belgic E coins supports this. He also says (II, 4, 7) that the Gaulish ruler Diviciacus claimed sovereignty over parts of southern England; quite what this meant in practice is unclear, but it suggests political ties of some significance. Caesar's account refers to the mid-first century BC, but there is no reason to think that these relationships did not start much earlier.

The changes described above were not all simultaneous. The first coins came into Kent in the second century, if not earlier; local coin production began at the end of the second century; imported amphorae started to appear in the first half of the first century, but other imported pottery not until after about 15 BC. The

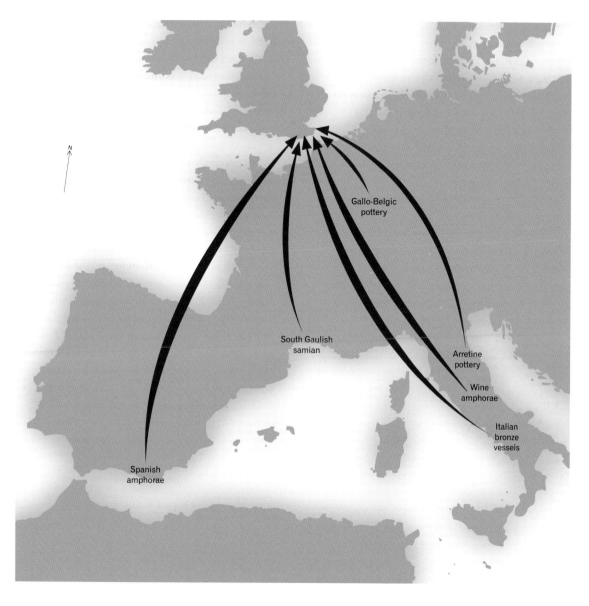

Gallo-Belgic pottery

South Gaulish samian

Arretine pottery

Wine amphorae

Italian bronze vessels

Spanish amphorae

date of the start of cremation burial may not have been the same as that for innovations in pottery. There were two centuries of change, not a single horizon, and these changes had begun well before the Roman conquest of Gaul and Caesar's expeditions to Britain. Perhaps the most important element was the influx of gold around 200 BC, the first for over 500 years; when it became available from the late third century BC onwards it transformed political possibilities.

It is also important to realise that the cross-Channel contacts did far more than just introduce imports. The most important changes were cultural, ideological and political, not material. The innovations in architecture noted above, such as rectangular plans and fired-clay building materials, represented the adoption of a fundamentally new way of organising the physical space in which social relationships were played out, as well as a major change to the perceived landscape of settlement. The proliferation of brooches and a concern for bodily hygiene suggest a major change in the human body and its external appearance in the structuring of human relationships. The importation and adoption of fine tablewares suggest, not just a fondness for Mediterranean wine, but a whole new manner of serving and consuming food and drink.

The key thing about imported objects such as amphorae, fine tablewares and bronze vessels for washing, is not that they represent flourishing commercial trade, but that they are the material symbols of a new way of life consciously espoused by at least some sectors of the population. Though the origin of many of these new ideas was ultimately Mediterranean, Kent's external contacts were not with the Roman world, but with the non-Roman peoples of north-western Europe, who were responding to changing political and economic circumstances.

It was also a period of political change. The centuries of the early and middle Iron Age had been marked by a total absence of any signs of social differentiation or political centralisation, whether in settlement patterns, architecture, burials or material culture. The appearance of a stratum of richer burials in the first half of the first century BC suggests a new pattern of society, in which certain individuals were able to establish positions of authority. Caesar (*D.B.G.* V, 22) mentions four rulers in Kent, but we know nothing further of them and the nature of their power is uncertain. Towards the end of the century the minting of coins with the names of men claiming to be kings marks a further stage in the evolution of political power. Caesar's expeditions of 55 and 54 BC had not resulted in the incorporation of Britain into the Roman Empire, but Roman influence was exercised indirectly through local client kings. The increasing use of Roman prototypes for local coinage suggests a detailed knowledge of Roman imperial ideology, and close contacts between the British ruling families and Rome (Creighton 2000). The coins circulating in Kent, as noted above, suggest that from early in the first century AD, if not before, rulers from other parts of

England held sway. There is no evidence that any unified political or cultural group foreshadowing the *Cantiaci* of the early Roman period existed in the Iron Age. On the contrary, the picture is one of diverse regional patterns of development within the county, and in particular the difference between east and west.

Acknowledgements

I would like to thank the University of Southampton and the Arts and Humanities Research Board (now Council) for funding a period of research leave which made it possible to read the huge archive of unpublished reports on the archaeology of Kent, without which this chapter could not have been written. I would also like to thank the staff of Kent County Council's Heritage Conservation team, especially John Williams, Lis Dyson, Simon Mason, Paul Cuming and Stuart Cakebread, for their help in making this archive available and for answering endless enquiries. It is also important to recognise the contribution of the many archaeologists whose work in recent years has transformed our understanding of the county's archaeology.

Roman Kent

by Martin Millett

This paper is dedicated to the
memory of Tom Blagg who
taught me and inspired my
interest in Roman architecture.

Introduction

Over the years there has been a series of general accounts written about Roman Kent (Jessup 1930; Haverfield *et al.* 1932; Blagg 1982; Detsicas 1983; also Andrews 2001; Williams 2003). In common with similar accounts of other areas of Roman Britain, most have been written from one particular perspective, generally trying to relate the archaeological evidence to the types of narrative history of events that characterise the classic histories of Roman Britain (Frere 1987; Salway 1981). Whilst this is a perfectly legitimate approach and one that has met with considerable success because of the richness of the historical texts relating to Kent, they do not do full justice to the archaeological evidence now available.

This account questions the tendency to assume that the changes that followed the Roman annexation of Britain in AD 43 were the product of deliberate Roman policy, or at the very least direct imperial influence. Instead it will seek to explain how Roman Kent developed as the product of a range of different interactions between the indigenous inhabitants themselves, and between them and the Roman state. It will thus explore a minimalist view of the power structure of the Roman Empire, based on the idea that the importance of Britain to Rome lay principally in the political kudos its acquisition provided to the emperor Claudius. Once Britain was in Rome's possession, it was generally left to its own devices and was of little interest or significance to those who governed the Empire, except as a place where military campaigning could be relied upon to provide prestige when this was politically expedient. This is not to deny that some economic advantage accrued from the annexation of Britain but rather to suggest that such advantage was not of great significance to the Empire. There is little evidence that the Roman state was interested in anything beyond ensuring that Britain did not create trouble for it and paid its dues via taxation. The administration of the province was thus left largely in the hands of trusted local aristocrats who ran local government on basically Roman lines, treating their tribal areas (*civitates*) as their local fiefdoms. Thus the nature of Roman influence was principally indirect, mediated through local collaborators, and experienced through the imposition of the infrastructure of roads and towns that were constructed as part of the process of control. Much that we label Roman was built not by incomers but rather by the indigenous inhabitants who, for a variety of reasons, chose to emulate the forms and styles of life and building that had spread across western Europe from the end of the first century BC onwards. It should be noted that few of these ideas emanated from Italy and most were adopted across western Europe at around the same period, even in areas like southern Gaul or the Iberian peninsula which had been under Roman control for a considerably longer period (Woolf 1995).

This essay thus attempts to provide a different type of account, which seeks to explore the dynamics of a changing society, discussing the archaeology of Kent in relation to this historical theme. Although it follows a broadly chronological structure, the intention is to explore the archaeological evidence in relation to issues of social and economic history rather than simply military and political events, which were largely irrelevant to the majority of the population. More significant for the lives of ordinary people were the changes in communications, settlement and trade, which can be seen as the accidental by-product of imperialism rather than its objective. Equally important is the challenge of understanding how the deliberate actions of individuals living in these changing circumstances influenced the patterns that emerged for their own purposes.

Before embarking on an exploration of these issues it is worth emphasising that the archaeological and textual evidence available from Kent is exceptionally good. There has been a wealth of excavations on a wide variety of different types of site. There have also been a number of studies which provide detail about the

5.1 The probable boundaries
of the *civitates* of Roman
Britain. These local
government areas reflected
Rome's understanding of the
Iron Age tribal groupings.

settlement and economy of the region (e.g. Pollard 1988). In addition, there is a variety of textual references which shed light on different aspects of the area, and these are supplemented by the evidence of known place-names and minor inscriptions. Although the different archaeological and historical sources of evidence all need to be read thoughtfully and interpreted with care, they provide some exceptional information. Thus, by comparison with even the richest period of prehistory, we are able to provide a very full account of the Roman period. In using archaeological evidence we need to be a little cautious in accepting published evidence at face value and we should be aware of its limitations, especially in the lack of evidence from areas like the Weald and the paucity of information about the agrarian economy. Similarly, we lack very good evidence for certain topics like the use of classical art or the nature of religious practice.

Finally, in this introduction it is important to consider defining the area that we are examining.

The tribal district or *civitas* that occupied the territory that is now Kent during the Roman period is generally known as the *civitas Cantiacorum* and the people are called the *Cantiaci* (as found in Ptolemy and the *Ravenna Cosmography*), meaning the people of *Cantium* (as used by Caesar and Strabo – Rivet and Smith 1979, 299-300) (ill. 5.1). It is important to appreciate that this terminology is the product of Roman administrative action, the logic of which should be understood if we are properly to evaluate the meaning of the *civitas* name. Rome's practice in governing her provinces was pragmatic, but in the same way that modern western governments conceive of the world in terms of nation states (however inappropriate this might be in continents like Africa), so Rome understood the world in terms of city-states occupied by self-governing peoples. The essence of the concept, which has its roots in Mediterranean civilisation, was that the landowning classes governed their territory through a series of civic institutions that were based at a central town.

When Rome annexed territories without such political institutions already in place, military commanders seem to have treated the peoples they engaged with in the same way and encouraged, or perhaps even sometimes assisted them to construct a town to act as their centre of government (Mann 1965). In Britain, Rome seems to have encountered some unstable social groupings, the product of local peoples forming a variety of different alliances depending on changing circumstances. Some such groupings were probably only formed in order to fight the Roman invaders, but Roman officials apparently assumed they were more permanent organisations and so treated them as though they were established tribal states. This is arguably what happened in the case of the *Cantiaci* at the time of the Claudian invasion. By treating the group as of permanent importance, and eventually vesting in it the powers of local government, it can be argued that Rome fossilised a particular political geography with enduring consequences (see below).

Despite the physical boundaries provided by the river Thames, its estuary and the English Channel, as well as the dense forests of the Weald, it is important to appreciate that the boundaries of the territory governed by the *civitas Cantiacorum* are not definitely known and may well have been rather fuzzy. The area is generally and reasonably considered to be essentially coterminous with the historic County of Kent, but we have no sound and detailed evidence to confirm this. Our best information comes from a variety of ancient geographical sources which list a number of settlements within the *civitas*. The *Ravenna Cosmography* (106, 36) cites Canterbury (Rivet and Smith 1979, 207) whilst Ptolemy's *Geography* (II, 3, 12) lists London, Canterbury and Richborough (Rivet and Smith 1979, 144). The uncertainties and potential conflicts with modern assumptions are well illustrated by Ptolemy's reference to *Londinium* as being within the *civitas*. Most modern maps place the northern boundary of the *civitas* along the Thames, assuming an error by Ptolemy. A wooden writing tablet, however, dated to 14 March AD 118 and found in London, records the sale of a piece of woodland at *Verlucionium* in the *pagus* or district of *Dibussu*[?] within the *civitas Cantiacorum*. This has been interpreted by Roger Tomlin (1996) as relating to land held in what is now the county of Kent. It seems equally plausible, however, that the wood lay in or close to *Londinium* itself, which was indeed administratively part of the *civitas Cantiacorum* (Millett 1996). This illustrates how we need to be very cautious in assuming that the political geography of Roman Britain necessarily resembled that of today.

The Iron Age inheritance

In considering the development in the Roman period of what is now Kent we should start from the assumption that it is a product of the continuity and transformation of Iron Age society. There are two perspectives from which this development can be viewed. Tim Champion has already explored developments in the century leading up to the Roman Conquest in AD 43 in the context of the evolving patterns of prehistoric society (see above). Several key themes seem to emerge. Firstly, there is a strong strand of evidence that suggests distinctions between the archaeological evidence from the west and east of the county. Secondly, there is burial evidence from the latest phases of the Iron Age indicating the development of significant social differentiation and the emergence of leaders whom we might loosely think of as tribal chiefs. The settlement evidence also suggests that coastal locations were becoming increasingly important. Finally, the excavated evidence from Canterbury indicates the emergence of some larger valley-bottom settlement sites which were important social foci although not recognisably towns.

To complement the archaeological sources we have glimpses of the Roman perspective from textual evidence. The principal source is Caesar's commentary on the Gallic Wars during which he brought an army to Britain in 55 and again in 54 BC (*D.B.G.*, IV, 20-28; V, 11-23). In reading this account we must appreciate that Caesar was not attempting to write an objective historical or geographical account, but rather the text was designed to help him fulfil his political ambitions at Rome. To the extent that it contains incidental information it is probably a reasonably reliable source, but elsewhere we need to be particularly sensitive to its political spin.

Caesar's text relating to the expedition of 54 BC provides two sets of information specific to Kent, geographical generalisations and specific political information. At one point (*D.B.G.*, V, 14), having repeated a stereotype about the underdevelopment of the barbarian Britons – which has little evidential value – he says that the most civilised inhabitants live in Kent (*Cantium*) and have a life-style that differs little from that of the Gauls. This statement should probably be treated with great caution as he is drawing a contrast with people he considers to be barbarians dwelling elsewhere. The archaeological evidence offers little support for any major contrast between the peoples of Kent and those elsewhere in southern Britain, where all the peoples seem to have shared cultural links with the near continent. Elsewhere in the same geographical description he says, in an aside, that *Cantium* lies on the corner facing Gaul and provides the landing place for nearly all shipping from Gaul and areas further east. This seems reasonable but we should again be careful about accepting it at face value, especially as earlier in his text (*D.B.G.*, IV, 20), he bemoans how little reliable information there was about Britain in Gaul, except from traders.

The specific political information provided at the end of his campaign in 54 BC (*D.B.G.*, V, 22) is perhaps more easily assessed. He mentions that *Cantium* is divided into four regions (*regiones*), with four kings (*reges* – Cingetorix, Carvilius, Taximagulus, Segovax) who were allied to Cassivellaunus, the leader of the Britons who had opposed him. By implication, these leaders were given peace terms by Caesar on his departure and the region presumably continued to owe allegiance to the Roman state thereafter (Creighton 2000). If we can assume that Caesar was correct in attributing these kings to the land of *Cantium*, and that this was essentially the same territory as represented by the later *civitas*, then we can speculate that it comprised a federation of independent kingdoms. This would be consistent with other evidence, which indicates the presence of loose federations of peoples rather than centralised states, but we should to be very cautious in assuming that the geographical limits of the area known as *Cantium* did not change in any way in the period between Caesar and the Claudian invasion of AD 43. Although it is impossible accurately to document the political and dynastic changes in the South-East in this period, it is abundantly clear that there were major boundary shifts in the tribal territories (Millett 1990, 20-28).

The evidence from recent studies of Iron Age coinage confirms that there were significant geographical distinctions in coin use across the county (Holman 2000). In particular it is clear that from the second century BC down to the Roman Conquest coin use east of the river Stour was much more common than further west. The numbers of coins found at sites like Canterbury, Rochester and Springhead certainly suggest the presence of major settlement foci. Excavations at Canterbury have revealed parts of a substantial late Iron Age nucleus probably founded in the second half of the first century BC, with evidence for continental trade links and for the minting of coins (Blagg 1995, 8-9). The character of this settlement is currently being debated, with the most recently excavated evidence suggesting that it may have been a sanctuary rather than an *oppidum* as previously thought (Bennett *et al.* 2003, 193). It is likely that some of the similar concentrations of coin finds elsewhere indicate other focal settlements and we should be wary of assuming that only places which remained of importance into the Roman period are potential late Iron Age centres. In particular the earthworks at Loose to the south of Maidstone and the concentration of Iron Age coinage in this general area seem to support the suggestion that there was a focal site here (Cunliffe 1982, 46-47). Equally, current work in the vicinity of Ashford suggests that there was one there too (below).

Recent excavations at Springhead have confirmed that this site was an important religious centre in the later Iron Age (Williams 2003, 223-24) and there are indications from the coins that the same may have been true of a site at Stoke near Rochester (Holman 2000, 227). In the east of the county it is clear that the temple at Worth was an important late Iron Age focus (Klein 1928; Hawkes 1940). This evidence indicates an increasing diversity of settlement types at the end of the Iron Age and makes it very difficult to reconstruct the social organisation of the region on the eve of the Roman Conquest. It is also important to appreciate that the settlements themselves were unlikely to have remained stable over long periods. For instance, there is some evidence from the coin finds (Haselgrove 1987,

5.2 Coin of Amminus, c. AD 40. Obverse: AM[MINVS] in a wreath. Reverse: DVNO and horse. This is perhaps an abbreviation for Durovernon, the Iron Age name for Canterbury or another place nearby.

139-45) and imported pottery (Blagg 1995, 11) to suggest a decline in the vibrancy of Canterbury towards the end of the Iron Age. In this context it is interesting to note that the latest Iron Age coinages include issues bearing the legend DVNO (ill. 5.2). This has conventionally been interpreted as referring to the *Durovernon* (later *Durovernum*), the Celtic name for Canterbury. The discrepancy in spelling, however, and the more easterly distribution of these coin issues have led to the significant suggestion that we should be seeking another site as the mint for these coins (Holman 2000, 216; see also Rivet and Smith 1979, 344 where the name is expanded as *Dunum*).

The Roman invasion and the establishment of the *civitas*

In recent years there has been considerable debate about the events surrounding the Roman invasion of AD 43. In particular, a number of authors have suggested that the conventional argument that the invasion landing took place at Richborough needs reconsideration (Hind 1989; Black 2000; Bird 2002). It has been proposed instead, either that Richborough was one of several landing points, with others further west in Sussex and Hampshire, or that the invasion landing took place in the Chichester area of Sussex rather than in Kent. The flaws in the various arguments in favour of a Sussex landing have been eloquently stated by Frere and Fulford (2001; cf. Sauer 2002), whilst Grainge (2002) has looked at the navigational difficulties involved with a Channel crossing from Boulogne to Sussex. Whilst the archaeological evidence in itself is incapable of resolving the issue definitively, the balance of probability remains that the invasion force landed in east Kent in the summer of AD 43. It is conventionally assumed

that the early Claudian ditches first excavated at Richborough in 1926-27 (Cunliffe 1968, 232-34) represent an invasion period fort, much of which has been substantially removed by erosion (Frere and Fulford 2001, 49; Philp 2002c), but recent fieldwork provides very strong grounds for doubting that the earthwork enclosure was anywhere near as extensive as the 57 hectare fortress sometimes suggested. The work indicates that the remains comprised a pair of ditches to protect the cliff top above the beach and not a full size encampment, and this must cast doubt on assumptions that have been made about the nature of the invasion itself (Millett and Wilmott 2003).

Whatever the details of the events in the summer of AD 43, it is clear that Richborough became an important supply base for the Roman army from the early 40s down to *c.* AD 85 (Cunliffe 1968) and was a primary port of entry into Britain through much of the Roman period (box, pages 142-143) Even with the development of the port at Dover around the beginning of the second century AD (below page 177), Richborough seems to have remained significant. This is shown by the evidence of the Antonine Itinerary, the British section of which begins at *Rutupiae* (Richborough) and includes the port as the terminus of its longest route, which extends to Birrens beyond Hadrian's Wall (Rivet and Smith 1979, 154, 157-60) (ill. 5.6). Equally, the monumental *quadrifrons* arch constructed around AD 80-90 (Strong 1968) was apparently located at Richborough because it was the ceremonial entry point into the Roman province (Millett and Wilmott 2003). It is worth emphasising that this arch 'rivals [in scale] all the great monumental arches constructed in the Roman world' (Strong 1968, 73). The events it commemorated have been the subject of some speculation but, in the absence of surviving inscriptions, it is not clear whether its massive construction, fine sculptural detail and expensive materials were to mark Domitian's 'completion' of the Conquest of Britain, to record the site of Claudius' landing or some other event. The considerable use of Italian

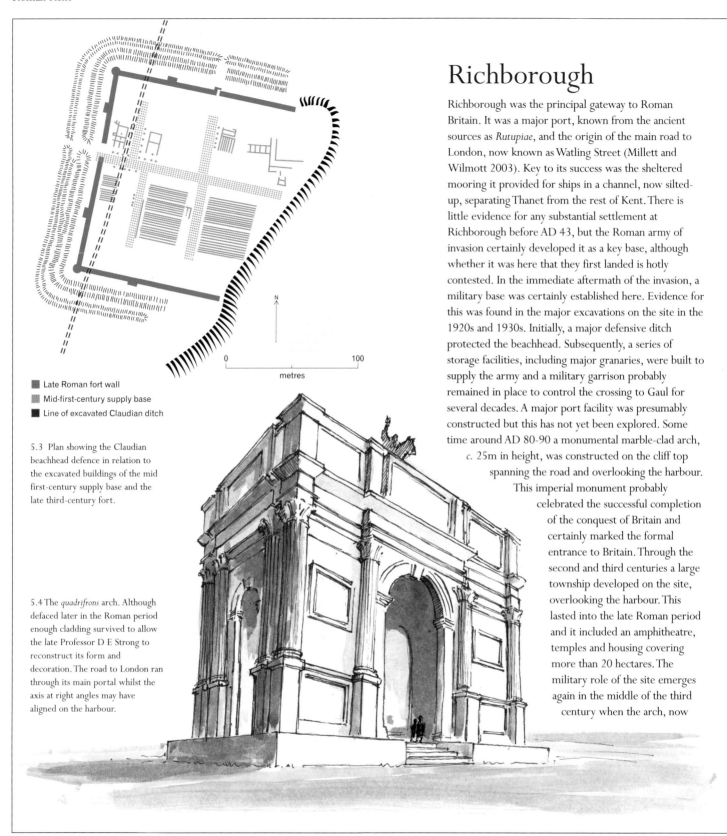

Late Roman fort wall
Mid-first-century supply base
Line of excavated Claudian ditch

5.3 Plan showing the Claudian beachhead defence in relation to the excavated buildings of the mid first-century supply base and the late third-century fort.

5.4 The *quadrifrons* arch. Although defaced later in the Roman period enough cladding survived to allow the late Professor D E Strong to reconstruct its form and decoration. The road to London ran through its main portal whilst the axis at right angles may have aligned on the harbour.

Richborough

Richborough was the principal gateway to Roman Britain. It was a major port, known from the ancient sources as *Rutupiae*, and the origin of the main road to London, now known as Watling Street (Millett and Wilmott 2003). Key to its success was the sheltered mooring it provided for ships in a channel, now silted-up, separating Thanet from the rest of Kent. There is little evidence for any substantial settlement at Richborough before AD 43, but the Roman army of invasion certainly developed it as a key base, although whether it was here that they first landed is hotly contested. In the immediate aftermath of the invasion, a military base was certainly established here. Evidence for this was found in the major excavations on the site in the 1920s and 1930s. Initially, a major defensive ditch protected the beachhead. Subsequently, a series of storage facilities, including major granaries, were built to supply the army and a military garrison probably remained in place to control the crossing to Gaul for several decades. A major port facility was presumably constructed but this has not yet been explored. Some time around AD 80-90 a monumental marble-clad arch, *c.* 25m in height, was constructed on the cliff top spanning the road and overlooking the harbour. This imperial monument probably celebrated the successful completion of the conquest of Britain and certainly marked the formal entrance to Britain. Through the second and third centuries a large township developed on the site, overlooking the harbour. This lasted into the late Roman period and it included an amphitheatre, temples and housing covering more than 20 hectares. The military role of the site emerges again in the middle of the third century when the arch, now

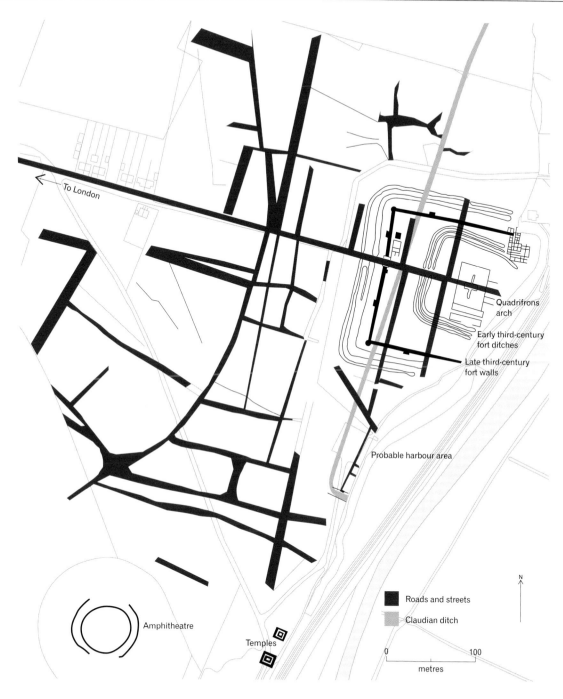

5.5 Plan showing the excavated forts, *quadrifrons* arch, and Claudian beachhead earthwork in relation to the streets of the extensive urban centre which developed during the middle Roman period. The plan was revealed by English Heritage through geophysical survey.

To London

Quadrifrons arch

Early third-century fort ditches

Late third-century fort walls

Probable harbour area

Amphitheatre

Temples

Roads and streets

Claudian ditch

N

0   100

metres

ruined, was converted to a watch-tower and enclosed within a ditched enclosure. Around AD 275 this was replaced by a new fort, enclosed within substantial stone walls. This was one of the series of installations constructed around the south-east coast which came to be called the Saxon Shore in the later fourth century. By then the *Legio II Augusta* was based at Richborough, and it is probably from here that they were withdrawn to Gaul in AD 406. Coin evidence shows that Richborough was one of the last places in Britain to be supplied with coinage, confirming that it remained a key government installation to the last.

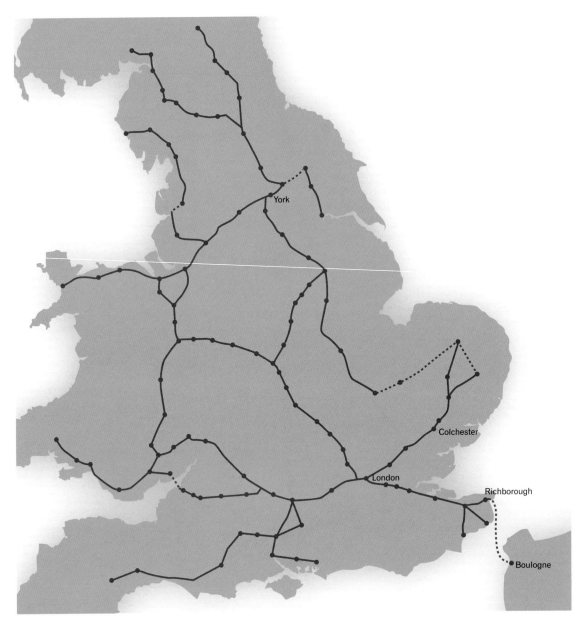

5.6 Map of Roman Britain showing the routes listed in the second-century Antonine Itinerary. The primary route from Gaul crosses from Boulogne to Richborough.

Carrara marble and the parallels between its decoration and that in contemporary Rome suggest that it was an imperial building project (Blagg 1984, 72-75). The approximate coincidence in the date of its construction with the earliest evidence for the development of Dover as a port may also be significant. Whatever the precise reasons, from the Conquest onwards Richborough developed as an important supply base, a port town and it again became a base for the military from the late third century right down to the fifth (see below).

Assessing why the military base was located at Richborough is key to understanding its origins and continuing importance. Discussions of the difficulties of navigating the English Channel clearly offer important evidence why an east Kent harbour was important (Grainge 2002), whilst an appreciation of the former coastal geography of the Wantsum channel shows why the general area was then appropriate as an anchorage (Hawkes 1968) (ill. 5.7). The coast of this part of Kent was at this stage dominated by a broad east-west channel which separated the Isle of Thanet from the mainland. The river Stour drained into it and its southern shore was characterised by a series of inlets and islets. It was on one of these, at the top of a low cliff, that the known Claudian encampment was built – presumably dominating both a safe anchorage and ground solid enough for beaching, loading and unloading ships. The geographical advantages of the area are obvious, but we should not ignore its previous history, even though this has not yet received the attention that it deserves, especially bearing in mind Caesar's comments cited above about the importance of east Kent ports. The area along the slopes overlooking the Wantsum channel was evidently very important for settlement at the end of the Iron Age and it seems highly likely that there were existing landing places or anchorages in the vicinity. The important Iron Age burial ground

excavated near Deal perhaps provides evidence for one site (Parfitt 1995) whilst there are hints of another at Worth (Klein 1928).

Equally significant is the recent collation of evidence of Iron Age coins from east Kent (Holman 2005; Cossburn 2001) which shows that there was a string of important late Iron Age settlements in this area; careful analysis of the dating of the groups of coins indicates that they were probably most intensively occupied in the period AD 20-40, immediately prior to the Claudian invasion. Our current understanding of the links between southern Britain and the Roman world during the late first century BC and the earlier part of the first century AD suggests intensive contact, not only through trading but also through strong ties of political obligation (Creighton 2000). It has long been appreciated

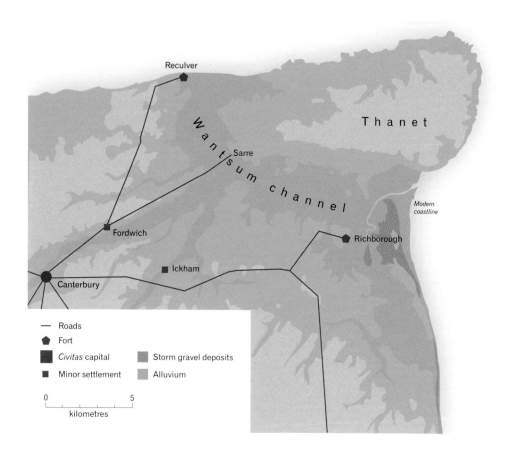

Roads
Fort
Civitas capital
Minor settlement
Storm gravel deposits
Alluvium

0   5
kilometres

5.7 Reconstructing the Roman coast. The Wantsum channel was largely open water, although a gravel spit constricted access to the east. Richborough, Reculver and Canterbury were thus all easily accessible by water.

that contacts with southern Britain intensified after Augustus' reorganisation of the Gallic provinces and from this stage onwards trading contacts with the Thames estuary became most important. It is within this context that we should understand developments around the Kentish coast, and especially the Wantsum channel which presumably became a focus for cross-Channel contacts with Roman Gaul. Against this background we can appreciate that Richborough was used by the Claudian army because the area was already well known and the Wantsum was regularly used by trading vessels. Indeed archaeological material from east Kent shows a variety of close links with northern Gaul, illustrating the frequency of such cross-Channel contacts.

Our understanding of this background is enhanced by an examination of the road network in northern Gaul, which was laid out from the Augustan period. One of the principal routes, running to the Channel at Boulogne (Drinkwater 1983, map 7), was most likely developed with the route to Britain in mind. In addition to responding to the established links with the island, there is evidence that Augustus was contemplating and preparing for an invasion (Cassius Dio, *Historia Romana*, 49, 38, 2; 53, 22, 5; 53, 25, 2), and it is in this context that we should understand the development of this military road through Gaul (ill. 5.8). Further preparations were made for the emperor Caligula's planned invasion in AD 40 (Suetonius *Caligula*, 44; 46). Although his actions are lampooned by his biographer, the construction of a lighthouse and presumably other infrastructure at Boulogne laid the ground for the campaign three years later. The key point from our perspective is that long-term preparations for contact with and the annexation of Britain had all focused on Boulogne, implying the use of the traditional route to east Kent and the Wantsum channel.

Developing contacts with Gaul also seem to have had an impact on settlement patterns elsewhere around the Kent coast. It is notable how a series of settlements that developed as focal places during the Roman period and have their origins in the later Iron Age are located on river estuaries. Even centres like Canterbury, which are today inland, were established on navigable stretches of rivers close to the coast. Communications by sea in the ancient world were dominated by short hops from one settlement to the next along the coast. Thus the growth in coastal trade probably helped enhance the importance of a number of places around the coast during the period leading up to and after AD 43.

The archaeological evidence from many of these sites in Kent is not all that clear because of the intensity of later settlement, but we also have information from Roman sources for the place-names used after the Conquest (following Rivet and Smith 1979). These provide some important clues to the establishment of a settlement pattern dominated by coastal locations. An element used in several names is *duro* which means 'enclosure'. There has been some discussion about whether the place-names containing this were Roman forts (Rivet 1980), but it seems more likely that the term generally refers to the pre-Roman topography. The name for Canterbury, *Durovernum*, meaning 'an enclosure by an alder swamp', can perhaps be associated with the excavated late Iron Age enclosure (Blagg 1995, 7-11). On the Medway estuary, Rochester was called *Durobrivae* (the enclosure by the bridge), and a place called *Durolevum* (enclosure by smooth-flowing water) is listed in *Iter II* of the Antonine Itinerary midway between Canterbury and Rochester. Although its location remains unconfirmed, it must lie close to water and a location in the area of Syndale Park/Ospringe, near Faversham and overlooking the Swale estuary, seems certain (Philp 1976; Wilkinson 2000; Sibun 2001). Further up Watling Street, Springhead was called *Vagniacis*, meaning 'a marshy place', and here recent excavations (Williams 2003, 223-24) have demonstrated the importance of the site in the later Iron Age. Roman settlements developed where Watling Street crossed the rivers Darent and Cray, but there is not yet evidence for Iron Age predecessors

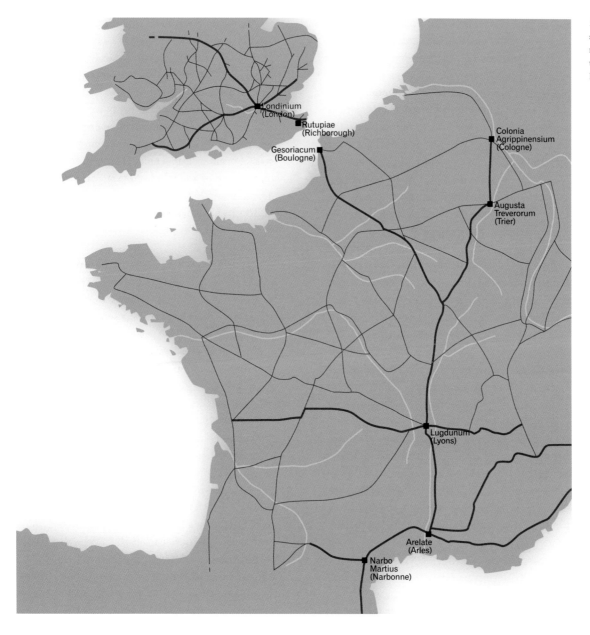

and the Roman name *Noviomagus*, or new market, certainly indicates some settlement reorganisation. (This settlement is presumed here to be at Crayford on Watling Street although Brian Philp has recently suggested that it lay at West Wickham and not on Watling Street (Philp 2000).) Elsewhere the importance of coastal navigation is reflected in other Roman place-names around the coast of Kent; whether or not this represents

earlier Iron Age usage is uncertain. Richborough, *Rutupiae*, means muddy estuary, *[Portus] Dubris* (Dover) also relates to water (the river Dour), whilst Lympne, *Portus Lemanis*, is named after a marshy river and the name for Reculver, *Regulbium*, refers to a great headland.

Along the north and east coasts of Kent it is tempting to see a settlement pattern at the end of the Iron Age focused on rivers and coastal inlets which provided an interface between the well-settled inland regions and the wider world. If we were to push this hypothesis further, we could relate individual social groups to each of the river valleys and perhaps see these as remaining focal in the later development of the settlement pattern during the Roman period (see below). This emphasis on coastal sites needs to be balanced by information from river valleys further inland where the evidence has, until recently, been rather more fragmentary. Although evidence from sites like Aylesford, Loose and Eccles on the edge of the Weald in the Medway valley suggests a significant centre or focus in these areas, detailed archaeological confirmation has been lacking. Recently, however, excavations at Brisley Farm, near Ashford, have revealed a pair of late Iron Age warrior inhumation burials associated with an enclosed farmstead which was presumably of importance in this period; it is interesting to note how the barrows raised over the burials were apparently revered well into the Roman period (Stevenson and Johnson 2004). Nearby, another pre-Conquest burial, this time a well-furnished cremation, has been found in a small cemetery adjacent to the Roman settlement that developed at Westhawk Farm (Booth and Lawrence 2000; Williams 2003, 225-7; below p.164). These sites hint at another social focus in the Stour valley, also located between the Downs and the northern edge of the Weald.

Although it is clear from later developments that coastal navigation remained important in the development of Roman Kent it is clear that overland communication was also significant from the period of the Conquest onwards. If we follow the conventional account of the Roman invasion, then the route followed by Watling Street was central to the invasion strategy, with the key battle being fought at the Medway crossing (Cassius Dio, *Historia Romana* 60, 20). Even if we cannot be as sure of this as some commentators insist, it is clear that the route was a primary one which was developed soon after the Conquest. The road was certainly in use by the time that London Bridge

was built, probably in AD 52 (Watson *et al.* 2001, 30-33), and *Londinium* was evolving as the provincial centre by the early 50s (Perring and Brigham 2000). It is also clear from the development of London that the Thames was a key artery for the transport of heavy materials. Indeed the overall distribution of Roman legionary bases in Britain shows that maritime communications were of central importance, hence the continuing importance of the supply base at Richborough. The itineraries, however, suggest that people rather than merchandise disembarked after a short sea crossing and continued their journeys overland.

The development of Watling Street (Margary 1955, route 1), connecting the estuaries along the Thames, created a new geography even though we can assume that it broadly follows an earlier route. Its emergence as a key road through the new province created a new focus for development, linking communities that had previously been comparatively inward looking and enhancing their connection with other parts of the Roman world. Equally, it seems to have changed the geographical framework from a series of separate valley-based communities to a broader network of interlinked settlements.

The other roads that developed in Kent connected various places to Watling Street. In the east, Canterbury became a hub, with roads eventually linking Reculver, Richborough, Dover and Lympne, all strategically important sites at different stages of the Roman occupation, and the alignments of the roads show some strikingly regular patterns (Parfitt unpublished) (ill. 5.9). Arguably the most ancient route (Margary 1955, route 130) followed the Stour valley from the Wantsum south-west to Canterbury and then the gap through the North Downs to the Weald. At Westhawk Farm, near Ashford, this road certainly dates to the pre-Flavian period on the evidence of the recently excavated roadside settlement. Here it met the road (Margary 1955, route 131) from Dover via Lympne, which ran along the southern flank of the Downs. This route does not continue

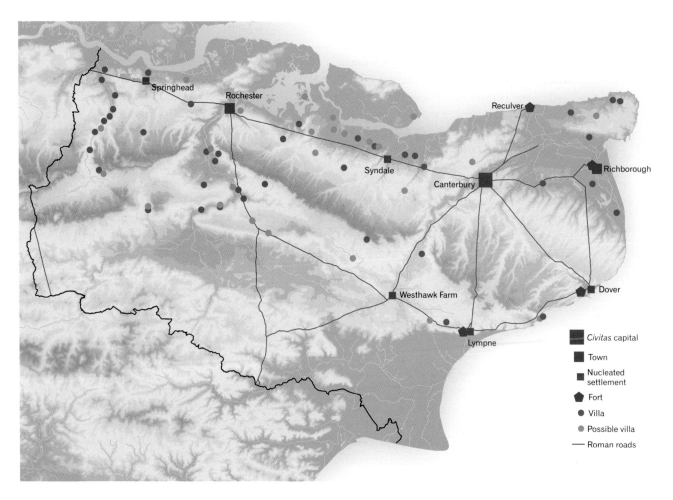

directly to the west, towards Maidstone, but seems to have followed the Stour route a little way southwards before resuming its westerly course (Booth pers. com.). The Stour road itself heads for the centre of the Weald to a point near Benenden. Both these routes intersect the road (Margary 1955, route 13) which ran south from Rochester, following the Medway valley through the North Downs and continuing across the Weald in the direction of Hastings on the south coast. Like the route south-west from Canterbury, this seems most likely to have followed a course that was also of significance during the Iron Age. Our information about the dates of construction of the principal roads is limited but, given their strategic significance, it seems likely that the main routes were laid out soon after the Roman annexation.

The route that connected Richborough to Canterbury (Margary 1955, route 10) is problematical for, although it should presumably have been developed at a very early date, its established route appears to be later and follows a somewhat irregular path. Subsequently Canterbury was linked with the newly developed sites of Reculver (*ibid.*, route 110), Lympne (*ibid.* route 12) and the later port at Dover (*ibid.*, route 1a), and Richborough with Dover (*ibid.*, route 100). An existing network of trackways and less formal routes, like that along the North Downs, also probably continued to be important.

The principal roads were certainly built at the behest of the Roman military, although whether they were constructed by soldiers or local people on their behalf is a matter which it is probably

5.9 Map of Kent showing the principal Roman settlements and villas. A large number of other rural settlements and farms are omitted for clarity.

impossible to resolve. Conventional ideas about the development of civilian areas of Roman Britain being the by-product of an initial military stimulus are not applicable to Kent. Here, as in other areas which had long been influenced by contacts with Roman Gaul, the stimulus for development after AD 43 seems largely to have been home-grown. The Roman military installations of the invasion period at Richborough have already been discussed. In addition there is good evidence for a fortlet of 0.4 hectares, dating to the mid-first century AD, beneath the later fort at Reculver (Philp 2005, 98-102; 192-3). Both these places very likely remained key to the supply strategy of the Roman army operating around the coast of Britain. Elsewhere in Kent the evidence for forts is less convincing, although a number of claims have been made. Since the aim of Claudius' generals was not to impose a military government but rather to govern indirectly through native rulers, the absence of strong evidence for long occupied forts is not unexpected. The strategy in most parts of southern England seems to have involved at most a short-term military occupation, with any forts housing auxiliary units of the army located to oversee established centres of native power.

Administrative control was soon passed to pro-Roman aristocrats who henceforth governed their tribal territory (*civitas*) on Rome's behalf. Any short-lived military sites are thus most likely to be found on or beside Iron Age centres. Indeed, in a number of instances elsewhere in Britain in the period following AD 43 soldiers were encamped within Iron Age sites and not in specially built forts (Millett 1990, 50 and illus. 15). Identifying such soldiers is very difficult as military equipment seems to have circulated widely amongst civilians in the province whilst excavators have sometimes been over-optimistic when trying to identify sections of ditch as parts of possible forts. However, the short term presence of soldiers at strategic locations, for instance at Canterbury or at sites along Watling Street, would not be surprising even if clear evidence has to date

not been forthcoming.

The key point in the development of Kent was thus the creation of the *civitas Cantiacorum*, not the establishment of any early military bases. The *civitas* centre was certainly *Durovernum Cantiacorum* (Canterbury), as the place-name appears in this form in the *Ravenna Cosmography* (Rivet and Smith 1979, 353). We have already noted that it was an important pre-Roman centre, even though it may not have been at the peak of its occupation at the time of the invasion. The selection of Canterbury as the administrative focus for the *civitas* should not be taken to imply that it was already the tribal centre, or even that *Cantium* was a single territorial entity. Indeed, as previously noted, there are good reasons for believing that it was not. The archaeological evidence would certainly seem to suggest that it was occupied by several geographically distinct social groups at the time of the invasion. The point is that these peoples were treated as one group – the *Cantiaci*, meaning the people of *Cantium* – by Rome, and that Roman administrators perceived Canterbury as the focal settlement. It may well have been a traditional meeting place, even if rivalled by other places at the time of the Conquest. Certainly the nearby hill fort at Bigberry Camp on the hill behind Canterbury may have fulfilled a similar role in the first century BC to the early first century AD (Thompson 1983). Once Canterbury was treated as the central place of the *civitas* the construction of the road system reinforced its geographical focus. To a lesser extent, it would appear that the same process took place at Rochester, where another road junction, together with the harbour and river crossing, assured the continued importance of *Durobrivae*.

Geographical factors are, however, only part of the story. What made the *civitas* was not the place but the people, in particular those indigenous leaders who chose to support the conquerors and remained to govern the territory on their behalf. It was they who not only created the new political entity but also presumably gained immense personal benefit from so doing. Whatever their individual motives, they clearly aspired to present themselves and their properties in a Roman fashion, adopting the Latin language, Roman ways of dressing and styles of building. To quote Tacitus (*Agricola*, 21), 'the Britons spoke of these innovations as civilisation when they were in fact symbols of enslavement'. It seems most likely that the indigenous aristocracy expected to gain favour from copying Roman ways, even though there is almost no evidence that the conquerors had a deliberate policy of encouraging this attitude. Instead, the pressures seem to have been more subtle, the wish to identify with those in power, the desire not to appear out of place, the compulsion to follow contemporary fashions, and the impulse to evolve new ways of distinguishing themselves from their perceived social inferiors.

In the archaeology of Kent we can see the impact of these early leaders through the various structures that they constructed. It is important to appreciate the significance of building forms at this period. Hitherto, people had lived in timber houses of modest scale, although the sophistication of their designs has too often been overlooked. Technical limitations meant that the internal areas that could be roofed over were limited and the absence of windows will have made the interior spaces gloomy. Although individual status was expressed through differences in building size, and presumably architectural detail, such differentiation was modest. Other modes of display, like burial ritual, were probably more important means by which Iron Age social elites defined their status. In these circumstances the introduction of new methods of building was particularly important, even though traditional forms of display certainly also continued. The changes occurred both in the new urban centres and also in the countryside.

When we consider the patterns of evidence in the period soon after the Conquest it is important not to start from presuppositions about the nature of sites, as recent work elsewhere in Britain is leading us to question their character (cf. Millett 2001). The rural evidence can be used first to illustrate this point. The villa is perhaps the most potent symbol of Roman archaeology. The very term conjures up images of luxury rural living. This certainly overplays the quality of even the most developed of the Kent villas, except in the later Roman period. When we look at those that emerge in the early Roman period they were generally comparatively modest. Nevertheless, we should not underestimate their importance as symbols of power, representing a new mode of building and expressing the Roman cultural aspirations of their inhabitants. In the past there has been a strong tendency to associate villas with changes in agricultural production and to assume a close connection with farming, even to the extent that some authors refer to all of them as 'villa estate' centres. These are key misapprehensions.

In the ancient world the ownership of land was important, not only as a way of holding wealth but also as a symbol of political power. Thus, under Roman systems of government, only those who held their wealth in land could hold political office, and we have nothing to suggest that this convention was not applied in the *civitas Cantiacorum*. As a result, those who had obtained wealth through a variety of means, through inheritance, trade, warfare or corruption, would generally hold it in the form of land. Powerful members of the establishment could thus own estates in a variety of places, including those where they were not usually resident. It is very likely that some land in Kent passed into foreign hands after the Conquest, although it is impossible to establish this in the absence of textual evidence. Given that such new landowners needed to earn cash from rents or the direct farming of the land, it is unlikely that the forms of settlement found on their land would have differed from those seen elsewhere. As elsewhere in Britain, there does not seem to be significant evidence for changes in agriculture at the period of the invasion, and only where there is a marked change in the buildings or in land boundaries can we even consider being able to identify changes in ownership.

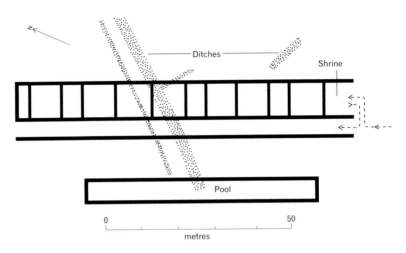

5.10 Eccles villa in the mid-first century in relation to Iron Age ditches. A single range overlooks a large pool. The different sized rooms suggest suites of two and three rooms occupied by separate social groups.

Whilst there can be no doubt that many of those who built villas also held large tracts of land, the construction of a house in a new architectural form represents a decision about how to expend wealth, not an indication of how it was obtained. To associate this surplus wealth solely with farming in the locale is to misjudge the complexity of contemporary society.

The pattern of early Roman villa development in Kent is striking in several aspects. First, there are comparatively few sites, with a total of perhaps eleven with good evidence for buildings dating to before AD 100. This is particularly interesting when one considers that the area was amongst the earliest annexed, yet the construction of these villas did not take place until two or three generations later. This must suggest that the fashion for the rural aristocratic retreat was slow to catch on, for reasons that are difficult to appreciate. The one major exception to this pattern is the earliest phase of the villa at Eccles, which dates perhaps to as early as AD 55, only a decade after the invasion (ill. 5.10). The villa overlooks the Medway where it cuts through the North Downs, very close to the important Iron Age cemetery at Aylesford (Evans 1890). It apparently overlies an Iron Age farmstead and one may perhaps assume the continuity of a centre of power after the invasion. The first structure was replaced about ten years later by a very substantial complex, comprising a range of rooms fronting a corridor (Detsicas 1991). This site is best seen as a symbol of *romanitas* having been adopted by one of those who had retained political power locally after the establishment of the *civitas*. Both the scale of the buildings and their design are impressive, especially given the very early date and topographic setting overlooking the river Medway. We should certainly see the Eccles villa as one that would have provided a spectacular display for its owner, whether to overawe subservient local residents or to impress those visiting from elsewhere in the Empire with its scale and contemporary design. Perhaps significantly, this villa lay in part of the Medway valley which later developed as one of the main foci for villas in the *civitas*.

The other villa that may have been in the possession of an early member of the cantonal elite is at Wingham about 10 kilometres east of Canterbury. The bath-house was excavated in the 1880s. A re-excavation of the villa in the 1960s suggested that its construction should perhaps be dated to the early second century (Jenkins 1985), but the mosaic in the bath-house appears to be of first century date and can be closely paralleled in *Gallia Belgica* (Smith 1978, 121). Whatever its precise date the evidence suggests a residence of some pretension, certainly appropriate to a local leader who lived close enough to make regular appearances at Canterbury.

Further villas were constructed during the period from about AD 70 until the end of the first century. Where modern excavations have taken place these villas can often be shown to have been built on settlements with origins in the Iron Age, suggesting that they were probably also built by aspiring indigenous leaders of the second generation. An extensively excavated site is that at Thurnham overlooking the Medway on the southern flank of the North Downs (Oxford Archaeological Unit 2000b) (box, pages 154-5). Here the remains of a comparatively modest

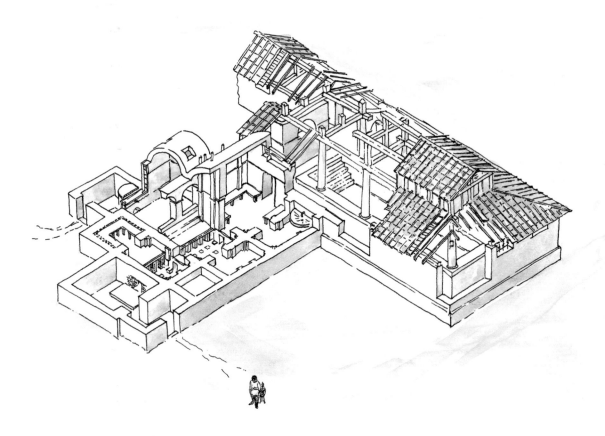

house with clay floors but plastered walls, dated to *c.* AD 70 or before, lay beneath a later and more pretentious stone rebuild, which belongs approximately to the end of the first century AD. The excavations show very clearly how the first-century villa was laid out to replace the round houses of an Iron Age enclosed farmstead.

One key question is thus why it took families at least a generation or two to aspire to this new style of architecture. Equally striking, however, is the fact that several of the first-century villas are characterised by the presence of bath-houses. The Roman habit of social bathing required both a sophisticated architecture and a developed knowledge of social customs. The construction of baths at villas like Eccles, Minster-in-Thanet, Wingham and Northfleet thus illustrates how deeply their owners had been imbued with new

social values (ill. 5.14).

The distribution of the earlier villas is also striking. Whilst one might have expected them to cluster around the emergent *civitas* centre at Canterbury, there is no evidence for them in its immediate vicinity, the nearest being perhaps at Wingham, Ickham or South Street near Herne Bay. That at Faversham is probably more closely associated with *Durolevum*. Villas are mainly clustered in the west of the modern county with groups in the Medway and Darent valleys in the hinterland of Rochester and Crayford respectively. It seems likely that we should associate these two clusters with different valley-based Iron Age communities. In this sense, their development suggests a strong continuity of social patterns, illustrating that Canterbury's existence did not bring a unity to the new *civitas*. More subtle

5.11 The fourth-century bath house at Eccles, one of the larger ones in a Kent villa. The range to the right contains a *piscina* or swimming pool. That to the left houses a standard suite of cold, warm and hot rooms with plunge baths.

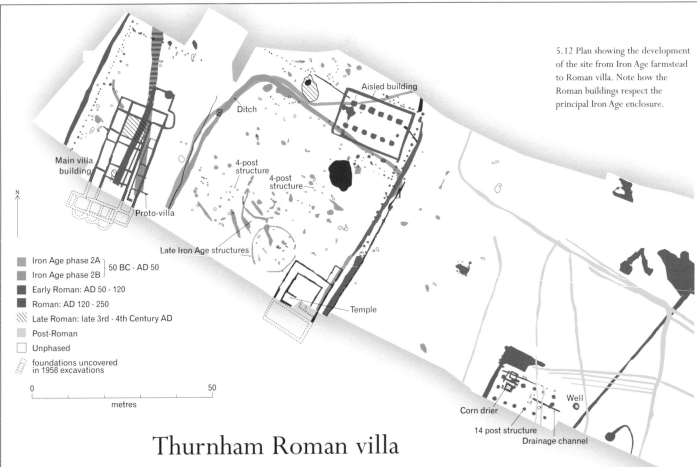

5.12 Plan showing the development of the site from Iron Age farmstead to Roman villa. Note how the Roman buildings respect the principal Iron Age enclosure.

Aisled building

Ditch

Main villa building

Proto-villa

4-post structure

4-post structure

Late Iron Age structures

Iron Age phase 2A
Iron Age phase 2B } 50 BC - AD 50

Early Roman: AD 50 - 120

Roman: AD 120 - 250

Late Roman: late 3rd - 4th Century AD

Post-Roman

Unphased

foundations uncovered in 1958 excavations

0 ————————— 50
metres

Temple

Well

Corn drier

14 post structure

Drainage channel

Thurnham Roman villa

5.13 The aisled building. Such structures were similar in scale to great medieval halls, with pairs of enormous posts to support tall roofs. They probably served some communal function.

The term villa is used to describe a variety of rural sites that adopted Roman architectural forms. They vary from palatial residences to well-appointed farms, with the latter being more typical. Tucked beneath the north Downs on the edge of the Weald, the villa at Thurnham is one such site. Originally discovered in the nineteenth century, then partly

dug when the Maidstone by-pass was built in 1958, it was more fully explored during the construction of the Channel Tunnel Rail Link (Pirie 1961; Oxford Archaeological Unit 2001). Like many such sites, its origins lie in an enclosed Iron Age farmstead, here with at least three substantial round houses.

Soon after the Roman conquest, a modest Roman-style house was constructed to one side of the earlier focus, within a newly constructed enclosure. The house is only partly preserved and, although modest, had used new modes of display, including painted wall plaster. At the front of the villa enclosure was a probable temple, although this identification is tentative as it has not been fully explored and no votive material has been identified. Early in the second century AD the first villa building was replaced by one on a larger scale, constructed in stone. This evolved through additions into a house with corridors on either façade, and a bath suite at one end.

5.14 The main villa building. The central range of rooms has a corridor to either side. Beneath that to the left can be seen the foundations of the first-century proto-villa.

The adoption of Roman-style bathing and living in a house with individual suites of rooms marks a significant social development with the inhabitants, whose way of living now identified them with the dominant elite culture of the Roman world.

Beyond the house, the excavations also provided excellent evidence for the adjacent farm. This included two large aisled halls, one within the enclosure, the other some distance to the east. Such buildings are often seen as of less significance than the main dwellings, and are sometimes dismissed as barns. This is a mistake, for although that to the east is clearly associated with agriculture, as it contains a so-called corn-drying oven, that within the enclosure was a majestic structure, comparable with a major medieval barn and associated with domestic evidence. It is best interpreted as a key building in the settlement, not a mere barn. Like other parts of the complex, it does not seem to have survived far into the fourth century.

evidence for this social distinction between the east and west of the modern county is provided by the patterns of use of household pottery, which show differences in the types used throughout the Roman period (Pollard 1988, 197).

In concentrating on the villa sites, we tend to ignore an array of other rural settlements. A glance at the map of known find-spots of Roman material from Kent shows that it was very widely settled and this is confirmed by the results of many of the evaluation excavations that have been undertaken in recent years. Some of these finds are probably from the margins of sites that would be recognised as villas if they were more extensive, but most derive from ordinary rural settlements that characterised much of the Romano-British countryside and typically comprised modest timber buildings. Even though these are difficult to understand through limited excavation, they are key to any understanding of settlement patterns. Most probably represent small-scale farming, whether by independent peasants or tenants of larger landowners. They certainly cannot be dismissed as mere subsistence farmers since the very presence of artefacts like Roman pottery implies that they were integrated into the provincial economy, albeit on a modest scale. Such ordinary sites are more typical of rural society than the larger villas.

Excavations at some of these sites provide insights into their character. At Bower Road, Smeeth, work in advance of the construction of the Channel Tunnel Rail Link revealed good evidence for the nature of one such site (Oxford Wessex Archaeology Joint Venture 2004). In the initial phases there were only ditches and pottery confirming Iron Age and earlier Roman activity. During the second century a timber building was constructed and this was replaced by a more substantial farmstead, built in the later second century but continuing in use into the fourth. Economic evidence from the site demonstrates that it operated as a mixed farm. Comparable sites of Iron Age to early Roman date have also recently been indicated at a variety of other sites, including

Charing (Keller 1990), Herne Bay (Hounsell and Ralph 2001), Harrietsham (Canterbury Archaeological Trust 1998), Tottingham Farm, Aylesford (Hutchings 1999), Saltwood (Williams 2003, 229) and Bradbourne House, East Malling (Ward 1997). The nature of these sites varies, but at all a mixed farming economy is likely to have been practised. Elsewhere more specialised economic functions may have given rise to different types of settlement. For instance, in the estuarine coastal areas or the north Kent Marshes and Romney Marsh, seasonal occupation probably allowed the pasturing of sheep and cattle as well as salt production (Cunliffe 1988). Associated settlement sites are poorly known, but one at Lydd has recently provided some evidence for an economy based on salt production (Priestley-Bell 2000).

If the rural evidence raises interesting questions, so too does the growth of urban centres. The principal problem is that the main sites lie beneath modern towns with the result that their earliest layers are extremely difficult to excavate on a large scale. At Canterbury (*Durovernum Cantiacorum*) a sequence of excavations since the 1940s has provided important evidence about early development. Part of the Iron Age settlement, founded at the end of the first century BC beside a crossing of the Stour, has been revealed by excavations in the Marlowe area (Blockley *et al.* 1995) and most recently in the Blackfriars excavation (Bennett *et al.* 2003). It included a series of round houses and an enclosure which is little different from other later Iron Age sites in south-east England, except for the concentration of goods traded sporadically from the Roman Empire. The character of the site does not seem to have been much affected by the Roman Conquest, although there is arguably evidence for a short-lived military fort (Bennett *et al.*, 1982, 25-30). This would suggest that those in power within the new *civitas* continued to live much as before and were not aspiring to develop a Roman style town until two or three generations after the Conquest. Evidence at sites elsewhere,

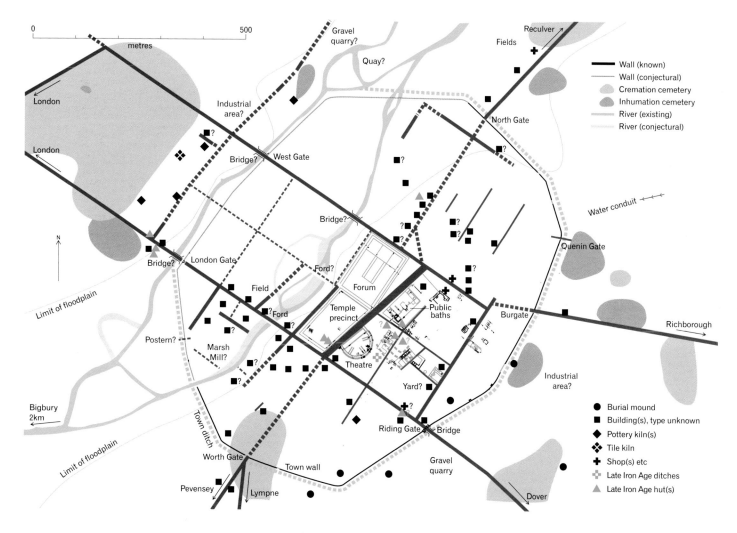

Labels within the map:

London
London
Industrial area?
Gravel quarry?
Quay?
Reculver
Fields
North Gate
Bridge?
West Gate
Water conduit
Quenin Gate
Bridge?
Bridge?
N
Forum
Burgate
London Gate
Ford?
Public baths
Field
Temple precinct
Limit of floodplain
Ford
Postern?
Marsh Mill?
Theatre
Yard?
Richborough
Industrial area?
Bigbury 2km
Town ditch
Riding Gate
Bridge
Worth Gate
Town wall
Gravel quarry
Pevensey
Lympne
Dover

metres 0 – 500

Legend:
Wall (known)
Wall (conjectural)
Cremation cemetery
Inhumation cemetery
River (existing)
River (conjectural)

● Burial mound
■ Building(s), type unknown
♦ Pottery kiln(s)
✚ Tile kiln
✚ Shop(s) etc
▦ Late Iron Age ditches
▲ Late Iron Age hut(s)

5.15 Overall plan of Roman Canterbury showing the street layout and principal buildings.

like Verulamium (Niblett 2001) and Silchester (Fulford and Timby 2000), indicates that this pattern was not unique to Canterbury. We should, however, be cautious, because there have not yet been substantial excavations in the presumed forum area of Canterbury where we might expect to find the earliest evidence for monumental buildings.

Major development at the centre of the town seems to date to *c.* AD 80-100 (ill. 5.15). The first buildings are timber but too little survives for us to obtain full details of their plans. Contrary to the expected stereotype, the Roman town does not develop with a strictly orthogonal street grid, and the layout of the streets suggests piecemeal

development, which does not start until after the beginning of the second century. The elements of planning that have been identified raise some interesting issues (Bennett 1989). Canterbury was at the hub of a series of roads and, following classical principles of urban design, we might expect the principal approach roads to determine the town's grid. This, however, is not the case and, as Wacher has noted (1995, 191), it is the road from Dover (Margary 1955, route 1a) rather than that from Richborough (route 10) which determines part of the grid. Given the late development of Dover (below), the grid cannot have been established until the second century. Furthermore, the layout of the grid shows clearly that it was adapted to a pre-existing topography, with the late first-century theatre and temple at an angle to the Dover road. Equally, the other axis of the town seems largely determined by the route that runs along the Stour valley. If the forum and basilica are positioned in the insula usually suggested (Bennett 1989, 125), it would appear that the main approach was designed to be along this route from the north-east. Equally, although the Richborough road (Margary 1955, route 10) approaches the town heading straight towards the ford, it seems to make an awkward intersection with grid. This raises a series of interesting questions about the early development of the town, perhaps indicating that the topography was determined by important features of the pre-Roman layout.

5.16 Reconstruction of a Corinthian capital from Canterbury, carved from Marquise limestone quarried near Calais. Dating to c. AD 70-100, it comes from a classical temple similar to that of Sulis Minerva in Bath.

It was not until the early second century that we have evidence for the town acquiring a full suite of public buildings (page 169). The only first-century monumental structure for which we have good evidence is the theatre, which was constructed with an earthen bank c. AD 80-90 (Frere 1970). It lay beside a temple complex which has only been partially excavated but is likely to have been contemporaneous, given the religious contexts in which many Roman theatres were created (Gros 1996, 272-98). This central area of Canterbury has produced one of the largest and most varied collections of imported

marble veneers from Roman Britain. These, together with fragments from Corinthinian capitals (ill. 5.16), show that there were magnificent public buildings here, including a classical temple on a scale and of a quality comparable with that at Bath (Blagg 1984, 66-71). In the absence of information about the development of the forum complex, we need to be cautious in drawing conclusions about the first-century development of the town, but the early date of the theatre and temple complex, together with the manner in which it influences the later street grid, implies the presence of an important cult centre. Sanctuary sites with facilities including theatres were a common feature in Gaul (Fauduet 1993, 103) and the site at Gosbecks adjacent to Colchester provides a good parallel in Britain (Hawkes and Crummy 1995, 95-105). If we put aside our expectations of what an early Roman town should be like, it is conceivable that we should understand the early development of *Durovernum Cantiacorum* primarily as a religious sanctuary rather than as a conventional town. If this does represent a continuity from the Iron Age we might speculate that Canterbury was chosen as the *civitas* centre because the religious centre was a neutral meeting point where different tribal groups came together. Such a location would also have been an appropriate one for conducting trade with those from outside. The construction of the temple and theatre complex with its fine architecture would have represented a considerable investment of resources, but equally perhaps represented a key symbol of new unity for the *Cantiaci* and their cultural links.

The proposition that sanctuaries were important in the early development of the *civitas* draws attention to the site at Springhead (*Vagniacis*), where recent work has shown that the second- and third-century temples beside Watling Street lay adjacent to a spring that had been a focal point for a major religious complex for a considerable period (Williams 2003, 223-24) (box, pages 160-1). Although less architecturally sophisticated than the sanctuary at Canterbury this too perhaps acted as a social focus for the people of the western part of the region. A substantial associated cemetery to the south-east at Pepperhill also indicates that site was an important regional centre (Oxford Archaeological Unit 2000a). Other temples with early origins, especially that at Worth (Klein 1928) and perhaps that at Boxted (Wilson 1973, 321-22), should be reconsidered in this light. We have comparatively little information about other nucleated sites. Potentially the most important, *Durobrivae* (Rochester), has provided very little evidence to indicate its character, although there are reasonable grounds for believing that it was a late Iron Age centre that continued in occupation into the early Roman period (Burnham and Wacher 1990, 76-78).

Given the evidence for only gradual adoption of fully Roman styles of status display in the first century AD, it is worth considering the extent to which traditional modes of expression also continued. One of the more remarkable features of Roman Kent is the proliferation of burial evidence. Although this provides a marked contrast with other parts of Britain where burials are surprisingly rare, formal burial seems to have been used for only a relatively small proportion of the population. This implies that only the more important people in the community were buried in a way that is archaeologically recoverable (Millett 1995, 121-31). The practice of elaborate burial is well attested in the later Iron Age (see Champion this volume) and there is considerable evidence that this tradition continued and evolved during the early Roman period. There is an unusual number of first- and second-century cremation burials from the territory that are furnished with an elaborate array of grave goods (Struck 2000, fig. 9.2). Such burials are important because they illustrate complex social customs, not only through the presentation of rich grave goods and the ashes of the deceased but also by the whole ritual of cremation and the collection of the ashes. The associated ceremonies provided important means for surviving members of the community to establish their social position after death (Pearce 2000). Even more striking is the array of elaborate funerary monuments that occur in Kent, including earthen barrows, mausolea and enclosed cemeteries (Struck 2000). These continue through the Roman period and are commonly associated with other important settlement foci. Thus there is an important group of barrows around the south-eastern edge of Canterbury, while the spectacular barrow at Holborough (Jessup 1955) lay only just across the Medway from the Eccles villa and close to another at Snodland. Best known from excavation is the fourth-century monumental circular mausoleum constructed on the site of a long-lived cemetery beside the villa at Keston (Philp *et al.* 1991; 1999). These monuments all made important and visible statements in the landscape about those who had been important in society. That they were probably key in establishing and maintaining powerful dynasties is suggested by the continued reverence shown to the graves of the late Iron Age warriors at Brisley Farm, Ashford (above pages 124, 126). Like sanctuary sites, such visible monuments are in the same tradition as those seen in parts of *Gallia Belgica* and *Germania*, perhaps stressing the cultural links of the *Cantiaci* with their continental neighbours.

The established *civitas*

The developments in the decades around the end of first century AD set the pattern for the subsequent growth of the *civitas*. The following years saw intensification of building in Roman styles, as well as the rapidly growing use of a range of objects in everyday life, even on the least sophisticated rural sites. This all provides evidence for what might loosely be described as economic prosperity. It is perhaps this growth that also led to some significant shifts in settlement patterns. If the first-century pattern seems generally to have been typified by a continuity of Iron Age patterns we can detect new trends from the second century onwards. In particular, there are strong indications that nucleated settlements beside the

Springhead

5.17 Springhead in the late second century. Although details of the road layout differ from the plan opposite, it provides a good overall impression of the likely character of the site.

The sanctuary at Springhead, *Vagniacis*, situated where Watling Street crosses the head of the Ebbsfleet valley, is now the best-explored such site in Britain. After some exploration during the nineteenth century, it was the subject of a series of excavations by the Gravesend Historical Society through the 1950s-1980s (Detsicas 1983, 60). Most recently, extensive excavations have been completed in advance of the construction of the Channel Tunnel Rail Link (Williams 2003, 222; to add Wessex Archaeology re CTRL forthcoming).

Sanctuaries are well known in Gaul, and like many of them, Springhead is focused on natural springs. In the late Iron Age a pond below them was enclosed by a substantial ditch, apparently designed to exclude people, but a ceremonial way was also created to lead visitors up the valley toward the springs. This provides clear evidence for an Iron Age origin although its monumentalisation did not occur until after the Roman invasion. There is no convincing evidence for a Roman fort and an enclosure sometimes seen as

military is more likely civilian. The site seems to have developed as a major religious focus in the first and second centuries AD, declining thereafter. At least seven temples were constructed on the southern side of the pool at the point where the Roman road turns to cross the valley. They are all in the so-called Romano-Celtic tradition and were associated with a varied series of votive deposits.

The temples acted as a focus for the development of a settlement with the construction of a series of houses, shops and workshops along the road frontage and a bathhouse set back from it. These facilities undoubtedly served the needs of those passing along the road, but the sanctuary was most likely their *raison d' être*. The focal role of the site is also reflected in the growth of cemeteries nearby. A monumental mortuary enclosure including stone sarcophagi lay just to the south-east of the site and a substantial cemetery containing more than 500 burials was excavated during the construction of the Channel Tunnel Rail Link.

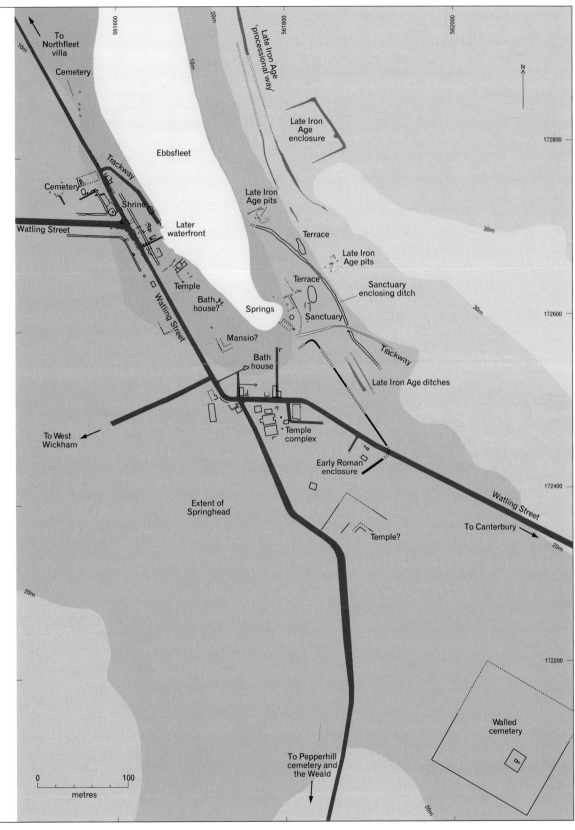

To Northfleet villa

Cemetery

Cemetery

Trackway

Shrine

Watling Street

Later waterfront

Ebbsfleet

Watling Street

Temple

Bath house?

Springs

Mansio?

Bath house

To West Wickham

Extent of Springhead

Temple complex

Early Roman enclosure

Temple?

To Pepperhill cemetery and the Weald

Late Iron Age 'processional way'

Late Iron Age enclosure

Late Iron Age pits

Terrace

Late Iron Age pits

Terrace

Sanctuary

Sanctuary enclosing ditch

Trackway

Late Iron Age ditches

Watling Street

To Canterbury

Walled cemetery

N

561600
561800
562000

10m

20m

10m

30m

30m

20m

20m

20m

172800

172600

172400

172200

0   100

metres

5.18 The sanctuary site developed around a spring as major focus of activity by the late Iron Age. In Roman times it became an important stopping point along the road from Canterbury to London, but its primary function was religious.

Roman roads were becoming more significant.

Such minor roadside sites are often difficult to understand because they were generally characterised by relatively insubstantial timber buildings that can only be understood in large-scale excavations. There have long been indications that the larger roadside sites like Springhead prospered from the second century onwards, although recent work suggests that this site was in decline by the third century (Williams 2003, 225). The large cremation cemetery at Ospringe, presumably associated with *Durolevum*, also seems to have had its *floruit* in the second and third centuries (Philpott 1991, 22). Similarly, the large settlement that grew up at Richborough probably reached its full extent at this period and there are hints of growth and development at a number of other important settlements like Dover. Such places fulfilled a variety of economic and social roles, acting as centres for communities living within a distance that could be covered in a day or so by foot. As such they formed a network that linked society together.

Until recently there has not been much good evidence from the smaller roadside settlements, but several excavations over the past decade have begun to provide important new information about their variety. One site at Monkton on Thanet was strung out alongside a sunken trackway but seems to have been relatively shortlived (box, adjacent). Excavation uncovered an array of unusual sunken-floored buildings which are difficult to parallel elsewhere in Roman Britain (Canterbury Archaeological Trust *et al.* 1996; Williams 2003, 227-28). Not far distant on the Roman road running north-east down the Stour valley from Canterbury a more extensive roadside site has been excavated at Hersden, revealing a complex plan and occupation which started during the later Iron Age. In the Roman period a planned settlement with regular house-plots and their associated burial grounds was laid out facing the road (Cross and Rady 2002; Williams 2003, 227).

Perhaps the best understood of these sites is

Monkton

The landscape of Roman Kent was dominated by agricultural settlements, mostly relatively unassuming farmsteads rather than villas. Such sites have not been as fully or as extensively explored as the larger or more sophisticated settlements, but there is enough evidence to suggest that they took a variety of different forms and fulfilled a range of economic roles. Generally, it has only been through development-led excavations that evidence about these sites has been forthcoming. On Thanet the overall distribution of sites can be seen fairly clearly, but there is only occasional information about the character of the rural sites. Road construction at Monkton has provided good evidence about one nucleated site, although it is unlikely to be typical given their huge variety (Canterbury Archaeological Trust *et al.* 1996; Clark forthcoming).

Unlike many rural sites which were individual farmsteads, this settlement spread out along a trackway, represented by a sunken way. Only a strip of land along the north side of this lane has been excavated and this revealed a sequence of enclosures and structures facing on to it, an arrangement not untypical of rural sites excavated elsewhere. The main difference comes in the type of buildings found as they mostly comprised rectangular sunken-featured buildings of a type more commonly seen in early medieval settlements. They are clearly Roman in date as the whole settlement seems to have been abandoned in the late second century. Amongst the abandonment debris was a large collection of agricultural tools, presumably indicating the nature of the site.

Because the excavation involved an unusually extensive exploration of the margins of the site, it also revealed a small shrine just beyond the edge of the settlement.

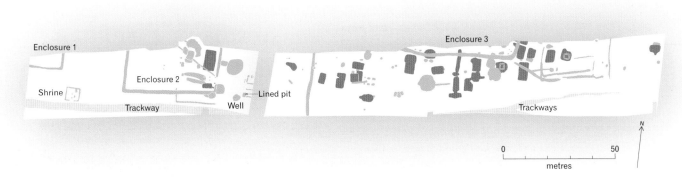

Enclosure 1

Shrine

Enclosure 2

Trackway

Well

Lined pit

Enclosure 3

Trackways

0   metres   50

N

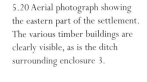

5.19 The buildings, grouped around a series of enclosures to the north of a trackway, perhaps indicate different social groups. A shrine is located beside the track towards the western limit of the site.

5.20 Aerial photograph showing the eastern part of the settlement. The various timber buildings are clearly visible, as is the ditch surrounding enclosure 3.

5.21 The sunken areas of some of the buildings. These structures presumably had earth and timber walls, with the sunken areas being the remains the floors.

that recently excavated at Westhawk Farm near Ashford (box, adjacent). It lies at the junction where the Roman road that follows the Stour valley up from Canterbury meets that running west from Lympne along the edge of the Weald. The site covers more than 20 hectares and includes several regular house plots on one side of the principal road and an open area with a probable shrine on the other. Its growth begins in the later first century and it continued in occupation into the fourth century, but seems to have declined in size after the about AD 250. There was a variety of productive activities on the site, including small-scale iron-working (Booth and Lawrence 2000; Booth 2001). This site raises a series of interesting questions about rural development in the middle of the Roman period, not least how many more similar sites may lie undiscovered. The overall character of the Westhawk Farm settlement appears unpretentious and largely dominated by timber buildings, although we should remain very conscious of the magnificent timber buildings with insubstantial foundations that dominated the architecture of this region in the later Middle Ages (Pearson 1994).

In common with some such settlements elsewhere in Britain and Gaul there is evidence for a formal planned layout which must imply some communal or imposed authority. Similarly, as at a number of sites, a temple provides the only evidence of public buildings (Millett 2001). In their preliminary discussion of the site Booth and Lawrence (2000, 481) raise the issue of whether the Westhawk Farm settlement might have fulfilled some function in controlling the exploitation of the Wealden iron (cf. below). Although it is well placed to have had some role in this industry it is also important to note the accumulating evidence for similar settlement agglomerations from across the north-western provinces, suggesting that they represent a more general economic phenomenon.

A key feature of these sites is a general absence

Westhawk Farm

The roadside settlement at Westhawk Farm near Ashford was unknown before its discovery as a result of excavations in advance of housing development in the late 1990s. It has been the subject of extensive excavation and an even larger-scale geophysical survey (Williams 2003, 225; Booth, Bingham and Lawrence forthcoming). This means that we have a better understanding of its layout than almost any other similar site in Roman Britain. It covers an area of more than 20 hectares and is a typical low-density roadside settlement. It seems to have developed as the economy of the Roman province expanded. In common with other settlements in Kent and in contrast to those in other regions, it seems to have flourished principally in the third century with decline in the fourth. Its development was intimately related to the importance of the Roman road from Canterbury to the port at Lympne, and, although there is no evidence that it was directly involved in the management of the iron-works in the Weald, its economic prosperity was partly determined by their rise and decline.

The layout shows that the settlement was partly a planned development, as there is clear evidence for the division of the area on the northern side of the road into regular plots. These enclosures contained a variety of ordinary timber houses and associated settlement features. In the area excavated, round houses of traditional Iron Age form outnumbered rectangular buildings, but overall the evidence suggests that the site was relatively undifferentiated socially, with ordinary families, presumably of indigenous people, living and working in an ordinary place. Indeed, it is the evidence that it provides for the lives of the common people which makes Westhawk important.

At the centre of the area investigated there is an area unoccupied by houses that can perhaps be seen as a central place for people to gather (A). It was not monumentalised, and is best compared with a village green rather than a market square. Situated to one side was a rectangular enclosure, which contained a structure in the shape of an elongated octagon orientated on the south-eastern entrance to the enclosure. This is interpreted as a temple or shrine (Booth 2001). As at other such sites, this temple is the only public building so far identified and appears to have been indigenous in form.

Excavated area ←

Excavated area ←

0   100
metres

N

5.22 Geophysical survey of the settlement. Note the extensive settlement along the road with a regular pattern of property boundaries to the north. To the south the plan is more complex, with side streets as well as other settlement enclosures.

5.23 The excavated area. There are various forms of building in enclosures beside the road. In open area A a rectangular enclosure contains an octagonal structure best understood as a temple. As in other similar settlements, communal or public buildings are so far absent.

A

A

Prehistoric
AD 43 - 70
AD 70 - 150
AD 150 - 200
AD 200 - 250
AD 250 - 350
AD 350 - 400
Post-Roman

0   50
metres

N

of higher-status dwellings and the presence of evidence for craft and industry, as well as frequently for small shrines. In some instances the settlements are located relatively close to a villa. This has led to the suggestion that their inhabitants may have been dependent on the villa owner (Millett 1990, 208-10). The general absence of evidence for social differentiation in them certainly points to occupation by a workforce that may have been dependent on a landowner, and the provision of shrines is reminiscent of later estate-villages that were given basic communal facilities. The site at Weshawk Farm is earlier in date than many of the other known sites and the absence of any known villa locally probably suggests a different origin, arguably developing from the existing social focus in this area as represented by the late Iron Age burials here and at Brisley Farm nearby (see above).

The structural evidence from another roadside settlement at Ickham is very much less easy to understand, since it was rescued during quarrying under difficult circumstances in the early 1970s (Bennett, Riddler and Sparey-Green forthcoming). It lay beside the Little Stour river, close to the ancient coastline on an otherwise unknown road, about half-way between Canterbury and Richborough. The three excavated water-mills have been widely discussed (Young 1981; Spain 1984, 119-22), but the other structures are little understood. Nevertheless, the site clearly had a major industrial role and evidence was recovered for the working of lead, pewter, copper and iron,

as well as woodworking, tanning and flax-processing. The site overlay an Iron Age farmstead and was certainly developing from the second century AD, but apparently had its *floruit* during the fourth century. Although the presence of military metalwork has led to the suggestion that the site was under the control of the army (Young 1981; Detsicas 1983, 177), the material may perhaps have been solely the product of scrap recycling (Bennett pers. comm.). Ickham lies close to a villa and may perhaps conform to the pattern of other nucleated later Roman settlements in Britain, which could have been developed under the control of important local landowners (Millett 1990, 205-11).

The growth of settlement agglomerations on the road system also raises the question of the character and functions of the principal urban foci. As in the earlier period we have little evidence from Rochester (*Durobrivae*), except that it was one of the places to receive defences in the later second or early third century, perhaps indicating that it held some importance for local administration (cf. Burnham and Wacher 1990,

5.24 The Roman town wall of Rochester, built in the earlier third century. The regular Roman *petit appareil* of Kentish ragstone is clearly distinguishable from later stone- and brickwork above. Town walls at that time were probably as much to express a town's status as for defence.

77-79) (ill. 5.24). As the walls enclosed an area of only about 7.5 hectares it seems unlikely to have been a very major population centre. More important for understanding the role of this town is surely its focal position within the region and its function as a river crossing and a port. Not only was there a significant group of villas in the Medway valley (see below), but the marshes at the estuary of the river and on the Cliffe peninsula were also the focus of important pottery and salt extraction industries (Monaghan 1987; Pollard 1988, 173-77). The exploitation of such agriculturally marginal areas for manufacturing is widespread in this period.

Pottery manufacture in this area has its origins in the Iron Age. Production seems to have started off on a modest scale, but through the first century AD a diversity of pottery was made in the area, with some of the material achieving a wide Thameside distribution. Around AD 120 there was a major change in the output of the Cliffe peninsula with the beginnings of production of one fabric of so-called black burnished ware 2 (BB2), the inspiration for which originally came from Dorset (Williams 1977). By the later second century BB2 was very widely distributed, dominating assemblages in London and spreading up the east coast to be amongst the principal pot types used on the northern frontier (ill. 5.25). The extent, however, to which the Kent products as opposed to those from Colchester were more distributed is not known. Indeed, why these unprepossessing ceramics achieved such a widespread distribution is unclear, but it seems most likely that their transport was incidental to other forms of trade; whether it can be associated with cereal grain being supplied to the army is not at all certain (cf. Pollard 1988, 198-99).

Whether or not it acted as an administrative centre for this part of the *civitas*, Rochester was clearly key to the social network of the Medway valley and thus presumably gained from control of trade passing from there into the Thames estuary. An indication of the scale of the trade originating from further up the Medway valley is provided by

5.25 Black burnished ware 2 cooking pots made in the Cliffe marshes and around Colchester from *c.* AD 120 were not only used locally but also taken up the east coast in large quantities, provisioning the Roman army on Hadrian's Wall and beyond.

♦ Kiln

▨ Distribution of black burnished ware 2 pottery

the distribution of Kentish ragstone. Probably quarried in the Maidstone area, it was used widely for major building projects, including the walls of Roman London and the late Roman coastal fortifications at Reculver, Richborough and Bradwell in Essex (Williams 1971, 172; Pearson 2002). A second-century barge containing a cargo of this stone, probably quarried near Allington on the Medway, sank near Blackfriars in London (Marsden 1994, 33-95) (ill. 5.26).

Canterbury was a much larger centre than Rochester, with some 53 hectares enclosed within its later third-century walls. Excavation of a fair

5.26 The Blackfriars barge, which sank in the Thames in the mid-second century, carrying Kentish ragstone from the Medway. It was a modest trading vessel probably typical of those operating up and down the Kent coast.

number of houses shows that it developed to become a significant centre for habitation. Although the majority of these appear to have been relatively modest in scale, recent investigations at Whitefriars have revealed much of a large and sophisticated courtyard house rebuilt in stone in the middle of the Roman period (Bennett *et al.* 2003, 193-94). Generally, however, there are few indications from finds such as mosaics to suggest any very large population of the wealthiest in the province. Civic buildings continued to be developed, with the public baths constructed in the early decades of the second century (Blockley *et al.* 1995), whilst the theatre was rebuilt about a century later (Frere 1970). This suggests that the town continued to act as a major focus for the *civitas* although, as in several other Romano-British towns, there is comparatively little evidence for commercial activity either within or around the town (Blagg 1995). For instance, as at other *civitas* centres, the production of pottery which began in the vicinity of the town in the first century seems to have ceased during the second century, as larger rural producers became dominant (Pollard 1988, 178-79). This contrasts with the industrial centre nearby at Ickham (see above).

The ports at Richborough and Dover also clearly developed as major harbour settlements. At Richbrough recent fieldwork has revealed something of the plan of the town (Millett and Wilmott 2003), whilst long-term work at Dover has shown that there was a major settlement outside the fort, within which was the impressive 'painted house', partially preserved within the rampart of the the late Roman fort (Philp 1989). Coastal and estuarine sites clearly had significant harbours although the evidence for them remains slight. Most interesting in this respect is the recently excavated site at Northfleet near the mouth of the Ebbsfleet, 2 kilometres north of Springhead. Occupation started in the later Iron Age and a structure, conventionally seen as a villa with a bathhouse, was constructed in the second century AD beside a substantial oak wharf. The

facilities were expanded during the later second century and there is good evidence for its use for trade down to the end of the Roman period. Evidence for various minor crafts and industries were uncovered during the excavation, and also evidence for a hard-standing below high-water level on which boats could have been beached (Williams 2003, 230-31; Foreman, pers. comm.). This site may best be understood as a small harbour and trading site rather than as a conventional villa and it is perhaps typical of what we should expect at other coastal inlets.

Despite the probability of frequent and close contacts across the English Channel there is comparatively little evidence for large-scale trade of common everyday commodities. For instance, although there is more imported pottery in Kent than found elsewhere in Britain, the numbers of pots involved seem to have been very small and little Romano-British pottery was exported (Fulford 1977, 35-62; Pollard 1988, 198-200). Evidence for cross-Channel traders is, however, provided by a series of altars from a shrine at Colijnsplaat near the mouth of the Rhine in the Netherlands. In addition to four dedicated by people who describe themselves as traders with Britain, one calls himself a *negotiator* [merchant] *Cantianus [et?] Geserecanuus* (Stuart and Bogaers 2001, 59, A9), comfirming the regularity of the trading link between the Rhine, Boulogne and Kent. Further direct evidence for seaborne trade is provided by the cargoes of second- and third-century samian pottery periodically brought up in fishing nets along this coast. The best-known wreck site is at Pudding Pan Rock, Herne Bay (Smith 1909). Recent systematic survey, together with an analysis of old finds, indicates that there is probably a series of Roman wrecks, not just one (Walsh 2000, 57, fig. 2).

The pattern of villa development established in the first century continues thereafter (ill. 5.9). The dearth of sites in east Kent persisted, with those that did develop being at some distance from Canterbury. The main concentrations continued to be in the Medway and Darent valleys and it is here too that those with more elaborate features like mosaics are mostly found. There is also a group in the area of the Swale in the hinterland of *Durolevum*, where it has been suggested that a system of regularly sized estates was laid out, although the evidence for formal organisation of the landscape is as yet inconclusive (Wilkinson 2000; Williams 2003, 231). Throughout the Roman occupation, villas are wholly absent from the Weald, except around the margins. The clustered distribution and the remarkable lack of villas in the vicinity of Canterbury is interesting and deserves explanation, especially because where there has been detailed survey work, in areas like Thanet, the landscape was densely occupied with rural sites, mostly farms that cannot really be called villas (Perkins 2001). Colin Andrews (2001, 25) has suggested that the absence of such evidence for Romanisation may have resulted from the depressive effect of the Roman military in the form of the *Classis Britannica* and the later fort garrisons. Whilst this suggestion is attractive it probably places too much emphasis on a comparatively small number of troops (see below). Another explanation is that there was a preference in the area around Canterbury for living in or near the town rather than in the countryside (Blagg 1982, 56). This also seems unlikely, given how little evidence we have for prestigious town houses, but this should not disguise the underlying point, that the absence of villas represents an important cultural choice, not the absence of an ability to invest in buildings.

In this context the character of the villas is also notable. Although there are large and developed villas (see below), others, like those recently excavated at Maidstone (Houliston 1999), Minster (Perkins and Parfitt 2004) and Thurnham (Oxford Archaeology Unit 2000b), are comparatively limited in scale and pretensions. Thurnham is not untypical with a modest corridor house and bath suite (begun in the late first century AD) facing on to a yard containing other impressive buildings, in the form of an aisled hall and a possible shrine,

beyond which lay the agricultural facilities. These prosperous structures lack evidence of architectural elaboration and this perhaps indicates that there was little competition between owners, at least in terms of building. The range of site types includes both the halls and those made up of multiple dwelling units (Smith 1997). These different architectural forms are difficult to understand in detail but they do suggest that villas were generally not simply occupied by individual families. In some at least several different social groups may have lived side by side in separate accommodation (e.g. Darenth or Eccles – Smith 1997, 156, 293). This raises difficult and interesting questions about the nature of social organisation, although the suggestion that such sites in multiple occupancy provide evidence for particular systems of inheritance remains problematic (Millett 1990, 197-99).

Other characteristics of the excavated villas are also important. Firstly there are few villa mosaics, even from the later period when they are more common elsewhere in Britain. Secondly, it has been observed that formal dining rooms (*triclinia*) are also uncommon (Black 1987, 53, 73). These features may suggest that the owners of the usual run of Kent villas were not participating in the social routine of entertaining guests to formal dinners at their rural homes as is generally assumed to have been typical in the later Empire. By contrast the number of villas with bathhouses attached shows that bathing in the Roman style did play a significant role in the lives of people in the region. This, together with the manner in which villas cluster in areas like the Darent valley, indicates that they were built for show, in order to make an impression from a distance and to demonstrate that their owners were members of the landowning elite which came to dominate the later Roman Empire.

There are a few larger and more impressive villas that do stand comparison with the best from other parts of Britain but these are only found far distant from Canterbury, mostly in the western part of the county. In particular, Lullingstone,

Eccles, Darenth and Folkestone are impressive sites. The villas at Lullingstone and Darenth, close together in the Darent valley, provide insights into the most elaborate. At Darenth the villa evolved from the early second to the fourth century, developing a gradually more elaborate plan (Philp 1984, 72-131) (ill. 5.27). In its most developed form the villa comprised a series of separate ranges of buildings, surely indicating multiple occupancy. Attempts to label buildings with particular functions like workers' accommodation (Black 1987, 52-53) are difficult to sustain, and it is better to look at it as an integrated complex made up from a series of dwelling houses. These were constructed around a trapezoidal courtyard that was given a strong element of axial symmetry as the complex developed. This made the central house the focal point of the architectural ensemble, at the head of which lay a grand ornamental pond. This layout is greatly enhanced by its landscape setting. Despite this elaborate architecture the villa has no single major reception room and even more curiously lacks mosaic floors.

By contrast the villa at Lullingstone further south down the valley is well known for its art (ill. 5.28). It comprises a remarkable complex of structures set on a south-east-facing slope overlooking the river (Meates 1979; 1987). It was excavated from 1949 to 1961 and is now ripe for a much fuller reconsideration than can be provided here. There is evidence for an underlying Iron Age settlement, with the Roman villa probably constructed c. AD 100. The early structure is modest, the only unusual feature being a cellar in the north-east corner. Such cellars seem very likely to have been constructed for religious purposes and, indeed, this is one of a cluster of similar structures found in northern Kent (Perring 1989). Not long after the construction of the main villa a circular building was put up on a terrace immediately to the north. Although generally interpreted as a shrine there is little evidence to support this idea. Subsequently, the house underwent a number of modifications,

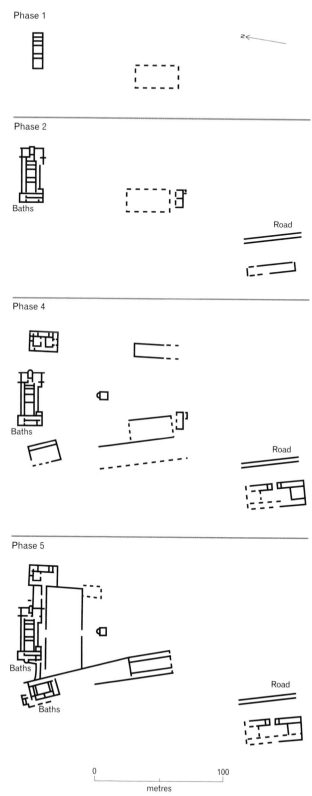

5.27 A simplified sequence for the Darenth villa from the late first to the late fourth century.
A modest structure, similar in plan to Eccles (ill. 5.10), becomes the core of the principal house and has a bath suite added at its west end. Other buildings are constructed in front. In contrast to Thurnham (ill. 5.11) the Darenth complex is given an architectural unity with a trapezoid plan making the main house the focus of the ensemble. As with other villas, the various buildings probably housed separate social groups: in particular note the second bath house to the west screened from the main courtyard by an enclosure wall.

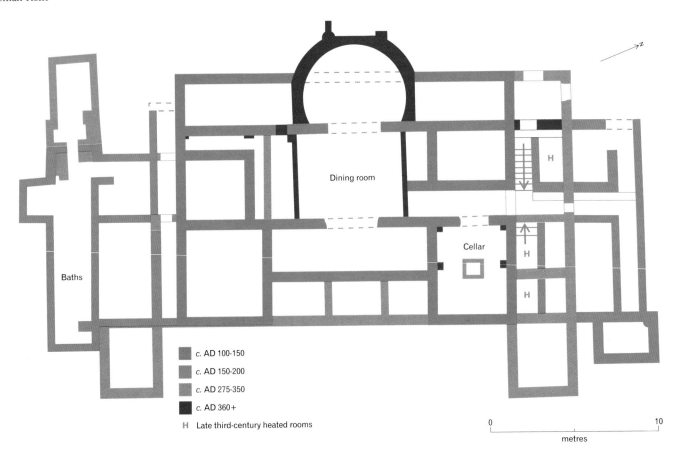

Baths

Dining room

Cellar

c. AD 100-150
c. AD 150-200
c. AD 275-350
c. AD 360+
H   Late third-century heated rooms

0   10
metres

5.28 The development of the main villa building at Lullingstone. It underwent various changes, culminating in the provision of a large central dining room with an apse. The late second-century additions at the north end of the villa were replaced in later remodelling. Some other rooms were also modified.

including the addition of a range of baths during the later second and third centuries. From this period too we have the fine wall-paintings of water nymphs in the cellar (Meates 1987, 8-9), as well as a very unusual pair of imported Greek marble portrait busts later deposited there (Toynbee 1964, 59-63). The busts were perhaps associated with the veneration of ancestors. There are other indications of religious activity from the earlier phases of the building. A very unusual hoard of ingots and a circular casting certainly appear to have been carefully buried as a foundation deposit. The ingots are in a very lead-rich copper alloy and there is some suggestion that they might represent melted-down statuary (Meates 1979, pl. XVIIID; 1987, 78-82). Similarly the pit interpreted by the excavators as relating to the tanning of leather (Meates 1979, pl. XXIID) may much more likely be associated with the so-called 'structured deposition' of animal remains now commonly related to Iron Age and Roman

religious practice.

At the beginning of the fourth century a mausoleum in a form like that of a Romano-Celtic temple was added to the terrace above the house. This contained a pair of burials, one of which was robbed in the later fourth century. That which survives intact, a male in his mid-twenties, had been packed in gypsum and placed in a lead coffin. This rite, sometimes erroneously associated with Christianity, was widespread amongst the elite in fourth-century Britain (Philpott 1991, 90-96). Scattered bones believed to derive from the robbed grave came from a woman, again in her twenties. The mausoleum also contained some very fine grave goods. In addition to a pair of flagons, one in bronze, there were glass vessels, a gaming set and a box inlaid with bone (Meates 1979, 127-32). The mausoleum must surely have been built for the burial of former owners of the villa, especially given the way in which the structure dominates the site, sitting on its terrace above. The excavator interpreted the structure as a temple-mausoleum, but despite the form of the plan the term does not seem very satisfactory, as major tombs were by definition places for paying homage to the gods and to one's ancestors. As we have seen earlier, major burial monuments are a recurrent feature of the Roman landscape in the *civitas* and it would seem that Lullingstone represents no more than the usual close association between the monuments of the living and those of the dead.

Perhaps fifty years later the house, which had remained modest by the standards of some villas, was transformed with the addition of an apse mosaic at the back of the principal reception room. The survival of this mosaic provides an usually clear insight into aristocratic culture of fourth-century Britain. The room is considered to be a dining room and it should be noted how the scenes on the floors were all designed to be viewed by those sitting in the apse. The floor of the main room is a carpet of abstract decoration, with a central panel containing busts of the four seasons surrounding Bellerophon riding Pegasus above the Chimaera. The apsidal room shows a swimming bull with Europa on its back, and above, on the threshold into the main room, is a text from Virgil (*Aeneid*, I, 50):

invida si ta[vri] vidisset ivno natatvs
ivstivs aeolias isset advsque domos

'If the jealous Juno had seen the swimming of the bull more justly would she have gone to the halls of Aeolus' (RIB, 2448.6) (ill. 5.29).

The key to appreciating the significance of this classical quotation lies in realising that its use implied both a depth of knowledge of Latin literature on behalf of the patron who commissioned the floor and also his or her assumption that guests would know enough of classical culture to appreciate this learning. By this stage in the fourth century those living at or dining in a villa like this were fully part of a classical cultural tradition that united the Roman Empire.

Finally the villa at Lullingstone has also

produced a remarkable set of wall-paintings from the last few decades of the fourth century (Meates 1987, 14-45) (ill. 5.30). These were recovered from rubble that collapsed into the cellar and derive from a room above at the north end of the villa (Meates 1979, 53). The paintings have been reconstructed to show a series of Chi-Rho monograms together with figures standing between columns and facing the viewer with their arms outstretched as *orantes* or people at prayer.

5.29 The fourth-century mosaic in the main dining room of the Lullingstone villa.

5.30 The fourth-century wall-paintings from the Lullingstone villa. The scenes were very heavily restored and there is now doubt about the reliability of this work which was influenced by early Christian paintings elsewhere.

These and other features of the paintings can be read as unique and convincing evidence that part of the villa was converted to a house church in the final decades of the fourth century (Liversidge and Weatherhead 1987).

Several key points emerge from this remarkable site. Firstly, despite the buildings themselves being relatively unpretentious, the decoration and finds give a very different impression both of the cultured lives of the inhabitants and also the combination of a fully classical taste with influences more typical of the northern provinces. It should equally be noted that although we describe the site as a villa, the range of structures present is not simply associated with farming. Throughout the use of the site there is a strong religious theme present, so the villa, in a sense, defies our modern categorisation. It is difficult to decide the extent to which the site at Lullingstone should be treated as unusual and how far fuller investigation of other sites might reveal complementary information.

When considering the best of the villa sites it is easy to forget that even the more modest represent the exception to the normal run of rural settlements that were without major stone buildings or obvious signs of display. In areas where detailed work has been undertaken it is clear that the landscape was heavily populated by families making their livings from farming and resident in such settlements. For instance, recent work on the Isle of Thanet suggests a density approaching one site per square kilometre (Perkins 2001). This is comparable to that noted in other parts of Roman Britain (Millett 1990, 183). If a similar density of sites can be postulated elsewhere in the county we can assume a substantial number of ordinary farmsteads. It is unfortunate that archaeological investigation of such sites has not often been on a scale sufficient to make them readily comprehensible, so we remain largely ignorant of their characteristics (see above page 156). The area about which we know least is certainly the Weald. Distribution maps suggest that this area may have been less densely settled and certainly the heavy clay-lands would not have been attractive for early agricultural practices, but we should be conscious of the comparative lack of archaeological field-work in the area and also that modern land use may be masking previous, more intensive utilisation of that landscape. Even if there was not intensive farming, the woodlands are certain to have been exploited. Older ideas that the production of iron may have led to large-scale deforestation (Cleere 1974, 177) ignore the long tradition of careful woodland management which seems unlikely to have been absent here, although evidence for it has not been found in analysis of the charcoal from Westhawk Farm (Booth pers. com.). An instructive comparison can be made with the iron- and pottery-producing areas in the lowlands of East Yorkshire, where the archaeological evidence shows that coppicing and pollarding were widespread. It is also interesting to note that settlement sites in that area do not generally produce Roman finds, except the pottery produced in their kilns (Halkon and Millett 1999, 221-28). In the absence of pottery manufacture, as in the Weald, we might well have a woodland population which is extremely difficult to locate archaeologically. This may explain some of the characteristics of much of the Weald in this period. Equally, it seems unlikely that the Weald was as densely occupied as other parts of the *civitas*, and we should also recall that the patterns of seasonal pasturing of pigs and other stock that may have been practised would have left little archaeological impression on the landscape.

Military aspects

One of the unusual features of the archaeology of Kent in comparison with other parts of southern Britain is the continued presence of the Roman military after the initial invasion period. It has already been noted that the harbour facilities were important both as a bridge to Gaul and for the provision of military supplies. It is in this context that we should understand the continued military

presence in the area, not as a result of any organised threat to the stability of the Roman province. The supply of the army and the suppression of piracy to ensure a secure Channel crossing provides the context for the presence of the *Classis Britannica*, the British fleet, which is well attested from Kent.

The *classis* has been the subject of a considerable literature although the evidence is comparatively limited. We have an inscribed altar dedicated to Neptune from Lympne (*Portus Lemanis*), put up by L. Aufidius Pantera, prefect of the fleet, in *c.* AD 135/45 (*RIB*, 66) (ill. 5.31). Although this is earlier than the surviving fort at Lympne (see below), it has often been taken imply the location of an earlier fort and a base for the fleet here (Cunliffe 1980, 227; see also Philp 1982). The presence of ceramic tiles stamped *CL[ASSIS]BR[ITANNICA]* (*RIB*, 2481) from the forts at Richborough and Dover, as well as Lympne, might suggest that they too were associated with the fleet (ill. 5.32). Only at Dover

5.31 The Lympne altar.
The text reads:
[NEP]TV[NO]/ARAM/L(VCIVS)
AVFIDIV(S)/PANTERA/PRAEFECT
[VS]/CLAS(SIS)BRIT(ANNICAE).
To Neptune, L. Aufidius Pantera, Prefect of the British Fleet, set up this altar.

5.32 Roof tile from Dover stamped CL.BR. – the *Classis Britannica* or British fleet. The significant distribution of such tiles in Kent indicates the active presence of the fleet in the area.

5.33 The Roman forts at Dover. The first two (early second century and *c.* AD 130) used the traditional playing card shape and are associated with the *Classis Britannica* but do not conform to a standard fort plan. The substantial stone wall of a late Roman fort with external towers was constructed over them just after AD 275.

do we have excavated remains of a fort of the appropriate period and only small numbers of tiles come from the other two sites.

At Dover (*Portus Dubris*) the first fort, constructed around the beginning of the second century, was not completed. It was replaced by a fort, *c.* 1.05 hectares in area, built around AD 130, which continued in use periodically until the early third century (Philp 1981; Wilkinson 1995) (ill. 5.33). The association of this fort with tiles stamped by the *Classis Britannica* has generally been taken as evidence that it was a fleet base, although there are reasons to reassess this conclusion. The fort is small and has an unusual layout and buildings in comparison with auxiliary forts. In the north-west quarter there are two granaries whilst in the south-east are three more or less fully excavated barrack blocks. The remainder of the fort comprises a series of strip buildings on the same alignment, most of which are also probably barracks; there are two further strip buildings just inside the northern rampart. Unlike ordinary military barracks the Dover buildings comprise eight single rooms rather than paired suites and none has identifiable officers' quarters. The fort is also unusual in lacking evidence for a headquarters building, although small-scale work in its south-west quadrant has revealed part of a possible commanding officer's house (Philp 1990). These features suggest that the fort was out of the ordinary and this raises questions

about the nature of its use. In his analysis of the fort the excavator argued that it was occupied by a unit of up to 700 men from the fleet (Philp 1981, 100-02). By contrast, in his review of the excavation report, David Breeze has suggested that a comparison of the barracks with those elsewhere implies a unit size of no more than 320 men (Breeze 1983, 374). In the absence of epigraphic evidence for the battle order of the *classis* (Starr 1941; Holder 1982, 132-33) it is difficult to evaluate what this means, as we simply do not know what to expect. A comparison with Boulogne (*Bononia* or *Gesoriacum*) is instructive. Here, there is good evidence for a much larger fort (*c.* 12 hectares) with standard types of barrack block (Seillier 1994). There is also a series of inscriptions recording the presence of

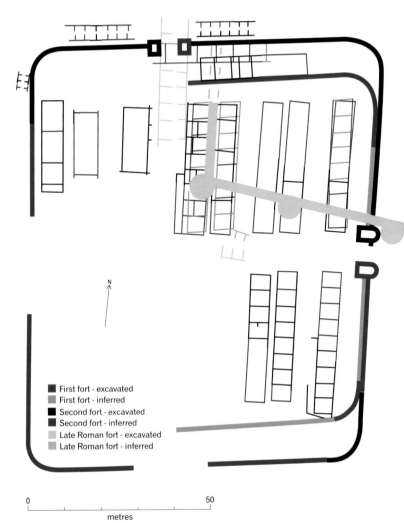

■ First fort - excavated
■ First fort - inferred
■ Second fort - excavated
■ Second fort - inferred
■ Late Roman fort - excavated
■ Late Roman fort - inferred

N

0 ⎿_____⏌ 50
metres

commanding officers of the fleet (Philp 1981, 114, Table A) and these lend support to the idea that Boulogne was the principal base of the *Classis Britannica*.

This raises the question of role and nature of the fort at Dover. As at Richborough and Lympne we should perhaps be cautious about assuming the fleet was based at a particular harbour rather than having been mobile and using different harbours for short periods. At one extreme one might suggest no more than the involvement of sailors in building work at Dover, since members of the fleet were involved in building work on the fort of Benwell and near Birdoswald on Hadrian's Wall (*RIB*, 1340, 1944-45). The scale of the fort at Dover does, however, suggest more substantial use which should probably be seen in the context of regular cross-Channel contacts.

The entry point to the province at Richborough was occupied by the so-called military supply base until sometime in the 80s when the huge *quadrifrons* arch was erected (see pages 142-3). By this stage a substantial harbourside town had grown up and this remained important through the Roman period (Millett and Wilmott 2003). From the late first until the early third century, however, Richborough seems to have lacked any military base and, when a small fort was constructed around the ruins of the arch in the early third century, it was not sufficiently large to have held a garrison of any size. By contrast Dover was clearly being developed as a major port. Rigold (1969) showed that the harbour here was probably begun in the Flavian period and the pair of lighthouses (that on the western hill having been largely obliterated by post-medieval fortifications) were not simply functional but made an important statement about Dover as the new entry point to the province (ill. 5.34). The construction of these facilities surely represents a deliberate plan to develop a harbour opposite that at Boulogne as a new key port of entry into the province, arguably around the beginning of the second century AD. This may also tie in with the priority given to the Dover road in

the development of the street grid at Canterbury (see above). It is within this context that we should perhaps examine the successive forts constructed from the Trajanic period onwards. Rather than seeing them simply as permanent naval bases, it is perhaps more likely that they served a series of complementary functions. Firstly, the fort provided a replacement for the earlier supply base at Richborough, a place where goods could be securely stored for onward transmission to the military and civil authorities. This role for Dover is attested by an altar dedicated by Olus Cordius Candidus, who is described as a *strator consularis*, a transport officer of the governor (Hassall and Tomlin 1977, 426-27). It may also explain some of the non-standard buildings in the fort that may have served as stores. Secondly, it could have provided quarters for the steady stream of officials, officers and

5.34 The Pharos or lighthouse within Dover Castle, one of a pair that stood on the hills on either side of the Roman harbour. Originally octagonal, its stepped profile rose *c.* 24m. Roman masonry survives to *c.* 19m and the round-headed arches represent original openings.

groups of soldiers who regularly passed to and fro across the Channel. If Philp is correct in his suggestion that the 'painted house' outside the fort formed part of a *mansio* (Philp 1989, 281-82), its function would presumably have been to provide accommodation for the more senior people travelling on official business, leaving the soldiers in transit to be housed within the fort. Finally, the fort probably did act as a secondary base for the men of the *classis* during spells of duty away from the base at Boulogne. As such it was probably the most significant of a range of harbours they used around the coast, including that at Lympne where we have seen that their commanding officer dedicated an altar. It thus seems that during the earlier Roman period, although the fleet was much in evidence, the fort at Dover is best understood as more than simply a naval base.

It is a paradox that the most plentiful evidence for the *classis* is provided by the stamped tiles which have been found on a series of sites associated with iron smelting (see *RIB*, 2481 for discussion). Most of these sites lie in Sussex, but an easterly group was located around what was then a complex of estuarine creeks where the rivers Rother and Brede flow into what is now Romney Marsh (Cleere 1974; Cleere and Crossley 1995). These sites include that at Beauport Park, as well as the Kentish site at Little Farningham, Cranbrook (Aldridge 2001). At some of these sites iron smelted from local ores was produced on a very significant scale and its manufacture was evidently of considerable importance to the regional economy. It has been estimated that the slag heap at Beauport Park alone is the waste from smelting 50,000-60,000 tons of iron. A total of 1,641 fleet tiles has been found here, together with a military-style bathhouse (Brodribb and Cleere 1988). This was built in the late second century and finally abandoned in the middle of the third century. Elsewhere the numbers of stamped tiles are significantly fewer. On the basis of the tiles it seems fair to assume that there was a close relationship between some of the iron production

sites and the *Classis Britannica*. The suggestion, however, that a substantial part of the industry was under the direct control of the fleet and that rights over iron were owned by the Roman state is entirely speculative (cf. Cleere 1974, 181, 188). Further, the idea that the Weald was some form of imperial estate (Cleere and Crossley 1995, 68) has no sound foundation and is probably based on a false assumption about the nature of imperially owned land (cf. Millett 1990, 120-21). An inscription from Beauport Park, taken to refer to a *vilicus* in charge of production (Brodribb and Cleere 1988, 261, fig. 11), is too fragmentary to allow any certain reading (Wright and Hassall 1971, 289), and in any case the term simply means bailiff, without any connotation of 'official' control. Roman military control over any metal production, apart from bullion, seems to have been very rare and there is little reason to assume that it was exercised in this case. More commonly the state seems to have bought its supplies from local producers, even though there may have been some reorganisation to enhance production.

Against this background we should surely see the evidence for the connections of the fleet with the Wealden iron industry in a more subtle way. The fleet was used for the supply of the Roman army throughout the province, and it is certain that the military consumed a significant quantity of iron. A coastal source for such a heavy material would have been particularly attractive to them, so we can understand why a site like Beauport Park may have developed as an important centre for supply. Whether production there was under direct military control, and whether it employed naval personnel or indigenous workers to smelt the ores, is probably unknowable. There are parallels for instance at Holt, Denbighshire (Grimes 1930), for manufacturing centres that produced a variety of goods like pottery for the military, and these perhaps provide the closest parallels for Beauport Park. It may be significant that the bulk of the *CLBR* tiles found in Britain was made from the Fairlight Clay quarried from very close to this site (Peacock 1977), suggesting that they may also have been manufactured at the same industrial complex. Away from the site at Beauport Park itself iron manufacturers almost certainly worked independently, perhaps selling to the state from time to time. The occurrence of smaller numbers of stamped tiles at sites like Little Farningham is probably the result of such trade. We may postulate, for instance, that independent producers smelted iron and transported it to sell at local trading centres, whether at military supply depots like Beauport Park or at other small riverine ports like that at Bodiam on the river Rother. As iron is very heavy, building materials like tile may represent cargo carried on empty returning boats or carts which were then sold or exchanged locally. It is through mechanisms such as this that stamped tiles can easily have been distributed across a large part of the region. The fact that they were stamped to show that they belonged to the state tells us no more than that the authorities were aware of the possibility of misappropriation. Bearing in mind more recent parallels for military surplus, we would be most unwise to equate the find-spots of tile with the presence of the fleet.

What is very clear from a variety of evidence is that, although the *Classis Britannica* was a constant feature of the region in the first to third century AD, its significance in the development of the region has probably been exaggerated: the number of sailors deployed was relatively modest, the ships are likely to have moved around the coast rather than being based only at Dover and, although the fleet utilised Wealden iron, this resource was probably exploited by a variety of users within a mixed economy. It seems equally clear that the use of Wealden resources declined around the mid-third century (Cleere 1974, 189) and the fort at Dover went out of use around AD 210 (Philp

5.35 Page from a fifteenth-century copy of the *Notitia Dignitatum* (Bod. Canon. Misc. 378), probably a reasonably accurate copy of the original, compiled c. AD 408. Note the insignia of the Count of the Saxon Shore, with pictograms of the forts under his command: Dover (*Dubris*), Lympne (*Lemanis*), Reculver (*Regulbio*) and Richborough (*Rutupis*).

1981). Since the latest mention of the *Classis Britannica* dates to the 240s there has been some tendency to associate its disappearance with a radical shift in official policy, perhaps a result of the disruptions of the third century, and to treat the later military archaeology of the region differently, referring to the forts as part of the 'Saxon Shore'. This, however, places too much emphasis on scant references in the textual sources and John Mann (1989) has instead emphasised the continuities involved.

The term 'Saxon Shore' is commonly deployed by archaeologists to refer to the late Roman forts around the southern and eastern coasts of Britain. In the case of Kent the forts included are Lympne, Dover, Richborough and Reculver. They are named in a late Roman text, the *Notitia*

Dignitatum, which provides the one and only source for the name of the Saxon Shore (ill. 5.35). It is a list of Roman officials which was compiled in its surviving form around AD 408, although it seems likely that it was drawn from official files, some of which were by then of some age. It was a bureaucratic document concerned with such things as pay and supplies – not a strategic description. The section that concerns us (*Notitia Dignitatum Occ.*) reads:

XXVIII Comes litoris Saxonici per Britanniam
   Sub dispositione viri spectabilis comitis litoris
   Saxonici per Britanniam...

      Praepositus militum Tungrecanorum, Dubris
      Praepositus numeri Turnacensium, Lemanis...

      Tribunus cohortis primae Baetasiorum, Regulbio
      Praefectus legionis secundae Augustae, Rutupis...

It thus lists the officials and their units under the command of the 'Count of the Saxon Shore'. The units concerned are of mixed character. At Dover (*Portus Dubris*) were troops presumably derived from one of the previously attested *cohortes Tungorum*, regular auxiliary battalions raised in the region around what is now Tongres in the first century AD, but it is not clear when they arrived in Kent (Holder 1982, 131; Jarrett 1994, 49-50). The other regular auxiliary unit was the *cohors I Baetasiorum* at Reculver (*Regulbium*). This unit is first known under Antoninus Pius and it had served on the Antonine Wall and at Maryport before moving to Reculver, perhaps in the earlier third century (Jarrett 1994, 54). The soldiers at Lympne (*Portus Lemanis*) were from a less regular type of unit, the *numerus Turnacensium*, that had been raised just across the Channel at *Turnacum* (now Tournai), perhaps as late as the 360s (Holder 1982, 132). Finally the garrison at *Rutupiae* (Richborough) comprised the *Legio II Augusta*, although it is likely to have been drastically diminished in size by this date. It is unclear whether they transferred to Richborough when

their Caerleon base closed at the end of the third century, but it is certain that the unit was split, with part of it serving as part of a mobile field army (Casey 1991, 20). It is clear from this mixture of units that the Count of the Saxon Shore had control of something rather more haphazard than we might expect from his grand title and we should bear this in mind when considering the development of what has sometimes been seen as a major defensive system. Equally, we should note that even if these units were up to strength, the total garrison of the forts cannot have exceeded perhaps 2,000 men.

It has commonly been assumed that the Saxon Shore command as described above was part of an organised system of defence that included forts in Gaul on the opposite coast of the Channel (Johnson 1976). It is equally assumed that the system had its origins in the third century and that the forts comprising it had generally been built during that period. This, however, seems improbable as we have no reason to assume that the command described in the *Notitia* is anything but a late fourth-century creation. As such, it is extremely unwise to use the term to refer to the forts around the shore of south-eastern Britain except at that date. If we turn to the archaeology of the forts themselves it is also evident that we should be very cautious about thinking of them as a planned system. The evidence from forts around the coast demonstrates that they were constructed piecemeal over a comparatively long period, perhaps more than 50 years (Cunliffe 1977; Maxfield 1989). The Kent sites illustrate the pattern well. Reculver is a fort with some typologically archaic features and is early in the series. The excavated evidence suggests that it was probably constructed in the late second century (Philp 2005, 206-18). It has produced an important building inscription but this dates its construction no more closely than to the period *c.* AD 200-60 (Mann 1977). The stone-built late Roman fort at Richborough is dated closely to *c.* AD 275 (Johnson 1970) and that at Dover probably dates to a little after *c.* AD 275

(Wilkinson 1995, 71-72). The poorly preserved fort at Lympne appears to have been built in the mid- to late 270s (Cunliffe 1980, 285). The forts were thus probably built over an extended period and should not be seen as a response to any single set of events, despite attempts to associate them with the usurper Carausius (AD 286-93). It seems more appropriate to see their building as part of a continuing response to the needs of maritime control through a long period and thus to associate them with the need to assure the security of shipping and military supply through unsettled times during the third century. Such a view stresses continuity of function, if not terminology, with the *Classis Britannica* (Mann 1989; Cotterill 1993). Only at a later stage, arguably around the time of the so-called Barbarian Conspiracy of AD 367, do we need to associate them with defence against a perceived threat from across the North Sea. Equally, there can now be no doubt that the late fourth-century name was associated with a barbarian threat, and certainly not the settlement of Saxon mercenaries as has sometimes been asserted in the past.

A concentration on presumed military strategy too often deflects us from a critical appreciation of the impact of even small military units on the local population. It has already been suggested that the number of men employed in the *classis* was small and that their impact has been overemphasised. When present in a port, however, the sailors will have brought, on the one hand, some direct spending power and, on the other, the sorts of social disruption still associated with gangs of young males. It is doubtful whether outside the ports they had much significant impact. As the epigraphic evidence suggests that the main fleet base was across the Channel in Boulogne, it seems improbable that there will have been the type of settlement of military dependants at any British site comparable to those that developed around the garrison forts on the northern frontier.

The later third- and fourth-century garrisons of the shore forts are supposed to have been manned by *limitanei*, settled frontier troops similar to those on the northern frontier. Other later Roman military units were higher-grade mobile units, which moved across the provinces to intercept and discourage any attackers. Such *comitatenses* may also have stayed in walled towns like Canterbury and Rochester at different times. One of the difficulties with the later Roman shore forts is that they provide little archaeological evidence for the installations that we might expect to find associated with more permanent garrisons, and this must raise the question of the extent to which they were used as such. On the northern frontier, forts contain a complex of buildings, including barracks, luxury houses for the commanding officer and headquarters buildings. Although the shore forts have impressive tall walls there is much less evidence for long sequences of substantial buildings indicative of occupation, except at Reculver (Philp 2005). The provision of what is surely a military amphitheatre at Richborough may imply that it was the intention to have a proper legionary base there, but generally the sites hint at a different story – emptiness. It may be that the garrisons (which are only attested from a very late date) were rarely up to strength or even in residence. Strategically this need not have been a problem, for the forts stood to inhibit attack, and even if the supposed military threats did not materialise, their tall walls, although empty, may have been effective in this role. These thoughts should certainly deter us from assuming that the military presence around the shore had anything like a major impact on society in the later Roman period.

Notwithstanding the apparent threats to the peace of the region the available evidence shows that the *Notitia* forts were not universally long-lived. The coins from Lympne indicate that it was largely abandoned by *c.* AD 350 (Reece 1989); equally, the coin list from Reculver has remarkably few fourth-century coins (Reece 2005). By contrast, the extraordinarily large number of coins from the period AD 388-402 at Richborough attests its continuing importance

5.36 Reconstruction of one of the Ickham mills. Their presence and extensive evidence for metalworking and other industry suggest a major supply base, probably associated with the Roman state.

5.37 Lead sealings from Ickham used on strings binding packages, sacks or bales. The various symbols (paired and single figures, horsemen etc, perhaps representing individuals, organizations or military units) identified their origins. Others, not illustrated, with military or imperial inscriptions, clearly relate to the Roman state.

into the fifth century (Reece 1981); recent evidence from Dover also confirms coin supply in this period, although it is suggested that the character of occupation changed through the fourth century (Wilkinson 1995, 75-77).

In laying emphasis on the coastal forts other important aspects of military influence in the region have perhaps been neglected. Throughout the Roman period there will regularly have been a variety of soldiers passing through the area and others seconded to the staff of the provincial governor will have been found on their duties in the *civitas*. It is probably wrong to assume that they were heavily involved in local administration as this was left to local communities, but it is all too easy to forget that the Roman Empire was a totalitarian state in which soldiers were regularly employed in government. For much of the time this presence is archaeologically undetectable yet there is one fascinating exception from Kent. The late Roman industrial site at Ickham beside the Little Stour river (Bennett, Riddler and Sparey-Green forthcoming) has produced several lead sealings of the periods AD 317-37 and 361-63 (*RIB*, 2411.22, 2411.25-27) (ills 5.36; 5.37). These derive from the breaking open of sealed sacks or bales, perhaps suggesting that materials were being processed here on behalf of the state,

although they may have arrived as scrap metal (Young 1981). The location of this roadside settlement close to Richborough and with easy maritime communications suggests continuity in the importance of east Kent for military supply into the later Roman period, and perhaps gives an indication of how changes in Imperial fortunes were affecting the region.

The decline of Roman power

There are considerable problems in understanding how the Roman period in Britain came to an end. Whilst we have reasonably good textual sources which enable us to see how the problems faced by Rome led to the progressive removal of military resources back to the Continent, the impact of these withdrawals on the people of Britain is very difficult to assess, not least because the cessation of regular bulk coin supplies in AD 388-402 means that it is very difficult to establish the chronologies of excavated sites (Millett 1990, 219-20). Whatever catastrophic events took place it seems very unlikely that the population realised that the withdrawal of troops in the first decade of the fifth century marked their final exclusion from the umbrella of the Roman world. The fort at Richborough was probably among the last Roman bases in Britain to have its garrison removed, and it is also in this part of Kent that direct contacts with Rome were re-established in AD 597 with the landing of the mission from Pope Gregory I led by St Augustine. In the intervening years it appears that most of classical society had disappeared from the region, even though Roman buildings had survived for reuse by the church. For instance, at Stone-by-Faversham – adjacent to the site of what had probably been *Durolevum* – a Roman mausoleum was converted to a church (Taylor and Yonge 1981). As at Canterbury, Rochester, probably Dover and Reculver, the Roman topography determined the sites of some of the earliest churches. Although Bede (*H.E.*, II.1) tells us that Roman churches were reused at Canterbury, there is nothing to suggest continuing Romanised communities.

The archaeological evidence for the late Roman to early medieval transition is disappointingly thin. Indeed, there is now very good evidence from a series of key sites (including Springhead, Thurnham villa, Monkton and Westhawk Farm) that occupation declined or ceased during the third century. The reasons for this remain unclear. Elsewhere, sequences continue later. At Canterbury extensive excavations have revealed a large area of the later Roman town (Blockley *et al.* 1995; Bennett *et al.* 2003). This work shows some evidence for decline from the middle of the fourth century, although it is difficult to be certain how we should generalise on the basis of the demolition of one house and the disuse of the public baths (Blagg 1995, 17-18). It appears that there was a relatively long period of gradual decline starting at this period and continuing into the fifth century, with piecemeal decay of the Roman infrastructure. The most important evidence comes from a group of grubenhäuser within the Roman town, which have sometimes been taken as evidence for an organised handover to Germanic mercenary soldiers. The evidence now suggests that there was a gap in occupation, with the earliest Saxon houses dating to the second quarter of the fifth century (Blockley *et al.* 1995, 280-335). Similarly, there is evidence of *grubenhäuser* and also timber halls from within the later Roman fort at Dover, although their context has not yet been fully published (cf. Wilkinson 1995, 57).

The nature of the process that led to the decline of the Roman city is a matter for speculation, but it is clear that the site remained focal because of its position on the road network. A hoard of late Roman silver, which gives some interesting insights into the latest phases of *Durnovernum Cantiacorum*, was found in 1962 just outside the walls on the western side of the city (Johns and Potter 1985, 312-52) (ill. 5.38). It was probably not deposited until at least the second decade of the fifth century and contained several coins, four silver ingots and a series of silver spoons. Two of the ingots are stamped (*RIB*,

5.38 Silver spoons from the Canterbury hoard. These plain examples, similar to those commonly in other late Roman hoards, have rat-tail handles, pear-shaped bowls connected by simple scrolls.

2402.12; 2402.9), the latter with a mark showing that it was produced in Trier. The spoons include one with a Chi-Rho symbol on the bowl, another decorated with a stag, and one which bears the inscription VIRIBONISM, perhaps 'viri boni s[v]m' – 'I belong to a good man' (*RIB*, 2420.48). Certain of these features suggest Christian associations, whilst the stamped ingots are of a type issued by emperors as donatives, a form of pay, to troops and officials. Whatever the reason for the hoard being hidden and not recovered, it hints at the continued presence of those associated with the Roman state into the fifth century. Other stamped ingots from Reculver (*RIB*, 2402.8) and Richborough (*RIB*, 2402.6), together with the evidence for the very late abandonment of the latter site, may suggest that officials were gathered in this part of Kent during the later fourth and early fifth centuries. The late use of Richborough is associated with the construction of a late Roman church in the north-west corner of the walled fort (Brown 1971). There are also plentiful coins of AD 388-402 from Rochester, suggesting a prolonged sequence there (Redfern 1978, 44-54). The excavations at Northfleet, in contrast to nearby Springhead, show a continuity of trading activity into the early decades of the fifth century (Williams 2003, 230-31), but good excavated evidence for the period is generally rare.

In the countryside the evidence is variable. The villa at Lullingstone continued in occupation into the early fifth century, when it was destroyed by fire (Meates 1979, 23-24). Other villas like Eccles and Darenth seem to have been inhabited up to the end of coin use in the early fifth century. Elsewhere, the coin sequences finish earlier, but it is not clear whether this implies abandonment or is simply a function of a reduction in coin circulation. Certainly the pottery evidence shows that trade networks persisted through the latter part of the fourth century, although local manufacture was in decline (Pollard 1988, 161-63). Whatever the details of specific sites it seems improbable that the population declined substantially over a short period; the challenge

that remains for archaeologists is to understand what happened to the civilian population living in the region through the last decades of the fourth and the early decades of the fifth centuries.

Acknowledgements

I am very grateful to Paul Booth, Keith Parfitt and John Williams for their comments on an earlier draft of this text. Thanks are also due to Paul Bennett, Rail Link Engineering, the Heritage Conservation Group of Kent County Council and Canterbury Archaeological Trust for access to unpublished material. I am also pleased to acknowledge the enormous work of generations of field archaeologists who have provided the evidence so briefly discussed here.

Anglo-Saxon Kent

by Martin Welch

Introduction

The fifth century saw a radical transformation of what became Kent, politically, socially and in terms of the physical landscape. Martin Millett in this volume has emphasised the minimalist intervention of the Roman state in the administration of the *civitas Cantiacorum*, and indeed of Britain as a whole, but many aspects of Roman civilisation had imprinted themselves on the underlying Iron Age culture. While significant elements of the Roman road network have survived to the present day, many of the physical manifestations of Rome's presence were already decaying in Britain during the fourth century. The Roman towns of Canterbury and Rochester remained essentially as walled defensive circuits and a few structures that escaped demolition, such as the stone theatre in Canterbury. Similarly, the visible Roman presence in the countryside also declined, as witnessed by the abandonment of villas and similar masonry structures.

By the end of the sixth century Kent had become a significant political force, whose rulers exercised hegemony over other kingdoms in southern and eastern England. The foundations were established for the settlement patterns we observe in Kent today; during the seventh and eighth centuries royal estates emerged, with the Church becoming a major landowner. A Christian mission led by St Augustine and received in 597 by King Æthelberht led rapidly to the foundation of bishoprics in both Canterbury and Rochester. This was followed by the establishment of minsters (monasteries) across Kent, each with its own large 'parish'. With the active encouragement of pious rulers such as Wihtræd (690/1-725), the Church became a dominant force in Kentish society and was ever more visible in the archaeology of its urban and rural landscape. It was much later, between the tenth and twelfth century, however, that the more localised parochial system with which we are familiar developed.

This chapter begins by reviewing the historical framework for the period, before exploring aspects of continuity and discontinuity in the landscape across the divide separating the Roman and Anglo-Saxon periods. The evidence for early Anglo-Saxon buildings and settlements is then considered, followed by an assessment of the more numerous cemeteries and burial sites that provide the basis for the emergence of a distinctive material culture in east Kent in the sixth and seventh centuries. The archaeology of the early Church and the development of the regional administration of the early kingdom are then described, before some final thoughts on possible future areas of research.

The historical framework

Despite the scarcity and general unreliability of our written sources, particularly for the fifth and sixth centuries, the Anglo-Saxon period is protohistoric rather than prehistoric, and only from the seventh century onwards is it fully historic. In order to understand Kent's political, social and economic development, an historical framework must be separated from the mythical overgrowth and we should also utilise the available archaeological evidence. This first section explores the emergence of the Kingdom of Kent into the historical record and in particular its relations with its powerful Frankish neighbours, drawing on written evidence, including the origin myths and the genealogy of the Kentish royal house.

Kent is a creation of the Anglo-Saxon period, replacing the Roman *civitas* of the *Cantiaci*. Initially the name Kent was restricted to the region east of the Medway, possibly a former sub-unit or *pagus* of the *civitas* (Detsicas 1983, 10 and 38-9). Before the end of the sixth century, however, Kent had expanded to include the western half of the historical county (Everitt 1986; Hasted 1778-99). The original extent of its Iron Age precursor *Cantium* (meaning a 'corner of land' or 'land on the edge') remains unknown, but it was probably rather larger than the Anglo-Saxon kingdom *c.* 600. Much has been made of the continuity implied by the Anglo-Saxon adaptation of the name of the *Cantii* or *Cantiaci* (Rivet and

Smith 1979, 299-300) to a name meaning 'the dwellers of Kent' (the *Cantware*). This need not, however, imply the annexation of the complete Roman *civitas*, though it might involve one of its component *pagi*. Archaeological evidence implies that the core of the Anglo-Saxon kingdom was centred in east Kent and that the region west of the Medway was added shortly before Augustine's mission from Rome. The appointment within Æthelberht's reign of a separate bishop for west Kent, based in Rochester, certainly supports this view (Brooks 1989, 68; Yorke 1990, 27). It was normal to have a bishop for each kingdom, implying that west and east Kent were originally independent kingdoms. Throughout the seventh and eighth centuries pairs of kings ruled Kent and the senior always governed its eastern half (Yorke 1983).

Historical tradition provides an origin myth for Anglo-Saxon Kent, which we have no means of testing using contemporary sources (Brooks 1989; Yorke 1990). Although the *Gallic Chronicle* of 452 records Saxons as taking control of Britain early in the 440s, it does not name a specific province, though Kent was probably involved. The *De Excidio* attributed to Gildas is another near-contemporary source, which portrays the Saxons as divine vengeance for British sins. This locates the first Saxon mercenary settlements in the eastern part of Britain and describes their successful rebellion and the appeal of the British to Aëtius in his third consulship. Clearly the Saxons remained a potent threat to the western British at the time its author was writing, either side of 500, but originally they might have been stationed anywhere between Kent and Yorkshire. We can accept or reject the traditions recorded for fifth-century events in Kent preserved in two much later texts, one of which has been referred to as a 'Kentish Chronicle' (Morris 1966, 157, n. 44; 1974, 37). These can be found in the *Anglo-Saxon Chronicle* (hereafter *ASC*) and the *Historia Brittonum* (hereafter *HB*) as composed in the ninth century. We also have the account provided in Bede's *Ecclesiastical History* (hereafter *HE*) written before

731. Names are provided for the leaders of the first Saxon mercenaries in Kent, but it is difficult to accept that two brothers bearing names more appropriate to horse deities (Hengest means a stallion and Horsa a horse) were really the first Saxon leaders here, invited in by a British ruler referred to as Vortigern (*ASC* 449; *HB c.* 31). Battles are recorded against the British in both east and west Kent at *Ægelesthrep* (perhaps Aylesford: *ASC* 455), *Crecganford* (perhaps Crayford: *ASC* 456), *Wippedsfleot* (*ASC* 465) and elsewhere (*ASC* 473; *HB c.* 44 and 45). It is reasonable to suggest that the Crayford battle was created to justify the later annexation of west Kent. The fact that the kings of Kent identified themselves with Hengest's supposed successor (or son) *Aesc* or *Oisc*, rather than with Hengest himself and called themselves the *Oiscingas* (*HE* II.5) must be significant. Hengest and Horsa may well have been borrowed from a common heroic folk tradition to fill a perceived gap in Kent's history. The presence of a Hengest in later Anglo-Saxon poetry implies that his name would resonate for an Anglo-Saxon audience. According to the *Finnsburg Fragment* Hengest becomes the leader of a warrior band in continental Frisia, whose lord has been treacherously slain and who bides his time before exacting revenge for his lord. It is not entirely clear from the poem whether he was a Jute or whether he could be linked to the Jutish settlement of east Kent as recorded by Bede (*HE* I.15). Interestingly there are relevant archaeological links between east Kent and Frisia in the fifth and early sixth centuries.

Oisc may be a further deity, rather than the historical ancestor of the Kentish kings; was Octa the son or the father of Oisc or was either Oisc or Octa really the father of Eormenric (also referred to as Irminric)? At least with Eormenric we can move from tradition into history, for he appears as the father of the first Christian ruler of Kent, Æthelberht, who died in 616-18. Eormenric shared his heroic Germanic name with a famous fourth-century ruler of the Goths (Ermanaric) and names beginning with *Irmin-* are common amongst the Franks. A contemporary source, the *Historia* written by Gregory, Bishop of Tours, mentions a king of Kent and the marriage of a Merovingian princess to a prince of Kent (IV.26; IX.26). She was the daughter of Charibert and Ingoberga and appears to be the Bertha named by Bede, with the prince being Æthelberht (*HE* I.25; II.5). If Eormenric was still king when Æthelberht married, then his own death should post-date 589 (Yorke 2002, 114). Æthelberht became an overlord or high king (*brytenwealda*) exercising authority (*imperium*) over other kingdoms across eastern and southern England (*HE* II.5). Following his own conversion, he could require the East Saxon and East Anglian rulers to accept baptism (*HE* II.3; 15), but it is unlikely that his influence ever reached as far north as Lindsey and the Humber, despite Bede's statement to the contrary. Æthelberht also guaranteed safe conduct for St Augustine to travel to the western end of the Thames basin to meet a delegation of British bishops. He was powerless to act, however, when those same British clerics rejected the authority of the Roman bishop (*HE* II.1) and his power was clearly waning well before his death. No subsequent king of Kent was able to match his authority, though we should not underestimate the political influence of his successors within south-east England during the remainder of the seventh century. It was presumably Eormenric who had laid the foundations for his son's success, though equally Æthelberht had risen to the occasion.

Æthelberht's son and heir Eadbald (616/18-640) was a pagan when he succeeded him, and his marriage to his stepmother shocked the missionary clergy of Canterbury and Rochester (*HE* II.5). This action, however, was probably designed primarily to gain access to the royal treasure she controlled as queen. When eventually he accepted the Christian faith, he put this wife aside and married a Christian Frank, Ymme (later anglicised in our sources as Emma). We do not know whether she was a royal princess like Bertha, or the daughter of a senior Frankish royal official, such as the mayor of the Neustrian palace (Brooks 1984, 64, n. 5). Such continuity of diplomatic links with the powerful Merovingian kings surely reflects an acceptance by Kent that it was better to recognise, than resist, Frankish claims to lordship. Nevertheless, by accepting baptism from Augustine, the emissary of the Bishop of Rome, rather than from a Frankish cleric such as the Bishop Liudhard, who served Bertha, Æthelberht was asserting a cautious independence from Merovingian authority. He avoided upsetting the Franks directly, trusting that their rulers had more important matters with which to concern themselves.

Kent seems to have reaped the benefits of diplomatic gifts and privileged access to traded goods from the Continent rather than inviting armed retribution by engaging in piracy or coastal raids on Frankish Gaul (Wood 1990, 95-6). Perhaps again, it was the potent threat of Kentish piracy that led the Franks to bribe Kent's rulers to

6.1 Imported seventh-century Frankish biconical wheelthrown vase from Updown, Eastry, grave 76:29.

6.2 Three sixth-century silver-gilt square-headed brooches of Kentish types from the Chessell Down (Isle of Wight) cemetery (approx. actual size).

6.3 Triangular early seventh-century copper-alloy buckle from Finglesham Grave 95 showing a naked warrior carrying two spears: a portrait of Woden (approx. actual size).

discourage any 'privateering'. Certainly archaeology confirms that east Kent enjoyed a 'favoured nation' status throughout the sixth century, if not earlier, and well into the seventh century. Its population possessed Frankish dress fittings, weapons and many other items, including, from the late sixth century onwards, imported wheel-thrown pottery (ill. 6.1). Archaeological evidence also links the Isle of Wight to Jutish east Kent in the sixth century (Arnold 1982a) (ill. 6.2). Wight was part of a Jutish province or kingdom based in Hampshire, according to Bede (*HE* I.15). There were contemporary Kentish settlements in Francia along the coastal margins between the Somme and Calais opposite Kent and in Lower Normandy opposite the Isle of Wight. A more distant, but key, site in the Saintonge region of south-west France has produced sixth-century Kentish finds (Haith 1988; Welch 1991; 2002; Yorke 2002).

Æthelberht's grandson Eorcenbert (640-664) issued the first and surprisingly late decree banning pagan worship in Kent (*HE* III.8) (ill. 6.3). He was succeeded by his sons Egbert (664-673) and Hlothere (673-685), but a tradition that Egbert had his cousins Æthelred and Æthelberht murdered at the royal hall in Eastry reveals the tensions underlying a seemingly smooth succession from father to son. Clearly Egbert feared that his brother's now adult sons possessed a strong claim to the throne and acted to remove them. Following the assassinations, he settled his dispute with his own kin by paying compensation in land on Thanet on which they would found a new monastery (Minster-in-Thanet: Rollason 1982, 9-11, 48; 1989; Yorke 1990, 35). A particularly violent period opens with the death in 687 of Eadric, a son of Egbert. It was eventually resolved by the succession of Eadric's brother Wihtræd in 690 or 691, and Wihtræd's long and successful reign saw the appearance of the third and final set of laws issued in Kent. The first laws were attributed, probably correctly, to Æthelberht and the second jointly to Hlothere and Eadric (Wormald 1999, 93-103). The third set reveals the ever-closer relationship of king and Church by the 690s. In 725 Wihtræd was succeeded by his sons Æthelberht II (died 762) and Eadbert, ruling jointly. Subsequently Sigered, who appears to have been a member of the East Saxon royal house, was king jointly with Eadbert in 762, but this arrangement ended by 764 when the Mercian overlord Offa chose to rule Kent himself. Offa's intervention here contrasts with the actions of his predecessor, Æthelbald, who had preferred to exercise indirect Mercian influence. Egbert II regained independence for Kent for several years after 776, but Offa was to rule again in person between 785 and his death in 796, while a two-year Kentish rebellion against Mercian rule, led by Eadbert Præn, was brought to a violent end in 798. Eventually, after 825, Mercian power over Kent and south-east England was replaced by West Saxon rule and Kent became a shire of the enlarged West Saxon kingdom, never again to have its own kings.

Under Æthelberht, Kent probably extended at least as far west as the south bank opposite London. According to Bede, he founded and built the first St Paul's cathedral in London, even though this city belonged to the East Saxons (*HE* II.3). The expulsion of its first bishop Mellitus by the East Saxons on Æthelberht's death (*HE* II.5) revealed the limits of Kentish authority, but a late seventh-century Kentish law code (Hlothere and Eadric, cap. 16) refers to the presence of the king's *wic-gerefa* in London, an official able to levy tolls on ships that reached London through Kentish seaways (Attenborough 1922; Blackmore 2002; Cowie 2000; Malcolm and Bowsher 2003; Wormald 1999, 102).

Opportunities to expand the Kentish kingdom, by absorbing what was to become Surrey, came and went within the seventh century (Hines 2004). Surrey's name means 'the southern region', but this is hardly an appropriate term for a territory the size of an early kingdom or later shire. A region (or *regio*) implies a sub-unit within a kingdom (or *provincia*), so initially this 'southern region' may refer to a much smaller territory centred on Chertsey (Blair 1991, 6-8, figs 4-5). Significantly, the Chertsey monastery was founded in *c*. 666 by Egbert of Kent (664-673), yet by the 670s, Surrey, London and the East Saxon kingdom were firmly under Mercian control. A *provincia* of the people of Surrey is mentioned in a Chertsey diploma (or charter) of 672 x 674 (Sawyer 1968, S1165) which records a grant of land by Frithuwold, a royal official (*subregulus*). He seems to have belonged to a noble family from the Midlands and is presented as governing the Surrey 'province' on behalf of his Mercian king Wulfhere (Blair 1989, 105-7). By analogy, the individual buried in an early seventh-century barrow chamber grave at Taplow in Buckinghamshire might well have been a Kentish 'prince' of the royal house, ruling the middle reaches of the Thames basin on behalf of Æthelberht (Webster 1992). Thus from the 670s onwards Kentish kings shared influence over London with the Mercian or

West Saxon overlords of their day, though clearly under Hlothere and Eadric they still exercised some real authority. By the eighth century, however, London had become a Mercian port, though its overlord Æthelbald was certainly prepared to issue trading privileges to several Kentish monasteries (Kelly 1992).

Our terminology for provinces and regions in the seventh to eighth century is taken from Bede. Often geographical prefixes (North, West, South, East and Middle) were combined with the ethnic label of Angles or Saxons. These names seem to have been created by clerical administrators in Canterbury, who needed to address letters to bishops in each converted 'province'. Their compass orientations make sense when we realise that they relate to Kent. In most cases we lack the earlier name, but the West Saxons had previously been the *Geuissæ* (Kirby 1991, 20-3; Yorke 1990, 132). In the *Tribal Hidage* document (Davies and Vierck 1974), the *Cantwarena* were assigned 15,000 hides (land units sufficient to support an extended family), which is half the 30,000 valuation of the more powerful kingdoms of the Mercians and East Angles. It is also more than double the 7,000 hides of a standard 'province' (e.g. the East Saxons). It may be that 7,000 hides were appropriate for each half of Kent, but if so, were the *Hæstingas* in the East Sussex Weald originally a Kentish people? The limits of their territory are indicated by three place-names, Hastingford (Farm) near Crowborough, Hastings itself on the coast and Hastingleigh (a woodland clearing), firmly in Kent on the Downs close to Wye. Of course, the latter might be an isolated outpost, but the Roman road system links the eastern Weald to Canterbury and Rochester rather than to Pevensey or Chichester (Detsicas 1983, fig. 7; Margary 1973: roads 13, 130 and 131). Following their defeat in 771, Offa arranged for the 'men of Hastings' to be attached to the South Saxon province and bishopric (Welch 1983, 274-5; 1989, 78-9), so perhaps the 'Jutish' *Hæstware* farmed part of Kentish Holmesdale and became the *Hæstingas* of Sussex only after 772.

Continuity and landscape from Roman to Anglo-Saxon Kent

The nature of the Anglo-Saxon transformation of Roman Britain into Anglo-Saxon England, whether by an extended and cumulative process of migration or through a takeover by a numerically small warrior élite leading to 'acculturation' of the native British population, is a fundamental question. The evidence for continuity, or its absence, between Roman and Anglo-Saxon Kent will be examined, looking at the distribution of settlement and burial sites in the landscape and the question of both Germanic migration and British survival.

It has been argued that the system of estates we find in manorial records for medieval Kent had its origins in the settlement patterns of the Roman period, and that Roman estates provided the basis for the estates granted during the seventh century to support new Anglo-Saxon ecclesiastical foundations (Brookes 2003, 88; Everitt 1986, 339-41). This does not necessarily prove continuity of landholding, so much as the dominance of the Roman road network in post-Roman Kent, as the communication nodes established at the junctions of roads, trackways and rivers inevitably attracted later occupation to the same locations as major Roman settlements. The best quality arable land was concentrated within two relatively narrow zones, defined by Everitt (1986) as the 'Original Lands'. These territories occupied the Foothills to the north of the Downs and Holmesdale south of the escarpment of the Downs. Woodland resources and grazing land were provided primarily by the North Down uplands and by the Weald, including the Chart hills on the southern edge of Holmesdale. A notable exception is provided by the woodlands of the Blean region, north of Canterbury, but smaller managed woods are indicated elsewhere across the Foothills and on Thanet by place-names such as Westwood. With such geological and landscape constraints, it is hardly surprising that broad similarities can be observed between the settlement patterns of the

Roman period and those of Anglo-Saxon and medieval Kent. Additionally there is no environmental evidence for large-scale abandonment of the farmed landscape or for radical changes in land use, such as a reversion from arable to woodland, between the fourth and eighth century.

If, however, we are expecting to find early Anglo-Saxon settlements and burial grounds continuing directly from their Roman precursors, the picture is distinctly patchy. While early Anglo-Saxon timber buildings have been revealed on or close to several Roman villa sites in west Kent, most recently at Northfleet near Gravesend, this need not imply that these villas were still operational estates. The Anglo-Saxon finds from the Northfleet sunken-featured buildings are sixth- and seventh-century, and continuity through the fifth and early sixth centuries cannot yet be demonstrated. Anglo-Saxon potsherds were found within the Lullingstone villa near Eynsford (Detsicas 1983, 184; Meates 1979; 1987). Villas are much less common east of the Medway, though decorated 'Jutish' hand-made pottery occurred amongst sherds recovered from the villa at Wingham, south-east of Canterbury (Detsicas 1983, 135; Myres 1977, 34-7, fig. 202.3221), suggesting fifth-century occupation. Still more recently a case has been made for Anglo-Saxon reuse, in the sixth to seventh century, of a substantial Roman stone aisled building at Deerton Street, west of Faversham. Its tiled roof was still intact when Anglo-Saxon hand-made and imported wheel-thrown potsherds and a mid-sixth-century small square-headed brooch were deposited on its floor (Paul Wilkinson pers. comm.; *British Archaeology* 80 (2005), 6). Again, the earliest burials of an Anglo-Saxon cemetery at the Eccles villa, near Aylesford (ill. 6.4), belong within the second half of the seventh century and if post-holes there represent a timber church, it will be an Anglo-Saxon one (Blair 2005, 236 n.229; Detsicas 1976). Archaeological evidence for the post-Roman Christian community implied by the *eccles* place-name (Brooks 2000, 239-40;

Hawkes 1973; Shaw 1994), and recognised by the Anglo-Saxon population, is still lacking. This is not the only place-name in Kent to indicate the continued existence of separate British and possibly Christian communities, as there are others, such as the Waltons located between Eastry and Woodnesborough (Hawkes 1979, 97).

Nevertheless, once Roman material culture, in the form of circulating coins and wheel-thrown, industrially produced pottery, had disappeared, the British population becomes archaeologically invisible. Only in recent decades has interest in excavating 'ordinary' Roman farming communities (both single farms and so-called 'villages') emerged (Detsicas 1983, 84-5; Hingley 1989). This may yet help the search for something similar in post-Roman Kent. There is a need to develop an appreciation of the typical building types from Romano-British settlements, to distinguish between British and newly introduced Anglo-Saxon methods of house construction (Hamerow 1999). Knowledge of how long British rural communities continued to inhume their dead within cemeteries first established in the third and fourth centuries remains very limited. Radiocarbon dates from the Queensford Mill

6.4 Later seventh-century copper-alloy buckle from Eccles Grave 19 with two knotted snake-like creatures in Style II (approx. actual size).

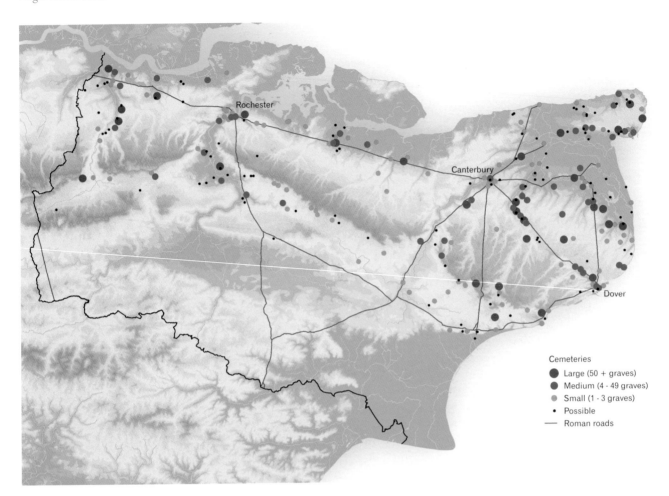

6.5 Distribution map of early Anglo-Saxon cemeteries in Kent: concentrated on the best farmland, except for sites either side of the Canterbury-Dover road.

Cemeteries
- ● Large (50 + graves)
- ● Medium (4 - 49 graves)
- ● Small (1 - 3 graves)
- • Possible
- — Roman roads

cemetery near Dorchester-on-Thames in Oxfordshire indicate Romano-British style burial continuing as late as the early sixth century (Chambers 1987); likewise burial in hobnail boots may have occurred as late as the sixth and seventh centuries at Shepton Mallet in Somerset (Leach 2001, 43-5, 208). As yet, there are no equivalent dates from Romano-British cemeteries in Kent, but high-accuracy radiocarbon dating may distinguish burials of the second half of the fourth century from those of the first half of the fifth. High-accuracy dating is expensive, but it has been applied successfully in resolving the chronology of seventh-century Anglo-Saxon burials (Scull and Bayliss 1999).

It should not be a surprise that the vast majority of known early Anglo-Saxon sites, principally cemeteries, are concentrated along what passes for a coastal plain between the former Thames marshes and the lower slopes of the North Downs, including the Isle of Thanet and the lower chalklands to the south of the Wantsum (ills 6.5; 6.6). Other sites are recorded in the sandy lowland zone between the escarpment of the North Downs and the Chartland at the edge of the Weald, or else occupy the more elevated land on either side of the three major rivers, the Darent, the Medway and the Great Stour, that cut through the Downs. Smaller river valleys also attracted settlement, for example the Dour valley inland from Dover (Evison 1987, text fig. 36) and the Lesser Stour or Nailbourne (Hawkes 2000, fig. 2). The extensive woodland of the Blean between Faversham and the Wantsum lacked both Roman villas and early Anglo-Saxon sites, despite its proximity to Canterbury. Colonisation and settlement of the higher chalklands by Anglo-Saxon communities began no earlier than the late

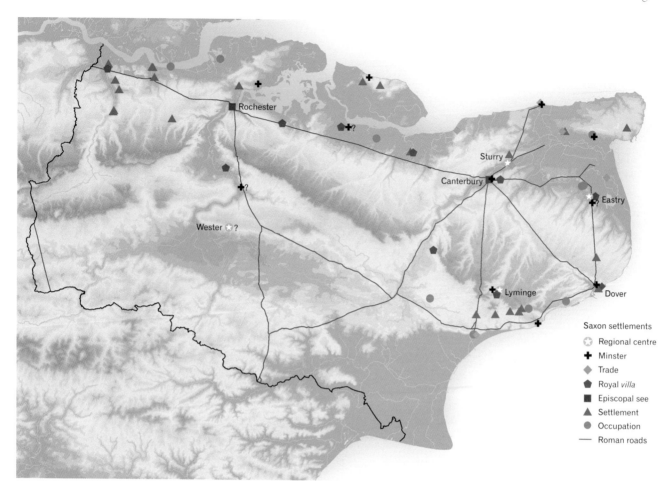

Rochester

Sturry

Canterbury

Eastry

Wester ☆?

Lyminge

Dover

Saxon settlements
- ☆ Regional centre
- ✚ Minster
- ◆ Trade
- ⬟ Royal *villa*
- ■ Episcopal see
- ▲ Settlement
- ● Occupation
- — Roman roads

sixth century (Brookes 2007), apparently discouraged by extensive areas of clay capping and major woodland. There is a particular concentration of seventh-century settlement represented by cemeteries either side of the Canterbury to Dover Roman road (Evison 1987, text fig. 36; Hawkes 1982a, fig. 28). Burial sites indicate that Anglo-Saxon colonisation of the Chartland at the margins of the Weald had also begun before the beginning of the seventh century, but it is not sufficient to suggest widespread occupation. Instead new finds of early Anglo-Saxon sites over the past thirty years have consistently confirmed the established patterns of settlement. Nevertheless, there are still areas within Kent where one might anticipate rather more archaeological evidence from between the fifth and seventh century. For example, on the Isle of Sheppey, despite the presence of a seventh-

century monastic foundation at Minster, only a couple of minor settlement sites have been located. While much of the island would have been uninhabitable marshland (Everitt 1986), modern redevelopment might have been expected to reveal rather more Anglo-Saxon material. The contrast with the number of early Anglo-Saxon sites on Thanet, where there was another seventh-century royal monastic foundation, could not be more marked.

The significance of Roman roads to early Anglo-Saxon settlement patterns has been demonstrated in a recent study (Brookes 2003, 87). Some 85% of Anglo-Saxon cemeteries were located within 1.2 km of a Roman road, a navigable river or the coast. The remaining 15% occur close to the ancient trackways that provided the most efficient routes for transhumance, in particular the herding of swine between the

6.6 Distribution of Anglo-Saxon settlements, discovered archaeologically or recorded in documents (regional capitals, episcopal sees, minsters and trading places).

principal farmland settlements of north Kent and their seasonal Wealden pastures. Place-names ending in -denn, recording these pastures, are confirmed in later manorial records (Everitt 1986; Jolliffe 1933; Witney 1976). Thus Tenterden in the Weald provided outlying pasture for Thanet, supplementing local salt-marsh pasture.

Brookes has explored the visibility of early Anglo-Saxon burial sites, which often incorporate Bronze Age barrows. These may have been invaluable landmarks to those travelling, whether along roads and drove-ways, or on ships around the east coast between Dover and Reculver (Brookes 2007, 68, fig. 33). The importance of sea transport should not be underestimated as east Kent forms a relatively narrow peninsula. Sheltered tidal waterways, notably the Wantsum and the Swale, would have been valuable routes. Several short creeks extend inland from the Swale to meet the main Roman road (Watling Street) between Rochester and Faversham; a better case for continuity between the Roman and the Anglo-Saxon periods can be made for nodal sites along this road, such as Milton and Faversham, than for many other locations (Everitt 1986).

Surprisingly, we have very little archaeological evidence for boats and ships within Kent between the fifth and the eighth century, although a number of sixth-century Kentish graves, all in cemeteries visible to coastal shipping, contained iron boat rivets, implying recycling of timber as coffin fittings (Brookes 2007; forthcoming a). The earliest substantial clinker-built ship from Kent was uncovered in the Graveney marshes by the Swale in 1970 and has been dated to the tenth century (Fenwick 1978). Investigation of beach markets and the earliest river harbours in Kent between the sixth and ninth century has hardly begun. In comparison with the extensive excavations at *Hamwic* (Southampton), *Lundenwic* (London) and *Gipeswic* (Ipswich) (Hill and Cowie 2001, 85-103; Scull 1997), the only place with a reasonably full assessment is the seventh- to ninth-century seasonal beach market and fishing site of *Sandtun*, near Lympne (Gardiner *et al.* 2001).

Recent fieldwork has located the probable site of Anglo-Saxon Fordwich, first mentioned in a charter issued by Hlothere in 675, as well as in a toll-remission document of *c*. 761 (Sawyer 1968, S7 and S29), and has also identified the settlement associated with the Sarre cemetery on Thanet, which may well have operated as a toll-levying station for sea traffic using the Wantsum Channel (Brookes 2007; forthcoming b). The original site of Sandwich, however, referred to in a mid-seventh-century context by the *Life of St Wilfrid* (ch. 13), remains to be discovered. Seasalter, to the west of Whitstable, might be *Harwich* (Baldwin 1992).

The four late Roman coastal forts might have been expected to produce evidence for continuity linking the fourth to the sixth century, but are disappointing in this respect. Only Richborough has produced clear evidence for military occupation at the very beginning of the fifth century. The prone weapon burial discovered north of its defences *c*. 1928-30 is probably that of a garrison officer (Böhme 1986, 515-6, Abb. 39-40; Bushe-Fox 1949, 80 pl. LXIII; Hawkes and Dunning 1961, fig. 5). Coins from Richborough imply that its garrison was being paid into the first decade of the fifth century (Reece 1968), which was probably when this man was buried. Unfortunately only the south-west corner of the fort at Dover has been excavated and fuller reports on the most recent excavations are still awaited. Anglo-Saxon occupation began no later than the early sixth century, but there is no particular evidence indicating continuity of occupation across the fifth century (Philp 2003). The Lympne fort suffered the first of three destructive landslides perhaps *c*. 540, with the second post-dating 700 (Hutchinson *et al.* 1985). *Sandtun* is effectively its successor from the seventh century onwards, but again continuity cannot be demonstrated (Gardiner *et al.* 2001, 265-7).

Equally, little is known archaeologically about the walled town at Rochester, controlling a bridge over the Medway, though an important Anglo-

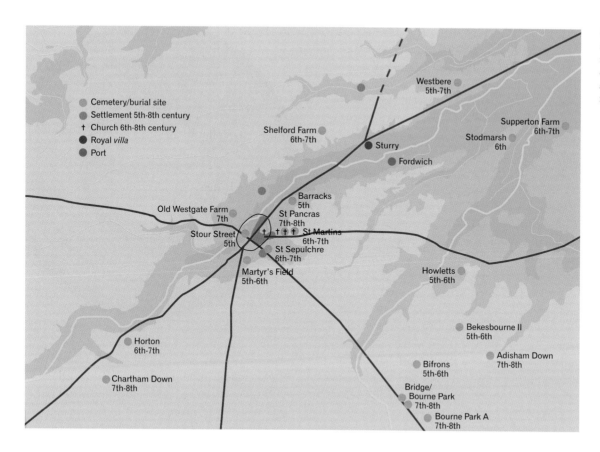

Cemetery/burial site
Settlement 5th-8th century
† Church 6th-8th century
Royal *villa*
Port

Westbere
5th-7th

Shelford Farm
6th-7th

Sturry

Supperton Farm
6th-7th

Stodmarsh
6th

Fordwich

Old Westgate Farm
7th

Barracks
5th

St Pancras
7th-8th

St Martins
6th-7th

Stour Street
5th

St Sepulchre
6th-7th

Martyr's Field
5th-6th

Howletts
5th-6th

Bekesbourne II
5th-6th

Adisham Down
7th-8th

Horton
6th-7th

Bifrons
5th-6th

Bridge/
Bourne Park
7th-8th

Chartham Down
7th-8th

Bourne Park A
7th-8th

6.7 Canterbury in its local setting with churches and minsters, extramural cemeteries, a trading settlement at Fordwich and royal centres at St Martin's and at Sturry.

Saxon cemetery was established nearby at Chatham around the end of the fifth century (Douglas 1793; Hawkes 1982a; 1990). By contrast, Canterbury has attracted virtually continuous archaeological excavation since the late 1940s, mostly concentrated in its south-east quadrant. The city has been presented as a case-study for overlap between late Roman and early Anglo-Saxon occupation (Frere 1966, 91-3, figs 18-20; Myres 1969, 95-7, fig. 40, map 7), but a reaction set in during the 1980s, with emphasis placed instead on the early depopulation and abandonment of much of the Roman town during the fourth century. This was signalled by 'dark earth' deposits that pre-date the earliest Anglo-Saxon occupation (Blockley *et al.* 1995). The first Anglo-Saxon structures were sunken-featured buildings cut into this dark earth, implying a new occupation on a rural scale within the Roman walled circuit (below, page 202). Not surprisingly

the pendulum is now swinging back and today's excavators seem anxious to re-establish continuity across the fifth-century divide (Bennett *et al.* 2003, 194). The Roman stone theatre on the Marlowe sites survived as a standing structure until late in the Anglo-Saxon period, but that hardly implies urban continuity. There is also some partial evidence for Anglo-Saxon use of Canterbury's Roman-period extramural cemeteries. The Scandinavian relief-decorated square-headed brooch from Martyr's Field to the south of the Roman walls was manufactured *c.* 500 (Chadwick 1958a, pl. Xa; Haseloff 1981, Taf. II.1; Hawkes 1982a, fig. 30). Later metalwork, including a jewelled pendant of the seventh century, indicates reuse of a second Roman cemetery to the west of Canterbury (Webster 1987) (ill. 6.7).

The official belts (*cingula*) issued to Roman officers feature in several Anglo-Saxon cemeteries

6.8 Fifth-century silver penannular quoit brooch from Sarre, Thanet: probably a product of a British metalworkshop in east Kent (approx. actual size).

in Kent (Evison 1981) and their dating has been established from coin-dated continental graves. The Milton 'simple' belt set is attributed now to the middle third of the fifth century (Böhme 1986, 495, Abb. 19.10-14; Hawkes and Dunning 1961, fig. 2; Hawkes 1989), making it more than probable that it belonged to an Anglo-Saxon war leader billeted in Kent. A contemporary burial (M8/A2) from Liebenau (Germany) illustrates the sort of weaponry that may well have accompanied the Milton belt (Böhme 1974, Taf. 27-8; Cosack 1982, Taf. 5-8). The strategic location of Milton at a creek running down to the Swale is significant. Similar belt sets in southern Britain occurred in comparable sites at Croydon and at Dorchester-on-Thames. Smaller and typologically later fixed-plate buckles represent the final type of Roman military belt fittings imported from the Continent in the middle of the fifth century. Details of the Kentish find-spot of a buckle from the Douglas collection have been lost (Trier-Samson Type: Böhme 1974, 71-3, Abb. 51-2; 1986, 495, Abb. 19.5), but two others are recorded from the Anglo-Saxon cemetery commanding the Wantsum at Sarre (Krefeld-Gellep Type: Böhme 1986, 508-9, Abb. 31.2 and 3, 44; Evison 1981, fig. 2b; Hawkes and Dunning 1961, fig. 20h). As with the Milton belt, these probably arrived in Kent worn by warriors from northern Germany (Welch 1993).

Again, we cannot ignore the belt fittings and brooches of the Quoit-Brooch Style (ill. 6.8). Some have favoured a south Scandinavian origin (e.g. Ager 1985; Chadwick 1961), and others a Frankish derivation, with roots in fourth-century Gallo-Roman metalworking (Evison 1965; 1968; 1981; Leeds 1936), but a consensus now exists for manufacture by 'British' workshops during the fifth century (e.g. Haseloff 1981; Inker 2000; Suzuki 2000; Welch 1983). Virtually every example in England comes from an early Anglo-Saxon burial, but a damaged openwork belt mount from Richborough is an exception (Cunliffe 1968, 94, pl. XXXV.104). This is matched by more complete versions from Andover (Cook and Dacre 1985, fig. 63.2, pl. XVII) and Alfriston (Evison 1965, fig. 23g; Welch 1983, fig. 40a). The Richborough find supports the case for regional manufacture in Kent and a late Roman metalworkshop existed nearby at Ickham (Young 1981; Bennett, Ridler and Sparey-Green forthcoming). Demonstrating that the Ickham smiths were responsible for Quoit-Brooch Style production is another matter, but the earliest examples do resemble late Roman models, whereas later items seem to have been designed for a newly established Anglo-Saxon clientele (Inker 2000, 51). Quoit-Brooch Style metalwork may well have been issued to 'Saxon' mercenaries billeted in Kent, in imitation of Roman practice of equipping troops with uniforms. Belt fittings would provide a substitute for the military *cingulum* and ring brooches (quoit and penannular forms) might have replaced military 'crossbow' brooches as cloak fasteners. Their Saxon warrior recipients seem to have regarded the brooches with distaste, however, and passed them on to their women, who sometimes combined them with an Anglo-Saxon female brooch, as at Lyminge Grave 10 (Evison 1965, fig. 28g-h; Welch 1983, 64-5).

British peasants possibly lived in structures so basic that they left virtually no trace, and adopted organic containers in place of pottery during the fifth century. Equally, a major depopulation episode across lowland Britain, including Kent, prior to the Anglo-Saxon settlement cannot be ruled out. It need not be just the landowners who fled Saxon rebellion in eastern Britain. Many of their tenants may have been forced to join them. British migration to the West Country and overseas to Armorica (Brittany) and Galicia (Spain) is recorded and Britons from Kent may well have participated. Alternatively a large residual population may have accepted Anglo-Saxon authority rather than abandon its land and this subservient population may have outnumbered the newcomers. Perhaps within a few generations this local population had become effectively Anglo-Saxon and was buried in Anglo-Saxon cemeteries. Unfortunately routine DNA analysis of ancient skeletons is still not common or reliable and the quality of bone survival in most Kentish cemeteries probably limits possibilities for future research (Mays and Anderson 1994). On the other hand, Y-chromosome DNA samples from living male populations in England confirm a major influx of men matched to those currently inhabiting modern Frisia in the northern Netherlands (Capelli *et al.* 2003; Weale *et al.* 2002). The Frisian islands, which were on the coastal migration route linking the Anglo-Saxon homelands to lowland Britain (England), seem to have been deserted in the fourth century and may well have been colonised by Saxon migrants moving westwards during the fifth century. Again, it is possible that semi-free peasants tied to the land they worked and referred to in the seventh-century Kentish laws as *læts*, and also the slaves or *theow*, might be descendants of the former British population. Establishing a relationship between the seventh-century Kentish *læts* and the third- or fourth-century Roman *læti* of Gaul and Italy remains problematic. The Roman *læti* were peoples settled on abandoned land, which they were required to

farm (Jones 1964, 60, 157 and 620). Unfortunately we lack any specific reference to *læti* in late Roman Britain, but then the relevant section for Britain seems to be missing from the *Notitia Dignitatum*. Perhaps *læti* had settled in south-east Britain, but the term *læt* seems to be restricted to Kent and it probably reflects Frankish influence over seventh-century Kent and the adoption of a Frankish model for its law codes (Wormald 1999). In any case, tenurial and legal status are not necessarily linked to ethnic identities, as those captured in warfare could be sold on as slaves (see the story of Imma: *HE* IV.22 [20]).

Anglo-Saxon cemetery archaeology can make its contribution to the migration debate, as the re-introduction of cremation to Britain centuries after its abandonment by Roman society must be significant. Hand-made pottery with specifically north German and Scandinavian forms was probably produced by women and may well provide a strong ethnic indicator (Haith 1997; Varndell and Freestone 1997, 37; Welch 1992, 109-10; Welsby 1997, 30). Likewise weapon burial may have an ethnic dimension in the fifth and sixth centuries (Härke 1992). The present author makes no apology for favouring large-scale migration into eastern Britain over an extended timescale and would point to archaeological evidence for the depopulation of regions within the continental homelands of the Anglo-Saxons during the fifth century (Welch 1992; 2003). Migration was a reality in protohistoric and early historic periods across continental Europe and there is a need to develop a theoretical basis for its interpretation using archaeological evidence.

Anglo-Saxon buildings and settlements in Kent

Despite the extensive archaeological investigations in Kent in recent years, only small rural settlements have been excavated apart from in Canterbury; the larger settlements found in some other counties are presently elusive (cf. Hamerow 2002). Sunken-featured buildings (also known in

German as *Grubenhäuser*) have been recognised from many excavations in Kent since the late 1940s, most notably in Canterbury (Blockley *et al.* 1995; Blockley *et al.* 1997, fig. 2; Frere and Stow 1983; Frere *et al.* 1987). This type of structure seems to have been introduced to lowland Britain from the Continent at the beginning of the Anglo-Saxon period. The relationship between these Anglo-Saxon sunken-featured structures and those of the second century AD excavated at Monkton on Thanet (Bennett and Williams 1997; see above page 162) is not entirely clear, but they appear to belong to different traditions (Hamerow pers. comm.). Rectangular earth-fast timber structures constructed at ground level have proved to be rare finds in Kent.

The Marlowe sites in Canterbury produced only two examples of post-built structures, both dated to the later seventh century. Building S9, 9m by 4m with a central pair of opposed doorways (Blockley *et al.* 1995, figs 145 and 148), fits a standard double-square module plan (James *et al.* 1984, figs 1 and 4). Although some archaeologists have argued for a British influence on this building type, similar structures occur across north-west Europe, particularly in the Netherlands (Hamerow 1999; 2002). Building S8 (9m by 7m) had well-spaced post-holes suggesting an open structure below its roof. Yet its 'weak' corner post-holes imply the use of horizontal timbers clasped by slender, earth-fast uprights, providing at least two reasonably solid wall corners. It was probably a workshop on the evidence for iron-working (Blockley *et al.* 1995, figs 145-6) and was replaced in *c.* 875-900 by S28, also associated with iron-working (Blockley *et al.* 1995, figs 181-2). It can be compared to contemporary workshops at Ramsbury in Wiltshire (Haslam 1980, 9-30, fig. 5). The only other Canterbury post-built structure, at 68-69a, Stour Street, was possibly of eighth-century date (Bennett 1980, 409).

The apparent absence of earlier post- or plank-based buildings within Canterbury probably reflects the poor survival of recognisable post-hole patterns due to later disturbance and also the restricted nature of sites generally available for excavation. Sunken-featured buildings are much easier to identify and large-scale excavations elsewhere, e.g. Mucking (Essex), suggest that there would be two to three sunken-featured buildings for every rectangular building (Hamerow 1993). By the mid-1990s, twenty-eight sunken-featured buildings had been recorded on the Marlowe sites, with a further six at the nearby Simon Langton Yard, implying some ten to fourteen ground-level buildings. All the sunken-featured buildings had been dug into a 'dark earth' horizon related to the abandonment of Roman buildings, combined with subsequent middening practices of a much-reduced population. Formation of the 'dark earth' began around the second quarter of the fourth century, with the construction of the first sunken-featured buildings around the middle of the fifth century (Blockley *et al.* 1995, 882-5). Most of the Canterbury examples feature a simple pair of post-holes, supporting a tent-like roof sufficient for a basic workshop. Variations can occur, however, with nine post-holes recorded from one building in Stour Street (Bennett 1980, 409, fig. 5). Two of the Canterbury structures were sited within ruined Roman masonry buildings and thirteen produced evidence that their pit bases formed their floors (Blockley *et al.* 1995, 463). Initially, in the fifth and sixth centuries there was a fluid pattern of shifting settlement, but more permanent occupation developed within fixed building plots during the seventh to eighth century. Thus small-scale, rural-style occupation was replaced by a more urban-like settlement, presumably linked to economic and social developments. As yet no equivalent settlement features are recorded within the Roman walled circuit of Rochester, though a similar picture to Canterbury might be anticipated.

Both sunken-featured buildings and substantial

rectangular buildings were excavated within the Roman coastal fort at Dover during the 1970s and 1980s (Philp 2003). Most of them are dated to the seventh century, including the largest of the sunken-featured buildings (N4). This was *c.* 8m by 4m and had been destroyed by fire, preserving a timber plank lining. It contained long strings of intermediate ring-shaped clay loomweights, typical of the middle Saxon period, and other finds include a copper-alloy workbox. Intermediate loomweights were present in other Dover sunken-featured buildings, although a sixth-century button brooch implies rather earlier occupation in the vicinity. Three successive sunken-featured buildings (S9) were cut into the fort rampart and are attributed to the sixth and seventh centuries on the basis of finds, including both amber and glass beads. By contrast building S11, containing bun-shaped loomweights, clearly belongs to the late Saxon period. A midden outside the fort's west wall produced a variety of finds, including a seventh-century gold finger (or thumb) ring, whose garnet setting contains a gold circlet inlay. Although this material may have come from the fort, there was possibly an extramural settlement adjacent to the fort's west wall, related to the early Anglo-Saxon cemetery on Durham Hill (Evison 1987, 169 and 177; Meaney 1964, 118), with a second cemetery on Priory Hill some 600m to the north-west (Evison 1987, text fig. 36; Meaney 1964, 176; Willson 1988, 81).

All the Dover rectangular buildings were trench-built, implying construction in the seventh century or later. The wall trenches of S10 contained horizontal timber beams into which timber uprights had been inserted; a similar charred beam from Bishopstone (East Sussex), structure 47, probably dates to the middle Saxon period (Bell 1977, 219-23, fig. 98; Gardiner pers. comm.). The S10 trenches had been dug through a stone and mortar floor, probably Roman in date though attributed by the excavator to a post-Roman phase. The relationships between floor surfaces and wall trenches for the timber buildings in the S14 complex can similarly be questioned. The structure is presented by its excavator as a timber church, first constructed in the seventh century and abandoned by the tenth century (Philp 2003, 58). It is attributed to the royal monastery first established by Eadbald in Dover during the 630s, re-founded within the Roman fort *c.* 696 by Wihtræd (Rigold 1977, 73), and replaced by the Norman stone church of St Martin le Grand, a short distance to the north. Although a so-called 'altar base' has been identified at the east end of a small central rectangular-cell structure (West Cell, Period I) and the *opus signinum* finish of the Period III floor is matched in seventh-century Kentish stone churches, a late seventh-century royal monastic church in Kent ought to be constructed in stone. This timber building also lacks the *porticus* side-chambers typical of stone churches, and a far more convincing case can be made instead for S14 representing two successive great timber halls. Each was built on a scale suitable for royal use and would have been maintained by a royal official (a *præfectus*) for periodic visits by the king's itinerant court to his royal *castellum* in Dover. These halls are comparable in scale to royal halls at Yeavering (Hope-Taylor 1977) and use construction methods found at Cowdery's Down (Millett and James 1983).

The first rural settlement in east Kent to reveal both sunken-featured and rectangular buildings is on downland some five kilometres north of Dover at Church Whitfield and dated to the sixth and seventh centuries (Parfitt 1996; Parfitt, Allen and Rady 1997, 7) (box, pages 204-5). North of Wainscott, across the Medway from Rochester (Rady *et al.* 2004), three successive enclosure ditches were associated with at least two, and possibly three, rectangular buildings. Structure 4 (*c.* 14m by 6m) had various early standard features such as pairs of post-holes for earth-fast upright wall planking, 'weak' corners and a double-square layout separated by central opposed doorways. Although Structure 5 was less

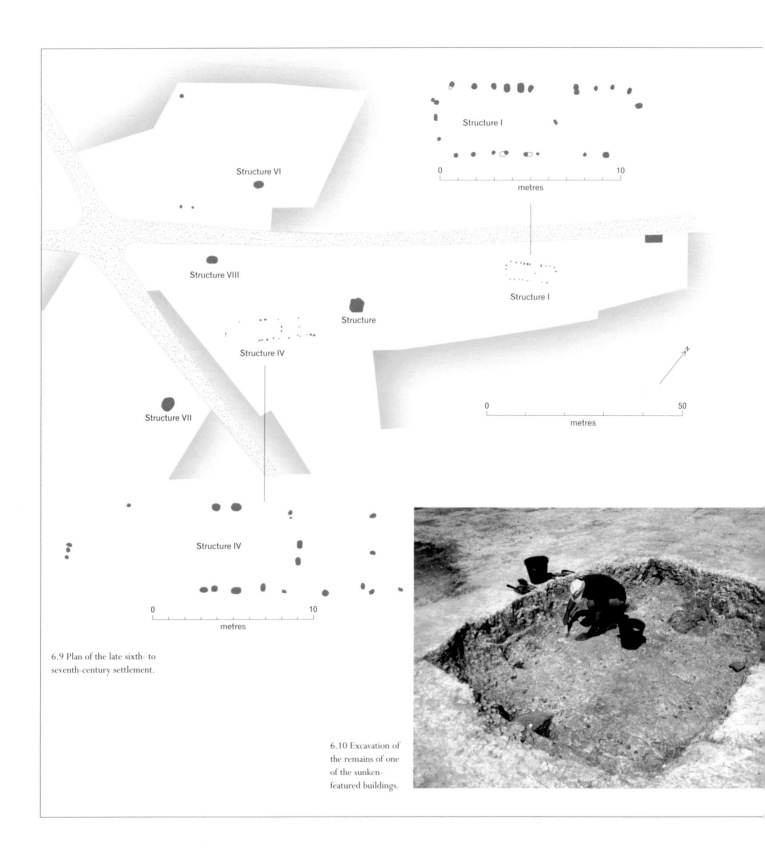

Structure VI

Structure I

Structure VIII

Structure I

Structure

Structure IV

Structure VII

Structure IV

0   metres   10

0   metres   50

0   metres   10

6.9 Plan of the late sixth- to
seventh-century settlement.

6.10 Excavation of
the remains of one
of the sunken-
featured buildings.

The Church Whitfield settlement

This site on the Downs to the north of Dover was one of the first to be excavated in east Kent that combined ground-level rectangular post-built structures with sunken-featured buildings (SFBs), both buildings being typical of early Anglo-Saxon rural settlements. There were two timber halls and four SFBs within the excavated area as well as a four-post structure which perhaps represented a granary. The site was probably a single farmstead or part of a small hamlet. Each hall may have housed a family unit, with the SFBs being used for industrial or similar activity.

Wheel-thrown pottery sherds of vessels imported from north-east France from the SFBs imply a late sixth- to seventh-century date range. These finds may, however, originate from surface middens used to backfill the SFBs when they were abandoned as buildings, rather than represent material lost during their occupation. Animal bones from the SFBs suggest that cattle, pigs and sheep were herded, butchered and consumed on site. Some hunting is indicated by roe deer bones and there were also fish remains.

The halls do not fit the dimensions normally associated with such structures in the seventh century, where a double-square module plan would be expected (James *et al.* 1984, fig. 4). Instead, they have a length more than three times their width, something more typical of the ninth century, if not later (Hamerow 2004, 302, fig. 11.1). It is not feasible to date such buildings using finds recovered from their post-holes and the dating of these halls has been derived from finds in the neighbouring SFBs. As so often, there were no visible traces of post-constructed fence-lines that might help to define contemporary household farm units and link the excavated buildings, as has been recorded on Hampshire chalkland at Chalton and Cowdery's Down (Welch 1992).

complete, a series of post-holes and flint post-pads demonstrate that it was less than 4.5m wide. Neither building produced direct dating evidence, but both have been attributed to the sixth to seventh century. Structure 6 was defined by an east-west beam trench on its south edge and by associated post-holes, but is more typical of later Anglo-Saxon buildings.

Another excavation in west Kent revealed a possible Anglo-Saxon rectangular post-built structure adjacent to the Darenth Roman villa. Two parallel rows of post-holes were set 5.2m apart, but there were no post-holes or trenches for the gable ends (Philp 1984, 81-2, 92-4, figs 23-4 and 26). The structure might be a simple double-square or a double-square separated by a central pair of doorways with an overall length of 10.4m or more. Its acceptance as Anglo-Saxon depends on the claimed preservation of a thin 'occupation layer' containing four hand-made potsherds. Yet occupation layers are rarely preserved in such timber buildings and no relationship appears to have been established between this layer and the post-holes. Rather, flints, broken Roman tile and potsherds in the post-holes strongly suggest that this was a late Roman-period structure. The 'pit' feature (3.88m by 2.28m), 25 metres to the south-east (*ibid.* 84, figs 24 and 28), containing a pair of post-holes and forty potsherds of Anglo-Saxon date, is convincing as a sunken-featured building, but three adjacent pits lack post-holes (*ibid.* 85-86), arguing against the same interpretation. A scattered group of definite sunken-featured buildings around the Northfleet Roman villa, south-west of Gravesend, has been dated to the sixth and seventh centuries. Although upland sites such as Church Whitfield are the norm, valley-bottom settlements such as Northfleet are recorded elsewhere, for example Abbots Worthy in Hampshire (Fasham and Whinney 1991) and Botolphs in West Sussex (Gardiner 1990a). A partially preserved watermill in waterlogged riverside deposits adjacent to the Northfleet Roman villa was an unexpected find (box, pages 206-7).

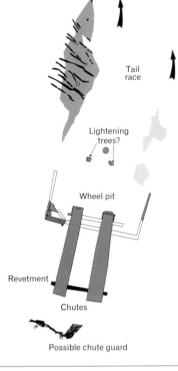

6.11 View of the penstocks and wheelpit; note the circular holes in the end of the penstocks which would have concentrated a jet of water.

Tail race

Lightening trees?

Wheel pit

Revetment

Chutes

Possible chute guard

0   metres   5

Wood
Wattle
Possible lightening trees
Possible wattle lined tail race

6.12 View of the penstocks from the mill pond. Note the sluice arrangements at the end of the penstocks to control the flow of water into the penstocks.

6.13 Plan of the mill showing how the water flow would be directed on to the two wheels via the chutes or 'penstocks'.

The Ebbsfleet watermill

An unexpected bonus of the reinvestigation of the Northfleet Roman villa site in advance of the construction of the new Ebbsfleet railway station was a partially preserved timber horizontal watermill. Two almost perfectly preserved wooden 'penstocks' were found *in situ*. They seem to have functioned as enclosed funnels to direct jets of water on to a pair of horizontal paddled wheels. On the basis of their location in the original tidal reach of the Ebbsfleet, Damien Goodburn (pers. comm.) has argued that the mill probably harnessed tidal water flows. The quality of the oak used suggests that the builders had to make do with second-rate timber resources, most probably a nearby stand of trees. Preliminary dendrochronology analysis indicates felling dates either side of 700 (689-719), but this need not date the excavated mill itself. The recycling of timbers from an earlier mill in one constructed rather later in the eighth century cannot yet be ruled out.

The earliest reference in Kent to a watermill, located at Chart, occurs in a charter issued by Æthelberht II in 762 (Sawyer 1968, S25). There is also a reference to a tidal mill by the Wantsum near Reculver, from an estate boundary clause dated to 949 (*ibid.*, S546; Gough 1992). The ninth-century watermill excavated at Tamworth in Staffordshire is well known (Rahtz and Meeson 1992) and several watermills across Anglo-Saxon England have now been subject to archaeological investigation. Of greatest relevance here is the unpublished mill from Old Windsor and another from the important monastic site of Barking Abbey, as both utilised water courses in the Thames basin. The excellent preservation of the Northfleet penstocks is exceptional, as they appear to be the first examples of such an early date to be recorded outside early Christian Ireland.

To date, four Roman villas in west Kent have produced early Anglo-Saxon structures: an isolated sunken-featured building at Lower Warbank, Keston (Philp *et al.* 1991, 133-5, figs 15, 30 and 39; 1999), another on the eastern edge of the Franks (Horton Kirby) villa (Webster 1976; 164) and the Northfleet and Darenth sites. A further isolated sunken-featured building was cut through Roman metalled surfaces at Springhead, but has yet to be dated. As insufficient fieldwork has taken place to establish whether early Anglo-Saxon settlement was particularly attracted to abandoned Roman villa sites, it may be that Anglo-Saxon rural settlements were more evenly distributed across the best arable land and we might expect that they would normally be located adjacent to their cemeteries (Tyler 1992, 79-81; Welch 1985b, 16-17). The currently visible pattern, though reinforced by the Orpington cemetery being adjacent to a Roman bathhouse and a metalled road (Philp and Keller 1995), may reflect a bias stemming from the fact that Anglo-Saxon settlement remains are relatively difficult to locate by fieldwork and much Anglo-Saxon evidence has come to light when investigating more archaeologically visible sites.

Returning to east Kent, a scatter of five sunken-featured buildings, with simple pairs of posts south of Manston Road in Ramsgate on Thanet, is attributed to the late sixth to seventh century (Wessex Archaeology 1996). Finds included copper-alloy tweezers and other toilet implements, iron knives and pottery, with both hand-made and imported wheel-thrown sherds. Iron slag and other debris indicate smithing nearby. Animal bone included sheep/goat (52%), with only two definite goat bones, cattle (30%), pig (13%) and horse (4%), in ratios similar to those from the settlement at West Stow, Suffolk (Crabtree 1989). The swine were probably pastured seasonally in the Weald, probably near Tenterden, as well as in managed woodlands on Thanet. Fish bones indicate some inshore fishing (ray, herring and flatfish), while shells imply beach collection of oyster (37%), mussels (27%) and limpets (27%), but these were probably not significant for the community's overall diet. Carbonised free-threshing wheats, hulled barley, rye, oats and peas were present. Hazelnut shells suggest woodland or scrub nearby and charcoal indicates exploitable stands of deciduous trees containing oak, maple and possibly hazel, but no wetland species such as willow or alder. Marginal woodland or more open areas with scrub are implied by dogwood, blackthorn and hazel. Mollusc species indicate the presence of fresh or brackish water, but also an open countryside. So this Anglo-Saxon community exploited the coastal margins as well as its immediate hinterland, though the absence of rectangular buildings implies that it was both marginal and subsidiary to a more substantial settlement in the vicinity. Whether the principal settlement was a hamlet or an isolated farm cannot yet be established, nor can we match it with any specific contemporary cemetery in the Ramsgate area. The site is invaluable for its report on the environmental evidence and similar quality evidence is needed urgently from sites across Kent, if we are to reconstruct the Anglo-Saxon rural economy.

A very unusual rural settlement on Glebe land at Harrietsham, immediately south of the downland scarp, has been attributed to the Anglo-Saxon period (Canterbury Archaeological Trust 1998). The wall foundations of its five rectangular aisled buildings consisted of medium to large flints set into linear trenches, with two rows of internal wall posts to support the roofs. Buildings 1 and 3 were of unknown length, but each was 13m wide. Aisled earth-fast timber structures are known from the Anglo-Saxon continental homelands (Zimmermann 1988; Hamerow 2002) and can be found occasionally in Anglo-Saxon England (e.g. Yeavering halls A2 and A4: Hope-Taylor 1977), but none has a low stone wall foundation, nor does the bow-sided building S15 at Portchester Castle (12.8m by 9.45m), dated to the late Anglo-Saxon period (Cunliffe 1976, 41-4, fig. 25). A late Roman date seems more plausible for Harrietsham and an apparent

sunken-featured building here was probably just a large pit.

An interesting sequence of sites in the Newington area to the west of Folkestone suggests continuous settlement between the sixth and ninth century, with a sunken-featured building at Biggin's Wood, another two sunken-featured buildings on Dolland's Moor, a rubbish pit at Cherry Garden Hill and a group of three pits at Cheriton Hill (Rady et al. 1989; Rady 1990). Nearby at Saltwood one of three isolated sunken-featured buildings is reasonably close to the easternmost of three Anglo-Saxon cemeteries. As at Manston Road near Ramsgate, however, the principal hamlets or individual farms associated with each of the Saltwood cemeteries have yet to be located. A single sunken-featured building on the northern edge of an early Bronze Age barrow near Ringlemere may well be associated with burials of the fifth to sixth century on its south side (Parfitt 2002; 2005). Establishing such relationships between the somewhat limited settlement evidence and the much more numerous contemporary cemeteries is essential if we are to develop a fuller understanding of settlement patterns and territorial organisation in Kent. Any assumption that settlements were sited within or close to later medieval and present-day hamlets or villages should be treated with caution. Rural agricultural settlements in pre-industrial societies were normally adjacent to their fields. They shifted as and when those fields became exhausted. Settlements could have been positioned, certainly initially, in the immediate vicinity of their cemeteries. In the case of the Kingston Down barrow field, this would imply a settlement adjacent to the main Canterbury to Dover Roman road rather than in the valley below, where the modern village of Kingston is located. For the settlement associated with the Finglesham (the 'prince's farm') cemetery, a hilltop rather than a valley location might again be indicated and the Old English place-name may have no link to the cemetery. Turning to the cemeteries inland from

Dover on the upper slopes of the Dour valley, it is possible that their communities occupied farms along the lower slopes of the valley bottom, as at the Northfleet Roman villa. Alternatively, these settlements could have utilised gently sloping land above their cemeteries, commanding access into the valley as well as exploiting their downland hinterland. Elsewhere across southern and eastern England, at such sites as Bishopstone (East Sussex), Mucking (Essex), Spong Hill (Norfolk), West Stow (Suffolk) and West Heslerton (North Yorkshire), early Anglo-Saxon settlements and cemeteries share adjacent locations. The regular spacing of contemporary settlements some 800m apart along the south edge of the Vale of Pickering around Heslerton may reflect its particularly favourable arable soils. With less productive land, a lower settlement density could be maintained. Focussed fieldwork projects are essential in any future exploration of settlement patterns for early Anglo-Saxon Kent.

Anglo-Saxon cemeteries and burial sites in Kent

Although settlement evidence is limited in Kent, cemeteries of the fifth to seventh century, with their wealth of grave goods, provide an outstanding resource for examining the origins and evolving social structure of Kent's population. This is of particular importance given the difficulty in separating myth from reality in terms of Saxon, Jutish and Frankish presence and influence. These issues are explored in some depth in this section.

Cemetery archaeology for the fifth to sixth century is fundamentally different in the two halves of the county. West Kent shares 'Saxon' characteristics with much of the rest of south-east England (Essex, Surrey, Sussex, etc.) and its roots are to be found in the fifth-century cemeteries of the Elbe-Weser coastlands in north-west Germany (Böhme 1986; Welch 1983). Female costume in west Kent is characterised by the wearing of saucer and disc brooches in matched pairs to fasten a peplos dress at the shoulders, with glass and/or amber beads strung between them. Weapon sets consist principally of single spears, but can be combined with small buckler-sized shields and additionally include high-status weapons such as axes or two-edged long swords (Evison 1965, figs 16-20, 22-23). Cremations are relatively common and usually utilise pottery vessels decorated in either a 'Saxon' or an 'Anglian' tradition. This duality reflects the presence of both pottery traditions in fifth-century 'Saxon' cemeteries beside the west bank of the Elbe (e.g. Issendorf: Weber 1998).

By contrast east Kent cemeteries are characterised by the development of a distinctive 'Kentish' material culture. Where copper-alloy cast dress fittings, with or without gilding, were the norm in west Kent, gilt cast silver was relatively common in the eastern half of the county. By the seventh century, however, this east Kentish material culture was being adopted in west Kent, reflecting the annexation of territory between the Medway and London in the later sixth century. Cremations, whether in a pottery urn or an organic container, are extremely rare east of the Medway in the fifth and sixth centuries. In terms of material culture, although both 'Saxon' and 'Anglian' influences are present amongst the earliest burials in east Kent, we also find a significant south Scandinavian element in the form of distinctive brooches, small gold pendants and hand-made pottery dating from the fifth into the sixth century. Traditionally this Scandinavian presence has been linked to Bede's statement that Kent was settled by Jutes from mainland Denmark (*HE* I.15), but recent research has pointed to the danger of over-simplistic interpretation (Kruse forthcoming; Sørensen 1999). A complicating factor is a major presence of Gallo-Roman and Frankish cultural material in east Kent in the later fifth and through most of the sixth century. Indeed it is through a combination of Scandinavian and Frankish elements that the uniquely blended Kentish tradition emerges during the sixth century; this was to be developed to its fullest extent during the seventh century.

6.14 Plan of the two early Anglo-Saxom cemetery areas at Buckland near Dover separated by a nineteenth-century railcutting: Buckland I excavated in the 1950s and Buckland II in 1994.

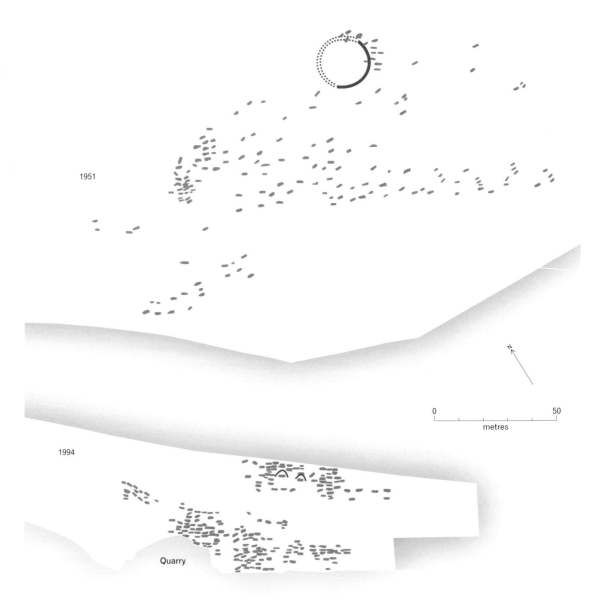

East Kent burial sites

Although burials provide the bulk of the archaeological evidence here up to the early eighth century, remarkably few sites have been adequately published and a few sites are continually referred to. Some of the most valuable published cemeteries, such as Kingston Down (Faussett 1856), Chatham Lines (Douglas 1793), Bifrons (Hawkes 2000) and Sarre (Brent J 1863; 1866; 1868; Perkins 1991a; 1992b), were excavated in the eighteenth and nineteenth centuries, though it is not always easy to relate finds in museum collections to published grave assemblages. Hawkes, however, demonstrated what can be done in separating the iron objects from the Bifrons and Sarre cemeteries (2000). Only a limited number of cemetery excavations have been adequately published within the second half of the twentieth century, including Lyminge II (Warhurst 1955), Buckland I near Dover (Evison 1987), Mill Hill near Deal (Parfitt and Brugmann 1997) and now Finglesham (Hawkes and Grainger 2006). A significant backlog of major projects awaits publication, including two sites in Broadstairs at St Peter's Tip (Hogarth 1973) and Bradstow School (Webster 1972; 1974; 1975). The rapid expansion of archaeological excavation since the introduction of developer funding during the 1990s has seen the investigation of several new cemeteries, including a new sector of Buckland (Parfitt and Haith 1995) (ill. 6.14). Publication of Buckland II should encourage re-evaluation of the Buckland I and Mill Hill reports, while the three cemeteries at Saltwood to the west of Folkestone, revealed in advance of the Channel Tunnel Rail Link, will be an important addition to the modern cemetery excavation corpus in east Kent (ill. 6.35).

A product of this uneven publication record is a distinct shortage of adequately recorded fifth-century grave groups from east Kent. There is particularly limited information about cremations, whether deposited in pottery urns or in organic containers, but a new site adjacent to an early Bronze Age barrow at Ringlemere, near Woodnesborough, has revealed several relatively early fifth-century inhumations as well as cremations. Its finds include a north German supporting-arm brooch (Mahndorf type) dating to the first third of the fifth century and an applied disc brooch (e.g. Böhme 1986, 568 Abb. 49 and 51-3). A significant number of later fifth-century graves were also excavated at Buckland II, compared to the few from Buckland I (Evison 1987, phase 1). Over time it should be possible to establish fifth-century phases for eastern Kent and relate these to the sixth-century scheme of thirty-year phases established for the richest female burials by Brugmann (1999). Fifth-century burials tend to be less well furnished, however, with fewer dress fittings, weapons and other finds compared to their sixth-century equivalents. There is also a greater diversity of material,

making the task of defining phases that bit harder. For the late sixth to early eighth century, a sequence of generation-length (thirty-year) phases is promised in the near future (C. Scull pers. comm.). Although based on a national sample, east Kentish graves will feature strongly in this project, which combines radiocarbon dates from human skeletons with computer-based seriation of the grave finds. In a recent survey, Brookes could list just three sites in east Kent producing convincing Anglo-Saxon cremation evidence (Hollingbourne, Westbere and Coombe near Woodnesborough (2002, 152)), with a further three possessing more circumstantial evidence (The Bayle (Folkestone), Old Westgate Farm (Canterbury) and Stodmarsh). Ringlemere has now produced fifth-century cremations and there are individual sixth-century examples from Saltwood and Lyminge II. Eventually, it should be possible to trace this minority burial practice from the earliest fifth-century phases into the later sixth century and the high-status Coombe burial group (Davidson and Webster 1967; Evison 1967).

The earliest cemeteries in east Kent

The cemeteries containing finds attributable to the later fifth century and the very beginning of the sixth century share a broadly coastal distribution, extending from Chatham Lines through to Milton and Faversham, with many more sites east of Canterbury along the rivers that fed the Wantsum channel, such as Westbere on the Stour and Howletts, Bekesbourne and Bifrons on the Nailbourne (Chadwick 1958b; Hawkes 2000), together with Thanet sites such as Sarre. Further south, cemeteries such as Finglesham, Mill Hill and Buckland also reflect this coastal pattern. The range of fifth-century objects recovered indicates mixed immigrants. They certainly included some Saxons, as indicated by some of the new Ringlemere finds, a chance find of a chipcarved 'supporting-arm' brooch from Eastry (Ager 1989) (ill. 6.15) and an applied disc brooch from Howletts (Evison 1978, fig. 2c-j). The five-spiral cast saucer brooch from Buckland I, Grave 48

6.15 Damaged metal-detector find of a 'chipcarved' supporting-arm brooch found near Eastry, but manufactured within the middle third of the fifth century in north-west Germany (approx. actual size).

6.16 Three Group II copper-alloy cruciform brooches from the Bifrons(Patrixbourne) cemetery: matched by brooches from Frisia and Jutland (approx. actual size).

to the very earliest forms, they share features implying manufacture in the second half of the fifth century, with burial no later than the early sixth century. They are also different in subtle ways from those found elsewhere in eastern (Anglian) England. Only some twenty-three cruciform brooches have been recorded from ten cemeteries in Kent, three of which, from two graves at Bifrons, have associated finds (ill. 6.16). Any future study must include alloy-analyses of the recent metal-detector and chance finds from east Kent. These have more than doubled the number of cruciform brooches for the region and cruciform brooches form nearly one third (32%) of all metal-detected brooch types from Kent (Richardson 2004, Table 3).

(Evison 1987, fig. 27), may not be as early as its excavator believed, but again implies a Saxon costume tradition. Angles were also present, e.g. the shoulder-bossed pot from Buckland I, Grave 87 (Evison 1987, fig. 40), and a fashion for relatively plain annular brooches may be attributable to the presence of Anglian women within its earlier communities (Parfitt and Brugmann 1997, 41; Chadwick 1958b, 39-40). The south Scandinavian component, however, has attracted particular attention because it can be related to the foundation myth of settlement by Jutes from mainland Denmark (present-day Jutland), as recorded by Bede in the early eighth century (*HE* I.15). Kent's cruciform brooches have been compared to examples from both Jutland (Hawkes and Pollard 1981, 323; Hines 1984, 245) and Frisia (northern Netherlands: Reichstein 1975). Its chain of islands provided sheltered seaways for westward migration from Jutland and north-west Germany. The admixture of Saxon, Angle and south Scandinavian elements visible in Kent's material culture might even have occurred in Frisia. Mortimer's analysis of the alloys of thirteen Kentish cruciform brooches revealed high levels of lead in five of them and similar lead levels occur in contemporary brooches of period (*Stufe*) D3 in Frisia (Mortimer 1990, 392-3). The possibility that many of the Kentish brooches were produced in coastal Frisia is thought-provoking. While Kentish cruciform brooches do not belong

The Jutes

By comparison with the fifth-century archaeological evidence for Saxon migrations from the Elbe-Weser coastlands, or of the Angles from Schleswig-Holstein via the Elbe estuary to southern and eastern Britain, it is not straightforward to construct an archaeological case for a Jutish migration. Not a single burial from east Kent can be identified with conviction as that of a migrant from Jutland according to Kruse (née Sørensen). Although there are

Brooches in early Anglo-Saxon Kent

Brooch fittings were a key feature of female costume in Anglo-Saxon Kent. They were functional dress fasteners as well as decorative fittings and have formed an invaluable key for archaeologists seeking to establish ranking in society and the relative dating of burials.

The earliest brooches from Anglo-Saxon Kent include a simple north-west German *Armbrustfibel* type, which is not too distant from a safety pin. A more developed version is the 'supporting-arm brooch' (*Stützarmfibel*), again imported from the Saxon region of north-west Germany (ill. 6.15). Such brooches fall within the broad category of 'bow brooches', as they have a raised bow linking the head- and foot-plate. Early forms of cruciform and so-called '**small-long**' brooches (ill. 6.16), both found in Kent between the mid-fifth and early sixth century, are typical of this category.

The most elaborate bow brooches in Kent are **square-headed brooches**. Cast in silver or copper-alloy with the upper decorated surface gilded, their decorative zones combine geometric designs with animal ornament and human or animal face masks (ills 6.2; 6.21; 6.22; 6.24; 6.25; 6.26; 6.28; 6.29). Their ornament has an angular etched effect referred to as relief-decoration or as chip-carved ornament. In earlier versions of such brooches imported from southern Scandinavia, the bow is extended and relatively thin. Later Kentish-made relief-decorated brooches have shorter, stronger and wider curved bars at the bow. Small and miniature versions of such brooches, referred to (unsurprisingly) as **small square-headed brooches**, were also produced in sixth-century Kent (ills 6.25; 6.40).

Round brooches, including solid disc and ring brooches, also feature. The ring forms are divided between those with a complete ring (**annular brooches**) and those with a narrow opening and end stops for the pin (**penannular brooches**). Simple annular brooches are associated with Anglian dress costume introduced from Scandinavia before the end of the fifth century and can have narrow cast or flattened sheet-metal rings. Basic penannular brooches are relatively rare in Kent, but brooches that combine broad annular rings with a subsidiary penannular ring seem to represent a product of British workshops in the Kent region. These so-called '**quoit brooch style**' brooches were usually made in silver with gilded elements and were decorated with animal, human mask and plant or geometric designs (ill. 6.8). They have been found throughout south-east England as far west as Wiltshire, but the finest examples are concentrated in Kent.

Disc brooches are another key category, particularly associated with the Saxons. Simple cast **disc brooches**, with decoration of concentric incised rings or rings of spaced small punched designs, date between the mid-fifth and mid-sixth century. A more elaborate type is ornamented by pressing a thin sheet-metal foil on to a die. A rim makes these brooches resemble a saucer and they have been referred to as saucer brooches, but they are more accurately described as **applied or composite disc or saucer brooches**. Their ornament includes geometric or animal designs. Fully cast **saucer brooches** represent the next stage of development (ill. 6.40). Early versions typically have a five-spiral coil chip-carved design derived from late Roman belt set designs. Later saucer brooches also have animal ornament, usually combined with geometric designs. **Button brooches** are miniaturised cast saucer brooches, typically with a central face mask design, though a few substitute a central garnet setting (ill. 6.19). They seem to originate in east Kent, combining Scandinavian-Kentish face-masks, but they rapidly spread across southern England and were exported to northern France and Belgium.

A wide range of brooches was imported from the Frankish world to Kent from the late fifth century onwards. They include garnet-decorated **rosette brooches** and bow brooches with semi-circular headplates with five or more non-functional knobs radiating from the plate (**radiate-headed brooches**) (ill. 6.21). The **Kentish square-headed brooches** were modified by the selective addition of individual small square, keystone, disc or triangular-shaped garnet slabs (ills 6.2; 6.22; 6.24; 6.26; 6.28; 6.29). Two silver gilt examples from Dover (Buckland) and Howletts each have a disc on the bow decorated with shorthand Style I animals and spaced garnet settings (ill. 6.29). If such a disc is detached and pin fittings added to the rear, a **Kentish jewelled disc brooch** is produced (ill. 6.24; 6.26; 6.28). The Kentish disc brooch developed from the first half of the sixth century, via **plated disc brooches**, through to the **composite disc brooches** of the seventh century (ills 6.30; 6.31). The structure of the composite brooches separated and bulked out thin gold sheets with paste infills to reduce the overall weight, permitting a larger and showier appearance. Shortages of gold and the breakdown in trade links with Indian sources for garnet and other semi-precious stones in the 560s led to the later versions of such brooches adopting copper-alloy frames to house recut tiny garnets.

It is not possible here to describe all the brooch types in use in early Kent, but an impression can be gained of the contrast between the earliest simply decorated and Roman influenced brooches and the most elaborate products of the first half of the seventh century, prior to the emergence of the 'Final Phase' fashions of the third quarter of that century.

cruciform brooches paralleled in Denmark and Frisia as well as hand-made pottery matched in Jutland and a wider North Sea community including Frisia, identifying grave groups in Kent that would be equally at home in contemporary Jutlandic cemeteries is another matter. There is also a limited number of elite female graves in Kent that contained large cast-decorated silver-gilt brooches, often together with small gold disc pendants or bracteates of Scandinavian type. In Denmark such brooches and pendants are found in hoards and never in graves. The combination of these symbolic Scandinavian dress items with Frankish and later with Kentish dress fittings is not matched in Scandinavia, but is a specifically Kentish phenomenon.

The typical contents of fifth-century burials at both Hjemsted (Ethelberg 1986; 1990) and Sejlflod (Nielsen 2000) can be contrasted with burials recorded in Kent. Pottery vessels occur in fewer than 10% of Kentish burials (Sørensen 1999, 173-5), but were numerous in inhumation graves in Jutland, where this pottery typically has handles. Only one handled pot is known from Kent, from Buckland II (Kruse forthcoming). Kruse has argued that only a dozen pots from Kent, sharing a hard, sandy fabric, mostly being small carinated or biconical vessels with out-turned rims, can be attributed to potters from Jutland (*ibid.*; Sørensen 1999). Some twenty-five pots from Kent are regarded instead as products of a wider North Sea region, including Frisia. They have biconical, carinated or rounded forms, can be plain or decorated and, where decorated, are usually burnished with horizontal grooves around the neck and vertical or chevron grooves around the shoulder or body. Kruse suggests that handles may have been going out of fashion by the sixth century in Jutland (Jensen 1985; Sørensen 1999, 63). Perhaps we have been too willing to assume that the 'Jutish' pottery of Kent (ills 6.17; 6.18), with its simple decoration, must belong to the fifth century, when much of it may be early sixth century. The late J N L Myres (1970; 1977,

6.17 Two handmade 'Jutish' pots with simple linear decoration from the Westbere cemetery (largest pot 151mm tall).

site by Mainman. On the other hand, if handmade pottery was primarily produced by women on a domestic scale, then few of these vessels are likely to have reached Kent through trading. They are possibly a better indicator of a south Scandinavian and perhaps Jutish origin for their female immigrant potters.

In fifth-century Jutland the corpse was normally placed in a coffin (plank-constructed at Sejlflod or a hollowed-out tree at Hjemsted), orientated east – west (WNW – ESE) with the head at the west end. As well as at least one handmade biconical handled pot decorated with linear grooved ornament, there would be a knife at the waist. Dress fittings such as silver clasps (Hines classes A and B), a copper-alloy brooch (often a cruciform brooch), a copper-alloy or iron pin, a copper-alloy or iron buckle and rivets from either a bone/antler comb or from class B clasps are found. Iron arrowheads and spearheads occur in male graves, but other weapons common in Kent, such as swords, axes and shield fittings (Härke 1992), are absent. While it is rare in Kent to be able to record a coffin, due to the soil conditions, at least east-west burial is common. Although a pair of brooches or a single brooch is a common feature in Kentish female costume, pins are rare before the seventh century, and clasps, typically at the wrists to fasten a long, narrow-sleeved tunic, are virtually unknown. Yet Scandinavian-type clasps were adopted as female dress fittings *c.* 500 throughout the Anglian regions of eastern England. Occasionally clasps manufactured in Anglian England appear in Kentish graves

6.18 Tall footed handmade 'Jutish' pottery beaker with vertical fluted ornament from near Canterbury (224mm tall).

115) drew particular attention to similarities between a tall beaker-shaped decorated vessel from the Bifrons cemetery (Hawkes 2000, fig. 38.9; Myres 1977, fig. 202) and a similar pot from Drengsted in Jutland. More recently, Mainman has argued that these pots were attempts to copy late Roman or post-Roman glass cone beakers (Macpherson-Grant and Mainman 1995, 866-7). Therefore the Bifrons 'beaker' and sherds from Wingham might be fashioned by a potter from anywhere around the North Sea margins and at least one similar pot has been noted from a Frisian

6.19 Seven gilt copper-alloy button brooches from the Bifrons(Patrixbourne) cemetery with Scandinavian human masks of the late fifth or early sixth century (approx. actual size).

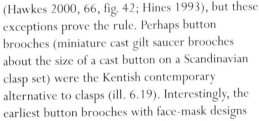

6.20 The 'Canterbury' gilt-silver Nydam style bow brooch: either imported from Scandinavia or made in Kent by a Scandinavian smith (approx. actual size).

bracteates also decorated in Style I (Axboe 1999; Bakka 1981; Hawkes and Pollard 1981). The previously only complete Nydam Style brooch from Kent (ill. 6.20), probably found in the Canterbury region, is now matched by a very similar brooch from a site in Gillingham (pers. comm. M Gaimster). Its manufacture would have been within the middle third of the fifth century, pre-dating some of the Kentish cruciform brooches (Bakka 1958, 9, fig. 2; Haseloff 1981, 140-1, Abb. 86; Jessup 1950, 11, pl. XIX.5). The earliest Style I brooches seem to be manufactured either side of *c.* 500, in the last two decades of the fifth century for the Jutlandic Group B version and in the first two decades of the sixth century for the Group C and related brooches. Too little is known about the burial context of the Martyr's Field (Canterbury) Group B brooch, but another Group B brooch was old, worn and repaired when deposited *c.* 525-30 in Finglesham Grave D3 (ill. 6.21). Its associations included three Scandinavian gold D bracteates and two recently imported Frankish brooch pairs (bird brooches and radiate-headed brooches) and a glass claw-beaker (Chadwick 1958b; Hawkes and Pollard 1981; Hawkes and Grainger 2006). Group C brooches could also be buried well after their manufacture, as at Bifrons Grave 41 (ill. 6.22). Here a massive three-piece brooch was deposited with both Kentish and Frankish dress fittings, implying a date of deposition as late as *c.* 550 (Hawkes 1981). Opinion remains divided as to which of these brooches were imported from Jutland and whether the Group C brooches were made by Scandinavian smiths operating in Kent. It is unfortunate that these brooches are so rare in Scandinavia. Although large relief brooches occur occasionally in graves in Norway and Sweden, they are never found in cemeteries within Denmark. The same holds true for the gold bracteates recovered in substantial numbers from hoards of precious metal in Denmark, sometimes with a large brooch. These hoards represent offerings to the same Nordic deities worshipped by Anglo-Saxon immigrants (Müller-Wille 1999).

(Hawkes 2000, 66, fig. 42; Hines 1993), but these exceptions prove the rule. Perhaps button brooches (miniature cast gilt saucer brooches about the size of a cast button on a Scandinavian clasp set) were the Kentish contemporary alternative to clasps (ill. 6.19). Interestingly, the earliest button brooches with face-mask designs also date to the very end of the fifth century (Avent and Evison 1982; Welch 1985a). These may well have signalled a Kentish Scandinavian identity as clearly as clasps elsewhere in England indicate an Angle.

Relief-decorated gilt-silver cast bow brooches were ornamented with cast animal, human and geometric designs either in the Nydam Style or more typically in Salin Style I (Haseloff 1974, 1981). Typically these occur in east Kent graves with gold

6.21 Dress fittings from Finglesham Grave D3 including a Scandinavian square-headed brooch, gold D bracteates, Frankish bird brooches and radiate-headed brooches (approx. half actual size).

6.22 Glass vessel and dress fittings from Bifrons Grave 41 with a Scandinavian-type square-headed brooch, a Frankish bird brooch and later Kentish-made brooches (approx. half actual size).

Hawkes viewed the gold bracteates from both Finglesham D3 and Buckland I Grave 20 as 'antiques' manufactured in the later fifth century, though not buried until *c.* 525 (Hawkes and Pollard 1981, 370). Die-links between the D bracteates worn on bead strings across the chest area in graves D3 and 203 at Finglesham suggested the curation of bracteates in a family chest and their burial with women of two successive generations. The obvious alternative would be periodic manufacture from stored or copied dies and possession of gold bullion ultimately derived from *solidi* coins to produce them (*ibid.*, 340-2 and 351-2). Hawkes noted other die-links within the pair buried in Bifrons Grave 29 and the bracteate from Bifrons Grave 64, within a trio from Sarre Grave 4, and between bracteates from Sarre Grave 90, Hérouvillette (western Normandy) Grave 39 and another from an undocumented 'Kent' site. A case can be made for some, if not all these gold bracteates being fashioned in Kent, rather than imported in the late fifth century from Jutland (Webster 1978). A silver foil from Bradstow School (Broadstairs) Grave 71 with a C bracteate die impression might suggest possession of a die, though C bracteates are more commonly found in Anglian England (Hines 1984; Kruse forthcoming). The D bracteate was the preferred signal for Jutish identity in Kentish burial dress. The importation of ready-made D bracteates from southern Scandinavia, carefully stored in treasure chests until selected as heirloom fittings to proclaim Jutish descent, remains a real possibility, but workshop evidence is needed to resolve this debate.

Both bracteates and relief brooches seem to bear religious images, with bracteates linked to the cult of Woden. The D bracteate portrays a bird-headed beast perhaps representing death or an evil power in the form of a monster, but alternatively the beast might depict the transformation of Woden into animal form (Sørensen 1999, 218). David Leigh has examined combinations of human masks and animal

quadrupeds on the relief brooches, including 'animal-men' or *Tiermenschen* (1984a; 1990). The latter could well be linked to shamanism with its transformations of human into animal. Women wearing these elaborate brooches and bracteates would have been leading actors in cult ceremonies, but determining whether such brooches were for everyday use, as the heavy wear on some of them suggests, or were limited to ceremonial occasions is not straightforward. The display of such brooches and bracteates involved conscious ethnic symbolism, but establishing whether these women were true descendants of Scandinavian migrants is another matter. It was perhaps more significant that Jutish ancestry was being claimed in an active process of ethnogenesis involving the leading social caste, utilising symbols of high material value (silver-gilt cast brooches and gold sheet pendants), ornamented with religious iconography (Behr 2000; Sørensen 1997). This fine metalwork may have been acquired by gift exchange with a south Scandinavian peer group, but might alternatively represent marriage alliances with Scandinavian families. The wearers were displaying their newly established status among the leading families of farming landowners in the coastal regions of east Kent. Interestingly, no problem was seen in combining Scandinavian status markers with either Frankish dress fittings (e.g. Finglesham D3) or later with locally made Kentish jewellery (e.g. Bifrons Grave 41).

Such graves can be viewed as 'founder burials', forming the focus for newly established cemetery communities. The Finglesham D3 female and the contemporary Grave 204 male weapon assemblage fit this model (Hawkes and Pollard 1981; Hawkes 1982b; Hawkes and Grainger 2006), but as most of the early sector of this cemetery was removed in chalk quarrying, the date of its earliest burials is uncertain. The so-called 'founders' may be descendants of fifth-century settlers and perhaps these families took at least two generations to feel sufficiently secure to advertise their status as landholders in their burial practice. Initially the ethnic symbols might have been passed on as unburied treasure to heirs rather than disposed of in the grave. It seems improbable that a south Scandinavian or Jutish origin was an entirely artificial concept, however, even if some of those buried with brooches and bracteates might have been Saxons, Angles or the products of mixed marriages, including some British component. As Hedeager has suggested, Scandinavian origin myths for Germanic peoples across Europe, as recorded in written sources from the sixth century onwards, can hardly have been invented overnight. Rather they would have been developed, altered and refined through oral tradition over many generations. There was probably an underlying tradition of a Jutish origin for key members of what emerged as the Anglo-Saxon elite in east Kent. This Jutish identity was then expanded to provide a focus for the social and political unification of what became its kingdom in the sixth century. These people symbolised their belief in that tradition in later fifth- and earlier sixth-century graves by wearing initially imported and later locally made dress accessories depicting Nordic religious iconography (Hedeager 2000, 25, 27, 49-50, 52). Behr has emphasised the importance of the religious role played by these leading women in sixth-century Kent, possibly even anticipating the functions that future abbesses of the Kentish royal house would play as the heads of monasteries within the seventh century (2000).

Kruse has drawn on anthropological theory to explain the pattern of Jutish material by arguing for a migration route or 'stream' (Anthony 1990, 903; 1992; 1997; Sørensen 1997, 169). This route would have extended between Jutland and Kent following the North Sea coastal waterways of north-west Germany and the Netherlands. She sees the migration as not a single event, but an extended process in which a small number of individuals, initially male warriors, took the first steps. Over time people went back and forth between Jutland, Frisia and Kent, which might help to explain why individual women buried

wearing distinctive Scandinavian dress fittings such as cruciform brooches seem to make their first appearance relatively late in the process. During the later fifth century the first settlers would have sent back to Jutland for brides or else acquired, by gift exchange, high-status metal dress fittings to present to young women as part of the betrothal and marriage process. They selected, from a wider range of dress items, a specific set of symbols that distinguished them as 'Jutes' from other Scandinavian immigrants to lowland Britain. Initially they used cruciform brooches and Nydam Style relief brooches, but subsequently these were replaced by Style I relief brooches and gold D bracteates, to which was added the button brooch. This repertoire contrasts with the range of brooches, bracteates and clasps adopted in the Anglian regions beyond Essex. The relative rarity of Jutlandic handmade pottery certainly implies that the number of female immigrants from Jutland may have been limited, but nevertheless they appear as a component of an incoming population. Additionally we can suggest that the first Jutes to settle in Kent may have travelled a shorter distance from Frisia or even from north-eastern France rather than from Denmark. Direct links with Jutland may even represent a secondary migration phase, helping to explain the lack of close parallels between burial costume and practices between Jutland and Kent. Undoubtedly the rarity of adequately recorded fifth-century burials from east Kent has hampered understanding, limiting our ability to assess items such as beads and buckles found with the cruciform brooches.

The two Bifrons graves mentioned earlier suggest that cruciform brooches will often have been associated with metal fittings imported from the Frankish world. Perhaps this implies that Kent's 'Jutes' arrived from north-east Gaul or other Frankish controlled territories nearby. Textile impressions derived from the corrosion products of metal dress fittings are a further source of evidence. Contrasts in weaves have been identified between Scandinavia, the Frankish regions and different English regions, including Kent (Jørgensen 1987, 307; 1992, 28). Weave patterns, the use of dyed colours and woven 'tartens', as well as of narrow patterned braids as edgings on collars, cuffs, hems and the front edges of jackets or coats, may have been as significant as ethnic labels to contemporaries as the brooches used to fasten them. Finally, the continuing importance of Scandinavian links with Kent in the later sixth century and on into the seventh century should be noted. This is witnessed by a brooch from Gotland (Sweden) in a rich grave at Eastry (Hawkes 1979) and the adoption and active development of Style II animal ornament in Kent (Speake 1980), though Nielsen (1999, 200) sees Style II as reaching Kent via Francia rather than through direct links with Scandinavia. Nevertheless, the continued manufacture of gold bracteates with Style II animal designs (Speake 1980, pl. 13) suggests a vibrant Germanic artistic

6.23 Triangular buckle from Sarre, Thanet, grave 68: its principal gold plate is decorated with interlaced Style II animals in gold filigree wire (approx. actual size).

tradition within Kent. The same can be argued for the adaptation of Style II on showy dress items imitating Frankish forms in the early seventh century, such as large jewelled composite disc brooches and belt sets with triangular plates and shield terminals to the tongue (*ibid.*, pls 6-8) (ill. 6.23).

The Franks

The extent of Frankish influence and immigration into east Kent has also dominated cemetery interpretation, notably in the publications of Evison. Undoubtedly significant quantities of Frankish-made items occur in Kent cemeteries between the fifth and seventh century, but large-scale Frankish settlement during the fifth and sixth centuries is harder to justify. Thus Brugmann could only identify three female graves that exclusively contained Frankish brooches (Mill Hill, Grave 92; Bekesbourne, Grave 19; Bifrons, Grave 21: Brugmann 1999, fig. 3.25 and Table 3.1; Hawkes 2000, figs 9-10). She noted that where Frankish brooches were present, they were not in the correct dress positions in comparison to contemporary continental burials. It seems that Kentish women did not understand how a continental Frank would use these brooches and that Kentish garments were differently tailored and difficult to adapt to the continental four-brooch fashion. Kentish sixth-century graves also lack other common Frankish dress fasteners and jewellery, such as hairpins, earrings and fittings for both garter and shoe mounts (Parfitt and Brugmann 1997, 116; Wieczorek 1996, Abb. 541 and 547 for continental examples). It seems that brooches were imported, rather than brides or migrants. Of course, arranged marriages across the Channel cannot be ruled out, but the evidence is underwhelming. At the same time, Frankish influence on the wealthiest female burials in sixth-century Kent is seen in the wearing of symbolic objects, such as strainer spoons and rock crystal balls in metal slings. These were often worn together, hanging from the waist in graves such as Lyminge 44 (ills 6.24-26), when in Francia either one or the other is found (Hinz 1966; Martin 1997). Narrow cloth braids with gold thread woven into them around the head provide another marker borrowed from the Frankish world (Crowfoot and Hawkes 1967). Iron weaving battens, representing the role of leading women as weavers in cloth production, are matched in graves in specific regions across western Europe, but are rare in England outside Kent (Harrington 2002; Chadwick 1958b, 30-5). Kentish society emulated continental practice, but adapted it.

A rather stronger case can be made for the presence of Frankish warriors in Kentish communities. Continental influence on the range of weapons between the later fifth and seventh century is clear, often accompanied by imported belt fittings. Evison has argued that at least four of the weapon graves from Buckland I (graves 22, 91, 65 and 56) would not look out of place in a Frankish cemetery (Evison 1987, 172, figs 41 and 76, 36 and 73, 31 and 72). Fine weapons were prized items across Europe in this period and if a man from Kent could acquire Frankish weapons, whether by gift exchange or by commercial trade, there is no way of establishing from his burial whether he was a Frank or local. Weapons such as spearheads with inlaid ornamentation would have been valuable acquisitions (e.g. Lyminge Grave 4: *ibid.*, 134 and 164). Distinctive items such as the socketed bill-hook, known as a *fauchard*, from a sixth-century grave at Buckland II, are very likely to be imports, but could also be copied by a Kentish smith. The throwing-axe known as a *francisca*, and also the axe-hammer, were clearly prestige weapons in the fifth to sixth century (e.g. Howletts: Evison 1965, 20, pl. 6b; Härke 1992, 105-6, n. 132, Abb. 6 and 14). Ownership of these weapons was certainly not exclusive to the Franks, whether on the Continent or in England (Welch 1983, 125-6). That the leading form of iron shield boss used to protect the fist at the centre of a leather-covered wooden buckler is the Group 3 convex cone form is not surprising. The Group 3 date range extends from the early sixth century into the early seventh in east Kent, and

6.24 Lyminge, grave 44: chain-linked pair of Kentish jewelled disc brooches, a pair of Kentish jewelled square-headed brooches, a rock crystal ball and a sieve spoon (approx. half actual size).

6.25 Bifrons grave 51: Kentish small square-headed brooch pair, Frankish bird brooches, a rock crystal ball and sieve spoon set (approx. half actual size).

some examples were continental imports, though many others were probably manufactured locally (Dickinson and Härke 1992; Spain 2000; forthcoming).

The barb-headed throwing spear, commonly

6.26 Sarre, Thanet, grave 4: glass bell beaker, Kentish jewelled disc brooch pair, two square-headed brooches, six gold D bracteates, a finger ring, crystal ball and sieve spoon (approx. half actual size).

referred to as the *angon*, seems, however, to be an imitation of a Frankish weapon rather than a Frankish import. The sixth-century Frankish *angon* has a head with a diamond-shaped section and barbs set close to the shaft, whereas those found in late sixth- or seventh-century contexts in east Kent have a flatter head and barbs set away from the shaft. The latter seem to belong to a Scandinavian barb-headed spear tradition represented in ritual weapon deposits at sites such as Nydam (Swanton 1973, 33-7). No true Frankish *angon* has been found in England (von Schnurbein 1974, 433) and Kentish throwing spears mostly occur in richer weapon sets after they have gone out of fashion in the Frankish Rhineland *c.* 580/90-610 (Nieveler and Siegmund 1999, 8). Burial practice may provide a better indicator of Frankish warrior presence. In particular, the continental practice of placing a spear in a downward-pointing position parallel to

the legs (in contrast to the standard Anglo-Saxon point up beside the skull) is normal for a barbed-headed spearhead in Kent and also occurs in a small number of graves with other spear types. Again, one must allow for Kentish adoption of continental practice, rather than assume automatically that all spear-down burials are continental Frankish migrants.

An interesting feature of sixth- to seventh-century cemeteries on Thanet is also found elsewhere within east Kent. The practice of contemporary grave robbing might represent a household seeking secretly to recover items that it felt obliged to place publicly in a family burial, avoiding loss of face. Alternatively it could be simple theft, implying an ability to sell on the stolen goods to unscrupulous foreign traders. This may have been easier to achieve on Thanet and in the eastern coastal region than elsewhere in Kent. Contemporary grave robbing is virtually unknown in the rest of Anglo-Saxon England and indeed across much of Kent, but was commonplace in Merovingian-period cemeteries across the Channel (Roth 1978). Over 14% of burials had been robbed at both Sarre and Lyminge II. The proportion of weapon graves robbed at Sarre was even higher (over 17%), implying that iron weapons were particularly valuable. At Broadstairs I, Finglesham and Polhill, though the proportion of robbed graves was low at respectively 2%, 3.5% and 1%, the percentage of robbed weapon burials was elevated to 8%, 7% and 6% (Härke 2000, 391-2, Table 5). Such weapons would have to be extracted quickly to avoid significant rust damage. This may suggest the presence of some Franks in these burial communities as well as some familiarity with continental burial customs, perhaps observed by Kentish traders visiting *Francia* and facilitated by Frisian and Frankish traders attending beach markets at Sarre and elsewhere.

Kentish counterparts to these Franks are indicated by a minority of graves in the cemeteries of north-east France between the Somme and the hinterland of Calais. Disc brooches appear at Vron in a phase dated *c.* 450 to 485/90 (e.g. Grave 159A: Seillier 2002, fig. 2), but are not found in sixth-century burials there. This raises the possibility that the origins of the Anglo-Saxon disc brooch are continental. From the late fifth century onwards there is a pair of Scandinavian square-headed brooches from Vron Grave 43 (Welch 2007) and also button brooches and small square-headed brooches manufactured in Kent. From *c.* 530/40, however, no more Anglo-Saxon dress fittings are recorded at Vron or Nouvion in Ponthieu, though three sites, Fréthun, Marquise-Hardenthun and Grenay, between Boulougne and Calais, provide evidence for continuing contact with Kent (Seillier 2002; Welch 1991). As in Kent, the graves containing Kentish female dress fittings may be of local women married to Kentish traders, but a Kentish ring-sword fitting from Grenay (Evison 1979) might reflect a real Kentish presence. The occasional presence of handmade pottery in cemeteries full of local wheel-thrown products may also be significant, though other continental Germans may be responsible for these pots. More detailed research is needed to explore these cross-Channel links and the relationship of these burials to 'Saxons' who, according to a historical source, settled around Quentovic on the river Canche (Welch 1991; 2002). That they are called Saxons rather than Jutes is not surprising, for it seems that the Franks used 'Saxon' to describe all the English peoples, just as contemporary Italian and Greek sources called them all 'Angles'.

Kentish culture and identity

The outstanding feature of Kentish fashions in the sixth to seventh century is the fusion of Scandinavian forms with continental modes of decoration. This is exemplified by the addition of garnets to Style I-decorated square-headed brooches and the application of Scandinavian ornament to continental forms, with Style II artwork appearing on triangular buckle-plates. A related aspect is the use of luxury materials, rarely available in the rest of England. Kentish square-headed and disc brooches were routinely cast in silver and ornamented with black niello inlaid zig-zag borders and garnets, while elsewhere gilt copper-alloy was the norm in the sixth century. Gold became available in increasing quantities

6.27 Gilton: sixth-century ring-sword pommel with a moveable ring attached (approx. actual size).

6.28 Finglesham grave E2: brooches from a mid-sixth-century female dress assemblage (approx. actual size).

from the late sixth century, making possible the production of the elaborate jewellery that typifies Kent through the first half of the seventh century, until replaced by silver again. The ability to acquire luxury materials and prestige items is what marks out east Kent from its Anglo-Saxon neighbours; the more prosperous Kentish households could emulate their continental neighbours in displaying their status and wealth in death as they had in life. Indeed the relatively high proportion of male weapon assemblages containing the most prestigious weapon of a two-edged sword at the Buckland I and Sarre cemeteries may reflect a special function for these two communities (Hawkes 1982a, 76) (ill. 6.27). Their leading men are seen as royal agents

enforcing tolls on traders landing at Dover or awaiting the change of tide at Sarre. The assemblage from Buckland Grave C with its balance set and fine ring-sword symbolises this interpretation, but it may be that other coastal communities were equally prosperous.

Although the jewelled square-headed brooch represents a relatively straightforward elaboration of a Scandinavian Style I brooch form (ill. 6.28) by local silversmiths, the creation of a small jewelled disc brooch by detaching the jewelled disc used to cover the bow of a large Kentish square-headed brooch reveals a genuine inventiveness. Examples of such square-headed brooches with a jewelled disc are recorded from Howletts and Dover, possibly Buckland (Evison

1987, 39-46; Leigh 1984b) (ill. 6.29). The new disc brooches were initially made in matched pairs to provide a local substitute for imported Frankish garnet disc brooches. They were to develop into a key regional symbol in Kentish female costume and before the end of the sixth century were being worn singly at the throat, imitating new Frankish dress fashions (Avent 1975; Parfitt and Brugmann 1997). They were further elaborated with the addition of separate gold plates decorated in filigree and more sophisticated jewelled settings; finally this led to the creation of the larger composite jewelled disc brooches typified by the masterpiece from Kingston Down Grave 205 (Faussett 1856, pl. I; Jessup 1950, pl. XXXIV, colour pl. A) (ills 6.30; 6.31). The breakdown of sea trade in cheap tabular garnet between India and the eastern Roman Empire in the 560s (von Freeden 2000) helps to explain the recycling of garnet in settings of ever-decreasing size on composite disc brooches by the second quarter of the seventh century. By then composite brooches were being made of ever paler gold from recently imported Frankish coins (Hawkes 1974), while tiny honeycomb copper-alloy cells containing recut garnets represent the ultimate stage in this

process. None of the shortages of raw materials detracts from the achievement of Kentish craftsmen in the seventh century, who made the best possible use of what was available to them. The Kentish jewelled disc brooches equal, and often improve on, the quality of the products found in continental Frankish cemeteries. To see anything still finer, one has to turn to the

6.29 Two jewelled square-headed brooches with a disc-on-bow from Dover and Howletts: products of a single sixth-century Kentish workshop (approx. actual size).

Far left:

6.30 Composite jewelled seventh-century disc brooch from Kingston Down grave 205, manufactured around the same time as the Sutton Hoo jewellery (approx. actual size).

Left:

6.31 Composite jewelled seventh-century disc brooch from the Sarre, Thanet, 1860 grave, associated with the necklace in 6.32 (approx. actual size).

6.32 Necklace from Sarre, Thanet, 1860 grave, of amethyst and glass beads with a central decorated coloured (millefiori) glass disc pendant and four gold solidus coins minted in Provence, southern France, and probably imported in the 610s (approx. actual size).

6.33 Milton Regis dress assemblage with a Christian gold pendant cross, a millefiori glass pendant with a miniature recut garnet border and a silver disc pendant with a cruciform design (approx. actual size).

6.34 Sibertswold grave 172: pendants from a necklet with two imported gold coins, two pendants setting single cabachon garnets, two setting single amethyst cabachons, two setting decorated coloured (millefiori) glass and a large gold disc pendant set with small cabachon garnets (approx. actual size).

craftsmanship of the Sutton Hoo jeweller (Bruce-Mitford 1978). The jewellery of the mid- to late seventh century is dominated by dress pins and metal beads often associated with amethyst beads (ills 6.32-34). These new fashions, influenced by Mediterranean and specifically Italian dress fittings, can be linked to the opening of

- ■ Bronze Age
- ■ Late Iron Age - Roman
- ■ Anglo-Saxon

0   100

metres

communications between a newly converted Kent and Rome. It may also reflect the conscious adoption by the Christian Angles of an identity as the new Romans ruling Britain as God's agents (Geake 1997). Other items such as workboxes and chatelaines made up of iron-linked bars are distinctive features of seventh-century female fittings. By the late seventh century burial of fully dressed individuals is becoming less common and on occasion coins are placed in the grave as a substitute for grave finds, while grave structures defined by ring-ditches in the seventh century may function as an alternative means of indicating the status of the dead (ills 6.35; 6.36; 6.37).

Cemetery organisation and social structure in east Kent

One area that deserves further research here is the organisation and social structure of its cemeteries. Adequately published plans are so rare that only a few preliminary observations can be made. The first is the frequency with which cemeteries are focussed on Bronze Age barrows. Modern excavation has revealed at Ringlemere part of a fifth- to sixth-century cemetery associated with an early Bronze Age barrow that produced a corrugated gold cup (Parfitt 2002). There are two contemporary sixth-century burial zones either side of a prehistoric round barrow on Mill Hill (Parfitt and Brugmann 1997, figs 4 and 24) and a substantial round barrow provides a focus for one sector of burial activity in the late sixth and earlier seventh centuries at the northern edge of Buckland I (Evison 1987, figs 103-5) (ill. 6.14). Twelve graves, respecting a number of Bronze Age barrows at Cliffs End, near Ramsgate, were excavated in 2004 (pers. comm. Wessex Archaeology). The most dramatic example is the group of three cemeteries excavated to the north of Saltwood (Glass 1999; 2000). There were five Bronze Age barrows in an east-to-west row and three acted as foci for Anglo-Saxon cemeteries.

6.35 Saltwood near Folkestone: excavation plan of the three neighbouring cemeteries dating to the sixth and seventh centuries centred on three Bronze Age barrows.

6.36 St Peter's Tip, Broadstairs, Thanet: excavation plan of a seventh-century cemetery featuring annular and penannular ring-ditches around selected graves.

0   10

metres

The other two were perhaps barely visible by the sixth century, but the initial suggestion that each cemetery represents a burial phase for a single community is an over-simplification. The eastern and western burial grounds were established within the sixth century and continued into the seventh century, while the central and largest cemetery seems to have been founded at the very beginning of the seventh century (ill. 6.35).

All the cemeteries mentioned indicate a considerable range in size, organisation and period of use, probably reflecting the agricultural viability of the settlements they served. In some cases, as at Mill Hill, a relatively small farming community shifted its settlement after some eighty to ninety years, representing just three generations. Soil exhaustion of its infield may have forced such a move, or possibly there was an opportunity to colonise fresh land elsewhere. One characteristic of many of the larger cemeteries is their extended use, implying stability and continuity for the agricultural community. Buckland I and II were founded in the later fifth century and burial continued into the early eighth century (Evison 1987; Parfitt and Haith 1995). Admittedly Hawkes has contrasted a prosperous small community represented by burials of the early to mid-sixth century at Finglesham and a more ordinary community of seventh-century graves, some of which were marked by penannular ring-ditches implying mounds (Hawkes 1982b; Hawkes and Grainger 2006). She suggested perhaps three generations of an elite family (the founder graves D3 and 204 in particular) together with their servants. Influenced by continental cemetery interpretations (e.g. Basel-Bernerring: Martin 1976), she envisaged this family either moving on elsewhere early in the second half of the sixth century, or else becoming impoverished. In a new study Duncan Sayer will demonstrate continuity of burial through the sixth century and the available plan does not indicate any significant break in burial sequence during the sixth century. Changes in

burial practice over time may provide an explanation for the apparent decline in wealth of this community.

There is an urgent need to publish several modern excavations of east Kent cemeteries established around the beginning of the seventh century. The cemetery of some 400 burials at St Peter's in Broadstairs (Hogarth 1973) is a key site (ill. 6.36), as is the smaller Updown site close to Eastry. The Downland barrow cemeteries of the late sixth and seventh centuries excavated in the eighteenth and nineteenth centuries by Faussett and others (Struth and Eagles 1999) also need to be made accessible in print. The wealth in terms of gold and silver jewellery, imported fittings including amethyst beads in the cemeteries of Kingston Down, Barfriston and Sibertswold, make it clear that these communities were even more prosperous than those in the prime arable regions to the north and south of the Downs.

It is generally accepted now that the differences in any given generation between the 'wealth' buried in a cemetery frequently reflect not so much differences in command of resources between households and families as ranking within those households. In each household the married couple that headed it were buried with the fullest honours in terms of grave dimensions, a barrow or some other substantial above-ground marker. They were dressed in their best clothing, perhaps lying on bedding and accompanied by items indicating their status, including imported vessels from the Continent of bronze, glass or wheel-thrown pottery. If a couple or individual lived beyond the age of forty-five, (when the mean age of death was typically in the early twenties) and had effectively been replaced by a successor pairing of child-bearing age, then their burial might be more simply furnished. Everyone else in the household would be accorded burial appropriate to their standing within the household. Servants and slaves, together with younger children, might be given the simplest treatment. The richest burials in the east Kentish cemeteries during the sixth and seventh centuries are appreciably better furnished than their equivalents elsewhere in England, but compared to their equivalents in the Frankish and Alamannic continent, they seem to match class C graves (Christlein 1973). These are defined by the presence of full weapon sets, horse equipment (particularly horse bits) and at least one bronze vessel for the men, and gold dress fittings together with some silver items and again a bronze vessel for the women. The richer sixth-century burials at Finglesham (graves D3, 204, 203 and E2) certainly fit the bill, as do their seventh-century equivalents at Kingston Down (graves 205, 299, etc.: Brenan 1991). Christlein saw the C graves as ranking below the elite graves of lesser royalty and the kings, the so-called 'princely' and 'royal' graves. Examples of Frankish royal burial include the barrow at Tournai attributed to Childeric (died 481) and the stone tombs of an adult female and a boy in a sixth-century mortuary chapel beneath Cologne Cathedral (Doppelfeld and Pirling 1966; Werner 1964; Wieczorek 1996). Princely burial is represented by the weapon assemblage, horse gear and household equipment in Krefeld-Gellep, Grave 1782 (Pirling 1974; Wieczorek 1996). The C graves seem to represent prosperous farmers or lesser nobility. They appear to be upwardly mobile in the sixth to seventh century and use the burial event to advertise their self-evaluation to neighbours who witness the funeral.

All this suggests that it is not fully justified to label as 'princely' burials three early seventh-century weapon assemblages accompanied by cast bronze bowls imported from the East Roman Empire (so-called Coptic bowls) in the central cemetery at Saltwood. The assemblages from the barrow chamber grave at Taplow (Buckinghamshire) and the recently excavated Prittlewell (Hirst *et al.* 2004) across the Thames from Kent show the full range of domestic equipment that marks the true 'princely' burials of the early seventh century. It may be more appropriate to regard the Saltwood men as particularly successful C-grave individuals and as prosperous local landowners. The one burial that has some claim to represent a 'princely' grave

within east Kent is the rather poorly recorded barrow cremation deposit from Coombe, dated to the second half of the sixth century (Davidson and Webster 1967; Evison 1967).

It is difficult to summarise in a few pages the sheer range of evidence from well over 150 burial sites across east Kent, but what is emerging from current research is the success of its farming communities. Initially settlements were established around the coastal margins and only secondarily expanded with the foundation of new communities in more inland areas to harness Kent's landscape resources, implying population growth. There is still much more to learn about the additional exploitation of coastal and maritime resources through fishing and trade in particular, and that trade will have probably included the export of slaves. Future settlement excavations and environmental archaeology are essential, but these issues can also be explored by studying patterns of cemetery wealth (see page 246: Brookes 2003).

West Kent burial sites

It is an irony that so much more is known about fifth-century burial from a handful of sites in west Kent than from all the sites recorded east of the Medway. Cemeteries here (ills 6.37; 6.38) share much in common with their Essex counterparts as at Mucking (Clark and Hirst forthcoming), their south London equivalents at Croydon (McKinley 2003) and Mitcham (Bidder and Morris 1959), more distant Surrey sites such as Guildown near Guildford (Lowther 1931; Hines 2004) and in Sussex at Highdown and Alfriston (Welch 1983). The core of this region is the Darent valley and its tributary the Cray. Tyler (1992, fig. 1) has mapped most of the early Anglo-Saxon burial sites as well as the settlements here.

The twenty-one cremations and sixty-four inhumations from Fordcroft in Orpington represent part of a larger burial ground (Palmer 1984; Tester 1968; 1969; 1977; Tyler 1992, 71-2, 73-5, fig. 1.16), invaluable for comparison with the Temple Hill, Dartford excavation finds of 2002 (O'Brien 2004). Surprisingly no cremations were located at Temple Hill, but three of its inhumations can be placed as early as the middle third of the fifth century by their continental dress fittings. A pair of 'supporting-arm' brooches (Perlberg Type) from north-west Germany accompanied a woman aged thirty-five to forty-five. They were manufactured within the first third of the fifth century (Böhme 1974: Stage (*Stufe*) II), but her age suggests burial as late as the 440s or 450s. A partially overlying grave contained a younger female aged twenty-five to thirty, wearing a single imported brooch. This was a small version of the Glaston Type whose date range overlaps that of 'supporting-arm' brooches. Only one adult male could be dated so early with its cast copper-alloy buckle. This was ornamented with stylised animal-head terminals either side of a narrow fixed plate. It is a crude copy of the official buckles issued to Roman army officers within the middle third of the fifth century (Stage III: Böhme 1986, 508-9, Abb. 31). Orpington Grave 74 also contained an early north-west German brooch, a damaged simple bow brooch (*Armbrustfibel*) of Stage I manufactured *c.* 400 (Böhme 1974, Abb. 51/52, Taf. 16, Karte 1). Originally misidentified as a 'supporting-arm' brooch (Hines 1999, 24, Abb. 7a-b; Palmer 1984, 20, fig. 7), it would have implied burial in the first decades of the fifth century, if it had been in fresh and undamaged condition. Instead it belongs with other old or heavily worn imports retained as heirlooms and ethnic symbols in later fifth-century burials within eastern England. More typically their manufacture occurred within 'Stage II' with even badly damaged 'Stage I' finds being extremely rare here, so the Orpington find is significant.

The second half of the fifth century is represented at Temple Hill by several burials. One contained a pair of simple disc brooches, beads, a copper-alloy bracelet with distinctive Quoit-Brooch Style ornament (matched by the Mucking Grave 631 bracelet) and a hand-made pot with four long bosses and linear decoration. Similar assemblages occur in Orpington Graves 51 and 58, with disc brooches associated with other fifth-century items, including a decorated pot (Dickinson 1979, 42-3). Although disc brooches ornamented with concentric circles or punched ornament can occur in Anglo-Saxon graves of the first half of the sixth century, their first appearance in southern England is around the middle of the fifth century. Two other graves at Temple Hill contained other early bossed pots with pedestal bases, but there were no fifth-century applied saucer brooches to match the pair from Orpington Grave 68. Both Orpington and Temple Hill have produced sixth-century cast saucer brooches in matched pairs and one of those also produced the rare feature of silver-wire slip-knot rings, mostly with a glass bead attached, as matched in Alfriston Grave 43 (Welch 1983, 82, fig. 20a). Specifically east-Kent manufactured items first appear early in the sixth century: a Kentish small square-headed brooch, a small rock-crystal ball in a silver sling and a unique, damaged silver disc brooch with two concentric rings of miniature framed human masks belonging to the Quoit-Brooch Style and manufactured within the fifth century (Chadwick 1961; Evison 1965, pls. 11b, 14d, 15b; 1968) occurred in one burial here. Similarly Orpington Grave 41 contained a young teenager wearing sixth-century Kentish fittings: a button brooch and a small square-headed brooch. Another Temple Hill female more unusually wore an early sixth-century Group III cruciform brooch (Åberg 1926, 39-42) with an 'antique' Roman 'trumpet' brooch. She may have arrived here from Anglian England for an arranged marriage.

Most male burials cannot be dated too precisely, but one Temple Hill grave contained a two-edged long sword (*spatha* type) with an attached free-moving ring on a copper-alloy staple. Swords with pommel ring attachments are a sixth-century east Kent development, inspired by continental fashions (Evison 1967; 1975) (ill. 6.27). By comparison with the fine sword from Buckland I, Grave C (Evison 1987, figs. 1-3), the Temple Hill sword is distinctly modest. A spear ferrule, but no spearhead, was recovered from

6.38 View of the cemetery during excavation: note the penannular ring-ditches that enclose so many graves.

6.37 Excavation plan of the cemetery.

N

Quarry

0   20

metres

■ Anglo-Saxon graves and features

The Anglo-Saxon cemetery near Cuxton

An Anglo-Saxon weapon burial was discovered in railway construction work in 1859 (Smith 1861), but the precise find-spot was not recorded. Archaeological work ahead of the Channel Tunnel Rail Link located what still survived of its cemetery, which was then excavated. There were perhaps originally some fifty individuals here (thirty-six excavated in 1998) buried within a hundred-year period. The site most likely represents a small, short-lived farming community consisting of two households. Their burial place had a commanding view across the Medway and both cemetery and settlement were probably visible from passing rivercraft.

The cemetery is characteristic of seventh-century Kentish burial grounds. Eleven graves were enclosed within penannular ring-ditches, most of which also had a marker post at the entrance gap. Such ringworks imply some sort of mound or platform, or at the very least a matching earth-and-chalk rubble bank within the ditch, which clearly mark the position of the grave above ground. The marker post might well have been carved and possibly painted, or else carried an emblem (Hogarth 1973). Although ring-ditched graves involved additional labour to construct, they do not necessarily enclose the best-furnished burials. Four produced no visible grave finds and two contained children. More unusual is the grave surrounded by ten small, spaced posts (Down and Welch 1990, 25-33, figs 2.4 and 2.12).

One burial contained a weapon assemblage to match the 1859 find: there was a spearhead, a shield boss with hand-grip and other shield mounts, a silver buckle ornamented with a *cabachon* garnet set in a gold mount, a small iron buckle and an imported roulette-decorated grey-ware pottery bottle. Two other weapon graves contained complete pots. One was associated with a spearhead, a copper-alloy small buckle and two knives, the other a spearhead and ferrule, together with two buckles, a silver pin and a knife. Weapon burial remained an active element in defining adult male status for longer in Kent than elsewhere in southern England (Härke 1992) and it is not surprising that another five graves at Cuxton contained either a shield and spear combination or just a spear.

Finds from other graves included Frankish-style belt sets. There are at least two relatively rich female dress assemblages with finds of necklaces, iron buckles, a silver ring, an iron chatelaine with keys, a pair of iron shears, knives and a double-sided antler comb, an iron firesteel, a copper-alloy 'workbox' and a Byzantine copper-alloy cylindrical 'needle-case'. Despite Cuxton's location beyond the western margin of the original kingdom of Kent and its distance from the east coast ports of Dover and Sandwich, this community enjoyed access to continental imports on an impressive, if limited, scale.

this grave, but its Group 3 shield boss belongs to a continental type introduced early in the sixth century (Dickinson and Härke 1992; Spain 2000). Two other burials produced shield fittings, but the rest contained spears broadly datable between the fifth and seventh century. In one, unusually, the spear was placed point downwards and parallel to the right leg, a continental practice possibly implying a Frankish migrant. Three spear graves were enclosed by annular or penannular ditches, indicating burial mounds fashionable in the later sixth and seventh centuries, but a fourth ring-ditch enclosed no visible burial. Turning to the pottery evidence, the cremation containers from Orpington represent the normal range found in the fifth and sixth centuries and include vessels of both continental Saxon and Anglian traditions. An unpublished stamp-decorated vessel from Otford has animal 'eyes' depicted on its three long bosses. It belongs between the late fifth and mid-sixth century and is similar to vessels from Northfleet and Mucking, though it is closer still to a pot supposedly from 'London' (Myres 1977, pl. Ia) and another from Alfriston, Grave 52 (*ibid.*, fig. 206). Perhaps then the 'London provenance' is reliable.

Mention must be made of two key assemblages from Darenth Park (Tyler 1992, 72-3, 75-6, map fig. 1.5), with Grave 4 containing a fifth-century mould-blown glass bowl manufactured in the Meuse region of Belgium, decorated with a Christian Chi-Rho symbol on its base (Webster 1981). Matched by two bowls from Westbere in east Kent (Jessup 1946, 17-19, fig. 2, pl. III.29; Werner 1957), most of these Christian bowls come from sites between the Seine and Rhine valleys. Two are recorded from north-west Germany, however, including one from Issendorf (Böhme 1976, 226, map on 211), so the Darenth bowl might well have arrived with a pagan Saxon migrant rather than from cross-Channel trade. A large silver-gilt square-headed brooch and a copper-alloy bossed-rim bowl (Wilson 1956; Hines 1997, 273, fig. 117a) are the other finds here. These bowls were prized imports from the

6.39 Dartford (Darenth Park) gilt silver great square-headed brooch of early sixth-century date (approx. actual size).

Frankish continent, typically found with lavish brooch sets (e.g. Alfriston Grave 28: Hines 1997, pl. 2b; Welch 1983, 69-2, figs 10-12). The Darenth/Dartford brooch is an early version modelled directly on Scandinavian examples (Hines 1997, 17-32, pl. 2a) (ill. 6.39) and symbolises the adoption of new fashions across 'Saxon' England at the beginning of the sixth century, when square-headed brooches with Style I animal ornament replaced north German chip-carved equal-arm brooches. No other large square-headed brooch has been reported from a west Kent site, perhaps reflecting the limited wealth of its communities; absence of fifth-century equal-arm brooches is equally curious, when so many occur just across the Thames at Mucking. Overall, the evidence implies settlement by mixed bands of Saxons and Angles from the Elbe region beginning in the 430s or 440s. Inter-marriage provides the obvious explanation for the presence of dress fittings from other Anglo-Saxon regions in the early sixth century, including limited contact with east Kent, matched by occasional finds of saucer brooches in east Kent, as at Lyminge Grave 39 (Warhurst 1955, pl. VIII) (ill. 6.40).

On occasion, early cemeteries could continue into the seventh century, as at Riseley Grave 56 (Tyler 1992, pl. I), whose jewelled gold pendants and amethyst beads match those from some of the richest east Kent burials (e.g. Sibertswold Grave 172: Meaney and Hawkes 1970, pl. VI) (ills 6.33; 6.34). Similarly the earliest burials in a small barrow field within Greenwich Park belong to the sixth century, though cemetery use extended well into the seventh century (Douglas 1793, 56n, 89-91; Struth and Eagles 1999, 40, figs 16 and 17) and an isolated seventh-century burial exists still further west at Deptford (Gaimster 2005; Philp and Chenery 1993). The most fully published cemetery of seventh- and early eighth-century date was located at Polhill near Sevenoaks and opposite Otford (Philp 1973; 2002a), but more recently a double cemetery above Springhead has been investigated. Most of the inhumations here were aligned east-west and laid out in irregular north-south rows, whereas earlier cemeteries usually reveal a variety of orientations. In both burial zones, however, there is a single north-south grave marking a special burial, as at Chamberlain's Barn II in Bedfordshire (Hyslop 1963, fig. 3). The smaller Springhead burial area contained just ten graves and may represent a family/household plot rather than a separate cemetery. Most of these contained finds including spearheads and knives, as well as a silver disc brooch with garnet settings related to east Kentish types and a rare item of a buckle from the eastern Roman Empire, reflecting the Mediterranean influences in seventh-century costume. Twenty-four graves were recorded in the second burial area. At its south-western edge there were five small penannular ring-ditches and one larger

6.40 Lyminge grave 39: a pair of Saxon gilt saucer brooches and a pair of Kentish small square-headed brooches (approx. actual size).

annular ditch. Three of these enclosed graves, two of which contained a knife, but then virtually every burial was accompanied by finds. These included another jewelled disc brooch similar to that in the first cemetery, silver pins, beads and a copper-alloy workbox. There were also two sceattas implying burial as late as *c*. 700. Weapons included a sword, a small single-bladed seax with a pommel, but no shield bosses or fittings, but then shields had become rare finds by the middle of the seventh century. Indeed the Polhill cemetery produced just one late shield boss of Group 7 (Philp 2002a, fig. 13.1).

The early ecclesiastical archaeology of Kent

Christianity was certainly present around the Thames estuary in late Roman Britain (Watts 1991, 217, figs 27 and 28), but does not seem to have survived the Anglo-Saxon takeover of southern and eastern Britain in an organised or meaningful sense (Blair 2005, 22-25, fig. 2). Augustine's mission from Rome in 597 was directed at an essentially pagan Kent with place-names commemorating cults of Woden, Thunor and others. Admittedly Augustine came across a cult of St Sixtus in or near Kent, but this was swiftly suppressed (*ibid.*, 13, 24, 29). The Gregorian mission's establishment of a literate Catholic Church is associated with profound changes in Anglo-Saxon social, economic and political organisation. In particular the introduction of a written record for land-giving (the diploma, more commonly referred to as a charter) was used to permit property to be alienated from family ownership as permanent gifts to the Church. Over time this led to radical changes in the nature of secular landownership, shaping the development of a landed aristocracy (Blair 2005, 84-91, 100-8; John 1964; 1966). The earliest surviving contemporary copy of such a charter records a grant of 679 to Reculver made

6.41 Charter issued in the name of King Hlothere to the Reculver minster in a single-sheet contemporary copy

by Hlothere (ill. 6.41), but their introduction may even go back to agreements between Augustine and Æthelberht (Brooks 1974).

The foundation of churches and monasteries constructed in stone, but possibly also using timber for some buildings between the end of the sixth and the eighth century, has been explored archaeologically. Early stone churches built to a fairly standardised simple plan were recognised well over a century ago in Kent. The most complete example survives within the Roman coastal fort at Bradwell (Essex), normally identified as the church dedicated here to St Peter by Bishop Cedd between 653 and 664 (Cambridge 1999, 208-9). Within Kent the closest equivalent is provided by a church within the Reculver fort. Built on land granted for a monastery in 669 by Egbert (664-673), its first abbot was the king's own mass-priest Bassa (see *ASC sub anno* 669; Brooks 1984, 180-6; Cambridge 1996; 1999, 208; Rigold 1977, 73, fig. 39). The only early church to survive as a roofed building in Kent is that dedicated to St Martin, overlooking Canterbury from a hill half a mile to the east. There is every reason to accept the tradition that this was the private chapel of the Frankish queen Bertha (Bede *HE* I.25), in which Augustine held services immediately after his first meeting with her pagan husband (Bede *HE* I.26). Bertha probably inherited her veneration of St

Martin from her mother Ingoberga (Yorke 2002) and it was Gregory, bishop of Tours, who prepared Ingoberga's will. This explains why Gregory twice mentions Ingoberga's daughter as married to a Kentish prince (*Histories* IV.26; IX.26; Wood 1994a; 1994b). Bertha was entombed in a *porticus* (side-chapel) dedicated to the same Gallic saint. Unfortunately we cannot be certain that the gold medallion pendant bearing her chaplain Bishop Liudhard's name was actually found in St Martin's churchyard (Blair 2005, 61, n. 200; Gem 1997, colour pl. 16; Grierson 1952; Webster and Backhouse 1991, 23-4, no. 5).

Bertha's principal residence was probably an adjacent timber hall complex, as St Martin's remained a royal manor as late as the ninth century (Sawyer 1968, S338; Sparks and Tatton-Brown 1987, 205). If there had been a royal residence within the walls of Canterbury, then her chapel would surely have been located there instead. Probably a trading settlement or *wic* had been developed between the Roman city walls and St Martin's and extended north-eastwards, perhaps as far as the river-port of Fordwich. A reference in a forged eleventh-century Canterbury charter (Sawyer 1968, S3) to a *Wyckengemearke* has been matched to archaeological finds, including Ipswich ware pottery, to justify this seventh- to ninth-century extramural *wic*. Similar material occurred at both *Lundenwic* (centred on Covent Garden, London) and at *Eoforwic* (Fishergate) at York (Hill and Cowie 2001).

Bede was informed that Bertha's chapel reused a still standing Roman church. The first phase of St Martin's possibly utilised the foundations and lower wall of a Roman structure, which it has been suggested was a mausoleum associated with an extramural cemetery adjacent to the Roman road east to Richborough (Toynbee 1953). Recent excavations, however, have produced no evidence for Roman burials (Rady 1987), so another possibility is the reuse of part of a Roman villa (Sparks and Tatton-Brown 1987). The ruined church at Stone-by-Faversham is often quoted as a comparable adaptation of a Roman funerary

monument, a Roman origin being widely accepted for its chancel (Cherry 1976, fig. 4.1; Fletcher and Meates 1969; 1977; Irvine 1875; Taylor and Taylor 1965, 575-7; Taylor and Yonge 1981). Perhaps, however, Bede had been misled and Bertha's small chapel was newly built by Frankish masons working under Liudhard's supervision. Expansion of St Martin's with a wider nave may belong within the seventh century, but no independent dating exists.

Recent excavations under the nave of Canterbury Cathedral certainly suggest that Bede's informant, Abbot Albinus (died 732), could not differentiate between an early seventh-century church and fourth-century Roman stone buildings. Bede states that a previous Roman church had been 'restored' in building the cathedral (HE I.33), and Krautheimer (as quoted by Blockley *et al.* 1997, 99-100) made the ingenious suggestion that the Latin verb *recupare* here implies that land on which a Roman church was believed to have stood had been granted by Æthelberht. The 1993 excavation revealed sections of wall separating the first church nave from a southern *porticus* as well as another *porticus* or *narthex* to the west. All its wall foundations had been dug through a layer of 'black earth' overlying previous Roman occupation datable no later than the fourth century, and in one place it even covered an abandoned Roman street (*ibid.*, 11-14, 95-100, figs 2, 3, 5, 35 and 36). Although only limited sections of the building fabric survived, Roman brick tile was present (*ibid.*, 12-13, fig. 9 sections 2 and 3). No trace of a Roman precursor was observed; if one had existed, it must have been located at the chancel end of the first church or still further east. Any such building would normally have been aligned with the Roman streets, but such an orientation would set it at a very awkward angle to the early seventh-century church. It seems probable that the reuse of Roman building materials and the use of Roman mortar technology misled Albinus into believing that this was a restored Roman church (*ibid.*, 99). In time this first cathedral was extensively rebuilt, most probably within the ninth century, but as yet no part of the neighbouring baptistery and funerary church dedicated to St John the Baptist in the mid-eighth century by Bishop Cuthbert has been traced (Blair 2005, 202; Brooks 1984, fig. 2).

Bede also refers to the foundation and construction of two further cathedrals by Æthelberht in association with St Augustine. It is usually assumed that the church dedicated to St Paul in London occupied the site of the present cathedral within the western end of the Roman city, rather than being in *Lundenwic* to the north of the Strand. The cathedral at Rochester shared its dedication to St Andrew with Pope Gregory's own monastery in Rome (*HE* II.3). Excavations in the 1880s revealed the foundations of an apsidal chancel and part of a rectangular nave at the present west end of Rochester Cathedral (Cambridge 1999, 204-5, 208, fig. 10.1; Livett 1889; Taylor and Taylor 1965, 518-9). It has been argued that this church is too small to be the first cathedral (McAleer 1999, 8-17, pls. 1-3), implying a larger church nearby and at least two aligned churches of the seventh to eighth century here. An attempt to reconstruct the first Canterbury cathedral from the incomplete plan of the contemporary extramural monastic church dedicated jointly to Sts Peter and Paul and the complete Reculver church foundations is open to criticism (Blockley *et al.* 1997, fig. 36; Cambridge 1999, 206) (ill. 6.42). Archaeologists have perhaps been too anxious to establish uniform features across the few available churches. As Roman law prohibited burial within the city walls, presumably the cathedral's *porticus* side chapels would not have contained tombs and this practice was apparently honoured in Canterbury until Cuthbert's eighth-century baptistery was built (Blair 2005, 202). Instead burial for the privileged few was a function of the Canterbury extramural monastic churches in the seventh century. Bede describes royal and episcopal tombs as initially restricted to their respective *porticus*, with Æthelberht and Bertha in the southern *porticus* of Sts Peter and Paul which was dedicated to St

Martin. The metropolitan bishops (later known as archbishops) from St Augustine onwards were interred in its northern *porticus* dedicated to St Gregory. Bede adds that Augustine (most probably died *c.* 604) had to be buried initially outside a still incomplete church and later tradition records that Bertha also died before her *porticus* was ready. By the time Bishop Theodore came to be buried here in 690 St Gregory's was full and his tomb had to be constructed within the nave. Remnants of three seventh-century episcopal tombs are still visible in the outer north wall of the demolished church (Gem 1992; 1997, colour pl. 12).

The royal tombs may well have been more extravagant than those of the first bishops, perhaps using stone coffins or sarcophagi, whether recycled Roman examples or Frankish imports shipped across the Channel. Stone-slab tombs containing a wooden coffin, as at the 'royal' sixth-century chapel under Cologne Cathedral, provide a further alternative (Doppelfeld and Pirling 1966; Werner 1964; Wieczorek 1996, 438-47, 931-5). Royal inhumations in the early seventh century might well contain appropriate dress fittings, weaponry and vessels, as occurred at the basilica of St Denis near Paris (Fleury and France-Lanord 1998). Later kings might have been buried in shrouds instead, leaving little more than a small pin or metal hook fastening, but inscriptions and the decoration of their sarcophagi would indicate their rank. Certainly by the eighth century senior clergy were being interred in sarcophagi at Canterbury, and Abbot Hadrian (died *c.* 709-10) is described as occupying a decorated white marble sarcophagus (Gem 1997, 105). Jænberht (765-92), a former abbot of Sts Peter and Paul, was the last of its metropolitan bishops to be buried in the old monastic church, for all subsequent archbishops followed the earlier example of Cuthbert by being entombed in the new baptistery adjacent to the cathedral. This change was to provide a lasting source of resentment for the monastic community of Sts Peter and Paul (later St Augustine's Abbey) against the cathedral community (Kelly 1997, 44).

Æthelbert's successor Eadbald (*c*. 616-640) and his Frankish consort Ymme (Brooks 1984, 64 and 341 n. 5) were buried in the *porticus* of a second monastic church dedicated to St Mary. The pairing of an apostolic church with a smaller church dedicated to the Virgin became a norm in Anglo-Saxon monasteries (Blair 2005, 200-1, fig. 24). An eleventh-century source informs us that other kings were buried in St Mary's, including Hlothere (died 685) and Wihtræd (died 725). Eleventh-century lead coffin plates with their names inscribed survive from re-interments following the Norman demolition of both churches. Abbots buried here included Hadrian in his marble sarcophagus, but very little has survived of St Mary's itself. The standing ruins of a two-cell church dedicated to St Pancras probably represent a third seventh-century monastic church here (Blockley *et al.* 1997, fig. 36; Cambridge 1999, 211-6, fig. 10.5; Gem 1992; 1997, 101-4, figs 39-41). Constructed on the same east–west axis, but rather further east again, it possessed a rectangular nave and a slightly narrower apse in its first phase (Cambridge 1999, 213-5, fig. 10.5). There may have been a small *porticus* on the south side of the chancel, possibly balanced by another to the north (Gem 1997, fig. 40: Period I; Jenkins 1976), but the walls were substantially rebuilt on the same plan in the second phase and three narrow *porticus* chapels were added to the north, south and west nave walls (Gem 1997, fig. 40: Period 2). Reused tile brick appears in both phases and its build is comparable to those of the early walls of the church of Sts Peter and Paul. As the second-phase construction levels sealed a burial accompanied by a *sceatta*, this rebuild presumably took place towards the middle of the eighth century. A case can be made for viewing the earliest church as a second-generation building to be placed between the construction of Sts Peter and Paul and a third generation one represented by the Reculver church (Cambridge 1999, 215-16). This is more convincing than arguing that St Pancras is a late-Roman church and even that it was Bertha's chapel (Jenkins 1976; Thomas 1981,

172-4). So Roman is the construction of the earliest Anglo-Saxon churches, recycling Roman brick, tile and stone, using Roman mortar types and flooring materials of *opus signinum*, that strong archaeological arguments are required to demonstrate Roman-period buildings.

The church of Sts Peter and Paul was united to St Mary's by Archbishop Wulfric's eleventh-century octagon, creating a single extended church (Cherry 1976, fig. 4.6), but prior to that we have three separate aligned churches. Liturgical processions and celebrations will have linked all three and may even have involved St Martin's church (Blair 2005, fig. 9; Kelly 1997, 37). Unfortunately very little is known about any other monastic buildings here or at any early monastery in Kent. Gem points to investigations in the 1920s to the north of the church of Sts Peter and Paul that revealed domestic structures pre-dating eleventh-century rebuilds. These included a detached rectangular structure underlying the later refectory and other buildings arranged around a cloister. Could these pre-date the tenth-century monastic reforms? Gem sides here with Potts against Clapham (Cramp 1976, 248-9; Gem 1997, 104, fig. 34). He expects substantial stone structures by the later seventh and eighth centuries, even if the earliest monastic buildings were of timber. (For Kent's early stone churches see box, pages 240-1)

Monasteries founded within the seventh century are recorded at Lyminge, Folkestone, Dover, Minster-on-Thanet, Reculver, Minster-on-Sheppey and Hoo. The latter was unusual in being a product of *Geuissan* (West Saxon) intervention by Cædwalla in *c*. 686-7 (Brooks 1984, 183). Seventh-century stone churches have been investigated at Lyminge and Minster-in-Sheppey, as well as Reculver. The foundations of a two-cell church with an apsidal chancel revealed in nineteenth-century excavations at Lyminge (Taylor and Taylor 1965, 408-9) appear to belong to a late seventh-century nunnery. The traditional association with Æthelburh, the royal widow of Edwin (*HE* II.20) may be explained by another

6.42 Comparative plans of the
early stone churches in Kent.
Grey walls are inferred.

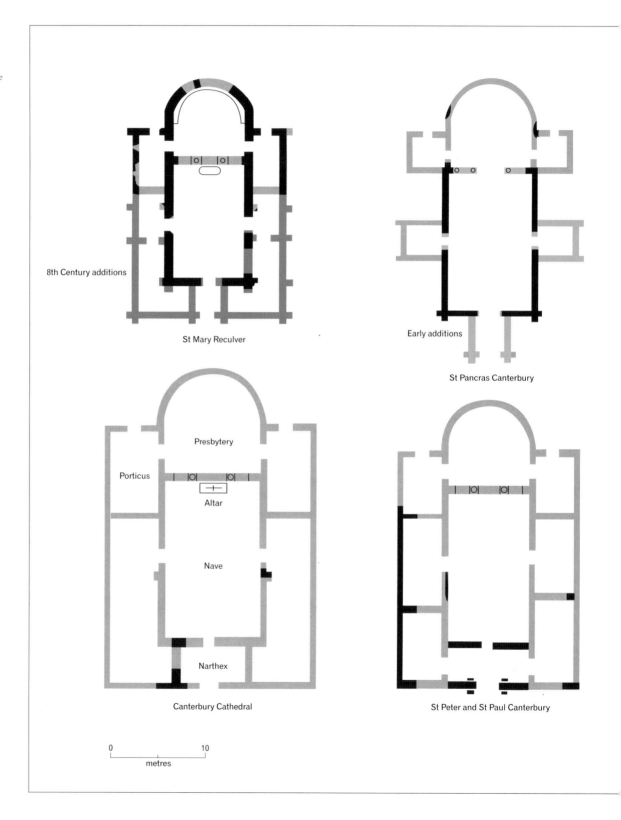

8th Century additions

St Mary Reculver

Early additions

St Pancras Canterbury

Presbytery

Porticus

Altar

Nave

Narthex

Canterbury Cathedral

St Peter and St Paul Canterbury

0   10

metres

Early stone churches in Kent

The earliest stone churches in Kent, built from the 590s onwards, seem to have followed a fairly standardised plan and were orientated east to west. A rectangular nave (the public area) was linked to a narrower chancel immediately to the east (the area reserved for the officiating clergy) by an arch or in some cases a set of triple arches. Typically the chancel terminated in a curved apse, with a stone bench around its inner wall to provide seating for the clerics. The principal altar was located near the east end of the nave before a screen in front of the chancel arch. The addition of side chapels to both north and south of the nave was common. Referred to by Bede as *porticus*, these 'chapels' did not form part of the church itself and therefore they could be used for burial. A further chamber or *narthex* might be added to the west of the nave.

There is some debate as to whether we should look to northern Gaul and Frankish masons for a model for these Kentish churches or rather to north Italy. The rarity of fifth- to sixth-century churches surviving in northern and western Gaul does not help. Certainly Eric Fernie saw shared features with fifth- and sixth-century churches in Ravenna (1983, 46, figs 13 and 14) and still closer similarities to churches in the Italian Tyrol, Switzerland and Austria (i.e. Altenberg, Sabiona, Romainmôtier, St Maurice d'Agaune and Laubendorf). Richard Gem, however, pointed to various churches along St Augustine's route through Gaul to Kent, mostly in southern Gaul (1997, 91-3, figs 28 and 29). These include an extramural basilica dedicated to the Apostles (Saint-Pierre) at Vienne, the basilica of St Justus at Lyon and the basilica of Saint-Martin at Autun built in the 590s. All these Gallic examples, however, are much more sophisticated structures than the Kentish churches. Eric Cambridge sees Italian features in the Reculver minster, a third-generation Kentish church (1999, 216-27). He accepts that the Ravenna characteristics here might have been transmitted via the Frankish Gallic world and suggests that both Italian and Gallic masons may have been brought over to Kent, just as both Italian and Frankish monks and priests participated in Augustine's mission.

Æthelburh (Wihtræd's queen) in a Lyminge charter of 697 (Cambridge 1999, 208; Sawyer 1968, S19; Witney 1984; Yorke 2003, 23, 197). The present church at Minster-in-Sheppey preserves Anglo-Saxon fabric in its north nave wall and has been attributed to a nunnery constructed after 664 (more probably *c.* 675-9) for Sexburh, daughter of Anna, king of the East Angles (Brooks 1984, 183-7; Cambridge 1999, 208; Taylor and Taylor 1965, 408-9). Although a secondary foundation to one at Milton Regis, the Sheppey nunnery became the senior house (Yorke 2003, 26). Roman coastal forts provided particularly attractive locations for monasteries with ready-made walls and ditches to demarcate them from the secular world. The site of the monastery at Dover supposedly founded by Eadbald in the 630s remains controversial. Later tradition placed it on high ground within the present royal castle. Wihtræd's foundation in the 690s was within the Roman fort, but a recent identification of its church with an excavated timber building complex (Philp 2003) has already been questioned here (see page 203). A late seventh-century royal monastic church would surely be built in stone, though the two successive large timber halls would not necessarily be out of place in a monastery (Blair 1996; 2005). Fortunately the excavations suggest that any Anglo-Saxon stone church here is likely to be well preserved. No secure archaeological trace has been recorded of an Anglo-Saxon church or monastery at Richborough, though it would be a suitable location for one (Rigold 1977, 71-2, fig. 35) and a late-Roman church has been identified here (Brown 1971). The third-century fort at Lympne was presumably too unstable to be developed as a minster site (Rigold 1977, 73), but an unusual basilican stone building incorporated into the present church at Lydd deserves a mention (Taylor and Taylor 1965, 405-8). Attributed a Roman date by some scholars (Fletcher and Jackson 1968; Fernie 1983, 72), others have preferred to see an Anglo-Saxon origin (Tatton-Brown 1989, 254). East Kent possesses unusually full documentation of its medieval churches and the *Domesday Monachorum* lists thirteen 'old minsters' for the Canterbury diocese in the late eleventh century. Christ Church cathedral and St Augustine's Abbey (formerly Sts Peter and Paul) at Canterbury have already been mentioned, together with Lyminge and Dover. The others have been identified as Charing, Eastry, Folkestone, Maidstone, Milton, Minster-in-Thanet, Teynham, Wingham and Wye. Not all these attributions are equally secure and in particular Eastry is open to question (Tatton-Brown 1988, fig. 22). Several minsters are at places that functioned as royal centres, notably Dover, Lyminge and Wye, suggesting a parallel administration of Church and state in Kent.

Not surprisingly, the chalices, patens and vestments of these churches have failed to survive the centuries, though in the 1530s Leland did record two crosses at St Augustine's Abbey that were said to be brought to Kent personally by Augustine (Heslop and Mitchell 1997, 67)! A forged charter records gifts from Pope Gregory to Æthelberht that were subsequently presented to the monastery of Sts Peter and Paul (Sawyer 1968, S4). The list included a silver platter, a gold sceptre or staff, a gold and gem-studded saddle and bridle, a silver mirror, a silken cloak and a decorated robe (Kelly 1997, 37). There is nothing improbable here, as two fine saddles were commissioned by King Dagobert in the seventh century from the famous Frankish goldsmith Eligius (Arrrhenius 1985, 96; Vierck 1974, 311). Neither these nor the manuscript books brought over from Rome in the seventh century have survived, with the possible exception of a sixth-century Italian book called the St Augustine's Gospels (Corpus Christi, Cambridge MS 286: Heslop and Mitchell 1997, 68-9, fig. 13, colour pl. 3; Webster and Backhouse 1991, 17-18, no. 1). Tradition may require it, but we cannot be certain that this book accompanied Augustine as the Anglo-Saxon marginalia added to it are no earlier than the eighth century (Tweddle 1995, 48: quoting Mildred Budny). There are eighth-century manuscript books attributed to a Kentish (probably Canterbury) *scriptorium*, including the *Vespasian Psalter* (BL Cotton MS Vespasian A.I: Alexander 1978, 55-6, no. 29; Heslop and Mitchell 1997, 69-72, colour pl. 4), the *Codex Aureus* (Stockholm Royal Library MS.A.135: *ibid.*, 56-7, no. 30) and the *Codex Bigotinus* (Bibliothèque Nationale, Paris MS lat. 281, 298: *ibid.*, 60, no. 34), but the *Barberini Gospel* (Vatican Library MS Barb. Lat. 570: *ibid.*, 61-2, no. 36) might be a Mercian or Northumbrian product (Webster and Backhouse 1991, 205, no. 160). Kent's monasteries, especially those at Canterbury, probably contained fine libraries that provided for the training of scribes and artists (Kelly 1997, 43-4). An academic 'school' at Canterbury inspired by Theodore and Hadrian, seems to have flourished in the seventh to early eighth century (Brooks 1984, 94-9), but little has survived in physical form. Even stone sculpture is rare, though some have assigned early dates to various stone fittings from Reculver. A seventh-century date seems appropriate for two architectural columns of Marquise limestone, possibly reusing Roman stone (Tweddle 1995, 162-3, ills 123-38), but the sculpture on one or more cross-shafts is more convincingly attributed to between the early ninth and early tenth century. Tweddle sees close parallels here with illuminations in the *Royal Bible* (BL MS Royal I. E.VI: Webster and Backhouse 1991, 217, no. 171) and favours the earlier part of the ninth century (*ibid.*, 46-61, ills 111-22), just beyond the period covered here.

Regions and lathes in Kent

Lathes, as described in the *Domesday Survey*, were the primary land divisions of Late Anglo-Saxon Kent, but when the Old English term 'lathe' first appears in the Rochester bridgework list of *c.* 975, it describes a royal manor (Aylesford) and a Domesday hundred (Eyhorne) rather than an eleventh-century administrative division. Lathe was thus a term that could be applied prior to the Domesday Survey to a range of jurisdictions (Brooks 1989, 69-70; Robertson 1939, 106-9, no. 52). Nevertheless Jolliffe's attempt to reconstitute the 'original lathes' of seventh-century Kent has remained influential. He believed that the land unit of the *sulung* (Kent's alternative to the Anglo-Saxon hide) was organised into multiples of 80 or 160, allowing him to map the earliest lathes (Jolliffe 1933, map opp. 95). Although Witney was critical of Jolliffe's methodology, he simply sought to produce a more refined reconstruction (Witney 1976, maps 4 and 5). In turn Witney has been followed by Everitt (1986) and Brooks (1989, table 4.1, fig. 4.2), while Blair has mapped all the original 'regions' (*regiones*) that enclosed the Weald in south-east England (1989, fig. 7.1; 1991, fig. 8; 2005, 154). These regions consisted of blocks of land (sometimes referred to rather misleadingly as multiple estates) that provided their communities with access to a range of landscapes and associated resources. In Kent these typically contained coastal or estuarine salt marshes, prime agricultural land including managed woodlands (in either the Foothills or the Holmesdale vale), and more extensive pasture with both open and woodland grazing land (either on the North Down uplands or on the Chart Hills). The regions also had access to swine pastures (*denns*), timber, building stone and iron-ore deposits in the Weald itself. In east Kent they could be double-banked, centred either on the Foothills or on Holmesdale for their best farmland, but all of them enjoyed access to the Weald, even communities on Thanet.

As Brooks (1989, 71-2) has pointed out, our attempts to work back from late historical sources to an earlier period present technical difficulties. The antiquity of the *Domesday Book* assessments of manors in *sulungs* listed under the *lathes* of Kent cannot be assumed, for we know that major changes in estate assessments took place between 1066 and 1086. Indeed Brooks has demonstrated that equally significant alterations occurred between the seventh and eleventh century, though the survival of documentation for these centuries is too patchy to permit confident modelling. A more cautious approach is taken now, exploiting the place-name and early historical evidence for royal regional centres between the sixth and eighth century.

Underpinning the *regiones* in each kingdom was the itinerant nature of early kingship. The progress of the royal household from one royal *villa* or *vicus* to the next was essential for the maintenance of a monarchy in a non-monetary rural economy. At each *vicus* the king's household consumed food rents, brought there on the hoof in the case of livestock, or by cart or boat in barrels and sacks, to await the king's arrival. During the royal visit, local people were required to perform traditional services, but in return the king became available to his people. He was there to settle disputes, administer justice and reward in front of witnesses those who served him well. The hierarchy of sites visited by Northumbrian kings on a seventh-century progress is described by Wilfrid's biographer in Latin as *civitates et castella vicosque*. The most important were the *civitates* and the *castella* (with *urbs* used as an alternative label) where a reeve or *præfectus* would have been a resident royal agent. In northern England these were typically earthwork-defended enclosures on a dominant hill or a coastal promontory (Alcock 1988; 2003, 49; Campbell 1979).

For Kent the equivalents are provided by the Roman stone-walled circuits at Canterbury and Rochester or on the coast at Reculver, Richborough and Dover. A reference to the king's hall (*sele*) and reeve (*wic-gerefa*) in London in the laws of Hlothere and Eadric is relevant (Attenborough 1922, cap. 16; Blair 2005, 272-3). At the bottom end are the unfortified *vici* and *villae*. There were many more of these and they could be relatively short-lived as royal places. Thus Bede observes (*HE* II.14) that Yeavering (*ad Gefrin*) had been a royal *villa* in Edwin's reign, yet by the time of subsequent kings it had been replaced by Milfield (*Maelmin*) (Hope-Taylor 1977; Welch 1992). Yeavering may have possessed a pagan religious shrine (Blair 2005, 54-7, fig. 7) that lost its significance when new Christian centres were developed. We do not know when or even whether royal halls or 'palaces' were constructed within the Roman walls of

Canterbury and Rochester in the seventh or eighth century. Perhaps an extramural location was always preferred, as certainly seems to be the case for Canterbury (Rady 1987, fig. 2). The successive great timber halls within the south-west corner of the Dover Roman fort (Philp 2003) support the case for a *castellum* 'palace' here, but might instead have been attached to a monastery (Blair 1996; 2005).

In the light of the possible relationship between the East Anglian royal *villa* mentioned by Bede at Rendlesham in Suffolk and the burial mounds at Sutton Hoo (*HE* III.22; Carver 1998; 2005), the documented presence of any 'royal' barrows in Kent would imply early royal centres in their vicinity. Unfortunately, both royal and princely burial sites of this period are absent from the archaeology of Kent. There are no equivalents to the Sutton Hoo barrows or to the Essex chamber graves at Broomfield (Meaney 1964, 85) and Prittlewell (Hirst *et al.* 2004). The nearest we possess is a poorly recorded sixth-century cremation deposit containing two swords from the Coombe barrow (Davidson and Webster 1967; Evison 1967). We can also note the exclusively Kentish character of the Taplow 'princely' barrow in south Buckinghamshire. This may well have been a Kentish prince governing the Middle Thames region on behalf of Æthelberht (Webster 1992). The rapid adoption by Kent's kings of Christian burial within the side chapels of a monastic church provides one explanation, with emulation first within the royal clan and then by Kent's aristocrats. As yet, we have not located the pre-Christian sixth-century and early seventh-century barrow burials of the ruling caste.

Meanwhile, place-names confirm that the earliest royal regional centres in Kent were not based on former Roman walled centres. Names ending in Old English *-gē* describe a centre for a district or region and are related to the modern German word *Gau*. Thus Lyminge is the capital of a region centred on the Wealden river Limen flowing into the Channel at Lympne and Hythe. It

retains its original spelling, yet Lyminge parish is well inland from both the coast and the river margins of the Weald. The other two documented *-gē* place-names have the modernised 'ry' ending. Sturry appeared as *Sturigao* in a forged charter (Sawyer 1968, S4) and must be the precursor of Canterbury as a regional centre for the Great Stour valley, the eleventh-century lathe being named after the *Burhwara* (the people of the *burh* of the *Cantware*). It seems Sturry may have been replaced as early as the 590s by a new royal *villa* on St Martin's Hill (Rady 1987). Both Sturry and St Martin's Hill were probably related to the emerging extramural trading and manufacturing *wic* complex of Canterbury (Sparks and Tatton-Brown 1987), and Sturry's location on the opposite bank to the medieval river port at Fordwich must be significant.

Eastry is the third of these *-gē* sites and a *regio Eastrgena* is referred to in 788 (Sawyer 1968, S128), whilst in other early ninth-century charters it appears as *Eastorege, Easterege and Eastraege* (Reaney 1961, 59; Sawyer 1968, S1264). The tradition that two princes were murdered on the orders of Egbert (664-673) in its royal hall (Rollason 1982; Yorke 1990, 25, 34-5) would allow us to take its existence as a royal *villa* back to the mid-seventh century. Its present village occupies a hilltop dominating the surrounding countryside at a key nodal point at the junction of a major Roman road between Richborough and Dover and a prehistoric trackway linking Sandwich to Wootton. There was probably a Roman roadside settlement here (Brookes 2003, 90) and perhaps a navigable river, a recurring feature of these royal centres, may have linked it directly to the east coast (Hawkes 1979, 96). Hawkes observed an impressive concentration of sixth- to seventh-century cemeteries as indicating a sixth-century origin for Eastry as a regional centre (*ibid.*, fig. 4.7). Although it remains possible that the former archbishop's manor house at Eastry Court was the site of the royal hall (*ibid.*, 95), exploratory excavation revealed nothing of relevance (Arnold

1982b). It seems more probable that its hall would have commanded a central hilltop location. The very existence of an 'eastern region' centred on Eastry implies a balancing 'western region'. The place-name of Wester (Linton parish) to the south of Maidstone, is conveniently close to the Medway (Brooks 1989, 69; Hawkes 1979, fig. 4.1) and Maidstone was an ancient minster foundation. If there was a *Westergē c.* 600, it was short-lived and much of its 'region' was to be incorporated into the lathe of Aylesford straddling the Medway. Further west, it seems highly probable that the Darent valley formed the core of an early administrative 'region' before the seventh century, but reconstructing the remaining 'regions' of west Kent is a more thankless task.

Returning to east Kent, however, a case has been made for adding Wye to the list of early 'regions' (Brooks 1989, 73, table 4.1, fig. 4.2). References to populations with a name ending in *-wara* provide the clue and the *Weowara* of Wye are matched by both the *Burhwara* of Canterbury and the *Limenwara* of Lyminge. Wye's name (*weoh*) implies a pagan cult centre and it is first documented as a royal vill by 762 (Blair 2005, 57, 278-9). Together with Lyminge, it is the only documented early regional centre for the Holmesdale *pays* in east Kent and both places would repay further archaeological investigation. Brooks has expressed scepticism that Faversham (*Febresham* in 815: Sawyer 1968, S178) was ever the centre of a region or lathe, but it was clearly an important royal centre in the seventh to eighth century. In the sixth to seventh century, it possessed an outstandingly rich cemetery (MacGregor and Bolick 1993; Smith 1923) and its unusual place-name incorporates a Latin loanword for a smith (*faber*). These facts have encouraged the suggestion that manufacturing may have been a key activity here, with fine metalwork fittings and perhaps even glass vessels being produced (Bruce-Mitford 1974; Evison 1982; Leigh 1980). Again, Brooks has cast doubt on Milton Regis as an early regional centre, viewing the half-lathe of Milton as a much later

creation. Milton and Rainham were, however, certainly important royal manors and there is a marked concentration of Anglo-Saxon burial sites around Milton creek comparable to Eastry's (Blair 2005, 278-9; Hawkes and Grove 1963, 36-8, fig. 3; Rigold and Webster 1970, 2-4, 17-18, fig. 1). The archaeology implies that Milton had become a very important place by no later than the sixth century.

Rather than attempt to establish the earliest regional boundaries along the coastal plain between Canterbury and Rochester, we should concentrate on the territories of these royal manors. Documentary, place-name and archaeological sources can be combined to demonstrate a series of estate centres at places such as Rainham, Milton, Teynham and Faversham, all of which developed initially within the early Anglo-Saxon period. The even spacing of such estate centres along Watling Street south of the Swale and in parallel along Holmesdale is a remarkable feature. It reflects the long thin hinterlands of arable and pasture resources assigned to each estate (Brookes 2007, fig. 35; Everitt 1986, map 3). Over the two centuries following the Christian mission there began a process of alienation of land on a hereditary basis from the royal estate that was to continue and help create the manorial patchwork recorded in the Kent *Domesday Book*. Grants of land recorded in Latin on charters written by the recipients, the minsters, initiated the process (Brooks 1974). The Church never dies, but merely replaces its chief executives, so written records were essential. In time the secular nobility came to view as unsatisfactory verbal statements of gift of food-rents from estates for one or more lifetimes. Landowners came to prefer all such grants to be recorded in writing (as bookland) and this led to the permanent alienation of estates from the royal lands. Naturally these grants were subject to conditions regarding obligations to the king, in particular military service, and in turn this formed the basis for the creation of a manorial and feudal aristocracy.

Archaeology's contribution to the future study of Anglo-Saxon Kent

Computers and the associated ability to manipulate large data-sets, particularly using geographical information systems to map the results, are having a major impact that will develop still further in the coming decades. A good example is provided by a published comparison of the distribution of wealth from furnished graves in east Kent cemeteries between the fifth and early eighth century and that of gold or silver coins between the seventh and ninth century (Brookes 2003, 93-5, figs 8.3 and 8.4). This has demonstrated a concentration of early buried wealth in a coastal zone centred on the Wantsum channel ports and on Dover, a pattern repeated with imports from the Frankish and Mediterranean worlds or with items produced by workshops within Kent. Inland wealth is focussed in particular on the Canterbury to Dover Roman road, a major route with many Anglo-Saxon cemeteries along it from the late sixth century onwards (Evison 1987, text fig. 36). These concentrations of disposable wealth deposited in graves can be related to a theoretical model that defines the distances over which a trader could afford to operate before incurring a financial loss (Brookes 2007; Plattner 1976; Stine 1962). Brookes has argued convincingly that Kent's extraordinary prosperity in the sixth to seventh century, by comparison to its Anglo-Saxon neighbours, is a result of the ability of its landowners to convert staple produce surpluses (grain, livestock and by-products such as leather and wool) into wealth by developing market mechanisms, notably in these eastern coastlands and along the Canterbury-Dover road. Initially this wealth can be measured in terms of bullion (silver and gold), rare materials (e.g. semi-precious stones) and imported items with a rarity value (e.g. copper alloy, glass and wheel-thrown pottery vessels). From the later seventh century onwards coin provides a more convenient substitute.

It is no accident that there is a marked concentration of graves containing equipment for assessing gold or silver bullion and coin in the coastal zone of east Kent. A touchstone for testing metal purity accompanied the balance and weight set from Gilton Grave 66. Sets of balances with weights are recorded from Dover at Buckland I (Grave C) and from two sites on Thanet, at Sarre (Grave 26) and Ozengell, while a burial at St Peter's, Broadstairs (Grave 76) produced balances without weights (Kent 1987; Scull 1986, fig. 14; 1990, fig. 9). Although weights and balances can have multiple functions, not all of which need be related directly to trade (Scull *op. cit.*), it seems reasonable to link their presence in east Kent to the development of a monetized society engaged in wealth conversion through trade. The considerable wealth of seventh-century communities buried in barrow cemeteries on the high downland near the Dover-Canterbury road may reflect an ability by pastoralists to generate surpluses from their herds and flocks more effectively than was possible for the arable farming communities of the Foothills and Holmesdale (Brookes 2007). Exploiting their access to ports at Dover and Sandwich, these downland communities converted these surpluses into wealth in metals, including copper as well as gold and silver, together with other luxury items. Through such mechanisms, these secondary communities that colonised the Downs in the late sixth century seem to have become more prosperous during the seventh century than populations based in the earlier and primary agricultural settlements of the Foothills and Holmesdale.

Turning to the coin evidence between the seventh and ninth century, we can link the 65 or more *sceattas* from Reculver (Blackburn 2003) to the eighth-century monastic ship-toll charters (Kelly 1992). Reculver, like other early minsters, owned trading vessels and it is reasonable to suggest that markets or fairs took place here and at other minsters. Casual coin loss would have been a direct result. Of course we cannot rule out some of the Reculver coins accompanying burials in its cemetery (Rigold 1977), but it seems probable that most were linked to commerce. Not quite so many coins for this period have been recovered from Richborough, but a metal-detector site 'near Canterbury' was another place where significant coin loss took place within this period (one gold shilling, nine *sceattas* and nine broad pennies) and it may relate to the extramural *wic* (Sparks and Tatton-Brown 1987). Overall the coin-loss pattern matches the earlier furnished-cemetery evidence and implies developing coastal and cross-Channel trade linked to the limited historical evidence for ports at Dover and in the Wantsum. Equally significant is the absence of coins from major estate centres elsewhere, such as Faversham, Milton, Rainham and Wye. It appears that a non-monetized economy still operated in these agricultural hinterlands away from the proposed east coast trading zone. The exception is Hollingbourne, which has produced seven seventh-century gold coins, twenty-six silver *sceattas* and nine later pennies. Hollingbourne seems to have become an important royal manor by the reign of Wihtræd (690/1-725), whose favoured manors were at Faversham and Milton (Witney 1982, 162). Its nodal location at the junction of trackways linking east to west Kent with north-south droveways between the Swale estate centres in the Foothills and their Wealden pastures made it a natural site for a market. There may even have been an early minster at Hollingbourne, which later appeared as a daughter house of Maidstone's minster, to contribute to its commercial development during the eighth century (Brookes 2003).

This exciting research has demonstrated the potential of quantifying archaeological evidence to throw new light on the economic development of early medieval society in England. It points up the process of change from a world where gift-exchange was used to legitimise the political and military social hierarchy to a more commercial and money-based society. Hitherto this has been principally the concern of the historian, but the new-found ability of archaeologists to manipulate large data-sets using computer technology has changed everything. In the near future, it should be possible to reassess fully the excavated data from sites in and around Canterbury and explore the emergence of its urban economy between the seventh and tenth century. Perhaps at some later stage the same might be attempted for Rochester and for the many small ports that played such a crucial role in developing the economy of Anglo-Saxon Kent. We are much closer now to understanding the mechanisms that might explain the precocious commercial development of east Kent, as its population exploited its proximity to the Frankish continent between the sixth and the eighth century. An ability to convert the surplus produce of its rural estates into portable wealth enabled its kings to become a dominant political force in southern and eastern England by the later sixth century. In the longer term its rulers could not compete with much larger kingdoms that could expand westward and northward at the expense of their British neighbours during the seventh and eighth centuries (in particular the West Saxons, Mercians and the Northumbrians). Kent reached as far west as London, but was hemmed in by the East Saxons to the north, by those who controlled Surrey to the west and by the South Saxons to the south-west. As a result, Kent came rather reluctantly under Mercian lordship during the eighth century and subsequently accepted more willingly West Saxon protection in the ninth century. The precise relationship of earlier kings of Kent to the Merovingian rulers of *Francia* in the sixth century remains a matter for further research (Wood 1992; 1994b), but it certainly seems to have worked to the advantage of the *Oiscingas* in Kent.

Acknowledgements

This chapter is dedicated to the memory of Sonia Chadwick Hawkes. Its author would like to thank the staff of the following organisations for their assistance: Archaeological Solutions, the British Museum, the Canterbury Archaeological Trust, the Channel Tunnel Rail-link Archaeology, the Heritage Conservation Group of Kent County Council, the Museum of London Archaeology Service, Oxford Archaeology, Pre-Construct Archaeology, Wessex Archaeology and the Kent Archaeological Field School. I am also grateful to the following individuals for sharing their research results with me: Stuart Brookes, Chris Fern, Sue Harrington, Andrew Richardson and Ian Riddler. If anyone feels omitted, I would appreciate their forgiveness, as compiling any survey of this scale inevitably puts the author in debt to many individuals. Finally I should like to thank the long-suffering editor John Williams and also my family for putting up with the long process of drafting and redrafting this contribution.

Bibliography

Abbreviations

ASC   *The Anglo-Saxon Chronicle*

DBG   Caesar, *De bello Gallico*

HB   *Historia Brittonum*

HE   Bede, *Historia Ecclesiastica*

RIB   *The Roman inscriptions of Britain, I, Inscriptions on stone*, T G Collingwood and R P Wright, 1965, Oxford.

         The Roman inscriptions of Britain, II, Instrumentum domesticum, S S Frere, M Roxan and R S O Tomlin, 1990-95, Stroud

Secondary sources

Åberg, N 1926. *The Anglo-Saxons in England*, Uppsala.

Ager, B M 1985. The smaller variants of the Anglo-Saxon quoit brooch, *Anglo-Saxon Studies in Archaeology and History* 4, 1-58.

Ager, B M 1989. An Anglo-Saxon supporting-arm brooch from Eastry, Kent, *Medieval Archaeology* 33, 48-151.

Aiello, L and Wheeler, P 1995. The expensive-tissue hypothesis: the brain and the digestive system in human and primate evolution, *Current Anthropology* 36, 199-221.

Akerman, J Y 1847. *An archaeological index to the remains of antiquity in the Celtic, Romano-British and Anglo-Saxon periods*, London.

Alcock, L 1988. *Bede, Eddius and the forts of the north Britons*, Jarrow.

Alcock, L 2003. *Kings and warriors, craftsmen and priests in northern Britain AD 550-850*, Edinburgh.

Aldridge, N 2001. Little Farningham Farm, Cranbrook, revisited, *Archaeologia Cantiana* 121, 135-56.

Aldridge, N 2005. A Belgic cremation cemetery and iron bloomery furnace at Jubilee Corner, Ulcombe, *Archaeologia Cantiana* 125, 173-82.

Alexander, J 1961. The excavation of the Chestnuts megalithic tomb at Addington, Kent, *Archaeologia Cantiana* 76, 1-57.

Alexander, J J G 1978. *Insular manuscripts, 6th to the 9th century*, London.

Allen, T 1999. Chartham Hatch, *Canterbury's Archaeology 1996-1997*, 12.

Allen, T 2002. Churchwood Drive, Chestfield, *Canterbury's Archaeology 1999-2000*, 23-7.

Allen, T, Parfitt, K and Rady, J 1997. Thanet Way, *Canterbury's Archaeology 1995-1996*, 24-7.

Allison, E 2005. Environmental archaeology, *Canterbury's Archaeology 2003-04*, 59-61.

Amos, E G J and Wheeler, R E M 1929. The Saxon-shore fortress at Dover, *Archaeological Journal* 86, 47-58.

Andrews, C 2001. Romanisation: A Kentish perspective, *Archaeologia Cantiana* 121, 25-42.

Andrews, P, Cook, J, Currant, A and Stringer, C, eds 1999. *Westbury Cave: the Natural History Museum excavations 1976-1984*, Bristol.

Anthony, D W 1990. Migration in archaeology: the baby and the bathwater, *American Anthropologist* 92, 895-914.

Anthony, D W 1992. The bath refilled: migration in archaeology again, *American Anthropologist* 94, 174-6.

Anthony, D W 1997. Prehistoric migrations as a social process, in *Migrations and invasions in archaeological explanation*, eds Chapman, J and Hamerow, H, British Archaeological Reports International Series 664, 21-32, Oxford.

Arnold, C J 1982a. *The Anglo-Saxon cemeteries of the Isle of Wight*, London.

Arnold, C J 1982b. Excavations at Eastry Court Farm, Eastry, *Archaeologia Cantiana* 98, 121-35.

Arrhrenius, B 1985. *Merovingian garnet jewellery: emergence and social implications*, Stockholm.

Arthur, P 1986. Roman amphorae from Canterbury, *Britannia* 17, 239-58.

Ashbee, P 1993a. The Medway megaliths in perspective, *Archaeologia Cantiana* 111, 57-111.

Ashbee, P 1993b. William Stukeley, the Kit's Coty Houses and his coves: a note, *Archaeologia Cantiana* 112, 17-24.

Ashbee, P 1997. Aylesford's Bronze Age cists and burials, *Archaeologia Cantiana* 117, 147-59.

Ashbee, P 1998. Coldrum revisited and reviewed, *Archaeologia Cantiana* 118, 1-43.

Ashbee, P 1999. The Medway megaliths in a European context, *Archaeologia Cantiana* 119, 269-84.

Ashbee, P 2000. The Medway megalithic long barrows, *Archaeologia Cantiana* 120, 319-45.

Ashbee, P 2003. The Warren Farm chamber: a reconstruction, *Archaeologia Cantiana* 123, 1-15.

Ashbee, P and Dunning, G C 1960. The round barrows of east Kent, *Archaeologia Cantiana* 74, 48-57.

Ashton, N M, Cook, J, Lewis, S G and Rose, J, eds 1992. *High Lodge: Excavations by G. de G. Sieveking 1962-68 and J. Cook 1988*, London.

Attenborough, F L 1922. *The laws of the earliest English kings*, Cambridge.

Avent, R 1975. *Anglo-Saxon garnet inlaid disc and composite brooches*, British Archaeological Reports British Series 11, Oxford.

Avent, R and Evison, V I 1982. Anglo-Saxon button brooches, *Archaeologia* 107, 77-124.

Axboe, M 1999. The chronology of the Scandinavian gold bracteates, in *The pace of change: studies in medieval chronology*, eds Hines, J, Høilund Nielsen, K and Siegmund, F, 126-47, Oxford.

Bakka, E 1958. *On the beginnings of Salin's style I in England*, Universitet i Bergen, Historisk-Antikvarisk Rekke 3, Bergen.

Bakka, E 1981. Scandinavian-type gold bracteates in Kentish and continental grave finds, in *Angles, Saxons and Jutes: Essays presented to J. N. L. Myres*, ed. Evison, V I, 11-38, Oxford.

Baldwin, R 1992. Seasalter: a problem borough in Domesday Kent re-examined, *Archaeologia Cantiana* 110, 237-67.

Barber, M 1997. Landscape, the neolithic and Kent, in *Neolithic landscapes*, ed. Topping, P, Neolithic Studies Group Seminar Papers 2, 77-86, Oxford.

Barber, M 2003. *Bronze and the Bronze Age: metalwork and society in Britain c.2500-800 BC*, Stroud.

Barber, M, Field, D and Topping, P 1999. *The Neolithic flint mines of England*, Swindon.

Barrett, J 1980. The pottery of the later Bronze Age in lowland England, *Proceedings of the Prehistoric Society* 46, 297-319.

Barton, R N E 1988. Long blade technology in southern Britain, in *The Mesolithic in Europe*, ed. Bonsall, C, 264-71, Edinburgh.

Barton, R N E 1991. Technological innovation and continuity at the end of the Pleistocene in Britain, in *The Late Glacial in north-west europe: human adaptation and environmental change at the end of the Pleistocene*, eds Barton, R N E, Roberts, A J and Roe, D A, Council for British Archaeology Research Report 77, 234-45, London.

Batteley, J 1711. *Antiquitates Rutupinae*, Oxford.

Behr, C 2000. The origins of kingship in early medieval Kent, *Early Medieval Europe* 9, 25-52.

Bell, M 1977. Excavations at Bishopstone, *Sussex Archaeological Collections* 115, 1-299.

Bell, M G 1983. Valley sediments as evidence of prehistoric landuse on the South Downs, *Proceedings of the Prehistoric Society* 49, 119-50.

Bennett, P 1980. 68-69a Stour Street, *Archaeologia Cantiana* 96, 406-10.

Bennett, P 1988. Archaeology and the Channel Tunnel, *Archaeologia Cantiana* 106, 1-24.

Bennett, P 1989. Canterbury, in *The Saxon Shore: a handbook*, ed. Maxfield, V A, Exeter Studies in History 25, 118-29, Exeter.

Bennett, P, Frere, S S and Stow, S 1982. *Excavations at Canterbury Castle*, The Archaeology of Canterbury Volume 1, Maidstone.

Bennett, P, Hicks, A and Houliston, M 2003. Canterbury Whitefriars: 'The Big Dig', *Current Archaeology* 185, 190-6.

Bennett, P, Macpherson-Grant, N and Couldrey, P 2007. *Excavations at Highstead, Chislet, Kent*, Canterbury.

Bennett, P and Williams, J 1997. Monkton, *Current Archaeology* 151, 258-64.

Bennett, P, Riddler, I and Sparey-Green, C forthcoming. *The Roman watermills and settlement at Ickham, near Canterbury, Ken*t, The Archaeology of Canterbury, new series.

Bennett, P J 1913. Coldrum monument and excavation, 1910, *Journal of the Royal Anthropological Institute* 43, 76-85.

Berger, A L, Imbrie, J, Hays, J D, Kukla, G J and Salzman, B, eds 1984. *Milankovitch and climate*, Dordrecht.

Bidder, H F and Morris, J 1959. The Anglo-Saxon cemetery at Mitcham, *Surrey Archaeological Collections* 56, 51-131.

Birchall, A 1964. The Belgic problem: Aylesford revisited, *British Museum Quarterly* 28, 21-9.

Birchall, A 1965. The Aylesford-Swarling culture: the problem of the Belgae reconsidered, *Proceedings of the Prehistoric Society* 31, 241-367.

Bird, D G 2002. The events of AD 43: further reflections, *Britannia* 33, 257-63.

Black, E W 1987. *The Roman villas of south-east England*, British Archaeological Reports British Series 171, Oxford.

Black, E W 2000. Sentius Saturnius and the Roman invasion of Britain, *Britannia* 31, 1-10.

Black, S B 2001. *A scholar and a gentleman: Edward*

Hasted, historian of Kent, Otford.

Blackburn, M 2003. 'Productive' sites and the pattern of coin loss in England, 600-800, in *Markets in early medieval Europe: trading and 'productive' sites, 650-850*, eds Pestell, T and Ulmschneider, K, 20-36, Macclesfield.

Blackmore, L 2002. The origin and growth of Lundenwic, a mart of many nations, in *Central places in the Migration and Merovingian period*, eds Hårdh, B and Larsson, L, Uppåkrastudier 6, 273-301, Lund.

Blagg, T F C 1982. Roman Kent, in *Archaeology in Kent to AD 1500*, ed. Leach, P E, Council for British Archaeology Research Report 48, 51-60, London.

Blagg, T F C 1984. Roman architectural ornament in Kent, *Archaeologia Cantiana* 100, 65-80.

Blagg, T F C 1995. The Marlowe excavations: an overview, in *Excavations in the Marlowe car park and surrounding areas*, eds Blockley, K, Blockley, M, Blockley, P, Frere, S S and Stow, S, The Archaeology of Canterbury Volume 5, 7-25, Canterbury.

Blair, J 1989. Frithuwold's kingdom and the origins of Surrey, in *The origins of Anglo-Saxon kingdoms*, ed. Bassett, S, 97-107, Leicester.

Blair, J 1991. *Early medieval Surrey: landholding, church and settlement before 1300*, Stroud.

Blair, J 1996. Palaces or minsters? Northampton and Cheddar reconsidered, *Anglo-Saxon England* 25, 97-121.

Blair, J 2005. *The church in Anglo-Saxon society*, Oxford.

Blancquaert, G and Bostyn, F 1998. L'âge du fer à Coquelles et Fréthun (Pas-de-Calais) (Fouilles du Transmanche 1986-1988), *Revue du Nord* 80, 109-37.

Blockley, K, Blockley, M, Blockley, P, Frere, S S and Stow, S 1995. *Excavations in the Marlowe car park and surrounding areas*, The Archaeology of Canterbury Volume 5, Canterbury.

Blockley, K, Sparks, M and Tatton-Brown, T 1997. *Canterbury Cathedral nave: archaeology, history and architecture*, The Archaeology of Canterbury, New Series 1, Canterbury.

Boast, E and Gibson, A 2000. Neolithic, Beaker and Anglo-Saxon remains: Laundry Road, Minster-in-Thanet, *Archaeologia Cantiana* 120, 359-72.

Boden, D 2004. Shelford Quarry, Broad Oak, *Canterbury's Archaeology 2002-2003*, 20-2.

Böhme, H W 1974. *Germanische Grabfunde des 4. bis 5. Jahrhunderts zwischen unterer Elbe und Loire: Studien zur Chronologie und Bevölkerungsgeschichte*, Munich.

Böhme, H W 1976. Das Land zwischen Elb- und Wesermündung vom 4. bis 6. Jh, *Führer zu vor- und frühgeschichtlichen Denkmäleren* 29, 205-26.

Böhme, H W 1986. Das Ende der Römerherrschaft in Britannien und die angelsächsische Besiedlung Englands im 5. Jahrhundert, *Jahrbuch des Römisch-Germanisches Zentralmuseum Mainz* 33, 469-574.

Booth, P 2001. The Roman shrine at Westhawk Farm, Ashford: a preliminary account, *Archaeologia Cantiana* 121, 1-23.

Booth, P, Champion, T, Garwood, P, Reynolds, A, Robinson, M and Munby, J forthcoming. *The archaeology of Section 1 of the Channel Tunnel Rail Link*.

Booth, P and Lawrence, S 2000. Ashford Westhawk Farm, *Current Archaeology* 168, 478-81.

Booth, P, Bingham, A and Lawrence, S forthcoming. *The Roman roadside settlement at Westhawk Farm, Ashford, Kent*.

Boube, C 1991. Les cruches, in *La vaisselle tardo-républicaine en bronze: actes de la table-ronde CNRS organisée à Lattes du 26 au 28 avril 1990 par l'UPR 290 (Lattes) et le GDR 125 (Dijon)*, eds Feugère, M and Rolley, C, Centre de recherches sur les techniques gréco-romaines, no 13, 23-45, Dijon.

Bowden, M 1991. *Pitt Rivers: the life and archaeological work of Lieutenant-General Augustus Henry Lane Fox Pitt Rivers, DCL, FRS, FSA*, Cambridge.

Bowen, D Q, ed. 1999. *A revised correlation of Quaternary deposits in the British Isles*. Geological Society Special Report 23, London.

Boys, W 1792. *Collections for an history of Sandwich in Kent. With notices of the other Cinque Ports and members, and of Richborough*, Canterbury.

Bradshaw, J 1966. Godmersham, *Archaeologia Cantiana* 81, liii.

Breeze, D J 1983. Review of Philp B J, The excavation of the Roman forts of the Classis Britannica at Dover, 1970-77, *Britannia* 14, 372-5.

Brenan, J 1991. *Hanging bowls and their contexts*, British Archaeological Reports British Series 220, Oxford.

Brent, C 1866. Bronze Age urn from Westbere, *Journal of the British Archaeological Asociation* 22, 241-2.

Brent, J 1860. *Canterbury in the Olden Time, from the municipal archives and other sources*, Canterbury.

Brent, J 1861. Roman cemeteries in Canterbury and some conjectures concerning its earliest inhabitants, *Archaeologia Cantiana* 4, 27-42.

Brent, J 1863. Account of the Society's researches in the Saxon cemetery at Sarr (Sarre), *Archaeologia*

Cantiana 5, 305-22.

Brent, J 1866. Account of the Society's researches in the Saxon cemetery at Sarr (Sarre), *Archaeologia Cantiana* 6, 157-87.

Brent, J 1868. Account of the Society's researches in the Saxon cemetery at Sarr (Sarre), *Archaeologia Cantiana* 7, 307-21.

Bridgland, D R 1994. *Quaternary of the Thames*, London.

Bridgland, D R 2001. The Pleistocene evolution and Palaeolithic occupation of the Solent river, in *Palaeolithic archaeology of the Solent river*, eds Wenban-Smith, F F and Hosfield, R T, Lithic Studies Occasional Paper 7, 15-25, London.

Bridgland, D R and Harding, P 1984. Palaeolithic artefacts from the gravels of the Hoo Peninsula, *Archaeologia Cantiana* 101, 41-55.

Bridgland, D R, Keen, D H, Schreve, D C and White, M J 1998. Quaternary drainage of the Kentish Stour, Fordwich and Sturry, in *The Quaternary of Kent and Sussex: field guide*, eds Murton, J B, Whiteman, C A, Bates, M R, Bridgland, D R, Long, A J, Roberts, M B and Walker, M P, 39-44, London.

Brodribb, G and Cleere, H 1988. The Classis Britannica bath-house at Beauport Park, East Sussex, *Britannia* 19, 217-74.

Brookes, S 2002. 'Landscapes, communities and exchange: a reassessment of Anglo-Saxon economics and social change AD 400-900 with special reference to Kent'; unpublished PhD thesis, University College London.

Brookes, S 2003. The early Anglo-Saxon framework for middle Anglo-Saxon economics: the case of east Kent, in *Markets in early medieval Europe: trading and 'productive' sites 650-850*, eds Pestell, T and Ulmschneider, K, 84-96, Macclesfield.

Brookes, S 2007. *Economics and social change in Anglo-Saxon Kent AD 400-900. Landscapes, communities and exchange*. British Archaeological Reports British Series 431, Oxford.

Brookes, S forthcoming a. Clench-nails from Anglo-Saxon cemeteries in Kent, *International Journal of Nautical Archaeology*.

Brookes, S forthcoming b. The Kentish Anglo-Saxon Emporia Project: excavations and survey at Fordwich, Kent, 1999-2000.

Brooks, N 1974. Anglo-Saxon charters: the work of the last twenty years, *Anglo-Saxon England* 2, 211-31.

Brooks, N 1984. *The early history of the church of Canterbury: Christ Church from 597 to 1066*, Leicester.

Brooks, N 1989. The creation and early structure of the kingdom of Kent, in *The origins of Anglo-Saxon kingdoms*, ed. Bassett, S, 55-74, Leicester.

Brooks, N 2000. Canterbury, Rome and the construction of English identity, in *Early medieval Rome and the Christian West: essays in honour of D. A. Bullough*, ed. Smith, J M H, 221-46, Leiden.

Brown, N 1988. A late Bronze Age enclosure at Lofts Farm, Essex, *Proceedings of the Prehistoric Society* 54, 249-302.

Brown, P D C 1971. The church at Richborough, *Britannia* 2, 225-31.

Bruce-Mitford, R 1974. *Aspects of Anglo-Saxon archaeology. Sutton Hoo and other discoveries*, London.

Bruce-Mitford, R 1978. *The Sutton Hoo ship-burial, Vol. 2*, London.

Brück, J 1995. A place for the dead: the role of human remains in late Bronze Age Britain, *Proceedings of the Prehistoric Society* 61, 245-77.

Brück, J 1999a. Houses, lifecycles and deposition on middle Bronze Age settlements in southern Britain, *Proceedings of the Prehistoric Society* 65, 145-66.

Brück, J 1999b. What's in a settlement? Domestic practice and residential mobility in early Bronze Age southern England, in *Making places in the prehistoric world*, eds Brück, J and Goodman, M, 52-75, London.

Brugmann, B 1999. The role of continental artefact-types in sixth-century Kentish chronology, in *The pace of change: studies in medieval chronology*, eds Hines, J, Høilund Nielsen, K and Siegmund, F, 37-64, Oxford.

Burchell, J P T 1933. The Northfleet 50 ft. submergence later than the Coombe Rock of post-early Mousterian times, *Archaeologia* 83, 67-91.

Burchell, J P T 1938. Two Mesolithic floors in the Ebbsfleet Valley of the Lower Thames, *Antiquaries Journal* 18, 397-401.

Burchell, J P T 1954. Loessic deposits in the fifty-foot terrace post-dating the main Coombe Rock of Baker's Hole, Northfleet, Kent, *Proceedings of the Geologists' Association* 65, 256-61.

Burchell, J P T 1957. A temperate bed of the last interglacial period at Northfleet, Kent, *Geological Magazine* 94, 212-14.

Burchell, J P T and Piggott, S 1939. Decorated prehistoric pottery from the bed of the Ebbsfleet, Northfleet, Kent, *Antiquaries Journal* 19, 405-20.

Burnham, B C and Wacher, J S 1990. *The 'small towns' of*

Roman Britain, London.

Bushe-Fox, J P 1925. *Excavations of the late-Celtic urnfield at Swarling, Kent*, Research Committee of the Society of Antiquaries of London Report 5, London.

Bushe-Fox, J P 1926. *First report on the excavations of the Roman fort at Richborough, Kent*, Research Committee of the Society of Antiquaries Report 6, London.

Bushe-Fox, J P 1928. *Second report on the excavations of the Roman fort at Richborough, Kent*, Research Committee of the Society of Antiquaries Report 7, London.

Bushe-Fox, J P 1932. *Third report on the excavations of the Roman fort at Richborough, Kent*, Research Committee of the Society of Antiquaries Report 10, London.

Bushe-Fox, J P 1949. *Fourth report on the excavation of the Roman fort at Richborough, Kent*, Research Committee of the Society of Antiquaries of London Report 16, Oxford.

Cambridge, E 1996. Reculver Abbey, in *The dictionary of art Vol. XXVI*, ed. Turner, J, 66-7, London.

Cambridge, E 1999. The architecture of the Augustinian mission, in *St Augustine and the conversion of England*, ed. Gameson, R, 202-36, Stroud.

Campbell, J 1979. Bede's words for places, in *Medieval settlement: continuity and change*, ed. Sawyer, P H, 34-54, London.

Cann, R 1988. DNA and human origins, *Current Anthropology* 17, 127-43.

Canterbury Archaeological Trust 1992. Interim report on work carried out by Canterbury Archaeological Trust, *Archaeologia Cantiana* 110, 357-81.

Canterbury Archaeological Trust 1996. Interim report on work carried out by Canterbury Archaeological Trust, *Archaeologia Cantiana* 116, 311-24.

Canterbury Archaeological Trust 1998. 'An archaeological investigation at the site known as Glebe Land, Harrietsham: interim report'; unpublished Canterbury Archaeological Trust report.

Canterbury Archaeological Trust and Trust for Thanet Archaeology 1996. Interim report on excavations in advance of the dualling of the A253 between Monkton and Mount Pleasant, Thanet, *Archaeologia Cantiana* 116, 305-10.

Capelli, C, Redhead, N, Abernethy, J K, Gratrix, F, Wilson, J F, Moen, T, Hervig, T, Richards, M, Stumpf, M P H, Underhill, P A, Bradshaw, P, Shaha, A, Thomas, M, Bradman, N and Goldstein, D B

2003. A Y chromosome census of the British Isles, *Current Biology* 13, 979-84.

Carver, M O H 1998. *Sutton Hoo: burial ground of kings?* London.

Carver, M O H 2005. *Sutton Hoo: a seventh-century princely burial ground and its context*, London.

Casey, P J 1991. *The legions in the later Roman Empire: the fourth annual Caerleon lecture*, Cardiff.

Chadwick, S E 1958a. Notes on an early Anglo-Saxon square-headed brooch from Canterbury, *Antiquaries Journal* 38, 52-7.

Chadwick, S E 1958b. The Anglo-Saxon cemetery at Finglesham: a reconsideration, *Medieval Archaeology* 2, 1-71.

Chadwick, S E 1961. The Jutish style A: a study of Germanic animal art in southern Britain in the fifth century AD, *Archaeologia* 98, 29-74.

Chambers, R 1987. The late- and sub-Roman cemetery at Queenford Farm, Dorchester on Thames, Oxon, *Oxoniensia* 52, 36-69.

Champion, T C 1975. Britain in the European Iron Age, *Archaeologia Atlantica* 1, 127-45.

Champion, T C 1980. Settlement and environment in later Bronze Age Kent, in *Settlement and society in the British later Bronze Age*, eds Barrett, J and Bradley, R, British Archaeological Reports British Series 83, 223-46, Oxford.

Champion, T C 1982. The Bronze Age in Kent, in *Archaeology in Kent to AD 1500*, ed. Leach, P, Council for British Archaeology Research Report 48, 31-9, London.

Champion, T C 2004. Exotic materials in the early Bronze Age of southeastern England, in *From megaliths to metals: essays in honour of George Eogan*, eds Roche, H, Grogan, E, Bradley J, Coles, J and Raftery, B, 48-52, Oxford.

Champion, T C 2007. Kent from 1500 to 300 BC, in *The earlier Iron Age in Britain and the near continent*, eds Haselgrove, C C and Pope, R E, 293-305, Oxford.

Charles, T 1843. Report on excavations at the Mount, Maidstone, *Journal of the British Archaeological Asociation* 2, 86-8.

Cherry, B 1976. Ecclesiastical architecture, in *The archaeology of Anglo-Saxon England*, ed. Wilson, D M, 151-200, London.

Christlein, R 1973. Besitzabstüfungen zur Merowingerzeit im Spiegel reicher Grabfunde aus West- und Süddeutschland, *Jahrbuch des Römisch-*

Germanisches Zentralmuseum Mainz 20, 147-52.

Clark, D and Hirst, S forthcoming. *Excavations at Mucking: two Anglo-Saxon cemeteries.*

Clark, J G D 1932. *The mesolithic age in Britain,* Cambridge.

Clark, P 2004a. Castle Road, Sittingbourne, *Canterbury's Archaeology 2002-2003,* 32-4.

Clark, P, ed. 2004b. *The Dover Bronze Age boat,* London.

Clark, P ed. 2004c. *The Dover Bronze age boat in context,* Oxford.

Clark, P ed. forthcoming. *Monkton – Mount Pleasant, Thanet: prehistoric, Roman and medieval discoveries on the Isle of Thanet 1994-1995.*

Clarke, A F 1982. The Neolithic of Kent: a review, in *Archaeology in Kent to AD 1500,* ed. Leach, P, Council for British Archaeology Research Report 48, 25-30, London.

Clarke, D L 1970. *Beaker pottery of Great Britain and Ireland,* Cambridge.

Clarke, D V, Cowie, T G and Foxon, A 1985. *Symbols of power at the time of Stonehenge,* Edinburgh.

Cleere, H 1974. The Roman iron industry of the Weald and its connexions with the Classis Britannica, *Archaeological Journal* 131, 171-99.

Cleere, H and Crossley, D 1995. *The iron industry of the Weald,* Cardiff.

Clinch, G 1908. Early man, in *The Victoria History of the County of Kent, Vol. I,* ed. Page, W A, 307-38, London.

Coles, B J 1998. Doggerland: a speculative survey, *Proceedings of the Prehistoric Society* 64, 45-82.

Coles, S, Hammond, S, Pine, J, Preston, S and Taylor, A 2003. *Bronze Age, Roman and Saxon sites on Shrubsoles Hill, Sheppey and at Wise Lane, Borden, Kent: a landscape of ancestors and agriculture by the Swale,* Reading.

Collis, J R 1977. Pre-Roman burial rites in north-western Europe, in *Burial in the Roman world,* ed. Reece, R, Council for British Archaeology Research Report 22, 1-13, London.

Colvin, H M 1959. An Iron Age hill-fort at Dover? *Antiquity* 33, 125-7.

Conway, B W, McNabb, J and Ashton, N, eds 1996. *Excavations at Barnfield Pit, Swanscombe, 1968-72.* British Museum Occasional Paper 94, London.

Conyngham, A and Akerman, J Y 1844. An account of the opening and examination of a considerable number of tumuli on Breach Downs, in the county of Kent, in a letter from Lord Albert Conyngham F.S.A. to John Yonge Akerman Esq. F.S.A.; followed by Mr. Akerman's remarks upon Lord Albert Conyngham's excavations, *Archaeologia* 30, 47-56.

Cook, A M and Dacre, M W 1985. *Excavations at Portway, Andover, 1974-5: Anglo-Saxon cemetery, Bronze Age barrow and linear ditch,* Oxford University Committee for Archaeology Monograph 4, Oxford.

Cook, J 1986. A blade industry from Stoneham's Pit, Crayford, in *The Palaeolithic of Britain and its nearest neighbours: recent trends,* ed. Collcutt, S N, 16-19, Sheffield.

Cook, J and Jacobi, R M 1998. Discoidal core technology in the Palaeolithic at Oldbury, Kent, in *Stone Age archaeology: essays in honour of John Wymer,* eds Ashton, N, Healy, F and Pettitt, P, 124-36, Oxford.

Cook, W H and Killick, J R 1924. On the discovery of a flint-working site of Palaeolithic date in the Medway Valley at Rochester, Kent, with notes on the drift-stages of the Medway, *Proceedings of the Prehistoric Society of East Anglia* 4, 133-49.

Cosack, E 1982. *Das sächsische Gräberfeld bei Liebenau, Kr. Nienburg (Weser): Teil 1,* Berlin.

Cossburn, P 2001. 'The Richborough environs: a study of social interaction, production and ideology'; unpublished BA dissertation, Department of Archaeology, University of Southampton.

Cotterill, J 1993. Saxon raiding and the role of the late Roman coastal forts of Britain, *Britannia* 24, 227-39.

Cotton, J and Wood, B 1996. Recent prehistoric finds from the Thames foreshore and beyond in Greater London, *Transactions of the London and Middlesex Archaeological Society* 47, 1-33.

Cowie, R 2000. Londinium to Lundenwic: early and middle Saxon archaeology in the London region, in *London under ground – the archaeology of a city,* eds Haynes, I, Sheldon, H and Hannigan, L, 175-205, Oxford.

Crabtree, P J 1989. *West Stow, Suffolk: early Anglo-Saxon animal husbandry,* East Anglian Archaeology 47, Ipswich.

Cramp, R J 1976. Monastic sites, in *The archaeology of Anglo-Saxon England,* ed. Wilson, D M, 201-52, London.

Creighton, J D 2000. *Coins and power in late Iron Age Britain,* Cambridge.

Cross, R and Rady, J 2002. Island Road, Hersden, *Canterbury's Archaeology 1999-2000,* 27-30.

Crowfoot, E and Hawkes, S C 1967. Early Anglo-Saxon

gold braids, *Medieval Archaeology* 11, 42-86.

Cruse, R J 1987. Further investigation of the Acheulian site at Cuxton, *Archaeologia Cantiana* 104, 39-81.

Cruse, R J and Harrison, A C 1983. Excavation at Wouldham, *Archaeologia Cantiana* 99, 81-108.

Cunliffe, B W 1968. *Fifth report on the excavations of the Roman fort at Richborough, Kent*, Research Committee of the Society of Antiquaries of London Report 23, London.

Cunliffe, B W 1976. *Excavations at Portchester Castle: Vol. 2, Saxon*, Research Committee of the Society of Antiquaries of London Report 33, London.

Cunliffe, B W 1977. The Saxon Shore – some problems and misconceptions, in *The Saxon Shore*, ed. Johnston, D E, Council for British Archaeology Research Report 18, 1-6, London.

Cunliffe, B W 1980. Excavations at the Roman fort at Lympne, *Britannia* 11, 227-88.

Cunliffe, B W 1982. Social and economic developments in Kent in the pre-Roman Iron Age, in *Archaeology in Kent to AD 1500*, ed. Leach, P E, Council for British Archaeology Research Report 48, 40-50, London.

Cunliffe, B W 1988. Romney Marsh in the Roman period, in *Romney Marsh: evolution, occupation, reclamation*, eds Eddison, J and Green, C, Oxford University Committee for Archaeology Monograph 24, 83-7, Oxford.

Darvill, T 1996. Neolithic buildings in England, Wales and the Isle of Man, in *Neolithic houses in northwest Europe and beyond*, eds Darvill, T and Thomas, J S, 77-112, Oxford.

Davidson, H R E and Webster, L E 1967. The Anglo-Saxon burial at Coombe (Woodnesborough), Kent, *Medieval Archaeology* 11, 1-41.

Davies, W and Vierck, H 1974. The contexts of the Tribal Hidage, social aggregates and settlement patterns, *Frühmittelalterliche Studien* 8, 223-93.

Dennell, R 2003. Dispersal and colonisation, long and short chronologies: how continuous is the early Pleistocene record for hominids outside East Africa? *Journal of Human Evolution* 45, 421-40.

Detsicas, A 1966. An Iron Age and Romano-British site at Stone Castle quarry, Greenhithe, *Archaeologia Cantiana* 81, 136-90.

Detsicas, A P 1976. Excavations at Eccles, 1975, *Archaeologia Cantiana* 92, 157-63.

Detsicas, A P 1983. *The Cantiaci*, Gloucester.

Detsicas, A P 1991. Excavations at Eccles: a progress report, *Archaeologia Cantiana* 107, 83-8.

Devoy, R J N 1978. Flandrian sea level changes and vegetational history of the Lower Thames Estuary, *Philosophical Transactions of the Royal Society* B285, 355-407.

Devoy, R J N 1980. Post-glacial environmental change and man in the Thames Estuary: a synopsis, in *Archaeology and coastal change*, ed. Thompson, F H, Society of Antiquaries of London Occasional Paper (New series) 1, 134-48, London.

Dewey, H and Smith, R A 1925. Flints from the Sturry gravels, Kent, *Archaeologia* 74, 117-36.

Diack, M 2003. North Foreland Road, Broadstairs, *Canterbury's Archaeology 2001-2002*, 25-6.

Diack, M, Mason, S and Perkins, D R J 2000. North Foreland, *Current Archaeology* 168, 472-3.

Dickinson, T M 1979. On the origin and chronology of the early Anglo-Saxon disc brooch, *Anglo-Saxon Studies in Archaeology and History* 1, British Archaeological Reports British Series 72, 39-80.

Dickinson, T M and Härke, H 1992. Early Anglo-Saxon shields, *Archaeologia* 110, 1-94.

Dines, H G 1929. The flint industries of Bapchild, *Proceedings of the Prehistoric Society of East Anglia* 6, 12-26.

Doppelfeld, O and Pirling, R 1966. *Fränkische Fürsten im Rheinland: die Gräber aus dem Kölner Dom, von Krefeld-Gellep und Morken*, Düsseldorf.

Douglas, J 1793. *Nenia Britannica: or a sepulchral history of Great Britain from the earliest period to its general conversion to Christianity*, London.

Down, A and Welch, M 1990. *Chichester Excavations 7*, Chichester.

Drinkwater, J F 1983. *Roman Gaul: the three provinces 58 BC-AD 260*, London.

Drower, M S 1995. *Flinders Petrie: a life in archaeology*, 2nd ed., Madison.

Dunning, G C 1966. Neolithic occupation sites in east Kent, *Antiquaries Journal* 46, 1-25.

Dyson, L, Shand, G and Stevens, S 2000. Causewayed enclosures, *Current Archaeology* 168, 470-2.

Eddison, J, ed. 1995. *Romney Marsh: the debatable ground*. Oxford University Committee for Archaeology Monograph 41, Oxford.

Eddison, J, Gardiner, M and Long, A, eds 1998. *Romney Marsh: environmental change and human occupation in a coastal lowland*, Oxford.

Eddison, J and Green, C, eds 1988. *Romney Marsh: evolution, occupation, reclamation*. Oxford University

Committee for Archaeology Monograph 24, Oxford.

Ellison, A 1981. Towards a socioeconomic model for the middle Bronze Age in southern England, in *Pattern of the past: studies in honour of David Clarke*, eds Hodder, I, Isaac, G and Hammond, N, 413-38, Cambridge.

Entwistle, R and Grant, A 1989. The evidence for cereal cultivation and animal husbandry in the southern British Neolithic and early Bronze Age, in *The beginnings of agriculture*, eds Milles, A, Williams, D and Gardner, N, British Archaeological Reports International Series 496, 203-15, Oxford.

Eogan, G 1994. *The accomplished art: gold and gold-working in Britain and Ireland during the Bronze Age*, Oxford.

Ethelberg, P 1986. *Hjemsted – en gravplads fra 4. bis 5. årh. e. Kr*, Haderslev.

Ethelberg, P 1990. *Hjemsted 2 – tre gravpladser fra 3. bis 4. årh. e. Kr*, Haderslev.

Evans, A J 1890. On a late-Celtic urn-field at Aylesford, Kent, *Archaeologia* 52, 178-92.

Evans, J 1860. On the occurrence of flint implements in undisturbed beds of gravel, sand and clay, *Archaeologia* 38 (ii), 280-307.

Evans, J 1881. *The ancient bronze implements, weapons and ornaments of Great Britain and Ireland*, London.

Everitt, A M 1986. *Continuity and colonization: the evolution of Kentish settlement*, Leicester.

Evison, V I 1965. *The fifth-century invasions south of the Thames*, London.

Evison, V I 1967. The Dover ring-sword and other sword-rings and beads, *Archaeologia* 101, 63-118.

Evison, V I 1968. Quoit-brooch style buckles, *Antiquaries Journal* 48, 231-4.

Evison, V I 1975. Sword rings and beads, *Archaeologia* 105, 303-15.

Evison, V I 1978. Early Anglo-Saxon applied disc brooches. Part II: in England, *Antiquaries Journal* 58, 260-78.

Evison, V I 1979. A sword pommel with ring-knob at Grenay, Pas-de-Calais, *Septentrion* 9, 37-9.

Evison, V I 1981. Distribution maps and England in the first two phases, in *Angles, Saxons and Jutes: essays presented to J.N.L. Myres*, ed. Evison, V I, 126-67, Oxford.

Evison, V I 1982. Anglo-Saxon glass claw-beakers, *Archaeologia* 107, 43-76.

Evison, V I 1987. *Dover: the Buckland Anglo-Saxon cemetery*, Historic Buildings and Monuments Commission for England Archaeological Report 3, London.

Fasham, P J and Whinney, R J B 1991. *Archaeology and the M3: the watching brief, the Anglo-Saxon settlement at Abbots Worthy and retrospective sections*, Hampshire Field Club and Archaeological Society Monograph 7, Winchester.

Fauduet, I 1993. *Atlas des sanctuaires Romano-Celtiques de Gaule: les fanums*, Paris.

Faussett, B 1856. *Inventorium Sepulchrale: an account of some antiquities dug up at Gilton, Kingston, Sibertswold, Barfriston, Beakesbourne, Chartham, and Crundale in the County of Kent, from A.D. 1757 to A.D 1773*, London.

Fawn, A J, Evans, K A, McMaster, I and Davies, G M R 1990. *The red hills of Essex: salt-making in antiquity*, Colchester.

Fenwick, V 1978. *The Graveney boat: a tenth-century find from Kent*, British Archaeological Reports British Series 53, Oxford.

Fernie, E 1983. *The architecture of the Anglo-Saxons*, London.

Feugère, M and de Marinis, R 1991. Les poêlons, in *La vaisselle tardo-républicaine en bronze: actes de la table-ronde CNRS organisée à Lattes du 26 au 28 avril 1990 par l'UPR 290 (Lattes) et le GDR 125 (Dijon)*, eds Feugère, M and Rolley, C, Centre de recherches sur les techniques gréco-romaines, no 13, 97-112, Dijon.

Field, D 1998. Round barrows and the harmonious landscape: placing early Bronze Age burial monuments in south-east England, *Oxford Journal of Archaeology* 17, 309-26.

Filkins, E W 1928. Excavation at Coldrum, *Antiquaries Journal* 8, 356-7.

Fitzpatrick, A P 1984. The deposition of La Tène Iron Age metalwork in watery contexts in southern England, in *Aspects of the Iron Age in central southern Britain*, eds Cunliffe, B W and Miles, D, Oxford University Committee for Archaeology Monograph 2, 178-90, Oxford.

Fitzpatrick, A P 1985. The distribution of Dressel 1 amphorae in north-west Europe, *Oxford Journal of Archaeology* 4, 305-40.

Fitzpatrick, A P 1997. *Archaeological excavations on the route of the A27 Westhampnett bypass, West Sussex, 1992. Volume 2: the late Iron Age, Romano-British and Anglo-Saxon cemeteries*, Wessex Archaeology Report 12, Salisbury.

Flemming, N C, ed. 2004. *Submarine prehistoric archaeology of the North Sea: research priorities and collaboration with industry*. Council for British Archaeology Research Report 141, York.

Fletcher, E and Jackson, E D C 1968. Excavations at the Lydd basilica, *Journal of the British Archaeological Association* 31, 20.

Fletcher, E and Meates, G W 1969. The ruined church of Stone-by-Faversham, *Antiquaries Journal* 49, 273-90.

Fletcher, E and Meates, G W 1977. The ruined church of Stone-by-Faversham: second report, *Antiquaries Journal* 57, 67-72.

Fleury, M and France-Lanord, A 1998. *Les trésors mérovingiens de la basilique de Saint-Denis*, Paris.

French, D A and Green, P W 1983. A late Iron Age site at Thong Lane, Gravesend, *Kent Archaeological Review* 73, 54-68.

Frere, J 1800. Account of flint weapons discovered at Hoxne in Suffolk, *Archaeologia* 13, 205-6.

Frere, S S 1954. Canterbury excavations, summer 1946. The Rose Lane sites, *Archaeologia Cantiana* 68, 101-43.

Frere, S S 1966. The end of towns in Roman Britain, in *The civitas capitals of Roman Britain*, ed. Wacher, J S, 87-100, Leicester.

Frere, S S 1970. The Roman theatre at Canterbury, *Britannia* 1, 83-113.

Frere, S S 1987. *Britannia: a history of Roman Britain*, London.

Frere, S S, Bennett, P, Rady, J and Stow, S 1987. *Canterbury excavations: intra- and extra-mural sites, 1949-55 and 1980-84*, The Archaeology of Canterbury 8, Maidstone.

Frere, S S and Fulford, M G 2001. The Roman invasion of AD 43, *Britannia* 32, 45-55.

Frere, S S and Stow, S 1983. *Excavations in the St. George's Street and Burgate Street areas*, The Archaeology of Canterbury 7, Maidstone.

Fulford, M G 1977. Pottery and Britain's foreign trade in the later Roman period, in *Pottery and early commerce: characterization and trade in Roman and later ceramics*, ed. Peacock, D P S, 35-84, London.

Fulford, M G 2003. *Lullingstone Roman Villa*, English Heritage guidebook, London.

Fulford, M G, Champion, T C and Long, A J, eds 1997. *England's coastal heritage: a survey for English Heritage and the RCHME*, London.

Fulford, M G and Timby, J R 2000. *Late Iron Age and Roman Silchester: excavations on the site of the Forum-Basilica 1977, 1980-86*, Britannia Monograph 15, London.

Funnell, B M 1995. Global sea-level and the (pen-) insularity of late Cenozoic Britain, in *Island Britain: a Quaternary persepective*, ed. Preece, R C, 3-13, London.

Gaimster, M 2005. Saxons in Deptford, *London Archaeologist*, 11(2), 31-7.

Gamble, C S and Steele, J 1999. Hominid ranging patterns and dietary strategies, in *Hominid evolution: lifestyles and survival strategies*, ed. Ullrich, H, 396-409, Schwelm.

Gardiner, M 1990a. An Anglo-Saxon and medieval settlement at Botolphs, Bramber, West Sussex, *Archaeological Journal* 147, 216-75.

Gardiner, M 1990b. The archaeology of the Weald: a survey and review, *Sussex Archaeological Collections* 128, 33-53.

Gardiner, M, Cross, R, Macpherson-Grant, N and Riddler, I 2001. Continental trade and non-urban ports in mid-Saxon England: excavations at Sandtun, West Hythe, Kent, *Archaeological Journal* 158, 161-290.

Garstang, J 1900. Excavations at Richborough, *Archaeologia Cantiana* 24, 267-72.

Garwood, P 2003. Round barrows and funerary traditions in late Neolithic and Bronze Age Sussex, in *The archaeology of Sussex to AD 2000*, ed. Rudling, D, 47-68, King's Lynn.

Geake, H 1997. *The use of grave-goods in conversion-period England, c.600-c.850*, British Archaeological Reports British Series 261, Oxford.

Gem, R 1992. Reconstructions of St Augustine's Abbey, Canterbury, in the Anglo-Saxon period, in *St Dunstan, his life, times and cult*, eds Ramsey, N, Sparks, M and Tatton-Brown, T, 57-73, Woodbridge.

Gem, R 1997. The Anglo-Saxon and Norman churches, in *The English Heritage book of Saint Augustine's Abbey, Canterbury*, ed. Gem, R, 90-122, London.

Gerloff, S 1975. *The early Bronze Age daggers in Great Britain and a reconsideration of the Wessex Culture*, Prähistorische Bronzefunde Abt. VI, Band 2, Munich.

Gibbard, P L 1995. The formation of the Strait of Dover, in *Island Britain: a Quaternary perspective*, ed. Preece, R C, 15-26, London.

Gibson, A, MacPherson-Grant, N and Stewart, I 1997. A Cornish vessel from farthest Kent, *Antiquity* 71,

438-41.

Gibson, M and Wright, S M, eds 1988. *Jospeh Mayer of Liverpool 1803-1866*. Society of Antiquaries Occasional Paper, new series 11, London.

Glass, H J 1999. Archaeology of the Channel Tunnel Rail Link, *Archaeologia Cantiana* 119, 189-220.

Glass, H J 2000. The Channel Tunnel Rail Link, *Current Archaeology* 168, 448-9.

Godfrey-Faussett, T G 1876. The Saxon cemetery at Bifrons, *Archaeologia Cantiana* 10, 298-315.

Godfrey-Faussett, T G 1880. The Saxon cemetery at Bifrons, *Archaeologia Cantiana* 13, 552-6.

Godwin, H 1962. Vegetational history of the Kentish chalk downs as seen at Wingham and Frogholt, *Veröffentlichungen des geobotanischen Instituts Zürich* 37, 83-99.

Gollop, A 2005. Westwood Cross, Broadstairs, *Canterbury's Archaeology 2003-04*, 18-9.

Gostling, W 1774. *A walk in and about the City of Canterbury*, Canterbury.

Gough, H 1992. Eadred's charter of AD 949 and the extent of the monastic estate of Reculver, Kent, in *St Dunstan: his life, times and cult*, eds Ramsay, N, Sparks, M and Tatton-Brown, T, 89-102, Woodbridge.

Grainge, G 2002. *The Roman Channel crossing of AD 43: the constraints on Claudius' naval strategy*, British Archaeological Reports British Series 332, Oxford.

Greatorex, C 2003. Living on the margins? The late Bronze Age landscape of the Willingdon Levels, in *The archaeology of Sussex to AD2000*, ed. Rudling, D, 89-100, King's Lynn.

Greenfield, E 1960. A Neolithic pit and other finds from Wingham, east Kent, *Archaeologia Cantiana* 74, 58-72.

Grierson, P 1952. The Canterbury (St Martin's) hoard of Frankish and Anglo-Saxon coin-ornaments, *British Numismatic Journal* 27, 39-51.

Grimes, W F 1930. Holt, Denbighshire: the works depot of the Twentieth Legion at Castle Lyons, *Y Cymmrodor* 41, 1-233.

Grinsell, L V 1992. The Bronze Age round barrows of Kent, *Proceedings of the Prehistoric Society* 58, 355-84.

Gros, P 1996. *L'architecture romaine: 1. Les monuments publics*, Paris.

Guttman, E B and Last, J 2000. A late Bronze Age landscape at Hornchurch, Greater London, *Proceedings of the Prehistoric Society* 66, 319-59.

Haith, C 1988. Un nouveau regard sur le cimetière d'Herpes (Charente), *Revue archéologique de Picardie* 3-4, 71-80.

Haith, C 1997. Pottery in early Anglo-Saxon England, in *Pottery in the making: world ceramic traditions*, eds Freestone, I and Gaimster, D, 146-51, London.

Halkon, P and Millett, M 1999. *Rural settlement and industry: studies in the Iron Age and Roman archaeology of lowland East Yorkshire*, Yorkshire Archaeological Society Roman Antiquities Section Monograph 4, Leeds.

Halliwell, G and Parfitt, K 1985. The prehistoric land surface in the Lydden Valley, *Kent Archaeological Review* 82, 39-41.

Hambleton, E 1999. *Animal husbandry regimes in Iron Age Britain: a comparative study of faunal assemblages from British Iron Age sites*, British Archaeological Reports British Series 282, Oxford.

Hamerow, H 1993. *Excavations at Mucking 2: The Anglo-Saxon settlement*, London.

Hamerow, H 1999. Anglo-Saxon timber buildings: the continental connection, in *In discussion with the past: archaeological studies presented to W A van Es*, eds Sarfatij, H, Verwers, W and Woltering, P, 119-28, Amersfoort.

Hamerow, H 2002. *Early medieval settlements: the archaeology of rural communities in north-west Europe 400-900*, Oxford.

Hamerow, H 2004. The archaeology of Early Anglo-Saxon settlements: past, present and future, in *Landscapes of change: rural evolution in late antiquity and the early Middle Ages*, ed. Christie, N, 301-16, Aldershot.

Hamilton, S 2003. Sussex not Wessex: a regional perspective on southern Britain *c.* 1200-200 BC, in *The archaeology of Sussex to AD 2000*, ed. Rudling, D, 69-88, King's Lynn.

Hamilton, S and Manley, J 2000. Hillforts, monumentality and place: a chronological and topographic review of first millennium BC hillforts in south-east England, *European Journal of Archaeology* 4, 7-42.

Härke, H G H 1992. *Angelsächsische Waffengräber des 5. bis 7. Jahrhunderts*, Cologne.

Härke, H G H 2000. The circulation of weapons in Anglo-Saxon society, in *Rituals of power: from late antiquity to the early Middle Ages*, eds Theuws, F and Nelson, J L, 377-99, Leiden.

Harrington, S 2002. 'Aspects of gender and craft production in early Anglo-Saxon England with reference to the kingdom of Kent'; unpublished PhD thesis, University College London.

Harris, J 1719. *The history of Kent*, London.

Harrison, A C 1991. Excavation of a Belgic and Roman site at 50-54 High Street, Rochester, *Archaeologia Cantiana* 109, 41-50.

Harrison, E R 1928. *Harrison of Ightham*, Oxford.

Haselgrove, C 1987. *Iron Age coinage in south-east England*, British Archaeological Reports British Series 174, Oxford.

Haselgrove, C 1988. The archaeology of British potin coinage, *Archaeological Journal* 145, 99-122.

Haselgrove, C 1997. Iron Age brooch deposition and chronology, in *Reconstructing Iron Age societies*, eds Gwilt, A and Haselgrove, C, 51-72, Oxford.

Haselgrove, C and Millett, M 1997. Verlamion reconsidered, in *Reconstructing Iron Age societies*, eds Gwilt, A and Haselgrove, C, 282-196, Oxford.

Haseloff, G 1974. Salin's Style I, *Medieval Archaeology* 18, 1-15.

Haseloff, G 1981. *Die germanische Tierornamentik der Völkerwanderungs-zeit: Studien zu Salin's Stil I*, Berlin.

Haslam, J 1980. A middle Saxon iron smelting site at Ramsbury, Wiltshire, *Medieval Archaeology* 23, 1-68.

Hassall, M W C and Tomlin, R S O 1977. Roman Britain in 1976 – Inscriptions, A, monumental, *Britannia* 8, 426-49.

Hasted, E 1778-1799. *The history and topographical survey of the county of Kent: containing the antient and present state of it, civil and ecclesiastical*, Canterbury.

Hasted, E 1797-1801. *The history and topographical survey of the county of Kent*, 2nd ed., Canterbury.

Haverfield, F J, Taylor, M V and Wheeler, R E M 1932. Romano-British remains, in *The Victoria History of the County of Kent, Vol. III*, ed. Page, W A, 1-176, London.

Hawkes, C F C 1940. The Marnian pottery and La Tène I brooch from Worth, Kent, *Antiquaries Journal* 20, 115-21.

Hawkes, C F C 1942. The Deverel urn and the Picardy pin: a phase of Bronze Age settlement in Kent, *Proceedings of the Prehistoric Society* 8, 26-47.

Hawkes, C F C and Crummy, P 1995. *Camulodunum Vol. 2*, Colchester Archaeological Report 11, Colchester.

Hawkes, S C 1968. Richborough – the physical geography, in *Fifth report on the excavations of the Roman fort at Richborough, Kent*, ed. Cunliffe, B W, Research Committee of the Society of Antiquaries

of London Report 23, 224-31, London.

Hawkes, S C 1973. Exhibits at ballots: finds from the Anglo-Saxon cemetery at Eccles, Kent, *Antiquaries Journal* 53, 281-6.

Hawkes, S C 1974. The Monkton brooch, *Antiquaries Journal* 54, 245-56.

Hawkes, S C 1975. Rare bronze escutcheon from Canterbury, *Kent Archaeological Review* 41, 6-8.

Hawkes, S C 1979. Eastry in Anglo-Saxon Kent: its importance, and a newly-found grave, *Anglo-Saxon Studies in Archaeology and History* 1, British Archaeological Reports British Series 72, 81-113.

Hawkes, S C 1981. Bifrons Grave 41, in *Die germanische Tierornamentik der Völkerwanderungs-zeit: Studien zu Salin's Stil I*, ed. Haseloff, G, 718-21, Berlin.

Hawkes, S C 1982a. Anglo-Saxon Kent c.425-725, in *Archaeology in Kent to AD 1500*, ed. Leach, P E, Council for British Archaeology Research Report 48, 64-78, London.

Hawkes, S C 1982b. Finglesham: a cemetery in East Kent, in *The Anglo-Saxons*, ed. Campbell, J, 24-5, Oxford.

Hawkes, S C 1989. The South-east after the Romans: the Saxon settlement, in *The Saxon Shore: a handbook*, ed. Maxfield, V A, Exeter Studies in History 25, 78-95, Exeter.

Hawkes, S C 1990. Bryan Faussett and the Faussett collection: an assessment, in *Anglo-Saxon cemeteries: a re-appraisal*, ed. Southworth, E, 1-24, Stroud.

Hawkes, S C 2000. The Anglo-Saxon cemetery of Bifrons, in the parish of Patrixbourne, East Kent, *Anglo-Saxon Studies in Archaeology and History* 11, 1-94.

Hawkes, S C and Dunning, G C 1961. Soldiers and settlers in Britain, fourth to fifth century, *Medieval Archaeology* 5, 1-70.

Hawkes, S C and Grainger, G 2006. *The Anglo-Saxon cemetery at Finglesham, Kent*, Oxford University School of Archaeology Monograph 64, Oxford.

Hawkes, S C and Grove, L R A 1963. Finds from the seventh-century Anglo-Saxon cemetery at Milton Regis, *Archaeologia Cantiana* 78, 22-38.

Hawkes, S C and Pollard, A M 1981. The gold bracteates from sixth-century Anglo-Saxon graves in Kent, in the light of a new find from Finglesham, *Frühmittelalterliche Studien* 15, 316-70.

Haycock, D B 2002. *William Stukeley: science, religion and archaeology in eighteenth-century England*, Woodbridge.

Hearne, C M, Perkins, D R J and Andrews, P 1995. The Sandwich Bay wastewater treatment scheme archaeological project, *Archaeologia Cantiana* 115, 239-354.

Hedeager, L 2000. Migration period Europe: the foundation of a political mentality, in *Rituals of power: from late antiquity to the early Middle Ages*, eds Theuws, F and Nelson, J L, 15-57, Leiden.

Helm, R 2003a. Bogshole Lane, Broomfield, *Canterbury's Archaeology 2000-2001*, 23-4.

Helm, R 2003b. Willow Farm, off Hooper's Lane, Broomfield, *Canterbury's Archaeology 2000-2001*, 22-3.

Heslop, S and Mitchell, J 1997. The arts and learning, in *The English Heritage book of St Augustine's Abbey, Canterbury*, ed. Gem, R, 67-89, London.

Hill, D and Cowie, R 2001. *Wics: the early mediaeval trading centres of northern Europe*, Sheffield.

Hill, J D 1997. 'The end of one kind of body and the beginning of another kind of body'? Toilet instruments and 'Romanization', in *Reconstructing Iron Age societies*, eds Gwilt, A and Haselgrove, C, 96-107, Oxford.

Hind, J G F 1989. The invasion of Britain in AD 43: an alternative strategy for Aulus Plautius, *Britannia* 20, 1-21.

Hines, J 1984. *The Scandinavian character of Anglian England in the pre-Viking period*, British Archaeological Reports British Series 124, Oxford.

Hines, J 1993. *Clasps, Hektespenner, Agrafen: Anglo-Scandinavian clasps of classes A-C of the 3rd to 6th centuries AD*, Stockholm.

Hines, J 1997. *A new corpus of Anglo-Saxon great square-headed brooches*, Woodbridge.

Hines, J 1999. Angelsächsische Chronologie: Probleme und Aussichten, in *Völker an Nord- und Ostsee und die Franken*, eds von Freeden, U, Koch, U and Wieczorek, A, 19-30, Bonn.

Hines, J 2004. *Sūl re-gē* - the foundations of Surrey, in *Aspects of archaeology and history in Surrey: towards a research framework for the county*, eds Cotton, J, Crocker, G and Graham, A, 91-102, Guildford.

Hingley, R 1989. *Rural settlement in Roman Britain*, London.

Hinton, M A C, and Kennard, A S 1905. The relative ages of stone implements of the lower Thames valley, *Proceedings of the Geologists Association* 19, 76-100.

Hinz, H 1966. Am langen Band getragene

Bergkristallanhänger der Merowingerzeit, *Jahrbuch des Römisch-Germanisches Zentralmuseum Mainz* 13, 212-30.

Hirst, S, Nixon, T, Rowsome, P and Wright, S 2004. *The Prittlewell Prince: the discovery of a rich Anglo-Saxon burial in Essex*, London.

Hodder, M A and Barfield, L H, eds 1991. *Burnt mounds and hot stone technology*, West Bromwich.

Hogarth, A C 1973. Structural features in Anglo-Saxon graves, *Archaeological Journal* 130, 104-19.

Holder, P A 1982. *The Roman army in Britain*, London.

Holman, D 2000. Iron Age coinage in Kent: a review of current knowledge, *Archaeologia Cantiana* 120, 205-33.

Holman, D 2005. Iron Age coinage and settlement in east Kent, *Britannia* 36, 1-54.

Holmes, T and Bennett, P 2003. Chilston sandpit, Lenham, *Canterbury's Archaeology 2001-2002*, 43-4.

Hope-Taylor, B 1977. *Yeavering: an Anglo-British centre of early Northumbria*, Department of the Environment Archaeological Report 7, London.

Houliston, M 1999. Excavations at the Mount Roman villa, Maidstone, 1994, *Archaeologia Cantiana* 119, 71-172.

Hounsell, D and Ralph, S 2001. 'Herne Bay High School new all weather pitch: an archaeological excavation. Interim site narrative'; unpublished Hertfordshire Archaeological Trust Report 996.

Housley, R A, Gamble, C S, Street, M J and Pettitt, P 1997. Radiocarbon evidence for the lateglacial recolonisation of northern Europe, *Proceedings of the Prehistoric Society* 63, 25-54.

Hurd, H 1909. On a late Celtic village near Dumpton Gap, Broadstairs, *Archaeologia* 61, 427-8.

Hurtrelle, J, Monchy, E, Roger, F, Rossignol, P and Villes, A 1990. *Les débuts du second âge du fer dans le Nord de la France*, Les dossiers de Gauheria 1.

Hutchings, P 1999. 'Archaeological evaluation Tottington Farm, Aylesford, Maidstone, Kent, Canterbury'; unpublished Canterbury Archaeological Trust report.

Hutchings, P 2003. Ritual and riverside settlement: a multi-period site at Princes Road, Dartford, *Archaeologia Cantiana* 123, 41-79.

Hutchinson, J N, Poole, C, Lambert, N and Bromhead, E N 1985. Combined archaeological and geotechnical investigations of the Roman fort at Lympne, Kent, *Britannia* 16, 209-36.

Hyslop, M 1963. Two Anglo-Saxon cemeteries at

Chamberlains Barn, Leighton Buzzard, Bedfordshire, *Archaeological Journal* 120, 161-200.

Inker, P 2000. Technology as active material culture: the Quoit-brooch style, *Medieval Archaeology* 44, 25-52.

Irvine, J T 1875. On the remains of Saxon or early Norman work in the church of Stone juxta Faversham, *Journal of the British Archaeological Association* 31, 249-58.

Jacobi, R M 1982. Later hunters in Kent: Tasmania and the earliest Neolithic, in *Archaeology in Kent to AD 1500*, ed. Leach, P, Council for British Archaeology Research Report 48, 12-24, London.

Jacobi, R M 1986. The contents of Dr. Harley's show case, in *The Palaeolithic of Britain and its nearest neighbours: recent trends*, ed. Collcutt, S N, 62-8, Sheffield.

Jacobi, R M 1999. Some observations on the British Upper Palaeolithic, in *Dorothy Garrod and the progress of the Palaeolithic*, eds Davies, W and Charles, R, 35-40, Oxford.

James, F 1899. Bronze Age burials at Aylesford, *Proceedings of the Society of Antiquaries of London* 17, 372-7.

James, S, Marshall, A and Millett, M 1984. An early medieval building tradition, *Archaeological Journal* 141, 185-215.

James, S and Rigby, V 1997. *Britain and the Celtic Iron Age*, London.

Jarman, C 2002. Glebeland, Marley Road, Harrietsham, *Canterbury's Archaeology 1997-1998*, 16-17.

Jarman, C 2005. Underdown Lane, Eddington, *Canterbury's Archaeology 2003-2004*, 14-16.

Jarrett, M G 1994. Non-legionary troops in Roman Britain: part one, the units, *Britannia* 25, 35-77.

Jenkins, F 1976. Preliminary report on the excavation at the church of St Pancras at Canterbury, *Canterbury's Archaeology 1975-6*, 4-5.

Jenkins, F 1985. The re-excavation of the Roman 'villa' at Wingham, *Archaeologia Cantiana* 100, 87-99.

Jensen, S 1985. A pit-house from Darum, *Kuml*, 111-21.

Jessup, F W 1956. The origins and first hundred years of the Society, *Archaeologia Cantiana* 70, 1-43.

Jessup, F W 1958. *A history of Kent*, London.

Jessup, R F 1930. *The archaeology of Kent*, London.

Jessup, R F 1932. Bigberry Camp, Harbledown, Kent, *Archaeological Journal* 89, 87-115.

Jessup, R F 1937. Excavations at Julliberrie's Grave, Chilham, Kent, *Antiquaries Journal* 17, 122-37.

Jessup, R F 1939. Excavations at Julliberrie's Grave, Chilham, Kent, *Antiquaries Journal* 19, 260-81.

Jessup, R F 1946. An Anglo-Saxon cemetery at Westbere, Kent, *Antiquaries Journal* 26, 11-21.

Jessup, R F 1950. *Anglo-Saxon jewellery*, London.

Jessup, R F 1955. Excavation of a Roman barrow at Holborough, Snodland, *Archaeologia Cantiana* 68, 1-61.

Jessup, R F 1975. *Man of many talents: an informal biography of James Douglas 1753-1819*, London.

Jessup, R F and Cook, N C 1936. Excavations at Bigberry Camp, Harbledown, *Archaeologia Cantiana* 48, 151-68.

John, E 1964. *Land tenure in England: a discussion of some problems*, Leicester.

John, E 1966. Folkland reconsidered, in *Orbis Britanniae*, ed. John, E, 64-127, Leicester.

Johns, C and Potter, T W 1985. The Canterbury late Roman treasure, *Antiquaries Journal* 65, 312-52.

Johnson, C 2003. Two late Iron Age warrior burials discovered in Kent, *Archaeology International* 6, 5-8.

Johnson, S 1970. The date of the construction of the Saxon Shore fort at Richborough, *Britannia* 1, 240-8.

Johnson, S 1976. *The Roman forts of the Saxon Shore*, London.

Jolliffe, J E A 1933. *Pre-feudal England: the Jutes*, Oxford.

Jones, A H M 1964. *The later Roman Empire, 284-602: a social economic and administrative survey*, Oxford.

Jones, G D B 1984. *Past imperfect: the story of rescue archaeology*, London.

Jones, R L and Keen, D H 1993. *Pleistocene environments in the British Isles*, London.

Jope, E M 2000. *Early Celtic art in the British Isles*, Oxford.

Jørgensen, L B 1987. *Prehistoric Scandinavian textiles*, Copenhagen.

Jørgensen, L B 1992. *North European textiles until AD 1000*, Århus.

Jumel, G and Monnier, J L 1990. Le gisement Paléolithique Inférieur de Saint-Malo-de-Phily (Ille et Vilaine): une confirmation géologique et archéologique, *Revue Archéologique Ouest* 7, 5-8.

Keller, P 1989. Quern production at Folkestone, south-east Kent: an interim note, *Britannia* 20, 193-200.

Keller, P 1990. *Charing near Ashford. Excavation of Iron Age and Romano-British farmstead sites at Bretts Sandpit, 1989*, Dover.

Kelly, D 1971. Quarry Wood Camp, Loose: a Belgic oppidum, *Archaeologia Cantiana* 86, 55-84.

Kelly, D 1987. Archaeological notes from Maidstone Museum, *Archaeologia Cantiana* 104, 350-67.

Kelly, D B 1992. The Mount Roman villa, Maidstone, *Archaeologia Cantiana* 110, 177-235.

Kelly, S 1997. The Anglo-Saxon abbey, in *The English Heritage book of St Augustine's Abbey, Canterbury*, ed. Gem, R, 33-49, London.

Kelly, S E 1992. Trading privileges from eighth-century England, *Early Medieval Europe* 1, 3-28.

Kendrick, T D 1950. *British antiquity*, London.

Kennard, A S 1944. The Crayford brickearths, *Proceedings of the Geologists' Association* 45, 121-69.

Kent, J P C 1987. The coins, in *Dover: the Buckland Anglo-Saxon cemetery*, ed. Evison, V I, Historic Buildings and Monuments Commission for England Archaeological Report 3, 180-1, London.

Kerney, M P, Brown, E H and Chandler, T J 1964. The late-Glacial and post-Glacial history of the chalk escarpment near Brook, Kent, *Philosophical Transactions of the Royal Society of London* B248, 135-204.

Kerney, M P, Preece, R C and Turner, C 1980. Molluscan and plant biostratigraphy of some late Devensian and Flandrian deposits of Kent, *Philosophical Transactions of the Royal Society of London* B291, 1-43.

Kinnes, I 1992. *Non-megalithic long barrows and allied structures in the British Neolithic*, British Museum Occasional Paper 52, London.

Kirby, D P 1991. *The earliest English kings*, London.

Klein, W G 1928. Roman temple at Worth, Kent, *Antiquaries Journal* 8, 76-86.

Kruse, P forthcoming. Jutes in Kent? On the Jutish nature of Kent, southern Hampshire and the Isle of Wight, in *Probleme der Küstenforschung im südlichen Nordseegebiet*.

Lambarde, W 1576. *Perambulation of Kent: conteining the description, hystorie and customs of that shyre*, London.

Lane, T W and Morris, E L, eds 2001. *A millennium of saltmaking: prehistoric and Romano-British salt production in the Fenland*, Sleaford.

Leach, P 2001. *Fosse Lane, Shepton Mallet 1990: Excavation of a Romano-British settlement in Somerset*, Britannia Monograph 18, London.

Leach, P E, ed. 1982. *Archaeology in Kent to AD 1500*. Council for British Archaeology Research Report 48, London.

Leeds, E T 1936. *Early Anglo-Saxon art and archaeology*, Oxford.

Leigh, D 1980. 'The square-headed brooches of sixth-century Kent'; unpublished PhD thesis, University College Cardiff.

Leigh, D 1984a. Ambiguity in Anglo-Saxon style I art, *Antiquaries Journal* 64, 34-42.

Leigh, D 1984b. The Kentish keystone-garnet disc brooches: Avent's classes 1-3 reconsidered, *Anglo-Saxon Studies in Archaeology and History* 3, 67-76.

Leigh, D 1990. Aspects of early brooch design and production, in *Anglo-Saxon cemeteries: a reappraisal*, ed. Southworth, E, 107-24, Stroud.

Leman-Delerive, G 1984. Céramique laténienne domestique de la région lilloise (Nord), *Gallia* 42, 79-95.

Levine, P 1986. *The amateur and the professional: antiquarians, historians and archaeologists in Victorian England, 1838-1886*, Cambridge.

Lewis, J 1723. *The history and antiquities, ecclesiastical and civil, of the Isle of Tenet in Kent*, London.

Liversidge, J E A and Weatherhead, F 1987. The Christian paintings, in *The Roman villa at Lullingstone, Kent. Vol. 2: the wall-paintings and finds*, ed. Meates, G W, Kent Archaeological Society Monograph 3, 11-40, Maidstone.

Livett, G M 1889. Foundations of the Saxon cathedral church at Rochester, *Archaeologia Cantiana* 18, 261-78.

Long, A J 1992. Coastal responses to changes in sea-level in the east Kent Fens and southeast England, UK, over the last 7500 years, *Proceedings of the Geologists' Association* 103, 187-99.

Long, A J, Hipkin, S and Clarke, H, eds 2002. *Romney Marsh: coastal and landscape changes through the ages*. Oxford University School of Archaeology Monograph 56, Oxford.

Long, A J and Hughes, P 1995. Evolution of the Dungeness foreland during the last 4000 years, *Marine Geology* 124, 253-71.

Long, A J and Innes, J B 1993. Holocene sea-level changes and coastal sedimentation in Romney Marsh, southeast England, UK, *Proceedings of the Geologists' Association* 104, 223-37.

Longworth, I H 1984. *Collared urns of the Bronze Age in Great Britain and Ireland*, Cambridge.

Lowther, A W G 1931. The Saxon cemetery at

Guildown, Guildford, Surrey, *Surrey Archaeological Collections* 39, 1-50.

Lubbock, J 1865. *Pre-historic times*, London.

Macgregor, A 1998. Antiquity inventoried: museums and 'national antiquities' in the mid-nineteenth century, in *The study of the past in the Victorian age*, ed. Brand, V, 125-37, Oxford.

MacGregor, A and Bolick, E 1993. *A summary catalogue of the Anglo-Saxon collections, Ashmolean Museum, Oxford*, British Archaeological Reports British Series 230, Oxford.

MacPherson-Grant, N 1969. Two Neolithic bowls from Birchington, Thanet, *Archaeologia Cantiana* 84, 249-50.

MacPherson-Grant, N 1980. Archaeological work along the A2, 1966-74, *Archaeologia Cantiana* 96, 133-83.

Macpherson-Grant, N 1989. The pottery from the 1987-89 Channel Tunnel excavations, *Canterbury's Archaeology 1988-89*, 60-3.

Macpherson-Grant, N 1991. A re-appraisal of prehistoric pottery from Canterbury, *Canterbury's Archaeology 1990-91*, 38-48.

Macpherson-Grant, N and Mainman, A 1995. Early to late Saxon [pottery], in *Excavations in the Marlowe car park and surrounding areas*, eds Blockley, K, Blockley, M, Blockley, P, Frere, S S and Stow, S, The Archaeology of Canterbury 5, 818-97, Canterbury.

Malcolm, G and Bowsher, D 2003. *Middle Saxon London: excavations at the Royal Opera House 1989-9*, London.

Mann, J C 1965. City foundations in Gaul and Britain, in *Britain and Rome: essays presented to Eric Birley*, eds Jarrett, M C and Dobson, B, 109-13, Kendal.

Mann, J C 1977. The Reculver inscription: a note, in *The Saxon Shore*, ed. Johnston, D E, Council for British Archaeology Research Report 18, 15, London.

Mann, J C 1989. The historical development of the Saxon Shore, in *The Saxon Shore: a handbook*, ed. Maxfield, V A, Exeter Studies in History 25, 1-11, Exeter.

Manning, W H 1972. Ironwork hoards in Iron Age and Roman Britain, *Britannia* 3, 224-50.

Margary, I D 1955. *Roman roads in Britain*, 1st ed., London.

Margary, I D 1973. *Roman roads in Britain*, 3rd ed., London.

Marsden, P 1994. *Ships of the port of London*, English Heritage Archaeology Report 3, London.

Martin, M 1976. *Das fränkische Gräberfeld von Basel-Bernerring*, Basel.

Martin, M 1997. Die goldene Kette von Szilágysomlyó und das frühmerowingische Amulettgehänge der westgermanischen Frauentracht, in *Perlen: Archäologie, Techniken, Analysen*, eds von Freeden, U and Wieczorek, A, 349-72, Bonn.

Masefield, R, Bayliss, A and McCormac, G 2004. New scientific dating of the later Bronze Age wells at Swalecliffe, Kent, *Antiquaries Journal* 84, 334-9.

Masefield, R, Branch, N, Couldrey, P, Goodburn, D and Tyers, I 2003. A later Bronze Age well complex at Swalecliffe, Kent, *Antiquaries Journal* 83, 47-121.

Matson, C 1962. William Rolfe: a noted Sandwich antiquarian, *Archaeologia Cantiana* 76, 180-5.

Maxfield, V A, ed. 1989. *The Saxon Shore: a handbook*. Exeter Studies in History 25, Exeter.

Mays, S and Anderson, T 1994. *Archaeological research priorities for human remains from south-east England (Kent, East and West Sussex and Surrey)*, Ancient Monuments Laboratory Report 56/94, London.

McAleer, J P 1999. *Rochester cathedral, 604-1540: an architectural history*, Toronto.

McGrail, S 1978. *Logboats of England and Wales, with comparative material from European and other countries*, British Archaeological Reports British Series 51, Oxford.

McGrew, W C, Marchant, L F and Nishida, T, eds 1996. *Great ape societies*, Cambridge.

McKinley, J I 2003. The early Saxon cemetery at Park Lane, Croydon, *Surrey Archaeological Collections* 90, 1-116.

Meaney, A L 1964. *A gazetteer of early Anglo-Saxon burial sites*, London.

Meaney, A L and Hawkes, S C 1970. *Two Anglo-Saxon cemeteries at Winnall, Hampshire*, Society for Medieval Archaeology Monograph 4, London.

Meates, G W 1955. *Lullingstone Roman villa*, London.

Meates, G W 1979. *The Roman villa at Lullingstone, Kent. Vol. 1: the site*, Kent Archaeological Society Monograph 1, Maidstone.

Meates, G W 1987. *The Roman villa at Lullingstone, Kent. Vol. 2: the wall-paintings and finds*, Kent Archaeological Society Monograph 3, Maidstone.

Megaw, B R S and Hardy, E M 1938. British decorated axes and their distribution, *Proceedings of the Prehistoric Society* 4, 272-307.

Mellars, P A 2004. Neanderthals and the modern human colonisation of Europe, *Nature* 432, 461-5.

Millett, M 1990. *The Romanization of Britain: an essay in archaeological interpretation*, Cambridge.

Millett, M 1995. *The English Heritage book of Roman Britain*, London.

Millett, M 1996. Characterizing Roman London, in *Interpreting Roman London: papers in memory of Hugh Chapman*, eds Bird, J, Hassall, M and Sheldon, H, 33-8, Oxford.

Millett, M 2001. Approaches to urban societies, in *Britons and Romans: advancing an archaeological agenda*, eds James, S T and Millett, M, Council for British Archaeology Research Report 125, 60-6, York.

Millett, M and James, S 1983. Excavations at Cowdery's Down, Basingstoke, Hampshire 1978-81, *Archaeological Journal* 140, 151-279.

Millett, M and Wilmott, A 2003. Rethinking Richborough, in *The archaeology of Roman towns: studies in honour of John S.Wacher*, ed. Wilson, P, 184-94, Oxford.

Mitchell, G F, Penny, L F, Shotton, F W and West, R G 1973. *A correlation of the Quaternary deposits of the British Isles*, Geological Society Special Report 4, London.

Moffett, L, Robinson, M A and Straker, V 1989. Cereals, fruits and nuts: charred plant remains from Neolithic sites in England and Wales and the Neolithic economy, in *The beginnings of agriculture*, eds Milles, A, Williams, D and Gardner, N, British Archaeological Reports International Series 496, 243-61, Oxford.

Monaghan, J 1987. *Upchurch and Thameside Roman pottery: a ceramic typology for northern Kent, first to third centuries AD*, British Archaeological Reports British Series 173, Oxford.

Money, J H 1960. Excavations at High Rocks, Tunbridge Wells, 1954-1956, *Sussex Archaeological Collections* 98, 173-221.

Money, J H 1968. Excavations on the Iron Age hillfort at High Rocks, near Tunbridge Wells, 1957-1961, *Sussex Archaeological Collections* 106, 158-205.

Money, J H 1975. Excavations in the two Iron Age hillforts on Castle Hill, Capel, near Tonbridge, 1965 and 1969-71, *Archaeologia Cantiana* 91, 61-5.

Money, J H 1978. Excavations in the two Iron Age hillforts on Castle Hill, Capel, near Tonbridge, 1965 and 1969-71: supplementary note, *Archaeologia Cantiana* 94, 268-70.

Moore, C 2002. Late Bronze Age, Romano-British and early/middle Saxon features at Hoo St Werburgh,

Archaeologia Cantiana 122, 259-74.

Morris, E L 1994. Production and distribution of pottery and salt in Iron Age Britain: a review, *Proceedings of the Prehistoric Society* 60, 371-93.

Morris, J 1966. Dark Age dates, in *Britain and Rome*, eds Jarrett, M G and Dobson, B, 145-85, Kendal.

Morris, J 1974. *The age of Arthur: a history of the British Isles from 350 to 650*, London.

Mortimer, C 1990. 'Some aspects of early medieval copper-alloy technology, as illustrated by a study of the Anglian cruciform brooch'; unpublished DPhil thesis, University of Oxford.

Muckelroy, K 1980. Two Bronze Age cargoes in British waters, *Antiquity* 54, 100-9.

Mudd, A 1994. The excavation of a late Bronze Age site at Coldharbour Road, Gravesend, *Archaeologia Cantiana* 114, 363-410.

Müller-Wille, M 1999. Das Frankenreich und der Norden, in *Völker an Nord- und Ostsee und die Franken*, eds von Freeden, U, Koch, U and Wieczorek, A, 1-18, Bonn.

Myres, J N L 1969. *Anglo-Saxon pottery and the settlement of England*, Oxford.

Myres, J N L 1970. The Angles, the Saxons and the Jutes, *Proceedings of the British Academy* 56, 145-74.

Myres, J N L 1977. *A corpus of Anglo-Saxon pottery of the pagan period*, Cambridge.

Needham, S P 1992. The structure of settlement and ritual in the late Bronze Age of south-east Britain, in *L'habitat et l'occupation du sol a l'Age du Bronze en Europe*, eds Mordant, C and Richard, A, 49-69, Paris.

Needham, S P 1996. Chronology and periodisation in the British Bronze Age, *Acta Archaeologica* 67, 121-40.

Needham, S P and Ambers, J 1994. Redating Rams Hill and reconsidering Bronze Age enclosure, *Proceedings of the Prehistoric Society* 60, 225-43.

Needham, S P, Bronk Ramsey, C, Coombs, D, Cartwright, C and Pettitt, P 1998. An independent chronology for British Bronze Age metalwork: the results of the Oxford Radiocarbon Accelerator Programme, *Archaeological Journal* 154, 55-107.

Niblett, R 2001. *Verulamium: the Roman city of St Albans*, Stroud.

Nielsen, J N 2000. *Sejflod – ein eisenzeitliches Dorf in Nordjütland*, Copenhagen.

Nielsen, K H 1999. Style II and the Anglo-Saxon elite, *Anglo-Saxon Studies in Archaeology and History* 10,

185-202.

Nieveler, E and Siegmund, F 1999. The Merovingian chronology of the Lower Rhine area: results and problems, in *The pace of change: studies in medieval chronology*, eds Hines, J, Høilund Nielsen, K and Siegmund, F, 3-22, Oxford.

Northover, J P 1982. The exploration of the long-distance movement of bronze in Bronze and early Iron Age Europe, *Bulletin of the University of London Institute of Archaeology* 19, 45-72.

O'Brien, L 2004. Early Anglo-Saxons in Dartford, *The Archaeologist* 52, 32-3.

Ogilvie, J D 1977. The Stourmouth-Adisham water-main trench, *Archaeologia Cantiana* 93, 91-124.

Oswald, A, Dyer, C and Barber, M 2001. *The creation of monuments: neolithic causewayed enclosures in the British Isles*, Swindon.

Otte, M 1990. The northwestern European plain around 18,000 BP, in *The world at 18,000 BP: Vol. 1, High latitudes*, eds Soffer, O and Gamble, C S, 54-68, London.

Ovey, C D, ed. 1964. *The Swanscombe skull: a survey of research on a Pleistocene site*, Royal Anthropological Institute Occasional Paper 20, London.

Oxford Archaeological Unit 2000a. Springhead Roman cemetery, *Current Archaeology* 168, 458-9.

Oxford Archaeological Unit 2000b. Thurnham Roman villa: new discoveries at an old site, *Current Archaeology* 168, 454-7.

Oxford Archaeological Unit 2001. 'Thurnham Roman villa, Thurnham, Kent, ARC THM 98, detailed archaeological works assessment report, final'; CTRL unpublished assessment report.

Oxford Archaeological Unit 2003. 'Beechbrook Wood, Hothfield, Kent, ARC BBW 00, targeted watching brief assessment report, final'; CTRL unpublished assessment report.

Oxford Wessex Archaeology Joint Venture 2004. 'Bower Road, Smeeth, Kent'; CTRL unpublished integrated site report.

Palmer, S 1984. *Excavation of the Roman and Saxon site at Orpington*, Bromley.

Parfitt, K 1990. Excavations at Mill Hill, Deal, 1982-1989: an interim report, *Kent Archaeological Review* 101, 9-18.

Parfitt, K 1994. A possible Bronze Age grave, Walmer, 1910, *Kent Archaeological Review* 116, 133-5.

Parfitt, K 1995. *Iron Age burials from Mill Hill, Deal*, London.

Parfitt, K 1996. Whitfield-Eastry bypass, *Archaeologia Cantiana* 116, 319.

Parfitt, K 1998a. A late Iron Age burial from Chilham Castle, near Canterbury, Kent, *Proceedings of the Prehistoric Society* 68, 343-51.

Parfitt, K 1998b. Neolithic earthen long barrows in east Kent: a review, *Kent Archaeological Review* 131, 15-21.

Parfitt, K 1998c. Some radiocarbon dates for prehistoric east Kent, *Archaeologia Cantiana* 118, 376-9.

Parfitt, K 2000. Three Iron Age weaving combs from Worth, *Kent Archaeological Review* 139, 198-200.

Parfitt, K 2002. Exceptional Bronze Age gold find in Kent (Ringlemere), *Current Archaeology* 179, 452.

Parfitt, K 2003. 'Observations on the layout of Roman roads in east Kent'; unpublished ms.

Parfitt, K 2004a. Honeywood Parkway, Whitfield, Dover, *Canterbury's Archaeology 2002-2003*, 31.

Parfitt, K 2004b. A round barrow near Haynes Farm, Eythorne, *Archaeologia Cantiana* 124, 397-416.

Parfitt, K 2004c. A search for the prehistoric harbours of Kent, in *The Dover boat in context: society and water transport in prehistoric Europe*, ed. Clark, P, 99-105, Oxford.

Parfitt, K 2005. 'Interim report on excavations at Ringlemere'; unpublished Canterbury Archaeological Trust report, Canterbury.

Parfitt, K, Allen, T and Rady, J 1997. Whitfield-Eastry by-pass, *Canterbury's Archaeology 1995-1996*, 28-33.

Parfitt, K and Brugmann, B 1997. *The Anglo-Saxon cemetery on Mill Hill, Deal, Kent*, Society for Mediaeval Archaeology Monograph 14, London.

Parfitt, K and Corke, B 2001. North Barracks, Deal, *Canterbury's Archaeology 1998-1999*, 26-7.

Parfitt, K and Corke, B 2003a. Crabble Paper Mill, Dover, *Canterbury's Archaeology 2001-2002*, 37-8.

Parfitt, K and Corke, B 2003b. The Dover-Deal bulk supply water main, *Canterbury's Archaeology 2001-2002*, 35-6.

Parfitt, K and Haith, C 1995. Buckland Saxon cemetery, *Current Archaeology* 144, 459-64.

Parfitt, K and Needham, S 2004. Ringlemere: the nature of the gold cup monument, *PAST (Newsletter of the Prehistoric Society)* 46, 1-2.

Parfitt, S A, Barendregt, R W, Breda, M, Candy, I, Collins, M J, Coope, G R, Durbridge, P, Field, M H, Lee, J R, Lister, A M, Mutch, R, Penkman, K E H, Preece, R C, Rose, J, Stringer, C B, Symmons,

R, Whittaker, J E, Wymer, J J, and Stuart, A J 2005. The earliest record of human activity in northern Europe, *Nature* 438, 1008-12.

Payne, G 1880. Celtic remains discovered at Grovehurst, in Milton-next-Sittingbourne, *Archaeologia Cantiana* 13, 122-6.

Payne, G 1883a. Bronze Age burial at Sittingbourne, *Proceedings of the Society of Antiquaries of London* 10, 29-30

Payne, G 1883b. Discovery of foundations of Roman buildings and other remains near Lower Halstow, Kent, *Archaeologia Cantiana* 15, 104-7.

Payne, G 1888. An archaeological survey of Kent, *Archaeologia* 51, 447-68.

Payne, G 1897. The Roman villa at Darenth, *Archaeologia Cantiana* 22, 49-84.

Peacock, D P S 1971. Roman amphorae in pre-Roman Britain, in *The Iron Age and its hill-forts*, eds Hill, D and Jesson, M, 161-88, Southampton.

Peacock, D P S 1977. Bricks and tiles of the Classis Britannica: petrology and origins, *Britannia* 8, 235-48.

Peacock, D P S 1982. *Pottery in the Roman world: an ethnoarchaeological approach*, London.

Pearce, J 2000. Burial, society and context in the provincial Roman world, in *Burial, society and context in the Roman world*, eds Pearce, J, Millett, M and Struck, M, 1-12, Oxford.

Pearson, A 2002. Stone supply to the Saxon Shore forts at Reculver, Richborough, Dover and Lympne, *Archaeologia Cantiana* 122, 197-220.

Pearson, S 1994. *Medieval houses of Kent: an historical analysis*, London.

Perkins, D R J 1985. The Monkton gas pipeline: Phases III and IV, 1983-84, *Archaeologia Cantiana* 102, 43-69.

Perkins, D R J 1988. A middle Bronze Age hoard from a prehistoric settlement site at St Mildred's Bay, Westgate-on-Sea, *Archaeologia Cantiana* 105, 243-9.

Perkins, D R J 1991a. The Jutish cemetery at Sarre revisited: a rescue evaluation, *Archaeologia Cantiana* 109, 139-66.

Perkins, D R J 1991b. A late Bronze Age hoard found at Monkton Court Farm, Thanet, *Archaeologia Cantiana* 109, 247-64.

Perkins, D R J 1992a. Archaeological evaluations at Ebbsfleet, Isle of Thanet, *Archaeologia Cantiana* 110, 269-311.

Perkins, D R J 1992b. The Jutish cemetery at Sarre revisited: Part II, *Archaeologia Cantiana* 110, 83-120.

Perkins, D R J 1994. 'An assessment/research design: South Dumpton Down, Broadstairs'; unpublished Trust for Thanet Archaeology report.

Perkins, D R J 1995. Report on work by the Thanet Trust for Archaeology, *Archaeologia Cantiana* 115, 468-74.

Perkins, D R J 1996. The Trust for Thanet Archaeology: evaluation work carried out in 1995, Hartsdown Community Woodland Scheme, *Archaeologia Cantiana* 116, 265-81.

Perkins, D R J 1997. A report on work by the Trust for Thanet Archaeology, *Archaeologia Cantiana* 117, 227-37.

Perkins, D R J 1998a. Kent International Business Park, Manston: excavations and evaluations 1994-97, *Archaeologia Cantiana* 118, 217-55.

Perkins, D R J 1998b. 'The proposed Asda superstore site, Westwood Road, Broadstairs: an archaeological evaluation report'; unpublished Trust for Thanet Archaeology report.

Perkins, D R J 1998c. A report on work by the Trust for Thanet Archaeology 1997-98, *Archaeologia Cantiana* 118, 355-71.

Perkins, D R J 1999. Late Neolithic and Bronze Age barrows: North Foreland, *Archaeologia Cantiana* 119, 373-4.

Perkins, D R J 2001. The Roman archaeology of the Isle of Thanet, *Archaeologia Cantiana* 121, 43-60.

Perkins, D R J 2004. Oval barrows on Thanet, in *Towards a New Stone Age: aspects of the Neolithic in south-east England*, eds Cotton, J and Field, D, Council for British Archaeology Research Report 137, 76-81, York.

Perkins, D R J and Gibson, A 1990. A Beaker burial from Manston, near Ramsgate, *Archaeologia Cantiana* 108, 11-27.

Perkins, D R J and Hawkes, S C 1984. The Thanet gas pipeline phase I and II Monkton parish, 1982, *Archaeologia Cantiana* 101, 83-114.

Perkins, D R J and Macpherson-Grant, N 1981. 'The Isle of Thanet Archaeological Unit: interim excavation reports 1977-1980'; unpublished report, Ramsgate.

Perkins, D R J, Macpherson-Grant, N and Healey, E 1994. Monkton Court Farm evaluation, 1992, *Archaeologia Cantiana* 114, 237-316.

Perkins, D R J and Parfitt, K 2004. The Minster Roman villa, *Current Archaeology* 193, 38-41.

Perring, D 1989. Cellars and cults in Roman Britain, *Archaeological Journal* 146, 279-301.

Perring, D and Brigham, T 2000. Londinium and its hinterland: the Roman period, in *The archaeology of Greater London: an assessment of archaeological evidence for human presence in the area now covered by Greater London*, ed. Kendall, M, 120-61, London.

Petrie, W M F 1880. Notes on Kentish earthworks, *Archaeologia Cantiana* 13, 8-16.

Philp, B J 1970. The Iron Age hillfort at Squerryes Park, Westerham, *Kent Archaeological Review* 22, 47.

Philp, B J 1973. *Excavations in west Kent 1960-1970: the discovery and excavation of prehistoric, Roman, Saxon and medieval sites, mainly in the Bromley area and in the Darent Valley*, Dover.

Philp, B J 1976. The probable site of Durolevum, *Kent Archaeological Review* 43, 62-4.

Philp, B J 1981. *The excavation of the Roman forts of the Classis Britannica at Dover, 1970-77*, Dover.

Philp, B J 1982. Romney Marsh and the Roman fort at Lympne, *Kent Archaeological Review* 68, 175-91.

Philp, B J 1984. *Excavations in the Darent Valley*, Kent, Dover.

Philp, B J 1989. *The Roman house with Bacchic murals at Dover*, Dover.

Philp, B J 1990. Major discoveries at Dover, 1990, *Kent Archaeological Review* 102, 25, 33-47.

Philp, B J 1991. Major Iron Age site discovered near Alkham, *Kent Archaeological Review* 103, 5-52.

Philp, B J 2000. Lost Roman town found at West Wickham, *Kent Archaeological Review* 141, 2-5.

Philp, B J 2002a. *The Anglo-Saxon cemetery at Polhill near Sevenoaks, Kent 1964-1986*, Dover.

Philp, B J 2002b. *Archaeology in the front line: 50 years of Kent rescue 1952-2002*, Dover.

Philp, B J 2002c. Richborough and the Claudian invasion base: new ideas on the erosion and layout, *Kent Archaeological Review* 148, 165-9.

Philp, B J 2003. *The discovery and excavation of Anglo-Saxon Dover: the detailed report on fourteen of the major Anglo-Saxon structures and deposits discovered in the centre of ancient Dover, during large scale rescue-excavation 1970-1990*, Dover.

Philp, B J 2005. *The excavation of the Roman fort at Reculver*, Dover.

Philp, B J and Chenery, M 1993. *Deptford, Lewisham: an outline report on rescue excavations in 1989 at the Broadway*, Bromley.

Philp, B J and Chenery, M 1997. *Hillside, Gravesend 1994-95: an outline report on a prehistoric and Romano-British site*, Dover.

Philp, B J and Keller, P 1995. *The Roman site at Fordcroft, Orpington*, Dover.

Philp, B J, Parfitt, K, Willson, J, Dutto, M and Williams, W 1991. *The Roman villa site at Keston, Kent: first report (excavations 1968-1978)*, Dover.

Philp, B J, Parfitt, K, Willson, J and Williams, W 1999. *The Roman villa site at Keston, Kent: second report (excavations 1967 and 1978-1990)*, Dover.

Philpott, R 1991. *Burial practices in Roman Britain*, British Archaeological Reports British Series 219, Oxford.

Piercy Fox, N 1969. Caesar's Camp, Keston, *Archaeologia Cantiana* 84, 185-200.

Piercy Fox, N 1970. Excavation at the Iron Age camp at Squerryes, Westerham, *Archaeologia Cantiana* 85, 29-33.

Piggott, S 1938. The early Bronze Age in Wessex, *Proceedings of the Prehistoric Society* 4, 52-106.

Piggott, S 1962. *The West Kennet long barrow: excavations 1955-56*, London.

Piggott, S 1974. The origins of the English county archaeological societies, *Transactions of the Birmingham and Warwickshire Archaeological Society* 86, 1-16.

Piggott, S 1985. *William Stukeley: an eighteenth-century antiquary*, revised ed., London.

Pilbrow, J 1871. Discoveries made during excavations at Canterbury in 1868, *Archaeologia* 43, 151-64.

Pirie, E 1961. Thurnham Roman villa, *Archaeologia Cantiana* 74, 162-70.

Pirling, R 1974. *Das römisch-fränkische Gräberfeld von Krefeld-Gellep 1960-1963*, Berlin.

Pitt Rivers, A H 1868. On some flint implements found associated with Roman remains in Oxfordshire and the Isle of Thanet, *Journal of the Ethnological Society of London* new series 1, 1-12.

Pitt Rivers, A H 1883. Excavations at Caesar's Camp, near Folkestone, conducted in 1878, *Archaeologia* 47, 429-65.

Pitts, M 1996. The stone axe in Britain, *Proceedings of the Prehistoric Society* 62, 311-71.

Pitts, M and Roberts, M B 1997. *Fairweather Eden: Life in Britain half a million years ago as revealed by the excavations at Boxgrove*, London.

Plattner, S M 1976. Periodic trade in developing areas without markets, in *Regional analysis 1: economic systems*, ed. Smith, C, 69-90, London.

Pollard, R J 1988. *The Roman pottery of Kent*, Kent Archaeological Society Monograph 5, Maidstone.

Pollard, R J 1991. Dressel 1 amphorae from Kent, *Journal of Roman Pottery Studies* 4, 52-8.

Powell-Cotton, P H G and Crawford, O G S 1924. The Birchington hoard, *Antiquaries Journal* 4, 223-6.

Preece, R C and Bridgland, D R, eds 1998. *Late Quaternary environmental change in north-western Europe: excavations at Holywell Coombe, south-east England*, London.

Preece, R C and Bridgland, D R 1999. Holywell Coombe, Folkestone, UK: a 13,000 year history of an English chalkland valley, *Quaternary Science Reviews* 18, 1075-125.

Pretty, E 1863. On the golden armillae in the Society's museum, *Archaeologia Cantiana* 5, 41-4.

Priestley-Bell, G 2000. 'Post-excavation assessment of Brett's Lydd quarry, Kent, part 11'; unpublished Archaeology South East report.

Proudfoot, E V W 1963. Report on the excavation of a bell barrow in the parish of Edmondsham, Dorset, England, 1959, *Proceedings of the Prehistoric Society* 29, 395-425.

Pryor, F 1998. *Farmers in prehistoric Britain*, Stroud.

Pryor, F 2001. *The Flag Fen basin: archaeology and environment of a Fenland landscape*, Swindon.

Pyke, J 1980. Greenhill Bronze Age site, Otford, *Archaeologia Cantiana* 96, 321-40.

Pyke, J 1981. A radiocarbon date for the Bronze Age site at Greenhill, Otford, *Archaeologia Cantiana* 97, 295-6.

Pyke, J and Ward, C P 1975. A middle Bronze Age burial at Otford, *Archaeologia Cantiana* 91, 185-7.

Rady, J 1990. Folkestone: Cheriton Hill, in Gaimster, D R M, Margeson, S and Barry, T, Medieval Britain and Ireland in 1989, *Medieval Archaeology* 34, 198.

Rady, J, Allison E, Anderson I, Bendrey R, Clark, P, Cotter, J, Holmes, T, Harrison, L, Lyne, M, McNabb, J, Macpherson-Grant, N, Pelling R, Riddler, I and Sparey-Green, C 2004. 'Archaeological work along the route of the Wainscott northern by-pass and at Four Elms roundabout 1992-1997'; unpublished Canterbury Archaeological Trust draft excavation report.

Rady, J, Leyland, M and Ouditt, S 1989. Folkestone: Cherry Garden; Newington: Dollond's Moor; Newington: Biggin's Wood, in Gaimster, D R M, Margeson, S and Barry, T, Medieval Britain and Ireland in 1988, *Medieval Archaeology* 33, 199-200.

Rady, M 1987. Excavations at St Martin's Hill, Canterbury, 1984-5, *Archaeologia Cantiana* 104, 123-218.

Rahtz, P 1958. Dover: Stembrook and St. Martin-le-Grand, 1956, *Archaeologia Cantiana* 72, 111-37.

Rahtz, P and Meeson, R 1992. *The Anglo-Saxon watermill at Tamworth*, Council for British Archaeology Research Report 83, London.

Reaney, P H 1961. Place-names and early settlement in Kent, *Archaeologia Cantiana* 76, 58-74.

Redfern, E H 1978. Coins: Roman, in Flight, C and Harrison, A C, Rochester Castle, 1976, *Archaeologia Cantiana* 94, 27-60.

Reece, R 1968. Summary of the Roman coins from Richborough, in *Fifth report on the excavations of the Roman fort at Richborough, Kent*, ed. Cunliffe, B W, Research Committee of the Society of Antiquaries of London Report 23, 200-19, London.

Reece, R 1981. The Roman coins from Richborough – a summary, *Bulletin of the University of London Institute of Archaeology* 18, 49-71.

Reece, R 1989. Lympne, in *The Saxon Shore: a handbook*, ed. Maxfield, V A, Exeter Studies in History 25, 152-7.

Reece, R M 2005. The coins, in *The excavation of the Roman fort at Reculver*, ed. Philp, B J, 103-13, Dover.

Reichstein, J 1975. *Die kreuzförmige Fibel*, Offa-Bücher 34, Neumünster.

Révillion, S and Tuffreau, A, eds 1994. *Les industries laminaires du Paléolithique Moyen*. Dossier du Documentation Archéologique 18, Paris.

Rhodes, M 1990. Faussett rediscovered: Charles Roach Smith, Joseph Meyer and the publication of the *Inventorium Sepulchrale*, in *Anglo-Saxon cemeteries: a re-appraisal*, ed. Southworth, E, 25-64, Stroud.

Richardson, A 2004. Portable Antiquities Scheme: Kent, *Medieval Archaeology* 48, 236-7.

Richardson, A 2005. *The Anglo-Saxon cemeteries of Kent*, British Archaeological Reports British Series 391.

Rigby, V 1995. Gazetteer of Gaulish imports in burials and cemeteries, in *Iron Age burials from Mill Hill, Deal*, ed. Parfitt, K, 179-93, London.

Rigold, S E 1969. The Roman haven of Dover, *Archaeological Journal* 126, 78-100.

Rigold, S E 1977. Litus Romanum – the Shore forts as mission stations, in *The Saxon Shore*, ed. Johnston, D E, Council for British Archaeology Research Report 18, 70-5.

Rigold, S E and Webster, L E 1970. Three Anglo-Saxon

disc brooches, *Archaeologia Cantiana* 85, 1-18.

Rivet, A L F 1980. Celtic names and Roman places, *Britannia* 11, 1-20.

Rivet, A L F and Smith, C 1979. *The place-names of Roman Britain*, London.

Roberts, M B and Parfitt, S A, eds 1999. *Boxgrove: a Middle Pleistocene hominid site*, London.

Roberts, M B, Parfitt, S A, Pope, M I and Wenban-Smith, F F 1997. Boxgrove, West Sussex: rescue excavations of a Lower Palaeolithic landsurface (Boxgrove Project B, 1989-91), *Proceedings of the Prehistoric Society* 63, 303-58.

Robertson, A J 1939. *Anglo-Saxon charters*, Cambridge.

Rodwell, W J 1978. Buildings and settlements in southeast Britain in the late Iron Age, in *Lowland Iron Age communities in Europe*, eds Cunliffe, B and Rowley, T, British Archaeological Reports International Series 48, 25-41, Oxford.

Roebroeks, W and van Kolfschoten, T 1994. The earliest occupation of Europe: a short chronology, *Antiquity* 68, 489-503.

Roebroeks, W and van Kolfschoten, T, eds 1995. *The earliest occupation of Europe*, Leiden.

Rollason, D W 1982. *The Mildrith legend: a study in early medieval hagiography*, Leicester.

Rollason, D W 1989. *Saints and relics in Anglo-Saxon England*, Oxford.

Roth, H 1978. *Zum Grabfrevel in vor- und frühgeschichtlichen Zeit: Untersuchungen zu Grabraub und „haugbrot" in Mittel- und Nordeuropa*, Göttingen.

Rowlands, M J 1971. A group of incised decorated armrings and their significance for the middle Bronze Age of southern England, *British Museum Quarterly* 35, 183-99.

Salway, P 1981. *Roman Britain*, Oxford.

Sauer, E 2002. The Roman invasion of Britain in imperial perspective: a response to Frere and Fulford, *Oxford Journal of Archaeology* 21, 333-64.

Sawyer, P H 1968. *Anglo-Saxon charters: an annotated list and bibliography*, London.

Scaife, R G 1987. A review of later Quaternary plant microfossil and macrofossil research in southern England, with special reference to environmental archaeological evidence, in *Environmental archaeology: a regional review. Volume II*, ed. Keeley, H C M, 125-203, London.

Schreve, D C, Bridgland, D R, Allen, P, Blackford, J J, Gleed-Owen, C P, Griffiths, H I, Keen, D H and White, M J 2002. Sedimentology, palaeontology and archaeology of late Middle Pleistocene River Thames terrace deposits at Purfleet, Essex, UK, *Quaternary Science Reviews* 21, 1423-64.

Scott Robertson, W A 1883. Traces of Roman occupation in and near Maidstone, *Archaeologia Cantiana* 15, 68-88.

Scull, C 1986. A sixth-century grave containing a balance and weights from Watchfield, Oxfordshire, England, *Germania* 65, 105-38.

Scull, C 1990. Scales and weights in early Anglo-Saxon England, *Archaeological Journal* 147, 183-215.

Scull, C 1997. Urban centres in pre-Viking England? in *The Anglo-Saxons from the migration period to the eighth century: an ethnographic perspective*, ed. Hines, J, 269-98, Woodbridge.

Scull, C and Bayliss, A 1999. Dating burials of the seventh and eighth centuries: a case study from Ipswich, Suffolk, in *The pace of change: studies in early-medieval chronology*, eds Hines, J, Høilund Nielsen, K and Siegmund, F, 80-8, Oxford.

Seillier, C 1994. *L'apport de l'archéologie*, Carte Archéologique de la Gaule: Le Pas-de-Calais 62/1, Paris.

Seillier, C 2002. Objets de type anglo-saxonne et migrations maritimes en Boulonnais et Ponthieu, in *Archéologie du littoral Manche – mer du Nord. II Le haut Moyen Age*, eds Curveillier, S and Seillier, C, Bulletin historique et artistique du Calisis no. 175, 29-47.

Shackleton, N J and Opdyke, N D 1973. Oxygen isotope and palaeo-magnetic stratigraphy of Equatorial Pacific Core V28-238: oxygen isotope temperatures and volumes at a 105 and 106 year scale, *Quaternary Research* 3, 39-55.

Shackleton, N J and Opdyke, N D 1976. Oxygen isotope and palaeo-magnetic stratigraphy of Equatorial Pacific Core V28-239, late Pliocene to latest Pleistocene, in *Investigation of Late Quaternary paleoceanography and paleoclimatology*, eds Cline, R M and Hays, J D, Geological Society of America Memoir 145, 449-64, Boulder.

Shand, G 2001. Ramsgate Harbour Approach Road, *Canterbury's Archaeology 1998-1999*, 18-22.

Shand, G 2002. Eddington Farm, Herne Bay, *Canterbury's Archaeology 1999-2000*, 18-23.

Shaw, R 1994. The Anglo-Saxon cemetery at Eccles: a preliminary report, *Archaeologia Cantiana* 114, 165-88.

Sibun, L 2001. Excavations at Syndale Park, Ospringe, *Archaeologia Cantiana* 121, 171-96.

Sieveking, G 1960. Ebbsfleet: Neolithic sites, *Archaeologia Cantiana* 74, 192-3.

Smart, P L and Frances, P D, eds 1991. *Quaternary dating methods – a user's guide*. Quaternary Research Association Technical Guide 4, Cambridge.

Smith, C R 1850. *The antiquities of Richborough, Reculver and Lymne, in Kent*, London.

Smith, C R 1852a. *Report on excavations made on the site of the Roman castrum at Lymne, in Kent, in 1850*, London.

Smith, C R 1852b. Roman villa at Hartlip, Kent, *Collectanea Antiqua* 2, 1-24.

Smith, C R 1861. *Collectanea Antiqua* V, 129-37.

Smith, C R 1874. Gold torques and armillae discovered in Kent, *Archaeologia Cantiana* 9, 1-11.

Smith, C R 1876. On a Roman villa near Maidstone, *Archaeologia Cantiana* 10, 163-72.

Smith, C R 1880. The Shorne, Higham and Cliffe marshes, *Archaeologia Cantiana* 13, 494-9.

Smith, D J 1978. Regional aspects of the winged corridor villa in Britain, in *Studies in the Romano-British villa*, ed. Todd, M, 117-47, Leicester.

Smith, I and Philp, B 1975. A new Neolithic site at Cheriton, Folkestone, *Kent Archaeological Review* 42, 42-5.

Smith, J T 1997. *Roman villas: a study in social structure*, London.

Smith, R A 1908. Anglo-Saxon remains, in *The Victoria History of the County of Kent, Vol. I*, ed. Page, W A, 339-87, London.

Smith, R A 1909. The diving operations on Pudding-pan Rock, Herne Bay, Kent and Gallo-Roman red ware recently recovered from the Rock, *Proceedings of the Society of Antiquaries of London* 22, 395-415.

Smith, R A 1911. A Palaeolithic industry at Northfleet, Kent, *Archaeologia* 62, 515-32.

Smith, R A 1923. *A guide to the Anglo-Saxon antiquities in the Department of British and Mediaeval Antiquities (British Museum)*, London.

Smith, R A 1933. Implements from high level gravel near Canterbury, *Proceedings of the Prehistoric Society of East Anglia*, 7:2, 165-70.

Smith, R A and Dewey, H 1913. Stratification at Swanscombe: report on excavations made on behalf of the British Museum and H.M. Geological Survey, *Archaeologia* 64, 177-294.

Smith, R A and Dewey, H 1914. The High Terrace of the Thames: report on excavations made on behalf of the British Museum and H.M. Geological Survey, *Archaeologia* 65, 185-212.

Smythe, C T 1842. Account of various Roman remains discovered in a field called the Slade in the parish of Boughton Monchelsea, in Kent, *Archaeologia* 29, 414-20.

So, C L 1965. Coastal platforms of the Isle of Thanet, Kent, *Transactions of the Institute of British Geographers* 37, 147-56.

So, C L 1966. Some coastal changes between Whitstable and Reculver, Kent, *Proceedings of the Geologists' Association* 77, 475-90.

So, C L 1971. Early coastal recession around Reculver, Kent, *Archaeologia Cantiana* 86, 93-8.

Somner, W 1640. *Antiquities of Canterbury, or a survey of that ancient citie, with the suburbs and cathedrall, etc.*, London.

Somner, W 1693. *A Treatise of the Roman ports and forts in Kent*, London.

Sørensen, P 1997. Jutes in Kent? Considerations on the problem of ethnicity in southern Scandinavia and Kent in the Migration period, in *Method and theory in historical archaeology (Papers of the 'Medieval Europe Brugge 1997' conference, Vol. 10)*, eds de Boe, G and Verhaege, F, 165-73, Zellik.

Sørensen, P 1999. 'A reassessment of the 'Jutish' nature of Kent, southern Hampshire and the Isle of Wight'; unpublished DPhil thesis, Oxford University.

Spain, R J 1984. Romano-British watermills, *Archaeologia Cantiana* 100, 101-28.

Spain, S 2000. 'The shield in early Anglo-Saxon Kent'; unpublished MA dissertation, University of York.

Spain, S forthcoming. The shields from the Anglo-Saxon cemeteries at Saltwood, Kent.

Sparks, M and Tatton-Brown, T 1987. The history of the ville of St Martin's Canterbury, in Rady, M, Excavations at St Martin's Hill, Canterbury, 1984-5, *Archaeologia Cantiana* 104, 200-12.

Speake, G 1980. *Anglo-Saxon animal art and its Germanic background*, Oxford.

Spurrell, F C J 1880a. On implements from the floor of a Palaeolithic workshop, *Archaeological Journal* 37, 294-9.

Spurrell, F C J 1880b. On the discovery of the place where Palaeolithic implements were made at Crayford, *Quarterly Journal of the Geological Society of London* 36, 544-8.

Spurrell, F C J 1883. Palaeolithic implements found in west Kent, *Archaeologia Cantiana* 15, 89-103.

Spurrell, F C J 1884. On some Palaeolithic knapping tools and modes of using them, *Journal of the Anthropological Institute* 13, 109-18.

Stanford, C B and Bunn, H T, eds 2001. *Meat eating and human evolution*, New York.

Starr, C G 1941. *The Roman imperial navy*, Ithaca, New York.

Stead, I M 1967. A La Tène III burial at Welwyn Garden City, *Archaeologia* 101, 1-62.

Stead, I M 1971. The reconstruction of Iron Age buckets from Aylesford and Swarling, in *Prehistoric and Roman studies*, ed. Sieveking, G de G, 250-82, London.

Stead, I M 1976. The earliest burials of the Aylesford culture, in *Problems in economic and social archaeology*, eds Sieveking, G de G, Longworth, I H and Wilson, K E, 401-16, London.

Stead, I M 1998. *The Salisbury hoard*, Stroud.

Stebbing, W P D 1934. An early Iron Age site at Deal, *Archaeologia Cantiana* 46, 207-9.

Stebbing, W P D 1936. Discoveries in the neighbourhood of Deal during 1936, *Archaeologia Cantiana* 48, 235-7.

Stebbing, W P D 1937. Bucket urns found near Deal, *Antiquaries Journal* 17, 73-6.

Stebbing, W P D and Cave, A J E 1943. Cherry Gardens Hill tumulus, Folkestone, *Archaeologia Cantiana* 56, 28-33.

Stevenson, J and Johnson, C 2004. Brisley Farm: the last Iron Age warriors of Kent? *Current Archaeology* 191, 490-4.

Stine, J H 1962. Temporal aspects of tertiary production elements in Korea, in *Urban systems and economic development*, ed. Pitts, F R, 68-88, Eugene, Oregon.

Stringer, C B 1985. The Swanscombe fossil skull, in *The story of Swanscombe Man*, ed. Duff, K L, 14-19, London.

Stringer, C B and Gamble, C S 1993. *In search of the Neanderthals: solving the puzzle of human origins*, London.

Strong, D E 1968. The monument, in *Fifth report on the excavations of the Roman fort at Richborough, Kent*, ed. Cunliffe, B W, Research Committee of the Society of Antiquaries of London Report 23, 40-73, London.

Struck, M 2000. High status burials in Roman Britain, in *Burial, society and context in the Roman world*, eds Pearce, J, Millett, M and Struck, M, 85-96, Oxford.

Struth, P and Eagles, B 1999. An Anglo-Saxon barrow cemetery in Greenwich Park, in *Patterns of the past. Essays in landscape archaeology for Christopher Taylor*, eds Pattison, P, Field, D and Ainsworth, S, 37-52, Oxford.

Stuart, P and Bogaers, J E 2001. *Nehalennia: Römische Steindenkmäler aus der Oosterschelde bei Colijnsplaat*, Leiden.

Stukeley, W 1724. *Itinerarium curiosum: Centuria I*, London.

Stukeley, W 1776. *Itinerarium curiosum: Centuria II*, London.

Suzuki, S 2000. *The Quoit Brooch style and Anglo-Saxon settlement: a casting and recasting of cultural identity symbols*, Woodbridge.

Swanscombe Committee 1938. Report on the Swanscombe skull: prepared by the Swanscombe Committee of the Royal Anthropological Institute, *Journal of the Royal Anthropological Institute* 68, 17-98.

Swanton, M J 1973. *The spearheads of the Anglo-Saxon settlements*, London.

Sweet, R 2004. *Antiquaries: the discovery of the past in eighteenth-century Britain*, London.

Tatton-Brown, T 1988. The churches of Canterbury Diocese, in *Minsters and parish churches: the local church in transition, 950-1200*, ed. Blair, J, 105-18, Oxford.

Tatton-Brown, T 1989. Church building on Romney Marsh in the later Middle Ages, *Archaeologia Cantiana* 107, 253-65.

Taylor, H M and Taylor, J 1965. *Anglo-Saxon architecture*, Cambridge.

Taylor, H M and Yonge, D D 1981. The ruined church at Stone-by-Faversham: a re-assessment, *Archaeological Journal* 138, 118-45.

Tester, P J 1965. An Acheulian site at Cuxton, *Archaeologia Cantiana* 80, 30-60.

Tester, P J 1968. An Anglo-Saxon cemetery at Orpington: first interim report, *Archaeologia Cantiana* 83, 125-50.

Tester, P J 1969. Excavations at Fordcroft, Orpington: concluding report, *Archaeologia Cantiana* 84, 39-77.

Tester, P J 1977. Further notes on the Anglo-Saxon cemetery at Orpington, *Archaeologia Cantiana* 93, 201-2.

Thomas, C 1981. *Christianity in Roman Britain to AD 500*, London.

Thomas, J S 1999. *Understanding the Neolithic*, London.

Thompson, F H 1983. Excavations at Bigberry Camp,

near Canterbury 1978-80, *Antiquaries Journal* 63, 237-278.

Thompson, F H 1986. The Iron Age hillfort of Oldbury, Kent: excavations 1983-4, *Antiquaries Journal* 66, 267-86.

Thompson, I 1982. *Grog-tempered 'Belgic' pottery of south-eastern England*, British Archaeological Reports British Series 108, Oxford.

Threipland, L M 1957. Excavations in Dover, *Archaeologia Cantiana* 71, 14-37.

Threipland, L M and Steer, K A 1951. Excavations at Dover, 1945-1947, *Archaeologia Cantiana* 64, 130-49.

Tomlin, R S O 1996. A five-acre wood in Roman Kent, in *Interpreting Roman London: papers in memory of Hugh Chapman*, eds Bird, J, Hassall, M and Sheldon, H, 209-15, Oxford.

Toynbee, J M C 1953. Christianity in Roman Britain, *Journal of the British Archaeological Association* 16, 1-24.

Toynbee, J M C 1964. *Art in Britain under the Romans*, Oxford.

Tuohy, C 1992. Long-handled 'weaving-combs' in the Netherlands, *Proceedings of the Prehistoric Society* 58, 385-7.

Tweddle, D 1995. The development of sculpture to *c.*950, & The date and stylistic context of the Reculver fragments, in *Corpus of Anglo-Saxon stone sculpture IV, South-east England*, eds Tweddle, D, Biddle, M and Kjølbye-Biddle, B, 31-45 & 46-61, Oxford.

Tyler, S 1992. Anglo-Saxon settlement in the Darent valley and environs, *Archaeologia Cantiana* 110, 71-81.

Tyers, P 1996. *Roman pottery in Britain*, London.

Vale, J 1987. Archaeological notes from Kent County Museum Service, *Archaeologia Cantiana* 104, 368-74.

Vallin, L and Masson, B 2004. Behaviour towards lithic production during the Middle Palaeolithic: examples from Hermies Le Champ Bruquette and Hermies Le Tio Marché (Pas-de-Calais, France), in *Lithics in action: Proceedings of the Lithic Studies Society Conference held in Cardiff, September 2000*, eds Walker, E A, Wenban-Smith, F F and Healy, F, Lithic Studies Society Occasional Paper 8, 6-25, Oxford.

van der Noort, R, Middleton, R, Foxon, A and Bayliss, A 1999. The 'Kilnsea-boat' and some implications from the discovery of England's oldest plank boat remains, *Antiquity* 73, 131-5.

van Doorselaer, A, Putman, R, van der Gucht, K and Janssens, F 1987. *De Kemmelberg: en keltische bergvesting*, Westvlaamse Archaeologica Monografieen III, Kortrijk.

Varndell, G and Freestone, I 1997. Early prehistoric pottery in Britain, in *Pottery in the making: ceramic traditions*, eds Freestone, I and Gaimster, D, 32-7, London.

Varndell, G and Needham, S 2002. New gold cup from Kent, *PAST (Newsletter of the Prehistoric Society)* 41, 2-4.

Vierck, H 1974. Werke des Eligius, in *Studien zur vor- und frühgeschichtlichen Archäologie*, eds Kossack, G and Ulbert, G, 309-80, Munich.

von Freeden, U 2000. Das Ende engzelligen Cloisonnés und die Eroberung Südarabiens durch die Sasaniden, *Germania* 78, 97-124.

von Schnurbein, S 1974. Zum Ango, in *Studien zur Vor- und Frühgeschichtlichen Archäologie*, eds Kossack, G and Ulbert, G, 411-33, Munich.

Wacher, J S 1995. *The towns of Roman Britain*, London.

Waddington, C 2004. *The joy of flint: an introduction to stone tools and guide to the Museum of Antiquities collections*, Newcastle upon Tyne.

Wait, G and Cotton, J 2000. The Iron Age, in *The archaeology of Greater London: an assessment of archaeological evidence for human presence in the area now covered by Greater London*, ed. Kendall, M, 101-17, London.

Walsh, M 2000. Roman maritime activities around Britain: what is the evidence and how might it be enhanced? in *TRAC99: Proceedings of the Ninth Theoretical Roman Archaeology Conference, Durham 1999*, eds Fincham, G, Harrison, G, Holland, R and Revell, L, 53-63, Oxford.

Ward, A 1997. 'Bradbourne House, East Malling, Kent. Revised post-excavation assessment report'; unpublished Canterbury Archaeologial Trust report.

Ward Perkins, J B 1938. An early Iron Age site at Crayford, Kent, *Proceedings of the Prehistoric Society* 4, 151-68.

Ward Perkins, J B 1944. Excavations on the Iron Age hillfort of Oldbury, near Ightham, Kent, *Archaeologia* 90, 127-76.

Warhurst, A 1955. The Jutish cemetery at Lyminge, *Archaeologia Cantiana* 69, 1-40.

Watson, B, Brigham, T and Dyson, T 2001. *London Bridge: 2000 years of a river crossing*, Museum of London Archaeology Service Monograph 8,

London.

Watts, D J 1991. *Christians and pagans in Roman Britain*, London.

Weale, M E, Weiss, D A, Jager, R F, Bradman, N and Thomas, M G 2002. Y chromosome evidence for Anglo-Saxon mass migration, *Molecular Biology and Evolution* 19, 1008-21.

Weber, M 1998. Das Gräberfeld von Issendorf, Niedersachsen. Ausgangspunkt für Wanderungen nach Britannien? *Studien zur Sachsenforschung* 11, 199-212.

Webster, L 1972. Broadstairs, Bradstow School, in Webster, L E and Cherry, J, Medieval Britain in 1971, *Medieval Archaeology* 16, 156.

Webster, L 1974. Broadstairs, Bradstow School, in Webster, L E and Cherry, J, Medieval Britain in 1973, *Medieval Archaeology* 18, 179.

Webster, L 1975. Broadstairs, Bradstow School, in Webster, L E and Cherry, J, Medieval Britain in 1974, *Medieval Archaeology* 19, 223.

Webster, L 1976. Farningham, in Webster, L E and Cherry, J, Medieval Britain in 1975, *Medieval Archaeology* 20, 164.

Webster, L 1978. Brakteaten: England, in *Reallexikon der Germanischen Altertumskunde 3*, 341-2, Berlin.

Webster, L 1981. Preliminary report on glass and pottery from Grave 4, in R M Walsh, Recent investigations at the Anglo-Saxon cemetery, Darenth Park Hospital, Dartford, *Archaeologia Cantiana* 96, 315-16.

Webster, L 1987. The gold pendant, in *Canterbury excavations: intra- and extra-mural sites, 1949-55 and 1980-84*, eds Frere, S S, Bennett, P, Rady, J and Stow, S, The Archaeology of Canterbury VIII, 282-4, Maidstone.

Webster, L 1992. Death's diplomacy: Sutton Hoo in the light of other male princely burials, in *Sutton Hoo: fifty years after*, eds Farrell, R and Neumann de Vegvar, C, 75-81, Ohio.

Webster, L and Backhouse, J 1991. *The making of England: Anglo-Saxon art and culture AD 600-900*, London.

Welch, M G 1983. *Early Anglo-Saxon Sussex*, British Archaeological Reports British Series 112, Oxford.

Welch, M G 1985a. Button brooches, clasp buttons and face masks, *Medieval Archaeology* 29, 142-5.

Welch, M G 1985b. Rural settlement patterns in the early and middle Anglo-Saxon periods, *Landscape History* 7, 13-26.

Welch, M G 1989. The kingdom of the South Saxons: the origins, in *The origins of Anglo-Saxon kingdoms*, ed. Bassett, S, 75-83, Leicester.

Welch, M G 1991. Contacts across the Channel between the fifth and seventh centuries: a review of the archaeological evidence, *Studien zur Sachsenforschung* 7, 261-9.

Welch, M G 1992. *The English Heritage book of Anglo-Saxon England*, London.

Welch, M G 1993. The archaeological evidence for federated settlement in Britain in the fifth century, in *L'armée romaine et les barbares du IIIe au VIIe siècle*, eds Vallet, F and Kazanski, M, 269-78, Paris.

Welch, M G 2002. Cross-Channel contacts between Anglo-Saxon England and Merovingian Francia, in *Burial in early medieval England and Wales*, eds Lucy, S and Reynolds, A, 122-31, London.

Welch, M G 2003. Migrating hordes? in *The land of the Dobunni*, eds Ecclestone, M, Gardner, K S, Holbrook, N and Smith, A, 65-7, Oxford.

Welch, M G 2007. La parure de la sepulture feminine 43 de Vron (Somme), Revue archéologique de Picardie, no. 1/2.

Welsby, D 1997. Early pottery in the middle Nile valley, in *Pottery in the making: world ceramic traditions*, eds Freestone, I and Gaimster, D, 26-31, London.

Wenban-Smith, F F 1995. The Ebbsfleet Valley, Northfleet (Baker's Hole), in *The Quaternary of the lower reaches of the Thames: Field Guide*, eds Bridgland, D R, Allen, P and Haggart, B A, 147-64, Durham.

Wenban-Smith, F F, 2001. LSS Excursion to Baker's Hole, Kent, *Lithics* 22, 55-7.

Wenban-Smith, F F 2004a. 'The Stopes Palaeolithic project: final report'; unpublished report prepared for English Heritage (available on-line from English Heritage Archaeology Data Service).

Wenban-Smith, F F 2004b. Handaxe typology and Lower Palaeolithic cultural development: ficrons, cleavers and two giant handaxes from Cuxton, in *Lithics* 25 (Papers in honour of R J Macrae), eds Pope M and Cramp K, 11-21.

Wenban-Smith, F F 2004 c. Bringing behaviour into focus: Archaic landscapes and lithic technology, in *Lithics in action: Proceedings of the Lithic Studies Society conference held in Cardiff, September 2000*, eds Walker, E A, Wenban-Smith, F F and Healy, F, Lithic Studies Society Occasional Paper 8, 48-56, Oxford.

Wenban-Smith, F F and Bridgland, D R 2001. Palaeolithic archaeology at the Swan Valley

Community School, Swanscombe, Kent, *Proceedings of the Prehistoric Society* 67, 219-59.

Wenban-Smith, F F, Allen, P, Bates, M R, Parfitt, S A, Preece, R C, Stewart, J R, Turner, C, and Whittaker, J E 2006. The Clactonian elephant butchery site at Southfleet Road, Ebbsfleet, UK, *Journal of Quaternary Science* 21(5), 471-83.

Wenban-Smith, F F, Bates, M R, Marshall, G D and Schwenninger, J L forthcoming. Recent fieldwork and new OSL dating results at Cuxton Lower Palaeolithic site, northwest Kent.

Werner, J 1957. Annexes I-V, in Breuer, J and Roosens, H, Le cimetière franc de Haillot, *Archaeologica Belgica* 34, 299-306.

Werner, J 1964. Frankish royal tombs in the cathedrals of Cologne and Saint-Denis, *Antiquity* 38, 201-16.

Wessex Archaeology 1996. 'Tesco site, Manston Road, Ramsgate, Kent: draft interim notes'; unpublished Wessex Archaeology report.

Wessex Archaeology 2002. 'Kingsborough Manor development, Eastchurch, Isle of Sheppey: watching briefs, evaluations and Phase 1, Stage 2 archaeological excavation'; unpublished Wessex Archaeology report.

Wetherall, D M 1994. From Canterbury to Winchester: the foundation of the Institute, in *Building on the past: papers celebrating 150 years of the Royal Archaeological Institute*, ed. Vyner, B, 1-21, London.

Wheeler, R E M 1929. The Roman lighthouses at Dover, *Archaeological Journal* 86, 29-46.

White, M J and Jacobi, R M 2002. Two sides to every story: bout coupé handaxes revisited, *Oxford Journal of Archaeology* 21, 109-33.

Whiting, W, Hawley, W and May, T 1931. *Report on the excavation of the Roman cemetery at Ospringe, Kent*, Report of the Research Committee of the Society of Antiquaries of London 8, London.

Whittle, A 1991. Wayland's Smithy, Oxfordshire: excavations at the Neolithic tomb in 1962-3 by R. J. C. Atkinson and S. Piggott, *Proceedings of the Prehistoric Society* 57, 61-102.

Whittle, A 1997. Moving on and moving around: Neolithic settlement mobility, in *Neolithic landscapes*, ed. Topping, P, Neolithic Studies Group Seminar Papers 2, 15-22, Oxford.

Wieczorek, A 1996. *Die Franken. Wegbereiter Europas*, Mannheim.

Wilhelmi, K 1977. Zur Funktion und Verbreitung dreieckige Tongewichte der Eisenzeit, *Germania* 55, 180-4.

Wilhelmi, K 1987. Zur Besiedlungsgenese Englands und des nordwestlichen Kontinent von 1500 vor bis Christi Geburt, *Acta Praehistorica Archaeologica* 19, 71-84.

Wilkinson, D R P 1995. Excavations on the White Cliffs Experience site, Dover, 1988-91, *Archaeologia Cantiana* 114, 51-148.

Wilkinson, P 2000. *The Swale District: an archaeological survey commissioned by Swale Borough Council*, Faversham.

Williams, D F 1977. The Romano-British Black-Burnished industry: an essay in characterization by heavy mineral analysis, in *Pottery and early commerce: characterization and trade in Roman and later ceramics*, ed. Peacock, D P S, 163-220, London.

Williams, H 1997. Ancient landscape and the dead: the reuse of prehistoric and Roman monuments as early Anglo-Saxon burial sites, *Medieval Archaeology* 41, 1-32.

Williams, H 1998. Monuments and the past in early Anglo-Saxon England, *World Archaeology* 30, 90-108.

Williams, J and Brown N, eds 1999. *An archaeological research framework for the greater Thames estuary*, Maidstone.

Williams, J H 1971. Roman building materials in south-east England, *Britannia* 2, 166-95.

Williams, J H 2003. New light on Roman Kent, *Journal of Roman Archaeology* 16, 219-36.

Willis, S 1994. Roman imports into late Iron Age British societies: towards a critique of existing models, in *TRAC 94: Proceedings of the Fourth Annual Theoretical Roman Archaeology Conference, Durham, 1994*, eds Cottam, S, Dungworth, D, Scott, S and Taylor, J, 141-50, Oxford.

Willson, J 1984. Rescue work at Wick Wood, Barham, Kent, *Kent Archaeological Review* 77, 166-74.

Willson, J 1988. Saxon burials from Priory Hill, Dover, *Kent Archaeological Review* 94, 81-92.

Willson, J 1993. A Bronze Age site on the Eastry by-pass, *Kent Archaeological Review* 112, 38-47.

Willson, J 2001. Kemsley Fields, near Sittingbourne, *Canterbury's Archaeology 1998-1999*, 32-3.

Willson, J 2002. The Street, Iwade, *Canterbury's Archaeology 1997-1998*, 23.

Wilson, D M 1956. An Anglo-Saxon grave near Dartford, Kent, *Archaeologia Cantiana* 70, 187-91.

Wilson, D R 1973. Roman Britain in 1972: sites

explored, *Britannia* 4, 271-323.

Wilson, T 1999. Scattered flints: lithic analysis during 1996-97, *Canterbury's Archaeology 1996-1997*, 36-8.

Winbolt, S E 1925. *Roman Folkestone*, London.

Witney, K P 1976. *The Jutish forest*, London.

Witney, K P 1982. *The kingdom of Kent*, Chichester.

Witney, K P 1984. The Kentish royal saints: an enquiry into the facts behind the legends, *Archaeologia Cantiana* 101, 1-22.

Wood, I N 1990. The Channel from the 4th to the 7th centuries, in *Maritime Celts, Frisians and Saxons*, ed. McGrail, S, Council for British Archaeology Research Report 71, 93-7, London.

Wood, I N 1992. Frankish hegemony in England, in *The Age of Sutton Hoo: the seventh century in north-western Europe*, ed. Carver, M, 235-41, Woodbridge.

Wood, I N 1994a. *The Merovingian kingdoms 450-751*, London.

Wood, I N 1994b. The mission of Augustine of Canterbury to the English, *Speculum* 69, 1-17.

Woodcock, A G, Kelly, D B and Cummins, W A 1988. The petrological identification of stone implements from south-east England, in *Stone axe studies, Vol. 2: the petrology of prehistoric stone implements from the British Isles*, eds Clough, T H M and Cummins, W A, Council for British Archaeology Research Report 67, 21-34, London.

Woodruff, C H 1874. On Celtic tumuli in east Kent, *Archaeologia Cantiana* 9, 16-30.

Woodruff, C H 1877. An account of discoveries made in Celtic tumuli near Dover, Kent, *Archaeologia* 45, 53-6.

Woodward, A 2000. *British barrows: a matter of life and death*, Stroud.

Woolf, G D 1993. The social significance of trade in late Iron Age Europe, in *Trade and exchange in prehistoric Europe*, eds Scarre, C and Healey, F, 211-18, Oxford.

Woolf, G D 1995. The formation of Roman provincial cultures, in *Integration in the early Roman West: the role of culture and ideology*, eds Metzler, J, Millett, M, Roymans, N and Slofstra, J, Dossiers d'Archéologie du Musée National d'Histoire et d'Art IV, 9-18, Luxembourg.

Wormald, P 1999. *The making of English law: King Alfred to the twelfth century*, Oxford.

Worsfold, F H 1927. Observations on the provenance of the Thames Valley pick, Swalecliffe, Kent, *Proceedings of the Prehistoric Society of East Anglia* 5,

224-31.

Worsfold, F H 1943. A report on the late Bronze Age site excavated at Minnis Bay, Birchington, Kent, 1938-40, *Proceedings of the Prehistoric Society* 9, 28-47.

Wright, E V 1990. *The Ferriby boats: seacraft of the Bronze Age*, London.

Wright, R P and Hassall, M W C 1971. Roman Britain in 1970: II inscriptions, *Britannia* 2, 289-304.

Wymer, J J 1968. *Lower Palaeolithic archaeology in Britain as represented by the Thames Valley*, London.

Wymer, J J 1982. *The Palaeolithic age*, London.

Wymer, J J 1995. The contexts of palaeoliths, in *Lithics in context*, ed. Schofield, A J, Lithic Studies Society Occasional Paper 5, 45-51, London.

Wymer, J J 1999. *The Palaeolithic occupation of Britain*, Salisbury.

Wymer, J J and Brown, N R 1995. *Excavations at North Shoebury: settlement and economy in south-east Essex 1500BC-AD1500*, East Anglian Archaeology 75, Chelmsford.

Yates, D T 1999. Bronze Age field systems in the Thames Valley, *Oxford Journal of Archaeology* 18, 157-70.

Yates, D T 2001. Bronze Age agricultural intensification in the Thames Valley and Estuary, in *Bronze Age landscapes: tradition and transformation*, ed. Brück, J, 65-82, Oxford.

Yorke, B A E 1983. Joint kingship in Kent, c.560-785, *Archaeologia Cantiana* 99, 1-20.

Yorke, B A E 1989. The Jutes of Hampshire and Wight and the origins of Wessex, in *The origins of Anglo-Saxon kingdoms*, ed. Bassett, S, 84-96, Leicester.

Yorke, B A E 1990. *Kings and kingdoms of Early Anglo-Saxon England*, London.

Yorke, B A E 2002. Gregory of Tours and sixth-century Anglo-Saxon England, in *The world of Gregory of Tours*, eds Mitchell, K and Wood, I N, 113-30, Leiden.

Yorke, B A E 2003. *Nunneries and the Anglo-Saxon royal houses*, London.

Young, C J 1981. The late Roman water-mill at Ickham, Kent, and the Saxon Shore, in *Collectanea Historica: essays in memory of Stuart Rigold*, ed. Detsicas, A P, 32-40, Maidstone.

Zimmermann, W H 1988. Regelhafte Innengliederung prähistorischer Langhäuser in der Nordseeanrainerstaaten, *Germania* 66, 465-88.

Index

Photographs of artefacts and sites, maps, illustrations, tables and graphs are denoted by page numbers in *italics*.